The
ENLIGHTENED
CUISINE

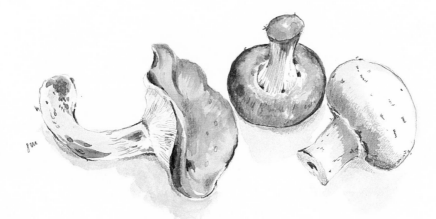

The
ENLIGHTENED
CUISINE

A Master Chef's Step-by-Step
Guide to Contemporary French Cooking

RENÉ VERDON
with Rachel H. Norman

Illustrations by Jacqueline Mallorca

Macmillan Publishing Company
New York

MACMILLAN PUBLISHING COMPANY
866 Third Avenue, New York, N.Y. 10022
Collier Macmillan Canada, Inc.

Library of Congress Cataloging in Publication Data
Verdon, René, 1924–
The enlightened cuisine.

Includes index.
1. Cookery, French.   I. Norman, Rachel H.   II. Title.
TX719.V46   1985   641.5944   85-11464
ISBN 0-02-621750-3

Macmillan books are available at special discounts for bulk purchases for sales promotions, premiums, fund-raising, or ed-ucational use. For details, contact:

Special Sales Director
Macmillan Publishing Company
866 Third Avenue
New York, N.Y. 10022

10   9   8   7   6   5   4   3   2   1

Printed in the United States of America

This book is dedicated to the memory of Edouard Nignon, a great chef and a poetical writer; and to my grandson Edwin who, like children everywhere, represents hope for the future.

CONTENTS

CONTENTS

PREFACE

The Enlightened Cuisine combines the professional techniques and skills that Chef Verdon applies in his kitchen to prepare foods for both his San Francisco restaurant, Le Trianon, and for himself. Not only is this book a welcome addition to the cook at home, it also includes original recipes never before published and presents the methods Chef Verdon uses to create his pastries.

Following the trend of eating fresher, healthier foods, Chef Verdon prepares elegant dishes that are lighter than any he has created before. He calls his new style of cooking "The Enlightened Cuisine"—*La Cuisine Eclairée.* Each chapter is an expanded version of one of his actual 2½-hour classes. Every category of cuisine has an introduction with tips concerning the instructions, is seasoned with culinary history related to the topic, and is spiced with the characteristics of the produce. Chef Verdon gives the processes and recipes for sauces required to make each dish or pastry. And each recipe is adapted for use with a processor or hand mixer.

Throughout this book, Chef Verdon provides lessons for classics that are seldom demonstrated. He begins with a preparation of *Consommé Clair,* from the first step of stock-making to clarification. He continues in thirteen chapters to explain the techniques and give all the steps necessary to prepare various *soupes* and potages; Brown Sauce to compound sauces; cream puff dough and gnocchi; hors d'oeuvres; first courses and salads; eight ways to prepare eggs; pie, tart, and cookie doughs, *crêpe* and noodle dough; seafood; meats and poultry; vegetables; pastry *(crème pâtissière)* and Bavarian creams, soufflés and butter creams; puff pastry, croissants, and brioche; as well as advanced pastries such as *Gâteau Génoise Mousseline* for *Gâteau Jacqueline* and Mango Mousse, and vacherins. He concludes with fourteen of his innumerable menus from over the past two decades.

René Verdon was one of the first chefs to popularize French cooking for Americans by introducing them to the subtleties of the classical style in which he was trained. He continued that tradition when he acted as executive chef of the White House from 1961 to 1966 and when he opened his own restaurant, Le Trianon, in San Francisco in 1972. He chose San Francisco for its European charm and because it offers the fresh seafood from the Pacific Ocean and the plentiful produce from the valleys of California. During the almost thirty years he has lived in the United States, Chef Verdon has traveled throughout all of the states to gather inspiration for new dishes and has worked to adapt American products to French cuisine.

Chef Verdon's ability as a teacher is reflected through the pages of this cookbook, whether he is making a Gratin of Peaches and Cream, Alsatian Poussin, Molded Mousses of Vegetables, or Fillet of Salmon with Whole Grain Mustard; and his passion for both French and American cuisines carries throughout his cooking.

We hope that you enjoy the book!

RACHEL H. NORMAN
September 1985

ACKNOWLEDGMENTS

First, I want to thank my husband, Dr. H. F. Norman, for his encouragement. I wish to acknowledge the invaluable assistance of Mr. Fred Hill, our agent; Mrs. Jacqueline Mallorca, our artist; and Dr. Carol A. Nimelstein, my daughter, one of our recipe testers and proofreaders.

I also want to thank Chef René for contributing his expertise in all facets of cuisine: from designing trays of pastries—*pâte à choux,* meringues, *tartes,* and *gâteaux*—just to assist Jackie in creating her drawings and watercolors for *The Enlightened Cuisine,* to his instant recall of culinary history and practical instructions found in the notes as well as in the recipes.

R. H. N.

NOTES from
MY KITCHEN

On entering my kitchen, the first object that might catch your eye is the hanging rack of shiny copper pots; next, you might notice the division of space into various centers for food preparation. With all of my equipment, I have very little space on my walls for ceramic molds or decorations, but I have found room to hang my favorite set of copper pots—they remind me of my native France!

The basic structure of my kitchen is built around the stove, refrigerator, and sink. This is called the work triangle. Of course, a restaurant kitchen will have larger, sturdier, and more numerous appliances than the ones usually found in a nonprofessional kitchen. I have installed refrigerators for vegetables, fruits, meats, and pastries. I have one tall refrigerator, with its temperature set at 65 degrees, that keeps certain foods—smoked salmon, oysters, salads—at the correct temperature for serving. I also have a walk-in refrigerator, with the temperature set at 48 degrees, where I store delicacies such as fresh morels, truffles, and prepared quenelles, and staples—vegetables, herbs, poultry, meat, and fish. Below the rack of copper and across from the convection oven and stoves along the back wall stands an elongated, stainless steel *bain-marie* with individual round spaces to hold containers of stocks and sauces in heated water. The lower floor has a meat locker, for both meats and two filled stockpots. My storage room in the basement keeps potatoes, onions, and shallots, and a large closet stores dry food—flour, sugar, rice, beans, and lentils. Shelves hold pastry and baking items such as parchment paper, doilies, and cardboard cake circles. Separate shelves hold olive oil, vinegar, and chocolate.

Although my kitchen is designed specifically for the professional chef, some of the basic concerns it services may be helpful to you in your kitchen. For example, you may want to use an area of your basement as a storage area or even turn part of it into an all-purpose pantry. Always be sure that your kitchen is properly ventilated, with hoods and fans for stoves, ovens, and cooktops. Try to locate the baking center in the coolest section of the kitchen: I have saved the corner farthest from the stoves to hang my pastry-making implements on the wall above the marble slab used to make and roll out various doughs. I keep the food processor in that area, and a butcher-block-topped table is a few feet away. It serves as an island, and when I need an extra dining area, it becomes a handy lunch table.

Across from this table, where I place my pastry trays of *Gâteau Génoise,* is a stainless steel counter on which I keep a professional-sized electric mixer, meat grinder, and slicer. My refrigerator-freezer sits next to the baking center.

If it is possible, try to have your sink and faucet next to the stove or cooktop, so you will be able to fill pots, cool off blanched vegetables, and rinse and drain pasta quickly. A dishwasher near the dining area in the home would save steps. Try to have counter tops next to the stove made of tile or a material such as stainless steel that can tolerate hot pots. You always want to be prepared for the emergencies that cooking can bring!

Although you may want to add as many conveniences as you can to your kitchen, you do not need a "dream" kitchen in which to learn the basic procedures I am going to demonstrate for *l'école de cuisine.* You'll add more sophisticated equipment as you can. It's more important to be able to make stocks, soups, sauces, doughs, and pastry and butter creams well and with confidence. One of the first steps toward doing this is to make planning ahead a natural part of your food preparation. It allows you to save all-important time and steps. In France, this is called *mise en place.*

Perhaps the reason the expression *mise en place* is heard more often in America today is because it has no exact English equivalent. It means, simply, that all the ingredients and preliminaries for a dish or a meal are set up as far in advance as possible. Vegetables are cleaned, peeled, and cut; meat, poultry, and fish are cleaned and trimmed; *bouquet garni* is tied; soup stocks and sauces are at hand; parsley is chopped; pots and pans are selected; and so on.

You will want to have your knives sharpened as well; the knife is a cook's primary instrument, used to peel and carve vegetables, to get to the inside of the edible parts of produce and foods—whether it's *foie gras* inside a goose or oysters inside of shells. The techniques and recipes for the lessons I have planned will require about eight knives: two for paring and chopping (a small paring knife and large chef's knife), two for boning (*filet de sole* knife for fish and one for poultry), a cleaver for chopping bone, a carving knife for meat, and a serrated bread slicer. A pastry knife for cutting and trimming *pâte feuilletée* is also necessary. And as you may know, the food processor is a rival of the knife as well as of the sieve for puréeing. I will talk about food processors in later chapters.

Although you may have your favorite types of pots and pans, I like tin-lined copper pots because copper is a better conductor of heat. However, food should not be kept or stored in copper. It tends to promote a condition called verdigris *(vert de gris)*—a green patina or crust of copper sulfate or copper chloride that forms on copper, brass, and bronze when exposed to air or sea water for long periods of time. Also, when the reddish color of copper begins to show through the tin lining *(étain),* the pot should be relined or retinned. Two new linings used for copper pots are stainless steel or nickel, both excellent but more expensive than tin. If you do not have copper pots, most heavy-bottomed pots are excellent: cast iron covered with enamel or club aluminum are especially good. But remember, aluminum will cause egg yolks to discolor. Always use a stainless steel pot with a copper bottom or cast iron with an enamel lining for beating eggs over heat.

The cast-iron skillet still has a place in my kitchen—I use the 10-inch skillet to caramelize the apples for my *Tarte Tatin,* the 8- or 9-inch one to bake *Pommes de Terre Anna,* and various sizes to sear and sauté meat. New cast-iron pans must be seasoned to prevent rust. Rub them with oil, clean out, pour in enough oil to coat the pan and bake in a 450-degree oven for about a half hour. Clean pan, dry, and rub with oil before putting away.

As someone who loves cooking, I always want to perfect the dishes I present. Experience and practice is the best way to know how to cook food properly. I am fondest of cooking when the food is, as the Italians call it, *al dente*—the area between undercooking and overcooking. This can differ from food to food, and even between different varieties of the same vegetable. For example, green asparagus can be served al dente, whereas white asparagus requires longer cooking.

Length of cooking time is especially important when you are preparing meat. Always take care to preserve the juices when cooking meat and poultry. When veal and chicken breast are cooked properly, a light pink liquid should trickle out upon cutting. (Since the white meat has no blood, the breast must be coated with flour to preserve the natural juices when sautéeing.) Be aware that legs take longer to cook. And, when meat is sautéed, the thickness of the cut determines the cooking time. Veal cut for scallopine is so thin that it will be cooked by the time it is turned over once in the skillet. An individual fillet of veal cut 1 to 2 inches thick requires different timing. One way to tell if meat is medium rare is to press the top: if it is still soft and springs back, it will not be overcooked or dried out.

These are just a few of my ideas on cooking. The rest will come in the chapters that follow. I hope that you will find the book useful and challenging: perhaps you will be inspired to try some dishes that you've never cooked before!

Welcome *(soyez le bienvenu)* and *à votre santé!*

RENÉ VERDON

Chapter One

SOUPS and POTAGES

Clear, Cream, and Puréed; Bisques;
My Classification of *Soupes*

B efore starting our first class on *soupes* and *potages* I wish to express a few thoughts I have gathered along the long path I traveled from my youth in the French provinces, to Paris, Deauville, across the Atlantic on the *Liberté* to New York City, where I was a chef in prestigious restaurants before being called to the White House. After five years executing many banquets for dignitaries, I traveled throughout all the states of America giving food demonstrations. Now that I am *chef de cuisine* of my own French restaurant in San Francisco, it is an added pleasure to share my techniques which help to produce the dishes that I serve here. I will teach the fundamentals and methods all aspiring cooks need to reach a certain perfection. Since music is the most exacting of the arts, demanding the greatest degree of excellence, I believe it is appropriate to compare the profession of chef with the four strings of a violin—to become a chef the four fields to conquer are *cuisinier,* cooking; *pâtissier,* pastry making; *boucher,* butchering; and *glacier,* ice cream making. Remembering that a violin has four strings will impress the student cook with a condensed classification of the various facets of *la cuisine.* After spending forty-five years in the kitchen, I still feel the music of my art when all the courses of a great dinner arrive at the table displaying harmonious colors, designs, and flavors.

When I started my trade in Nantes before World War II, I was first an apprentice in a restaurant kitchen for three years, with two more years in *pâtisserie.* I worked fifteen hours a day, six days a week. In the 1980s this training program is considered too long: it is usually replaced by enrolling in a professional cooking school for at least one year with some additional months. My impression is that too much of the student's time is spent in class, even though the teachers are well qualified. The student chef or *commis* should spend two years in apprenticeship with two days of each week in school. The authentic atmosphere and real work in a restaurant kitchen is the best teacher of all—to learn what it is to peel; to clean various vegetables; to handle and identify meats; to clean, bone, and fillet fish; to make mistakes. When the errors are crucial for that day's meals, they become indelibly etched in the aspiring cook's fingers and brain. The palate is being developed by tasting each time a finger is put in the sauce. When hovering above a pot, one's nose soon becomes trained as to its contents, whether they are too sour or might be burning. Soon the time comes to learn how to improve: to discover how a sauce that has curdled can be repaired, the different ways to thicken a sauce or make it lighter with just a little water from the faucet.

When I was an apprentice, I mixed a fish sauce with a meat sauce, for which I received a kick in the *derrière*. The memory of this has stayed with me to the extent that I always taste a sauce first before mixing it into another saucepan. Recently, I was talking with a chef whose assistant put salt instead of sugar over some apples. What a catastrophe! The poor fellow was so embarrassed he contemplated giving up his job, not because he was discouraged, but because he was so conscientious. If the culinary establishment gave stars as the army does, I would have given him one star. He deserved the opportunity to prove his ability and love for his trade; for without the former there can be little hope to achieve, and without the latter there can be no pleasure in one's craft.

Since the process of evolution takes place in the world of food just as it does in other spheres of nature, I have always been aware of the newest cooking trends. I continue to change my style of cuisine to please the "gourmets" and connoisseurs for whom I cook. It is a reciprocal process—chefs need people with discriminating palates to inspire them, just as they improve the taste of their devotées. Neither chefs nor gourmets are born overnight. It is by the everyday practicing, changing, experimenting with a new dish over and over again, correcting mistakes, that haute cuisine is forged into an art *sans fin*.

The best introduction to cuisine is the preparation of a rich stock overflowing with aromatic ingredients. Although soup stock is a most basic preparation, it can become an elaborate course when turned into a *Bisque de Homard* (p. 25) or a *Consommé à la Reine-Jeanne* (p. 10). Always starting from stock, advancing to clarification (p. 7), the fanciest soups emerge from *Consommé Clair*. Produced from everyday stock is *Potage Parisien* (p. 19) made from cut vegetables; *Vichyssoise* (p. 19) made of puréed vegetables with cream; and *Potage Crème Germiny* thickened with egg yolks and cream. My classification of *soupes* and *potages* (p. 16) has organized the characteristics of classic soups.

Different words meaning stock *(fond de cuisine)* actually represent the same gelatinous liquid: whatever difference there was between broth and bouillon has been lost. However, there is a distinction between 1) white stock *(fond blanc)* made from veal shanks, knuckle, and rib bones, or poultry bones which have not been browned before using in stock, and 2) brown stock *(fond brun)* made from veal bones browned in the oven with aromatic vegetables. To make brown stock I add herbs, water, and dry white wine. Veal bones are more desirable for they contain more gelatin than beef bones. Left-

3

over bones, meat, and vegetables for stock are thrifty and soul-satisfying ingredients; but freshly purchased meat of beef, veal, and chicken with their bones are more nutritious and flavorful.

Fish stock and fish soup are prepared in a way similar to broth, but more fish meat must be used for fish soup than meat used in beef or poultry soup. And fish stock and *fumet* are cooked only one half hour, in contrast to beef and poultry stock (p. 6), which is cooked for 8–12 hours. Fish stock is naturally more clear than a fish soup because it is strained without pressing the cooked fish and vegetables.

Experience has taught me that beef and chicken bones will always make a clear consommé, while veal bones will create a cloudy consommé. It is possible to make a consommé so clear that it does not have to be clarified. However, if the stock should become cloudy when gelatin is added to *Consommé à la Madrilène,* for example, or while making aspic, one will have to clarify it. Pork or veal blood were used for clarification in the past, but the method I use today is with egg whites (not beaten) and ground neck meat, which contains a large amount of blood (p. 7). I prefer to use veal stock for all cream soups because veal bones have more gelatin; it gives a velvet texture to the finished soup.

In case *Potage Crème Germiny* (p. 14) becomes too thick when it is cold, I dilute it with cold veal stock. This changes the consistency to resemble a cream sauce. It is usually more difficult to thicken soups than to thin them. However, one of the more simple ways to thicken soup is with raw rice. This is given in Step 6 under Lobster Bisque (p. 26). Leftover rice also can be put in the blender with a soup. Egg yolks will thicken soup when mixed in a little stock before stirring into a finished bisque. But they will change the color, causing it to look like a *Velouté Soupe.* The correct proportion of four other thickening agents is 1 tablespoon thickener to 2 tablespoons liquid:

1. Cornstarch (made from corn meal)—always dilute with a little water or liquid such as sherry, Cognac, or white wine. It gives a quick thickness. Add gradually to soup, stirring with a whisk. Stop adding cornstarch when soup is thick enough.
2. Potato starch or *fécule* (made from potatoes)—use the same way as cornstarch.
3. Arrowroot (made from the root and rhizomes of tropical plants)—add the same way.
4. *Beurre manié* (made from an equal amount of flour and butter blended together)—1 tablespoon of butter mixed with 1 tablespoon of flour. Do *not* use in a clear soup. Can be used for a bisque or a cream soup.

Almost more than any other course, the choice of soup for a menu reflects the season of the year. In winter a hot, hearty soup such as a garbure is appropriate, while in summertime a cold soup, such as cream of sorrel, is in tune with the weather. A well-made soup tests the ability of the cook to present a beautiful color and to preserve the flavor of the ingredients with a careful use of seasonings. It also tests resourcefulness, as the stems and leaves of vegetables which would otherwise be wasted are used. The stems of morels and oyster mushrooms, for example, can be sautéed with chopped shallots, garlic, and parsley, then reduced with sherry and cream to be added to a bouillon or consommé. Leftover bread can be used in garlic soup *(Soupe à l'Ail,* p. 27) or onion soup.

Five Different Types of Garnishes for Soups:

1. Various herbs and vegetables used as garnishes are given in the recipes for *soupes* in this lesson.

2. Other embellishments come from breads—day-old French and Italian breads make croutons (cut in cubes and sautéed in butter), or sliced as toast, buttered, or sprinkled with oil and cheese or chopped garlic.

3. Most doughs enliven soups: *pâte à choux* piped in tiny puffs or profiteroles; *crêpes* with chopped *fines herbes* in the batter, cooked and shredded. *Pâte feuilletée* is cut in elongated shapes, twisted, and flavored with cheese called *sacristains,* whereas *allumettes* are cut into strips and filled. They are served on separate plates, not in the soup. Puff pastry is also used as the cover for *soupe en croute.*

4. *Pâte à nouille* provides noodles which are usually pre-cooked to avoid clouding a clear soup. Pasta cut in dozens of sizes and shapes or filled like ravioli has almost taken the place of standard noodles.

5. Delicate garnishes are fashioned from miniature quenelles, meringues, and custards cut into ornamental shapes called *royales.*

The pageant of history has wrapped its romantic cloak about soups—a parade of international soups would include *pot-au-feu* for France, minestrone for Italy, won ton and bird's nest soups for China, and borscht for Russia. Fruit soups evoke the Scandinavians, gazpacho stands for Spain, Scotch broth recalls Scotland, mutton broth, England; while mulligatawny claims India, goulash reminds one of Hungary, and America has vegetable soup, Boston clam chowder, navy bean soup, and chicken gumbo. The parade is far from exhausted. The humble *potage* derived its name from the pot in which the meat and vegetables were cooked to create a meal. The fact that soup often serves as a meal in France and elsewhere proves its value and adaptability. It has played an indispensable role in the history of cuisine similar to that of bread, and it is revered for its restorative powers generated from the nourishing meats and vegetables responsible for its aromatic "nose." With the exception of strongly flavored turnips, parsnips, and cabbage, and the spice ginger (to be used with discretion), almost every vegetable can be featured in soup. Leeks are related to soup stock as shallots are to sauces—their unforgettable perfume is responsible for the label "chef's secret ingredient."

The only soup that can be served either at the beginning of the meal or at the end is fruit soup (p. 27). It is served either hot or cold. Mixed fresh fruit soup, fairly thick, flavored with red or white wine, contains peaches, strawberries, pineapple, rhubarb, apples, pears, and oranges (white pith and seeds removed) all cooked together with sugar to taste, water, and 2 cloves. Wine enhances all fruit soups, as do some liqueurs. Cherry soup made with consommé is popular in France and Hungary, where apple and apricot soups are also found. In America individual fruit soups are made from cantaloupe, cranberries, avocados, and peaches; banana soup is made in the West Indies.

Now, action will take the place of words, as *l'école de cuisine* begins with a large tray filled with fresh beef and veal bones plus aromatic vegetables to make stock which will be clarified to become *Consommé Clair*.

Clarified Soup Stock   *Consommé Clair*

Natural gelatin exists in veal, beef, and chicken bones. Knuckle bones, cracked, are preferred for their aspic; but leftover or trimmed bones can be used. Bones frozen for the purpose of making stock are acceptable.

INITIAL INGREDIENTS FOR STOCK (FOND)

4–6 pounds veal, beef, or chicken bones or all three
8 or more quarts of water
2 tablespoons salt
3 pounds brisket of beef
2–3 pounds beef or veal shanks or both with meat on
2 carrots
2 celery stalks

2 onions, cut roughly
2 leeks, with most of green cut off and discarded
6 parsley stems
Bouquet garni—2 sprigs thyme, 2 bay leaves, 3 parsley sprigs wrapped in the green of the leek and tied
2 tablespoons crushed peppercorns

6

1. Blanch bones first by covering with cold water. Bring to a boil and skim the fat. Stop the cooking, drain bones in a colander, and wash off.
2. Using a large stainless steel or porcelain-lined pot, put in bones with 2 tablespoons of salt. Add brisket of beef and beef or veal shanks with meat on them for flavor. Cover with water 3 or 4 inches above bones and meat. The amount of water could be as much as 8 quarts. More water can be added later on.
3. Bring to a boil, skim off foam, and add aromatic vegetables which have first been cut in 2-inch lengths. Put in herbs and seasonings. Bay leaf and thyme are used sparingly because of their strength (too much bay leaf will give a bitter taste to the bouillon or *fond de cuisine*).
4. Simmer 12 hours, skimming fat off occasionally.
5. If stock is made a day ahead, it should be cooled uncovered to prevent a fermentation of the flavor. When it has reached room temperature, stock should be covered and refrigerated. It will be very easy to remove fat the next day after it has solidified on top of the jelled stock—*dégraisser:* to remove fat or scum from the surface of soup stocks, *soupes,* and sauces.
6. After fat has been removed, stock can be frozen in pint and quart Mason Ball jars or other appropriate containers.

Makes about 6 quarts (15–20% of stock is lost while simmering).

How to Clarify Stock (Bouillon) to Make *Consommé Clair*

3 quarts stock (fond)
1½ cups chopped parsley
1½ cups celery stalks and leaves
1½ cups chopped carrots
1 leek, cut up
*1 onion, chopped—include dry skin
 to give a natural coloring*
*1 shallot, roughly chopped with its
 dry skin peelings to give it color
 "like a field of wheat"*

*2 egg whites per 1 quart of stock (egg
 shells and whole eggs can be used)*
1 pound lean ground beef
*1 to 1½ tablespoons gelatin to
 1 quart of stock if needed*
*2–3 fresh tomatoes, which add color
 to stock (optional)*
*Salt and pepper to taste, after
 clarification*

1. Use large stockpot with capacity to hold more than 3 quarts liquid for the stock which has been degreased. Pour in stock. Add quartered or diced tomatoes, if used.
2. Make a *mirepoix* of all coarsely diced or chopped vegetables found in list of ingredients, by placing in a large bowl.

7

3. Mix egg whites, *do not beat,* into *mirepoix.*

4. In a separate bowl cover 1 pound of ground beef with water before putting in soup stock. This draws out the juice or blood, which serves as a clarifier. Neck meat can be used, as it has a lot of juice. Add ground meat with its blood, *mirepoix,* and egg whites to stockpot.

5. If this consommé is needed for a soup which requires gelatin or for aspic, 1 to 1½ tablespoons of powdered gelatin to 1 quart of stock can be added at this stage. It can also be sprinkled on top of clarified consommé later instead of in Step 4.

6. Bring stock to a boil. As soon as the stock comes to a boil, do not stir anymore! Turn heat to low. Use a soup ladle to lift foam gently to outer edge of pot occasionally. Do not cover!

7. Simmer for 1 hour. The longer the consommé cooks, the more color it acquires. Since egg whites remove flavor, ground meat helps to bring back the flavor. The consommé is finished when the vegetables and meat start to sink down. Taste to correct salt and pepper.

8. To determine if enough gelatin has been used, put some liquid in a shallow bowl and refrigerate. Chilling will reveal consistency.

How to Strain the *Consommé Clair*

Place a wet cotton towel over a large bowl and slowly pour the liquid through. If any specks of fat remain, repeat the straining process. It should be completely free of fat, and clear.

Some Uses for *Consommé Clair*

1. Cold jellied consommé, chopped on a towel, is used to decorate platters of cold meat, chicken, and fish (aspic made with fish stock). Thin sheets of *gelée* can be cut out in various designs for the same purpose. Aspic must be tested first for correct consistency as explained in Step 8 of "How to Clarify Stock."

2. When aspic reaches the stage of becoming just cool enough to congeal, it is applied to coat *pâtés,* cold *Suprêmes de Volailles,* and other poultry and meat dishes such as Mousse of Ham or any dish to be glazed for a buffet table.

3. White Chaud-Froid Sauce (p. 56)

4. Eggs in Aspic *(Oeufs en Gelée)*

Five Consommés with Garnishes
Cinq Consommés Garnis

Jellied Consommé Madrilène   *Consommé à la Madrilène*

1½ cups tomato pulp (with fresh tomatoes)
6 cups Consommé Clair *with gelatin added (p. 6)*

Port wine, sherry wine, or *Cognac to taste*

1. Peel and chop fresh tomatoes. Purée in food processor, strain seeds and skin.
2. *Consommé Clair* should have just enough gelatin to make a soft gel. Test by chilling a small amount of soup. Mix tomato purée in heated consommé. Add port, sherry, or Cognac to taste. After an alcoholic beverage *(alcool)* has been added, the liquid soup may lose some of its thickness. If it does, it will be necessary to add more gelatin.
3. Chill *Consommé Madrilène* until it jells. Serve in small chilled soup cups with handles. If no *alcool* has been added, serve with a wedge of lemon.

Serves 6–8.

Consommé with Caviar   *Consommé Romanoff*

The same soup as *Consommé Madrilène* but topped with sour cream and about 1 teaspoon of any kind of caviar. Golden whitefish caviar can be used.

Consommé with Herbed Pancake Strips   *Consommé Célestine*

2 crêpes (p. 157) with chopped truffle and chives in batter
1 quart Consommé Clair *(p. 6)*

1 tablespoon tapioca
2 teaspoons chopped chervil

1. Make crêpes ahead of time as described in list of ingredients. One crêpe makes 2 servings.
2. Heat consommé and thicken with about 1 tablespoon tapioca, just enough to give a velvety sheen or quality to soup.

9

3. Shred or julienne crêpes and add to heated consommé. Sprinkle chopped chervil atop finished soup.

Serves 4.

Italian Consommé Mille-Fanti Soup

Consommé Italien
Soupe Mille-Fanti

¼ cup fine fresh bread crumbs
¼–½ cup grated Parmesan cheese
2 eggs, beaten

Pinch nutmeg
Salt and pepper to taste
1 quart consommé or stock

1. In a bowl mix fresh bread crumbs, grated cheese, and beaten eggs. Add seasoning. If mixture is too thick (bread acts like a sponge and soaks up liquid), add a little cold stock, about ½ cup.
2. Bring consommé to a boil, and slowly pour mixed ingredients into soup. Cover and cook slowly for 2 minutes. Stir with a whisk before serving.

Serves 4.

Consommé with Quenelles

Consommé à la Reine-Jeanne

1 quart consommé
1 tablespoon tapioca
12 or more small Chicken Quenelles
  (see following recipe)

1 tablespoon chervil leaves
Salt and white pepper to taste

Simmer consommé with tapioca 5–7 minutes; it is added to give a velvety texture to soup, not to thicken it. When ready to serve, taste for salt and pepper and garnish soup with very small Chicken Quenelles and chervil leaves.

Serves 6–8.

Chicken Quenelles   *Quenelles de Volaille*

*3 ounces white meat of chicken,
  uncooked*
1 egg white
Pinch nutmeg
Salt and pepper to taste

½ cup heavy cream
½ teaspoon glace de volaille, *reduced
  clear chicken stock (optional)*
*Few grains of cayenne pepper
  (optional)*

1. In a meat grinder using fine blade or food processor using steel blade, finely grind raw, boned chicken. *If using processor:* Add egg white, processing just long enough to incorporate (a few seconds). Season with nutmeg, salt, and pepper, and add cream quickly. Be careful not to overprocess, for mixture will turn to butter. Test flavor of quenelle by first poaching one. A little *glace de volaille* and a few grains cayenne pepper can be added. Chill in refrigerator.

2. *To make quenelles without a processor:* Put finely ground chicken in a mixing bowl, set bowl over ice, beat in egg white using a wooden spoon, and slowly fold in cream. Season with nutmeg, salt, and pepper. If flavor is too bland, add a little cayenne pepper and *glace de volaille,* the size of one-half of a filbert. Chill mixture 2 hours in refrigerator before shaping into small quenelles.

3. Shape quenelles like small olives using 2 teaspoons or pastry bag fitted with plain ½-inch tip. Poach 4–5 minutes in simmering water as directed in Step 5 for Salmon Quenelles (p. 189). Serve leftover quenelles as a garnish for meat.

Makes approximately 24.

Soups That Do Not Require
Consommé Clair

Cream of Asparagus Soup   *Potage Crème d'Asperges Vertes*

2 tablespoons butter
2 tablespoons flour
1 quart chicken or veal broth, heated
*1–2 bunches fresh asparagus stems,
  peeled*

1 pint heavy cream or half and half
*Salt and freshly ground white pepper
  to taste*
Diced croutons

11

1. Use a heavy saucepan to make a *sauce velouté:* melt butter, stir in flour with wooden spoon or wire whisk, and cook on medium low heat for 5 minutes. Slowly pour in hot broth, stirring with whisk to prevent lumps from forming.

2. Add peeled asparagus stems cut into small pieces. (Save tips and upper stalks to be steamed and served with a first or main course.)* Simmer asparagus stems in broth for ½ hour.

3. Purée soup in blender or food processor. Strain, if necessary, to give a smooth appearance. Do not force through the strainer (*chinois*). Add cream, which can be put in before or after straining.
   Reheat on low heat or in double boiler. Serve with diced croutons.

Serves 4–6.

* A few asparagus tips can be blanched until *al dente* or used raw and sliced thinly on the diagonal to use for garnish.

Cream of Mushroom Soup   *Potage Crème de Champignons*

If cultivated mushrooms are aged, they will acquire a wild mushroom flavor. Fresh as well as dried shiitake mushrooms are now in the markets. Wild mushrooms, such as morels (les morilles), *porcini (Italian), or* cèpes *(French) can be used to make a Cream of Mushroom Soup.*

2–3 tablespoons butter
2 small onions, chopped finely
1 pound fresh mushrooms, cultivated or wild, chopped finely, or 5 ounces dried, wild mushrooms, cleaned and chopped finely
2 tablespoons flour
4 cups chicken or *veal broth*
1 pint half and half or *light cream*

Salt and freshly ground pepper to taste
1½ teaspoons lemon juice
2 tablespoons sherry (optional)
1–2 tablespoons chopped parsley
White or *French bread, toasted and diced, served separately*
2 egg yolks (optional)

1. In a deep saucepan, melt butter and simmer onions and mushrooms slowly for 5 minutes on low heat.

2. Stir in flour with wooden spoon, and cook on low heat for 2 minutes.

3. Warm broth and slowly add to mushrooms, stirring with a whisk. Bring to a boil and simmer for 20 minutes. A double boiler can be used.

4. At this point, soup can be strained; however, pieces of onion and mushroom add to flavor. To finish, stir in cream. Lemon juice and sherry can be

12

added, if desired. Check seasoning. Sprinkle chopped parsley on top of each bowl of soup before serving. Serve with diced toast.

5. If a richer soup is preferred, add 2 egg yolks mixed with cream at the end. In that case, reduce flour to 1 tablespoon.

Serves 6–8.

To clean dried mushrooms:

Soak in warm water about ½ hour, drain, rinse under cold water. Use a coffee filter to strain some of the water in which mushrooms are soaked to add to soup for more flavor. Cut off and discard tough stems.

Cream of Sorrel Soup (Cold Soup)

Potage Crème Germiny (Potage Froid)

4 egg yolks
½ cup heavy cream
1 pint consommé or veal broth, cold
Salt and freshly ground white pepper
   to taste

8–10 leaves sorrel, shredded
2 teaspoons butter

1. Put yolks in a mixing bowl and pour in cream, mixing with a whisk. Slowly pour in cold consommé or veal broth, stirring with a whisk. Add salt and freshly ground white pepper to taste.

2. Pour soup into a copper pot or heavy saucepan, place on high heat, and whisk until foam disappears or soup coats a wooden spoon. Chill.

3. Pour through a fine strainer or *chinois* (French conical strainer) into a porcelain or non-staining bowl. Refrigerate until ready to serve.

4. Clean sorrel in the same way as spinach. Remove the center vein with stalk and shred. Sauté in 2 teaspoons butter until wilted, about 1 minute, and let cool. Just before serving, add shredded sorrel to chilled soup—½ tablespoon per cup.

Serves 4.

NOTE: If soup has separated the next day, it has been cooked too long. Blend it again with a whisk. Taste to correct seasoning.

13

Cream of Sorrel Soup (Hot Soup)

Potage Crème Germiny (Potage Chaud)

The hot Cream of Sorrel Soup is made the same way as the cold except the broth should be boiling when it is poured into the egg yolk and cream mixture. When reheating, do not allow soup to boil. Add prepared sorrel as soon as soup is thickened. If not serving soup immediately, keep warm in double boiler.

Serves 4.

Soup with Red and Yellow Bell Peppers

Potage aux Piments Rouge et Jaune

*1 medium size red bell pepper,
   roasted, peeled, and seeded
1 medium size yellow bell pepper,
   roasted, peeled, and seeded
Oil to coat peppers
2 tablespoons julienne of red and
   green peppers for garnish*

1 quart Potage Parisien *prepared
   through Step 3 (p. 19)*
¹/₂ cup half and half, sour cream, or
   plain yogurt *

1. To skin peppers: Coat peppers with oil and place in a shallow baking pan in a 450–500-degree oven. When blistered and slightly burned on one side, turn on other side. When both sides of peppers are slightly burned and have baked without collapsing (about 20–25 minutes), remove, and let peppers steam enclosed in a brown paper bag for a few minutes. Peel off thin skin while peppers are still hot, using a paring knife. (Peppers can be blackened over a flame as an alternative method.)

2. Julienne a few slices red and yellow peppers to garnish soup. Reserve. Purée rest of peppers in 1 pint of *Potage Parisien* at end of that recipe, Step 3. Mix with rest of potage.

3. Thin potage with ½ cup cream or to taste. When ready to serve, garnish with julienned peppers. Serve hot or cold.

Serves 4.

14   * If sour cream or yogurt is used, do not reheat (will cause soup to curdle).

Cold Cucumber Soup

Potage Crème de Concombres Froid

3 medium cucumbers
1 medium leek, white part with a
little green
2 tablespoons butter
2 bay leaves
1 tablespoon flour
3–4 cups chicken stock, heated

Salt to taste
Freshly ground white pepper to taste
1 cup half and half or light cream
Juice of ½ lemon, or to taste
Fresh dill, chopped, to taste
6 teaspoons sour cream

1. Peel 2 cucumbers and slice ¼ inch thick. Clean leek and slice ½ inch thick. Sauté both in butter with bay leaves on low heat until tender but not brown.

2. Using a wooden spoon, stir in flour and cook for 2 minutes without browning. Add warm stock, salt, and pepper to taste. Simmer for 20–30 minutes.

3. Press mixture through a sieve, or purée in a blender or food processor. Chill in refrigerator until ready to finish.

4. Remove seeds from third cucumber and grate. Just before serving stir into chilled soup with cream, lemon juice, and dill. Taste to correct seasoning.

5. Serve in chilled cups with a teaspoon of sour cream on top.

Serves 6.

Oxtail Soup à la Française

Potage Queue de Boeuf à la Française

1 oxtail, cut in 1-inch slices
2 carrots, sliced thick
1 celery stalk, sliced thick
1 onion, sliced or chopped
1 leek, cleaned and sliced lengthwise
1 bay leaf
Pinch thyme
2 cloves
1 teaspoon whole black pepper
Salt to taste
2 tablespoons sherry (optional)
Choose one of these thickeners:
1 teaspoon arrowroot, cornstarch
(fécule), or potato flour mixed
with 2 tablespoons water, stock, or
sherry

GARNISH:
1 tablespoon carrots, diced or
trimmed into small balls
1 tablespoon turnip, diced or
trimmed into small balls
1 tablespoon green peas
(All diced vegetables steamed or par-
boiled)

15

1. Cut oxtail in 1-inch slices and brown in baking pan in 375–400-degree oven with carrots, celery, and onion, turning once, about 40 minutes. Drain off accumulated fat.
2. Transfer to soup pot and cover with water at least 1½ inches above ingredients. Add leek, bay leaf, thyme, cloves, whole black pepper, and salt to taste. Remove grease as it accumulates to create a clear stock *(dégraissage)* and simmer until meat is tender, about 2½–3 hours.
3. Remove oxtail bones and take off meat. Reserve it for soup. Strain stock and thicken slightly with arrowroot, cornstarch, or potato flour mixed with water, stock, or sherry.
4. Garnish with diced carrots, turnips, and green peas, steamed until tender. Add meat from oxtail bones and sherry, if desired.

Serves 4.

NOTE: Like any consommé, stock can be chilled to remove fat at Step 3, or any remaining fat can be removed by skimming a paper towel over the surface.

Classification of *Soupes* and *Potages* by *le Chef Potager* (Clear soups, *consommés clairs,* not included)

Soups with Cut Vegetables/*Potages Tailles*

Any soup or potage with *cut,* not puréed, vegetables served in a tureen or bowl of soup. I prefer to use water instead of stock in order to preserve the taste of fresh vegetables used in soup.

Vegetable Grower's Soup   *Soupe Maraichère*

½ cup minced leeks, white part only
2 teaspoons butter
1½ cups peeled and thinly sliced potatoes
Salt and freshly ground pepper to taste
¼ cup vermicelli

¼ cup shredded lettuce
¼ cup cleaned and shredded sorrel
½ cup half and half
2 teaspoons butter (optional)
1 teaspoon chervil leaves
French bread, thinly sliced and toasted

16

1. Simmer minced leeks in 2 teaspoons butter in covered pot about 5 minutes. Pour in 6 cups water, potatoes, salt and pepper to taste, and simmer for ½ hour.
2. Just before serving add the vermicelli, shredded lettuce, and sorrel and cook for ½ minute. Finish with ½ cup cream, a little butter if desired, and 1 teaspoon chervil leaves.
   Serve thinly sliced toasted French bread separately.

Serves 4–6.

Cultivator Soup / *Soupe Cultivateur (Potage Paysanne)*

2–3 small carrots
1 small turnip
6 tablespoons leek, white part only
2 tablespoons onion
¼ cup white cabbage

3 tablespoons butter
2½ ounces bacon, diced
½ cup peeled and sliced potatoes or
  ¼ cup rice
Salt to taste

1. Prepare vegetables *paysanne* style: Cut carrots, turnip, leek, and onion in large dice. Shred cabbage and simmer in butter with diced vegetables, salted to taste, in covered pot for 5 minutes on low heat. Add 6 cups of water, and simmer for ½ hour.
2. Blanch bacon in boiling water for 2 minutes.
3. Twenty minutes before serving, add potatoes *or* rice and blanched bacon to soup.

Serves 6–8.

Cream of Vegetable Soups/*Potages Crèmes des Lègumes*

Any soup composed of puréed vegetables and thickened with cooked rice or another starch vegetable (see following recipes).

17

Jackson Soup   *Potage Jackson*

*1 cup flageolet beans (green dried
    beans from France)*
1 cup peeled and diced potatoes
2 tablespoons quick-cooking tapioca
*Salt and freshly ground pepper to
    taste*

½ cup half and half or *heavy cream*
*4 tablespoons julienne of leek for
    garnish*

1. Soak beans overnight in 2 quarts water. Drain, add 6 cups fresh water, and simmer for 1½ hours.
2. Add diced potatoes ½ hour before beans are done. Purée in batches in blender or food processor.
3. Soak quick-cooking tapioca in ½ cup water for 5 minutes, bring to boil, stir, and let stand 15 minutes.
4. After puréeing soup, return to pot and stir in cooked tapioca, add salt and pepper to taste and ½ cup cream. Heat through and serve garnished with julienne of leek.

Serves 6–8.

Ambassadors Soup   *Soupe Ambassadeurs*

*4 pounds (about 1 quart) unshelled
    fresh peas*
5 cups white stock or *consommé*
*Salt and freshly ground white pepper
    to taste*
*3 tablespoons cleaned and shredded
    sorrel*

3 tablespoons shredded lettuce
3 tablespoons butter
2 tablespoons rice, cooked in stock
1 tablespoon chervil leaves
¼–½ cup half and half or *heavy
    cream*

1. Make Purée of Fresh Pea Soup, called Saint-Germain *(Potage Purée de Pois Frais, dite Saint-Germain):* Cook 1 quart fresh peas in ½ cup simmering water, covered, until done—about 7 minutes. Drain, purée through a sieve or in food processor using steel blade, and dilute in pot with 5 cups white stock. Season with salt and white pepper to taste.
2. Sauté sorrel and lettuce in butter for 2 minutes. Add to hot *Potage Purée de Pois Frais* with 2 tablespoons cooked rice, chervil leaves, and cream. Check seasoning.

18   Serves 6–8.

Cream of Leek and Potato Soup

Potage Parisien

1–2 leeks, cleaned and chopped
2 tablespoons butter
1 tablespoon water
2 potatoes, Idaho or other baking variety
Salt and freshly ground pepper to taste

4 cups water or *stock* (optional)*
½ cup milk and ½ cup cream (approximate amount) or *1 cup milk* or *cream*

1. To clean leek cut off root, split leek in four pieces lengthwise, and soak in cold water. Chop fine including some of green top.
2. In a 3-quart saucepan, simmer leek in butter and water, covered, for 5–7 minutes until transparent.
3. Peel potatoes and cut into fine dice. Add 4 cups water, salt, and diced potatoes to saucepan with sautéed leek. Boil fast for ½ hour, skimming while cooking. Potatoes should disintegrate. Use whisk to mix soup. Add pepper to taste. Serve hot.
4. Thin the potage with milk, cream, or half milk and half cream.
5. Leftover soup can be turned into *Vichyssoise:* Purée soup in blender and chill. Add half and half according to desired thickness.

Serves 4–6.

* Stock can be used, but it will diminish flavor of the leeks.

Cream of Leek and Potato Soup with Sorrel

Potage Santé

1 tablespoon butter
½ cup sorrel leaves
4 cups Potage Parisien *prepared through Step 3 (p. 19)*

1 egg yolk
1 cup heavy cream or *half and half*

1. Clean sorrel leaves, removing center vein; shred and sauté in butter. Add to *Potage Parisien*.
2. In a bowl mix egg yolk and cream with a whisk. To prevent curdling, mix a little hot soup into cream before pouring cream and yolk mixture into hot *Potage Santé*.

Serves 4.

Watercress Soup

Potage Crème de Cresson

1 bunch watercress, leaves and tender stems only
1 quart Potage Parisien *prepared through Step 3 (p. 19)*

½ cup heavy cream or *half and half*

1. Clean and chop watercress. Add to *Potage Parisien* at Step 3 when finely diced potatoes are put in soup.
2. Finish the same way as *Potage Parisien* in Step 4—thin with desired amount of cream. Taste to correct seasoning.

Serves 4.

Garbure Soup

Potage Garbure

This broth originates in the Béarnais district (the province of Béarn). Preserved goose or *confit d'oie* can be one of the ingredients or cured ham or pork sausage. Vegetables and herbs provide the basic flavor: cabbage, thyme, garlic, parsley, marjoram, green beans, peas, potatoes, dry white or lima beans. Since the soup should be thick, it can be puréed. The very fine purée left in the sieve (¼ cup of purée) is mixed with 1 to 2 egg yolks, 3 tablespoons of grated cheese, and salt and pepper placed on toasted French bread and browned under broiler.

Serve the bread on a plate lined with a doily or on top of the soup.

NOTE: Another version of this farmer's soup, classified as a *potage taille,* is based on the style in which the vegetables to be served are cut, called *grossier batonets*—the root vegetables are peeled and cut in about 1¾-inch chunks.

Cream Soups/*Potages à la Crème*

These soups are thickened by egg yolks, not by a roux.
Potage Crème Germiny (p. 13)

Velouté Soups/*Potages Crèmes Veloutés*

The base of these soups is chicken consommé or veal stock thickened with a roux.

Potage Crème d'Asperges Vertes (p. 11)
Potage Crème de Champignons (p. 12)

Fish Soups/*Soupes de Poissons*

How to make fish stock *(le fond de poisson)*:

1 tablespoon butter
1 tablespoon oil
1 onion, sliced or minced
1 rib of celery and leaves, sliced
2 sprigs parsley
1 sprig thyme
1 bay leaf
Several mushroom stalks and
  trimmings

Juice of 1 lemon
1/2 teaspoon peppercorns
2 cups water
2 cups dry white wine
2 pounds bones and trimmings of
  fish or amount cook has left over.
  The head can be used.*

1. In a pot heat butter and oil and sauté briefly onion, celery, parsley, thyme, bay leaf, mushroom stalks, lemon juice, and peppercorns. Place fish bones and trimmings on top.

2. Cover fish and vegetables with equal amounts of water and wine: 2 cups water to 2 cups white wine. If red wine is used, omit lemon juice.

3. Simmer, partially covered, skimming several times. After sufficient flavor has developed, in about 30 minutes, strain stock.

Makes about 3½ cups.

Use in sauces and as stock for fish soups.

* Oily fish such as salmon are not recommended for fish stock except in red wine fish stock. There, head of salmon is acceptable.

Fish Stock Concentrate

Fumet de Poisson

1 large onion, minced
½ cup mushroom parings
3 sprigs parsley
1 sprig thyme
½ bay leaf
5 pounds bones and trimmings of fish: sole, whiting, sea perch, haddock, halibut, turbot, or red snapper

1 pint dry white wine
Juice of ½ lemon
1 tablespoon peppercorns

1. Place vegetables and herbs on bottom of pot. Arrange fish bones on top to prevent sticking.
2. Pour wine over fish bones, add 2½ quarts of water, juice of ½ lemon, and the peppercorns. Do *not* add salt. Fish has natural salt. Simmer for 30 minutes.
3. Strain through a fine sieve.
4. *Fumet de Poisson* can be frozen in ice cube trays to remove in small amounts, or it can be frozen in plastic 1-pint containers or Mason Ball jars.

Makes approximately 2 quarts.

NOTE: If stock is reduced to 1 pint, a *demi-glace de poisson* will be obtained.

Fish Soup

Soupe de Poissons

Basic method for preparing fish soup: Strain fish stock. The specific fish chosen for soup is cooked as directed with ingredients given, puréed with the stock in a blender, and then put through a sieve. Before serving, small chunks of cooked or uncooked fish are added to specific soup.

2 onions, chopped
2 leeks, white part with a little green
2 tablespoons olive oil
2 tomatoes, chopped
2 garlic cloves, crushed
2 pounds fish: red snapper, rockfish, rex sole, sea bass, porgy, or other saltwater fish
2 fennel stalks or 1 teaspoon fennel seeds

1 bay leaf
Pinch thyme
Pinch saffron
Tiny pinch cayenne pepper
2 quarts water
Garlic croutons—French bread, cubed, sautéed in butter with 1 garlic clove in pan
La Rouille (see recipe below)
Salt (optional)

1. In a large pot sauté onions and leeks in olive oil until soft. Add tomatoes and garlic and cook on medium heat for several minutes.
2. Pour in 2 quarts water with fish and rest of seasonings. Cook on medium low heat for 20 minutes. Purée in a blender or in small batches in a processor. Pass through a strainer or *chinois*. Reheat and serve with a bowl of garlic croutons and *Rouille* put in a sauceboat.

Serves 8–10.

Rouille Sauce   *La Rouille*

2 garlic cloves
2 red pimentos, small size, dry
  Spanish kind, or 2 canned
  pimentos with a few drops Tabasco
  sauce
1 slice French bread

2 tablespoons Soupe de Poissons
(see recipe above)
1 egg yolk
⅛ teaspoon saffron threads
¼ cup olive oil
Salt and freshly ground pepper to
  taste

Put first six ingredients in blender or food processor and process just until mixed. Slowly add olive oil drop by drop with machine running. Add salt and freshly ground pepper to taste.

Rouille can be made the old-fashioned way with mortar and pestle.

Makes approximately ½ cup.

Mussel and Scallop Soup   *Soupe de Moules et Pétoncles*

1 tablespoon olive oil
1 onion, julienned
1 leek, julienned, white part only
2 tomatoes, skinned, seeded, and
  diced
1 clove garlic, crushed
Pinch saffron
3 ounces red snapper fillet
1 teaspoon Cognac
1 cup white wine for stock (wine for
  steaming mussels, optional)

1 pound mussels, cleaned, dégorger,*
  if necessary
1 pint fish stock
3 egg yolks
1 cup half and half or *light cream*
3 ounces scallops, diced small, or *bay*
  scallops, unsliced
Salt and pepper to taste
Sliced bread rubbed with garlic clove

* Put one mussel in 350-degree oven for 2 minutes or until it opens. If it is sandy, soak mussels overnight in salted water, turning twice, to let them reject sand.

23

1. Heat olive oil in heavy pot, put in julienned onion and leek, and cook on low heat without browning for 5–8 minutes. Add diced tomato, crushed garlic, pinch of saffron, and diced red snapper. Flame with Cognac.

2. Pour in white wine, then fish stock, and simmer for 10 minutes.

3. Scrub mussels with wire or stiff brush under running water. Remove byssus or "beard." Discard any with open shells. Steam mussels in a small amount of water or wine, covered, for about 5 minutes, removing them as they open. Discard any bivalves that do not open. Cut out tough hinge or adductor muscles and discard black edging. Add mussels and the juice from shells to soup.

4. Put egg yolks in a large pot, pour cream over yolks, mix with a whisk; then pour hot soup in, stirring with a wooden spoon on low heat—the same method used to make *Crème Anglaise* (p. 287). Do not boil! Consistency should be light and creamy.

5. Just before serving add the scallops, which will cook enough in the hot liquid off heat. They should not be overcooked. Taste for salt and pepper. Since there is salt in the fish and mussels, it is better to salt when soup is finished.

Serves 6–8.

Variation: Serve with sliced bread rubbed with garlic, sprinkled with olive oil, and toasted.

Some Useful Facts about Mussels *(Moules)*:

1. Mussels are bivalve mollusks belonging to marine family *Mytilidae* found in salt water. Freshwater mussels belong to family *Unionidae*.

2. Only certain species of sea mussels are suitable for eating—most common species is the blue or edible mussel *(Mytilus edulis),* occurring in Europe, eastern North America, and as far south as North Carolina. The blue mussel has been introduced to our Pacific Coast, where it supplements the California mussel *(M. californianus).* Since *M. edulis* is present in polar to cool temperate waters everywhere, it is now believed to be a worldwide species with minor variations.*

3. Mussels are cultivated on a large scale in Europe by two methods: suspension between surface and sea bottom on stakes, *bouchot* method, and on sea bottom by seeding.

* A. J. McClane and Arie de Zanger, *The Encyclopedia of Fish Cookery* (New York: Holt, Rinehart & Winston, 1977), p. 200.

4. As with clams and oysters, mussels can be toxic if taken from polluted water or when feeding on dinoflagellates. Mussel beds are monitored and closed to fishing whenever this condition occurs. Pacific coast mussels are quarantined from May 1 through October.

5. Live mussels keep their shells tightly closed and should have a fresh, briny smell; open-shelled mussels should be discarded. The two halves fit together tightly to protect them from their deadly enemy, the starfish.* Live mussels covered with seaweed or damp cloth under refrigeration will last 24 hours. To prevent mussels from opening, cover with a weight, such as a stone or brick. Cooked, shelled mussels will keep under refrigeration no longer than 1 day. When they are covered with their own juice, they will keep several days.

* Shirley Ross, *The Seafood Book* (New York: McGraw-Hill, 1980), p. 129.

Lobster Bisque   *Bisque de Homard*

1 or 2 live lobsters, total weight 4 pounds. Lobsters can have parts missing.
4–6 tablespoons butter or vegetable oil or ½ of each
1 cup finely chopped onions
1 cup finely chopped carrots
1 cup finely chopped celery
1 clove garlic, minced
3–4 shallots, finely chopped
6 tablespoons Cognac
4–6 parsley sprigs
1 tablespoon tomato paste

2½ cups dry white wine
4–5 cups fish stock or light chicken stock
2 tablespoons whole white or black peppercorns
1 green leaf of leek (top of small green leek)
Bouquet garni—1 sprig thyme, 1 bay leaf, sprig parsley wrapped in green skin of leek and tied
2 tablespoons raw rice (cooked rice can be used if it is plain cooked)
1 cup heavy cream or half and half

1. To prepare raw lobster: Dip head of lobster in boiling water holding lobster by tail for a few seconds. Cut off claws and crack them. Insert knife in abdomen cutting through shell toward the head, then cut toward the tail. Press lobster apart, separating halves. Cut tail into four pieces cross-wise. Remove the sand sac or stomach from the head and discard along with the intestinal tract. Reserve juice or blood of lobster, also the green tomalley, which is the liver, and the roe or "coral" of the female lobster. There is very little waste in lobster—the meat in the head is excellent and full of protein, as is all lobster meat.

25

2. Put butter or oil or both in a heavy skillet on medium heat. Sauté *mirepoix* of onions, carrots, celery, garlic, and shallots until partially cooked. On high heat add the lobster, cooking until the shells are bright red. The color comes from the carotene in the shell.

3. Pour in half of the Cognac and flame lobster. Be careful in case flame should flare up. Remove lobster from pan.

4. Add tomato paste, white wine, fish stock, peppercorns, leek, and *bouquet garni.* Cover pot and simmer for 15 minutes. Strain out vegetables.

5. While stock is simmering in Step 4, remove meat from shells and claws and reserve. Crush all shells in food processor or pound until crushed. Simmer crushed shells in stock for about 20 minutes. Strain out in a sieve.

6. Add uncooked rice and whisk in tomalley and coral to strained soup. Cook on low heat until rice is done, about 20 minutes. Purée in blender, then strain through a Chinese cap *(chinoise)* or use cheesecloth *(étamine).*

7. Bring soup back to a boil. Lower heat, add remaining 3 tablespoons of Cognac, about ½ cup lobster meat cut into small or large dice, and cream. Taste to correct seasoning. If more thickness is desired, a little cornstarch (p. 4) or *beurre manié* (p. 4) can be used.

8. The reserved lobster meat can be served cold in a salad or heated and served with a sauce* accompanied by rice.

Serves 8.

NOTE: *Bisque d'Ecrivisses, Bisque de Crabes,* and *Bisque de Crevettes* are made the same way as *Bisque de Homard* with the exception of Step 1, which describes how to cut up the lobster and reserve the tomalley, roe, and its blood or juice.

* Before adding the cream to the Lobster Bisque in Step 7, *Sauce Américaine* can be made by removing some of the soup, to serve as sauce, at the end of Step 6. Or, when cooked lobster meat is added, it becomes Lobster à l'Américaine *(Homard à l'Américaine)* with chopped fresh tarragon included. A different sauce can be created by using chopped basil, chives, and a dash of vanilla.

Peasant Soups/*Soupes des Paysans*

Garlic Soup   *Soupe à l'Ail*

Bread soup (panada soupe) *is one example of a peasant soup, as is this garlic soup.*

9 cups water *or* stock
5 ounces crushed cloves garlic
   (2–3 heads)
2 sprigs sage
2 cloves

Salt and pepper to taste
20 slices French bread, small slices
Grated Gruyère cheese *or* half
   Gruyère and half Parmesan
Olive oil

1. Place in a pot: water, crushed cloves of garlic, sage, cloves, salt, and pepper. Bring to boil and allow to cook gently for 15 minutes.
2. Meanwhile, sprinkle the French bread with grated cheese and place in 350-degree oven for a few minutes to melt the cheese.
3. Place croutons in a soup tureen, sprinkle with a little olive oil, and pour soup over them through a fine strainer, lightly pressing the ingredients. Let bread soak and swell for 2 minutes before serving.

Serves 10.

Dessert Soups/*Soupes pour le Dessert*

Two-Tone Fresh Fruit Soup   *Soupe aux Fruits Frais aux Deux Couleurs*

FIRST SOUP:
1½ quarts water
6 tablespoons sugar
4 whole cloves
Pinch each of cinnamon and nutmeg
6 peaches, peeled and sliced
6 apples, peeled and cut up
1 grapefruit, peeled, pithed, separated
   into segments

2–3 slices pineapple, peeled and cut
   up
1 orange, peeled, pithed, and
   segmented
2 cups dry white wine *or* Barsac *or*
   Sauternes for a sweeter taste

27

1. Put water, sugar, cloves, cinnamon, and nutmeg in a large pot, bring to a boil, and add all of fruit and simmer until fruit begins to soften. Add white wine and simmer until fruit is soft, about 10 minutes longer.

2. Take off heat, remove cloves, and reserve 2 cups liquid from pot. Purée rest of soup in processor in small batches. Chill.

Makes 3 quarts.

SECOND SOUP:
2 cups liquid from first soup   *3 peaches, peeled and sliced*
1 cup blueberries   *¹⁄₄ cup blueberries for garnish*
¹⁄₂ cup strawberries   *6 strawberries, sliced, for garnish*

1. Bring soup to a boil, add fruit, and simmer until fruit is soft. Purée and chill. This soup will be a deep blue color in contrast to the peach-like color of the first soup.

2. How to serve, or the presentation: Hold a piece of foil or cardboard in center of individual soup bowl so that bowl is divided into two equal halves (see illustration below). Pour first soup into one side, pour second soup into other side. Carefully remove divider. Drop a few blueberries and sliced strawberries into lighter colored soup for garnish.

    Also serve as a summertime luncheon soup.

Makes 1 quart; the two soups together serve 10–12.

Le Pot-au-Feu

The words *pot au feu* mean pot on the fire, and the dish itself has been called a stockpot. It is appropriate here to compare a *Pot-au-Feu* to stock, for if a cook can make a substantial stock, he or she should find making this related dish almost as worthwhile. Since the meat in the *Pot-au-Feu* is a main course dish, more meat and less bones are used than for stock; and its stock can be clarified to use as a clear consommé *(Consommé Clair)* as well. The meats used for *Le Pot-au-Feu* are chuck, short ribs, brisket *(poitrine),* and beef or veal shank bones.

The same title is used for fish cooked in stock: *Le Pot-au-Feu de Poisson ou de la Mer.*

Traditional condiments to be served with both *soupes* and put in little dishes are: gherkins, whipped cream blended with horseradish. rock salt *(à la croque au sel)* and prepared mustard, mild or hot and spicy. The vegetables cooked a short time with the meat are also served.

The National Dish of France   *Le Pot-au-Feu*

Since some of the instructions for pot-au-feu *are different from the ingredients for stock in the Clarified Soup Stock recipe, Steps 1–6 (p. 7), here are the ingredients and steps to make my version of* Le Pot-au-Feu:

2–3 quarts stock (more can be used or water can be added to stock) or 4 quarts water or more, if preferred
1 teaspoon salt, or to taste
6 cracked peppercorns
2–3 pounds brisket or chuck roast
4 pounds short ribs of beef
3–4 veal shanks or 1–2 beef shanks (if veal shanks are unavailable)
2 onions stuck with cloves (1 unpeeled onion browned in oven)
1–2 leeks, white part with a little green included
2–3 celery ribs, cut up
1–2 large carrots, cut up
1 bouquet garni *(p. 6)*
1–2 cloves garlic (optional)

Vegetables to serve with meat as a main course to cook later:

24 baby carrots
16 small turnips
8 parsnips, trimmed in uniform oval shapes
1–2 celery roots, peeled and trimmed into 1½-inch chunks or oval shapes
16 baby leeks, cleaned and tied in bunches
16 small red potatoes or 6–8 large white potatoes, peeled and trimmed into 1¾-inch chunks or ovals
1 head cabbage, cut in wedges parboiled separately
Croutons, toasted, or *sliced French bread*
Parsley sprigs for garnish

29

1. Bring stock or water to a boil, put in beef and the veal shanks for several minutes to seal in juices and retain moisture of meat. Reduce heat to simmer, skim off foam and scum. Add rest of ingredients *except* vegetables for serving with the meat.

2. Cook meat just long enough to become tender, approximately 2½ hours; remove and keep warm. Strain, degrease stock, and boil down to concentrate the flavor, if desired. Stock can also be clarified (p. 7) for other uses such as consommés, aspics, sauces. If this dish is started with a well-made stock, a more flavorful soup will be ready to serve in a shorter cooking time.

3. The small vegetables listed in ingredients to be served with meat should be peeled, trimmed uniformly, parboiled (optional), cooked in stock just long enough to become tender, and removed. To reheat meat and vegetables before serving, pour some stock over them. Drain before serving on a large heated platter.

4. Serve clear soup as a first course with fresh or toasted French bread. Fresh parboiled noodles or julienned vegetables can be added to the soup. Slice the beef and arrange rest of meat with freshly cooked vegetables on a large heated platter for the main course. Decorate platter with parsley sprigs. Garnishes are given on page 113.

Serves 8.

Petite Marmite Henry IV with Chicken
Petite Marmite Henri IV avec Volaille

Made in an earthenware pot called a *marmite,* this bourgeois soup dish originally included an old bird which required longer cooking and had more flavor—it was an economical way to use a laying hen past its prime. Today, a tender roasting chicken (first browned in the oven) is preferred. When served in a restaurant, it is given an elegant presentation—vegetables such as carrots, turnips, celery, leeks are cut in small rectangular pieces, edges trimmed, with seven sides, cooked in consommé separately, and served with the chicken. Beef is always cooked in the soup stock with the chicken. Since I have found carrots grown in America to be sweeter than carrots grown in Europe, I blanch them to remove a little of this sweetness before putting them in stock.

Chapter Two

SAUCES

Brown, White, Warm, and
Cold Emulsified;
How to Use *Sauce Brune* in
Compound Sauces for Sautéed Meats

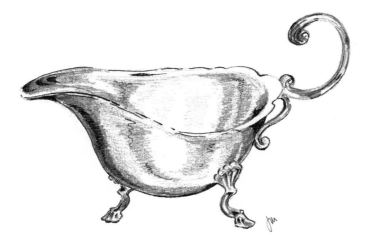

Saucemaking gives me the first opportunity to teach by comparison—the experience of making stock for *Consommé Clair* is applied to the same process for Brown Sauce. It is mainly an ingredient in sauces, not a main course dish such as soup. Brown Sauce *(Sauce Brune),* classified as a *Grande Sauce* or a *Sauce Mére,* plays an indispensable role in the completion of many great sauces. In the same way stock is begun, I collect a fresh assortment of bones and aromatic vegetables for the first step in making *Sauce Brune.* However, I place them in a shallow roasting pan to brown for about an hour on high heat; I do not do this for *Consommé Clair,* which is produced from a white stock *(fond blanc).* Although soup stock is not thickened in the final stage, Brown Sauce is thickened for immediate use. This does not apply to *potages* which are thickened with a light purée of starchy vegetables, rice, tapioca, or dried beans either cooked separately or in the soup.

I thicken my Brown Sauce with cornstarch or arrowroot which creates a shiny sauce. I no longer prefer flour as a thickener, for it produces a cloudy sauce. The deep brown color and richness of flavor come from the browned bones and vegetables, which are listed on page 39. To explain often-used terms which are interrelated, *demi-glace,* meaning "half glaze," is actually the middle stage between the liquid brown stock *(fond brun)* and the third stage, *glace de viande,* or meat glaze, an extremely reduced meat stock viscous enough to cut with a knife when chilled. Regardless of the true meaning, Brown Sauce is often called *Demi-Glace* in the culinary world. *Glace de Viande* (p. 40), an enrichment to put in sauces of meat or poultry dishes, is made from fresh or previously cooked beef or veal bones and additional chicken bones. Due to the prolonged cooking of the strained stock which results in this extreme viscosity, it can be preserved under refrigeration for months or frozen like Brown Sauce when prepared in advance.

Main course dishes are prepared very quickly and efficiently when Brown Sauce is on hand to serve as a base—just enough to give shine and body to the sauce that is poured around the meat. A few such dishes are Veal or Chicken Cordon Bleu (p. 43), Steak *Bordelaise* or *au Poivre* (p. 47), *Filets de Boeuf Baies de Cassis* (p. 48), and *Magret de Canard Baies de Cassis* (p. 244).

As Chef *Saucier* this is the proper time to discuss the role of wine—how it should be blended into sauces to add complexity and bouquet and how it enhances other categories of French cuisine. I always believe the finer the wine that is selected for the sauce or cooking pot, the greater is the sauce. Another conviction is that the same wine used in the kitchen to prepare the dish should be served at table. A red Burgundy or heavy Bordeaux are a wise choice for steak and roast sauces; a Bordeaux such as Pomerol, St. Emilion or a California Cabernet Sauvignon marry with veal; and a white Burgundy such as a Meursault, Pouilly Fuissé, or a good California Chardonnay harmonize with poultry. Sweet wine and port served with foie gras in aspic at the beginning of a dinner enrich the taste experience.

The five main uses of wine in cooking are:
1. As an ingredient in uncooked and cooked marinades for meat
2. In court bouillon for poaching fish, in braised meat and poultry dishes, in stews
3. For deglazing the pan in which meat, poultry, or fish were sautéed or roasted
4. To finish a sauce, wine, usually fortified, is added, in which case the sauce would not be brought back to a boil again
5. For pastries and desserts, fortified wines and liqueurs are listed in chapters on *les pâtisseries*.

Dishes serving as examples of the fourth use are Veal Madeira, Veal Piccata, Veal Calvados (with cream), Beef with Madeira Sauce (p. 43), and Braised Salmon with Champagne Sauce (p. 54). Fortified wines are sherries (Malaga, Jerez) and Madeira. *Alcohols* added to sauces are brandy, Cognac, Calvados, Armagnac, and Marc de Bourgogne. Wine used in dessert sauces such as Sabayon Sauce, the French version of the sweet Italian dessert Zabaglione, can be dry white wine finished with a liqueur or rum, Marsala, sherry, Madeira, or Champagne without other flavoring.

I do not want cooks to believe a tasty sauce always requires Brown Sauce —the sediment or brown bits that are left in the degreased pan can substitute for Brown Sauce. Add a little chopped shallots, a little wine, water, or lemon juice (lemon juice for veal or chicken) and deglaze the pan on medium high heat. I finish the sauce with a dab of butter and a little cornstarch mixed with liquid, if more thickness is desired. However, if the sediment is too dark after sautéeing the meat, the sauce will have a bitter taste and should not be used.

My sauce for Roast Leg of Lamb *(Gigot d'Agneau)* is little more than a pan sauce using the natural lamb juices. The delicate lamb flavor would be

33

lost if a thickened Brown Sauce were added. In advance, I prepare a lamb stock from the lamb bones. Ask the butcher for some extra lamb bones for stock and place these under the lamb while it is roasting. The hip bone and end of spine should be removed from the leg as well as excess fat. Insertion of garlic slivers in the meat is optional. Rub the outside of the lamb with fresh or dried rosemary, and roast in a 350-degree oven 15 minutes to the pound for medium rare meat. Add a *mirepoix* (p. 39) when the lamb is half done; this provides steam around the meat and prevents the vegetables from becoming overcooked. To test for doneness use your finger to penetrate the flesh along the leg bone where the hip bone has been removed. If meat is lukewarm, the lamb should be medium rare, and will register about 135 degrees on an instant thermometer (p. 206). When done, remove the lamb and place on a platter on the back of a large fork or inverted plate. This will raise the lamb above platter to stop the cooking and allow air to circulate. Turn lamb over once to distribute juices equally. All meat, steak, or roasts should be rested this way. Roast chicken and turkey should be tilted so that the juices will go into the breast as soon as they are removed from the oven.

To finish the sauce, the subject from which I have wandered, strain pan juices reserving the vegetables. Degrease, add warm stock, return the vegetables to pan, and reduce sauce for a few minutes. Again, strain sauce removing vegetables, taste to correct seasoning, and serve in a warm sauceboat. I do not add wine to lamb sauce, for it detracts from its unique taste. Pour sauce around sliced lamb on dinner plate, *not* on top of lamb, which would recook the sauce. Leftover cold, sliced lamb can be served with mayonnaise or other cold sauces with herbs. Chopped cooked lamb can be used to make Moussaka or stuffed eggplant.

When Roast Prime Rib of Beef *(Côtes de Boeuf Rôti)* is served with its natural juice, the French lend elegance to the name by calling it *jus de rôti.* If the roast is served with a more elaborate sauce such as *Sauce Madère, Bordelaise,* or *Périgueux,* this change should be stated in the title of the dish. To roast prime rib, place extra bones under and around the beef, add cut-up aromatic vegetables and cook in a 400-degree oven 15 minutes to the pound for a rare roast. The instant thermometer reading should be 120–130 degrees (see chart, p. 206). Remove roast from pan to rest 30 minutes before carving. Degrease sauce, add just enough beef stock to make the amount of sauce needed, simmer for about 5–10 minutes, strain, season to taste, and serve in a sauceboat.

During the Renaissance, sauces began to emerge in the form they have today, although at that time they were often served as a separate dish. The next stage of sauces was with solids—*Blanquette de Veau, Boeuf Bourguignon,* and other stews. Restaurateur and author Raymond Oliver felt that sauces came to represent the value of a country's cuisine. He wrote that England had only one sauce (which was mint), whereas France had hundreds of sauces. From the diversity of France's thirty-two provinces many sauces have become part of the language of cuisine: *Sauce Beurre Blanc Nantais* and *Sauce Bretonne* from Brittany; *Sauce Pistou, Sauce à l'Ail à la Provençal,* and *Sauce Provençal* from Provence; *Sauce Bordelaise* from Bordeaux; *Sauce Bourguignonne* from Burgundy; *Sauces Périgueux* and *Périgourdine* from Périgord; *Sauce Normande* from Normandy (this sauce contains a blond roux, stock, cider, white wine or egg yolks, cream and butter); *à la Niçoise,* a style of sauce from the Côte d'Azur, using anchovy flavor and tarragon; *Sauce Nantua* from Franche-Comte; and *Sauce Béarnaise,* first made in the restaurant Pavillon Henry IV in Saint-Germain-en-Laye outside Paris.

If names make new sauces, there are in America, especially California, varietal wines which have replaced French titles—for *Sauce Bordelaise* there is Napa Valley Cabernet Sauvignon Sauce (the Cabernet is softened with Merlot), for *Sauce Bourguignonne* there is Pinot Noir or Zinfandel Sauce, and for *Sauce Champagne* there are *méthode champenoise* wines used to make sauces for chicken, veal, and seafood, an example being Blue Point Oysters with Champagne Sauce.

The study of cuisine adds to our knowledge of history when we learn about distant origins of plants and how they relate to the culinary customs of diverse people. A colorful example is the story of the cocoa tree, *Theobroma cacoa,* Theobroma meaning "food of the gods."[*] Native to Central and South America, the beans were first used by the Aztecs not only in religious rites and as a form of currency, but processed into a drink reputedly much loved by Montezuma II.[†]

Chocolate contains theobromine, a strong stimulant related to caffeine. It is believed that cocoa beans and the recipe for the royal chocolate drink were taken back to Spain by the conquistador Hernando Cortes where it was kept a court secret from the rest of Europe for one hundred years. In spite of this effort, hot chocolate became a popular drink in fashionable society throughout Europe—there are many beautiful silver and painted porcelain chocolate pots and cups still extant in museums to prove it. The British opened the first "chocolate house" in 1657. It was the Europeans who thought of turning chocolate into a food: the English made the first chocolate bar in 1847, the Swiss were the first to make milk chocolate, and the Dutch invented the cocoa press and a process called "dutching" which makes chocolate more digestible.

[*] The cacao tree was named by the Swedish scientist Carolus Linnaeus.
[†] Mitchel Beazley Publishers Limited, eds., *The World Atlas of Food* (New York: Simon & Schuster, 1984), p. 80.

The ever inventive Italians thought of putting ground unsweetened chocolate in a sweet-sour sauce for wild boar *(Bistecchine di Cinghiale);* a modern recipe for this sauce includes 3 ounces of grated chocolate, 3 tablespoons sugar, 4 bay leaves, ½ pint wine vinegar, 3 ounces white raisins, 3 ounces pitted prunes, a pinch of ground cinnamon or nutmeg, and 1 tablespoon flour.* The sauce is made to this day! Legend has it that some Spanish nuns cloistered in Mexico were the first to make *Molé Poblano,* a turkey dish with a rich sauce of Mexican chocolate, spices, chiles, and seeds, because a distinguished bishop arrived unexpectedly. They simply combined all they had in their kitchen to make a festive dinner for him. It's a nice story, but it seems more likely that the local inhabitants had long before thought of this combination using their own local ingredients. Molé sauce is also served with chicken, beef, and pork. Some Western chefs are experimenting with the use of cocoa or chocolate as an ingredient in poultry and meat sauces.

Pertinent to the subject of sauces is the revelation that the grasses, grains, and berries on which animals and birds feed affect their flavor. This, in turn, influences the choice of herbs and berries chefs put in the sauces to serve with certain birds and meat. Lambs that graze on aromatic grasses near Mont Saint-Michel in Normandy are called *agneau de pré-salé,* the salty flavor of their meat coming from the salt marshes there. Pauillac on the Gironde is not only noted for its milk-fed baby lamb *(agneau de lait)* but also for the weaned lambs that feed in the salt meadows. In the Béarn, *Sauce Paloise* (p. 61) made with mint is served with the local herb-flavored mountain lamb. Since thrush or Grieve eat grapes when ripe, fresh grapes are added to their sauce; or the birds are wrapped in vine leaves before they are braised. Similarly, quail favor juniper berries, so that dried juniper berries are appropriate in their sauce.

To go a step further, historians reveal that in the nineteenth century gourmands ate Ortolan (small birds found in central and southern Europe) with dinner napkins over their heads, in the manner of old-style photographers, to get the full flavor of the delicate birds!

Leaping forward to our modern era, contemporary taste prefers fresh produce—meat, poultry, fish—quickly grilled, sautéed or braised and arranged artistically on individual plates. The sauces for this *nouvelle cuisine* style of cooking frequently are composed of vegetable or fruit purées, fruit vinegars, and reductions of meat, poultry or fish essences. Thickened without flour, they are apt to use more butter, cream or eggs. That explains the reason two flourless traditional sauces, *Les Sauces Beurre Blanc* and *Vin Blanc,* are so often served with *nouvelle cuisine* dishes for fish, while *Demi-Glace* is

* Ada Boni, *Italian Regional Cooking* (New York: Bonanza Books), p. 287.

used for meat. My conviction still holds that student cooks are obliged to learn the classic sauces before experimenting with "new" methods.

On my trip to France in 1982–83 I found a new direction called *cuisine bourgeoise* which had displaced *nouvelle cuisine*. When I returned to France in 1984, the current style was called *classique nouveau*, "cooking of the day," or *cuisine naturelle*. Despite these new titles—and granted that innovations create enthusiasm—there is no substitute for basic training in any art, including that of cuisine. One of the dishes I had in a restaurant on my last trip was a new version of foie gras, which was too raw for my taste; however, I did enjoy the Crayfish à la Nage and another dish of fresh black mushrooms and sliced black truffles sautéed in butter, finished with truffle juice. The *Rouget Sauce Vièrge* and *Rablé de Lièvre* or Saddle of Hare with six thin slices of potato were successful presentations of *classic nouveau* style.

In another restaurant I was served a salad with foie gras, sweetbreads, truffles, and *Pommes Gratin Savoyard* on a separate plate. A woodcock *(bécasse)* was served so raw I'm sure it would not have pleased American tastes. It is almost as if chefs feel that they must be like fashion designers who present a new line of clothing for every season of each new year. One plate set before me of fanned out, rare duck slices was tastefully garnished in the new sparse style, but the *Sauce Poivrade, subric* of vegetables, and mousseline of sole and salmon also presented have been established classics for over one hundred years. Instead of confusing diners with new titles for cuisine, I would rather believe that there are only two kinds of cooking—good and bad.

The real revolution in cuisine is more evident in *la pâtisserie*. Less sugar is used in *gâteaux,* pastry creams, and pastry sauces such as *crème anglaise*. In the same vein, fewer eggs are incorporated while more purées of fresh fruits—called *coulis* perfumed with liqueur or *alcool*—are found lining the dessert plate. One or two tablespoons of red or black currant jam are added to give a smooth thickness to fresh fruit sauces. It was on my last visit to France that I found *Gâteau Génoise Mousseline,* which is taught in Chapter 12 (p. 326).

It seems as if the contemporary kitchen is in danger of developing an "Esperanto cuisine" based on a borrowing and melding of techniques from Oriental, European, Mexican, Indian, and Middle Eastern countries resulting in a loss of the traditions and national spirit these regions have upheld for centuries. When foreign influences become too pervasive, the roots of national cuisines are muted. If this habit continues, scholarly cooks will need to become archeologists to trace the sources of the dishes they have learned to cook. A new anthropology of cuisine will develop in the classroom.

It is Frédy Girardet in Crissier, Switzerland, whose fresh approach and total devotion to his craft have contributed a successful method called *cuisine spontanée* or spontaneous cooking.* He takes notice of the nuances found in the market's produce each day to inspire a chef's gastronomic mind. Cooking should never become dull, he feels, and should always be free of routine gestures. The cook should let intuition influence his culinary skills. This method can only be effective if all the preparatory work is done ahead (*mise en place,* p. xvi), such as partial blanching, steaming of vegetables and fruits; and if liquids or *fonds de cuisine* are concentrated and reduced earlier in the day. That way the chef is free to complete the dish swiftly in order to preserve the integrity of the food and to design its composition on the plate. All his stocks, chicken, veal, and fish, are reduced to jelled essences *(glace de viande),* rather than maintaining stockpots at a simmer for hours. The alert chef not only watches and listens to his food, he also uses the pressure of his fingers to judge the degree of doneness. The degree of cooking tolerated by vegetables, fruit, or meat is decided by touching the produce when it is raw as well as during cooking. These precepts belong in all aspiring chefs' kitchens, where every meal should be as new and slightly different as a fresh pear or bunch of grapes.

Attention! I have digressed from the subject of *Les Sauces.* I feel as if I have just flown to France and back to California through my discussion.

In order for Brown Sauce to remain in the repertoire of "cooking of the day" or *classique nouveau* cuisine, I do not use flour as a thickener, nor do I simmer the stock as long as in the past. The aromatic vegetables used in the stock for this basic sauce are cut in irregular chunks. This *couper* reminds me of a French kitchen slang phrase *couper en coin de rue.* The literal translation is "cut like a street corner" and means not to peel vegetables and to cut them in irregular shapes. This rough style of cutting vegetables contrasts strongly with the fine julienned vegetables chefs use for garnish.

I probably have found Brown Sauce (p. 39) more useful than any other sauce in my kitchen. *Glace de Viande* might be in a close second position. Although *Sauce Tomate* is a common sauce, its brilliant color and herbal fragrance win it a high place in my cuisine. In this chapter twelve sautéed meat dishes follow these three sauces, all of which are completed with Brown Sauce.

Next are the four other mother sauces *(Les Sauces Mères* or *Les Sauces de Base).* The title of each sauce includes its label—that of a basic sauce, made with milk or stock, or a compound sauce; a basic emulsified sauce made with eggs and butter or an emulsified sauce made with eggs and oil plus some of their indispensable variations.

* "Frédy Girardet: Swiss Master of Spontaneous Cooking." Article based on interview by Roy Andries de Groot. *Cuisine Magazine,* February 1984, pp. 15 and 18.

Sauce Hollandaise and Mayonnaise are better understood if they are first made by hand. The dictionary defines an emulsion as "a dispersion of fine particles or globules of a liquid in a liquid," the physical chemistry taking place when emulsified sauces are made by hand or produced in a blender or processor. The main differences between the two machines are that the processor is faster, and newer models have a greater capacity than the standard blender for the home kitchen.

Brown Sauce   *Sauce Brune*

6 pounds or more beef and veal knuckle and joint bones with some meat *

MIREPOIX:
1 celery rib, cut in irregular large chunks
1 onion, cut in irregular large chunks
1 carrot, cut in irregular large chunks
1 bay leaf
1 teaspoon thyme
1 bottle (one-fifth size) dry white wine to 3 quarts water, or ¼ amount of dry white wine to ¾ amount of water

1 small can tomato paste
1 teaspoon salt (approximate amount)
½ teaspoon black peppercorns (can be cracked)
Parsley stems
Kitchen Bouquet, by the teaspoon (optional)
1–2 tablespoons cornstarch

1. Wipe off meat and bones with a damp paper towel before browning.

2. In a large, shallow roasting pan brown bones for 1 hour in 400–425-degree oven, adding *mirepoix* the last quarter hour. Salt and pepper meat before placing cut-up vegetables on top and around meat, thereby creating steam for cooking the meat.

3. When all the vegetables have partially browned, take roasting pan from oven, and with a slotted spoon remove bones to drain in a colander.

4. Put bones and vegetables in a large stockpot. Pour off fat from roasting pan, deglaze with a little water or wine, and pour into stockpot. Add tomato paste, salt, peppercorns, white wine, and water. As soon as stock comes to

* Be sure to use veal shank bones; they have more gelatin than beef bones, which are also included. Amounts can be doubled if more Brown Sauce is required.

a boil, lower heat to a simmer. Remove foam *(dépouiller)* as it forms by running soup ladle around top. Add parsley stems after first skimming the stock. Also remove any fat *(dégraisser)*.

5. Simmer for 8–9 hours. Do not cover! Remove scum occasionally.

6. After the stock or sauce has finished simmering, remove as much fat as possible before straining into a canister type pot. Defat again, and reduce if more than half the original amount of stock is left—about 2½ quarts of the liquid is required. Before sauce is thickened it can be frozen, or frozen after it is thickened by spooning into ½ pint or pint Mason jars. Small jars of *Sauce Brune* can be thawed out quicker than large ones. Clean plastic ice cube trays are also useable.

7. To correct the color: If stock is too red while simmering, add more water. If it is not brown enough after being reduced, add some more brown color by using Kitchen Bouquet—1 teaspoon or just a little more.

8. The best thickening agents are arrowroot or cornstarch, which make a clear, shiny sauce. The use of flour will make a cloudy sauce.

9. Brown Sauce is also called *Demi-Glace* after it is reduced and thickened. The way to add cornstarch is to dissolve 1 or 2 tablespoons of cornstarch in 3 tablespoons of cold water, bring sauce to a boil, and while stirring with a large spoon or soup ladle pour cornstarch slowly from above until the sauce is thick enough. To get the right consistency it may be necessary to use more cornstarch dissolved in water.

   Do not use a whisk to stir in cornstarch, as it could cloud the sauce. It is possible that natural gelatin from the veal bones will give enough thickness to require only a small amount of thickener.

Makes approximately 2½–3 quarts.

Meat Glaze   *Glace de Viande*

*10–12 pounds beef and veal bones
   with some meat attached, plus
   leftover chicken carcasses
1 onion, thickly sliced
1 carrot, thickly sliced
2 pounds aromatic vegetables—
   chopped onions, carrots, celery
   ribs, and parsley leaves*

*2 tablespoons tomato paste,
   4 tablespoons tomato purée, or
   2 cups overripe fresh tomatoes,
   unpeeled and cut in quarters*

1. In a large low-sided roasting pan place bones with thickly sliced onion and

carrot. Brown in a 450-degree oven, stir once, and bake about three quarters of an hour.

2. In a large stockpot place chopped vegetables, browned bones with vegetables, tomatoes, and cover with water. Do not salt. Simmer for 12 hours or overnight, adding a little water, if necessary, to keep contents covered.

3. Strain out bones and vegetables, return stock to pot, and skim off fat. Simmer until liquid is reduced by half, continuing to remove fat and scum as necessary.

4. Place stock in smaller pots as it reduces. Continue to cook on low heat until it is brown and syrupy—thick enough to coat a spoon. Pour into a small Mason jar, cool, and refrigerate or freeze.

5. Three quarts of stock will make about ½ pint of *Glace de Viande*. One tablespoon Meat Glaze added to 1 cup of hot water will create 1 cup of flavorful brown stock.

6. Mixed with the right amount of Madeira wine, it can be a substitution for *demi-glace* sauce served with roast or sautéed meats, or it can be brushed on to glaze the meat. Meat Glaze added by spoonfuls gives body and flavor to soups, sauces, stews, meat, and poultry dishes.

NOTE: A *glace* is a reduction of a liquid stock to an extract made from any type of meat or fish stock.

Tomato Sauce   *Sauce Tomate*

2 tablespoons oil
2–4 onions, chopped
2 cloves garlic, smashed
1 celery rib, cut up
1 carrot, sliced
1 tablespoon flour
3–4 pounds fresh, overripe, or
    canned tomatoes (use 1 small can
    tomato paste if there are not
    enough tomatoes)

1½ teaspoons salt
Pinch of pepper
1 bay leaf
1 sprig thyme
2 teaspoons sugar
1 quart beef or chicken stock

1. Heat the oil in a large heavy pot or saucepan and sauté the onions, garlic, celery, and carrot until lightly browned. Stir in flour and cook for about 1 minute.

2. Wash tomatoes, cut into chunks, and add to browned vegetables. Add salt.

41

3. Stir in remaining ingredients and simmer for 1–2 hours. This amount of cooking time helps kill acidity of tomatoes.

4. If a smooth sauce is required, put through a sieve or a *chinois*. Taste to correct seasoning.

Makes approximately 5 cups.

Uses: As an enrichment in Brown Sauce; as a sauce to serve with pasta, broiled fish, meat, and vegetable dishes.
Variations: Herbs such as tarragon, basil, and chervil can be added.

Twelve Sauces and Meat Dishes Using Brown Sauce
Douze Sauces et Plats de Viande en Servant de Sauce Brune

Bordelaise Sauce Prepared for Steak Bordelaise and Ground Beef

Sauce Bordelaise Préparé pour Entrecôte et Emincé de Boeuf

1½ inch thick filet mignon, 6 ounces; porterhouse, 12 ounces; club sirloin, 8 ounces; or chateaubriand (for two), 14 ounces, trimmed of fat
3–4 tablespoons Clarified Butter (p. 66, optional) or 2 tablespoons butter and 2 tablespoons oil

Salt and pepper to taste
2 shallots, finely chopped
1 tablespoon butter
½ cup dry red wine, preferably a Bordeaux or Cabernet Sauvignon
½ cup Brown Sauce (p. 39)
¼ cup fresh beef marrow, cut in small pieces (optional)

1. Choose a heavy sauté pan just large enough to hold steak comfortably. Preheat pan with clarified butter or half butter and oil. Salt and pepper meat just before putting in pan.

2. Sear steak on one side, turning only once when half cooked. Sauté on high heat until medium rare—approximately 8 minutes for 1½ inch thick steak. Test for doneness by pressing finger on top of meat: if meat is soft, it will be rare. Remove from pan, place on warm serving plate, and keep warm.

3. To make sauce, pour off fat, put chopped shallots in pan with 1 more tablespoon butter, and cook on medium heat for 1 minute. Add the red wine, reduce by one quarter, and stir in Brown Sauce. Just before serving, pour sauce around steak.

4. If marrow is to be served on top of cooked steak, ahead of time, cut

marrow in small pieces, poach in a small amount of boiling water or stock for 2 minutes.

Serve with fried potatoes, potato purée (p. 267), *Pommes de Terre Noisette* (p. 269), *Gratin de Pommes de Terre Dauphinoise* (p. 269), or *Savoyarde* (p. 270) and steamed green vegetables. This sauce goes well with meat loaf.

Serves 1–2.

Wine Merchant's Sauce   *Sauce Marchand de Vin*

3 tablespoons butter
3 tablespoons minced shallots
3/4 cup dry red wine: Cabernet Sauvignon, Zinfandel, or *Pinot Noir*

3/4 cup Brown Sauce (p. 39)
Salt and pepper to taste

1. Heat 2 tablespoons of the butter in a small heavy saucepan on medium heat. Add the minced shallots and cook until tender but not brown.
2. Add red wine and reduce sauce over high heat to half the original amount. Be careful—the wine will flame!
3. Stir in Brown Sauce, bring sauce to a boil, and simmer for several minutes. Taste to correct seasoning. Just before serving stir in 1 tablespoon butter. This sauce is similar to *Sauce Bordelaise,* but it does not include beef marrow. Place on bottom of plates to serve as a mirror.

    Serve with beef, venison, grilled or poached swordfish, halibut, turbot.

Makes 1 cup sauce, enough to serve 4.

Madeira Sauce Prepared for Veal Cordon Bleu   *Sauce Madère*

2 veal scallops, 2–3 ounces each— the best cut is la noix de veau, *veal from the leg, which has no bone*
1 slice prosciutto, Parma, or *dry ham such as Bayonne*
1 thin slice Gruyère cheese to fit inside veal
1 egg

Salt and pepper to taste
2 tablespoons oil and 1 tablespoon butter (approximately)
2 tablespoons flour
1/2 cup fresh bread crumbs
1/4 cup Madeira (dry sherry or *Sauce Tomate, p. 41, may be substituted for Madeira)*
1/2 cup Brown Sauce (p. 39)

43

1. Place the two pieces boneless veal in a plastic bag and pound until very thin—about ⅛ inch thick. Arrange ham and cheese between the two pieces of veal.
2. Beat egg slightly, mix with salt, pepper, and 1 teaspoon of the oil. First, dip stuffed veal in flour; second, coat with egg mixture; third, coat with fresh bread crumbs.
3. In heavy pan heat the oil and butter and sauté veal about 2–3 minutes on each side over medium heat, uncovered. Remove veal and place on heated serving platter.
4. Deglaze sauté pan with Madeira, reducing juices by half. Stir in Brown Sauce. Taste to correct seasoning. Pour sauce around Veal Cordon Bleu. Serve at once.

Serve with *petits pois,* asparagus tips, diced zucchini (stir fried), or *subric* of a green vegetable (p. 276). When meat or poultry is breaded, it is not necessary to serve a starch.

Sauce Madère can be served with Roast Prime Rib of Beef (p. 34), Roast Poussin or Pheasant, Tournedos Rossini, and broiled or sautéed small cuts of meat and poultry.

Serves 1.

VARIATIONS: When chopped truffles are added to *Sauce Madère,* it becomes *Sauce Périgourdine.* When diced foie gras and truffles are added to *Sauce Madère,* it becomes *Sauce Périgueux.*

Chicken Cordon Bleu can be made with a breast of chicken cut in half from a 2–3 pound fryer. For Turkey Cordon Bleu use uncooked, small slices of turkey breast.

Pepper Sauce   *Sauce Poivrade*

MIREPOIX:
1 large carrot
1 large onion
1 rib celery
1 tablespoon butter
1 tablespoon oil
1 bay leaf
1 sprig thyme
6 parsley stems
1 cup marinade (p. 209)
¼ cup red wine vinegar

1 tablespoon crushed black peppercorns
1 quart Brown Sauce (p. 39)
6–8 tournedos or 6–8 sirloin steaks, 8 ounces each, or 2–3 racks of lamb marinated 24–48 hours (p. 221)
1 cup leftover uncooked marinade from meat to be served with Sauce Poivrade

1. A stronger venison taste will result from longer marinating—48 hours as opposed to 24 hours. Instructions with ingredients for uncooked marinade are on page 209.

2. Make a *mirepoix* of the carrot, onion, and celery—cut in small dice, sauté in butter and oil over medium heat in a heavy saucepan with the bay leaf, thyme, and parsley stems for about 10 minutes.

3. Add the marinade, red wine vinegar, and crushed peppercorns; reduce until flavor is concentrated, about 10 minutes.

4. Add all of the Brown Sauce and reduce again on medium heat until consistency of sauce is thick enough to coat a spoon and has a shiny appearance. Put through a fine strainer *(étamine)*.

Makes 1 pint, enough for 6–8 tournedos (2–4 tablespoons of sauce served to 1 person).

Leftover uncooked marinade can be cooked and stored in refrigerator for reuse.

Pepper Sauce or *Sauce Poivrade* for Smaller Amounts of Marinated Meat

1 small carrot
1 small onion
½ rib celery
½ tablespoon butter and ½ tablespoon oil
1 bay leaf
1 sprig thyme
3 parsley stems
½ cup marinade (p. 209)
1½ tablespoons red wine vinegar

½ tablespoon crushed peppercorns
2 cups Brown Sauce (p. 39)
2 tournedos or *2 sirloin steaks, 8 ounces each,* or *a rack of lamb, well trimmed of fat. Marinate the desired meat for 24–48 hours in refrigerator—a stronger venison taste will result from longer marination. See instructions on page 209.*

1. Make a *mirepoix* of vegetables by cutting the carrot, onion, and celery in small dice. Sauté in butter and oil with the bay leaf, thyme, and parsley for 10 minutes.

2. Add ½ cup strained marinade, red wine vinegar, and crushed peppercorns and reduce by half to concentrate flavor.

3. Add Brown Sauce and reduce again by about half until consistency of sauce is thick and shiny. Strain and keep warm while cooking meat.

45

Makes 1 cup, enough for 3–4 tournedos (2 tablespoons of sauce served to 1 person).

Leftover sauce should be refrigerated with plastic wrap over the surface. It can be frozen and reheated in a double boiler.

Sauce Diane for Tournedos, Venison, Marinated Ribs, or Loin of Lamb

Sauce Diane is prepared in the kitchen, whereas Steak Diane is usually prepared in the dining room. However, I do not consider a dining room the proper place to sauté—the fire is never hot enough and the smoke, fumes, and flame are an annoyance. Flaming is acceptable if a dish must be served in that style.

2–3 tablespoons Sauce Poivrade
  (p. 44)
1–2 tablespoons heavy cream,
  whipped

1 teaspoon red currant jelly
(optional)

Ingredients given are for 1 serving of meat. One cup of sauce serves 4–6 people: 8 ounces *Sauce Poivrade* with ½ cup heavy cream, whipped.

Steak Diane   *Steak La Déesse de la Chasse*

12 ounces steak, boneless sirloin or
  filet mignon, 1 inch thick
1–2 tablespoons butter
½ teaspoon minced shallots
2 tablespoons Cognac
2 tablespoons sherry

1 tablespoon A-1 Sauce (optional)
½ teaspoon Dijon mustard
¼ cup Brown Sauce (p. 39)
2 tablespoons sour cream
Salt and pepper to taste
1 tablespoon minced fresh parsley

1. Cut steak in half, pound between two sheets of waxed or freezer paper until it is half its original thickness.

2. Using a chafing dish or sauté pan placed on a burner or Coleman stove, heat butter and sauté steak for about 30 seconds on each side. Cooking time depends on degree of heat from cooking element. Remove steaks and keep warm on a platter.

3. Add minced shallots, sauté ½ minute, add Cognac and sherry and flame.

Stir in A-1 Sauce, mustard, Brown Sauce, sour cream, salt and pepper to taste, and minced parsley.

4. Return steak to sauté pan just long enough to turn over in sauce using tongs or a fork put in side of steak to avoid loss of juice. Serve as soon as possible.

5. First put sauce on serving plate as a mirror with steak on top, or serve sauce in a sauceboat *(saucier)*.

   Serve with plain spätzle, pasta, or rice and a blanched, julienned green vegetable such as string beans or Swiss chard, or carrots, turnips, leeks, celery.

Serves 2.

Pepper Steak   *Steak au Poivre*

1 steak, New York cut or *boneless*
  sirloin, 1¹/₂ inches thick
20 black peppercorns or *2 teaspoons*
  green peppercorns
Salt
2–3 tablespoons butter or *half butter*
  and half oil

1–2 tablespoons brandy or *Cognac,*
  warmed
¹/₂ cup Brown Sauce (p. 39)
¹/₄ cup light or *heavy cream*

1. Trim excess fat from steak. Crush black peppercorns with a cleaver or crush green peppercorns with back of a wide knife. Salt steak just before dipping in crushed peppercorns, coating as much of the steak with the peppercorns as possible.

2. Use a heavy sauté pan just large enough to hold meat comfortably. Heat butter on high; put in steak, searing on one side for half the cooking time, about 4 minutes. Turn once to sear other side, sautéing about 4 more minutes until steak is medium rare. Test for doneness by pressing finger on top of steak—if it is soft, it will be on the rare side.

3. Remove from pan and keep warm. If black peppercorns were used, remove, as they tend to stick in the teeth. (Green peppercorns are soft and will not do this, so they do not have to be removed from steak.)

4. Pour off most of fat, add warm brandy to sauté pan, and flame. Stir in Brown Sauce and cream. Cook quickly, about 1 minute, and pour around steak on serving platter.

Serve with Soufflé Potatoes *(Pommes de Terre Soufflées,* p. 262), fried potatoes *(pommes de terre frites), Pommes Darphin* (p. 264), or *Pommes de Terre Dauphine* (p. 81), and green vegetables such as beans or sugar snap peas, steamed.

Serves 1.

Huntsman Sauce (Hunter's Sauce) — *Sauce Chasseur*

1 tablespoon butter
1 tablespoon oil
1 cup minced mushrooms
1 tablespoon minced shallots
½ cup dry white wine, Pinot Blanc or Chardonnay
1 cup Demi-Glace or *Brown Sauce (p. 39)*

½ cup Tomato Sauce *(p. 41)*
Salt and pepper to taste
Pinch chopped fresh tarragon
1 tablespoon finely chopped fresh parsley

1. Heat butter and oil in heavy saucepan and sauté minced mushrooms until lightly browned. Add minced shallots and sauté 1 minute.
2. Add white wine and reduce by half on medium high heat. Add Brown Sauce and Tomato Sauce, stirring until blended. Salt and pepper to taste.
3. Stir in chopped tarragon and parsley.
    Serve with fillet of beef, roast chicken, or small cuts of sautéed or broiled meat and poultry. If meat is broiled or grilled, put sauce on bottom of plate to serve as a mirror.

One pint of sauce serves 6–8, 4 tablespoons to a person.

Fillets of Beef with Black Currants — *Filets de Boeuf Baies de Cassis*

1 tablespoon butter
4–6 fillets of beef, 5 ounces each

INGREDIENTS FOR SAUCE:
1 tablespoon sugar
1 tablespoon raspberry vinegar
1 tablespoon black currant liqueur (crème de cassis)

Salt and pepper to taste

1 cup Brown Sauce *(p. 39)*
½ cup fresh black currants or canned baies de cassis au sirop

48

1. In a heavy skillet melt butter, sauté fillets on high heat, turning once or twice, until they are cooked rare to medium rare, about 5–8 minutes. Remove fillets and place on a serving platter in a warm area of the kitchen.

2. Degrease pan, add first four ingredients for sauce, deglaze pan on medium heat, then strain sauce. Add black currants, bring just to a boil, and pour over fillets.

   Serve with steamed fresh snow peas, fresh pears poached in white wine, Madeira, and green peppercorns.*

   This rich sauce is also outstanding with sautéed breast of duck (*Magret de Canard,* p. 244), leg of venison, fillet or rack of venison, top round from leg of wild boar, loin of pork.

Serves 4–6.

* Peel, core, and halve 4 fresh firm pears such as Bosc, and poach until tender in dry white wine flavored with 2 tablespoons port or dry Madeira (Sercial), and 4 teaspoons green peppercorns. Slice evenly, leave slices attached to stem, and fan out lightly for serving—one-half pear per person on dinner plate. In earlier days, when cooked pears were served, the half with the stem was given to the guest as a courtesy.

Veal Scallopine   *Fine Escalope de Veau*

An Italian lady who traveled 200 miles every week to attend l'Ecole de Cuisine asked me to prepare Veal Scallopine and Veal Saltimbocca. Now, two more meat dishes using Brown Sauce are added to le répertoire of les cuisiniers. Each dish is prepared for one person using veal taken from the leg, which is considered the most tender meat.

1 veal scallop, veal cutlet, or *loin or rib-eye chop (3–4 ounces)*	*1 tablespoon oil*
2 teaspoons flour	*2 mushrooms, sliced*
Salt and pepper to taste	*2 tablespoons Madeira* or *Marsala wine*
3 tablespoons butter	*¼ cup Brown Sauce (p. 39)*

1. Cut veal into four pieces before or after pounding. Place veal scallop or chop between two pieces of waxed paper or in a plastic bag. Pound gently with a flat instrument such as a cleaver or meat pounder *(batte).*

2. Place flour, salt, and pepper on paper, and put veal on top of seasoned flour. Pat a little flour on top of meat just before cooking. Do not prepare veal in advance because veal juices will go into the coating.

3. Preheat sauté pan with 1 tablespoon butter and oil; sauté veal, turning

49

once, being careful not to overcook. It should remain soft in the center when done.

4. Remove veal and place on warm serving dish in a warm oven. Add 1 or 2 tablespoons butter and sauté sliced mushrooms. Add wine and Brown Sauce. Cook on medium high heat for about 1 minute. Pour over veal and serve.

Serve with plain pasta, buttered linguine or fettuccine, and a green vegetable.

Serves 1.

Veal Saltimbocca   *Fine Escalope à la Saltimbocca*

1 veal scallop cut from leg,
  3 ounces, ¹/₂ inch thick*
2 slices prosciutto
1–2 thin slices Mozzarella or
  Provolone cheese
4 sage leaves
1¹/₂ teaspoons flour

2 tablespoons butter
¹/₂ teaspoon finely chopped shallots
¹/₄ cup Marsala, dry white wine, or
  Madeira
¹/₂ cup Brown Sauce (p. 39)
Salt and pepper to taste

1. Place veal between two pieces waxed paper, gently flatten with a metal pounder, and cut in four pieces. Salt and pepper veal lightly, as the ham and cheese are salty.

2. Cut prosciutto into four pieces the same size as the veal, place on top of each piece of veal, then place a thin slice of cheese, and finally a fresh sage leaf. Roll up, secure with toothpick, and dust lightly with flour.

3. In a heavy pan heat the butter and sauté the veal, turning several times, until just done, about 5 minutes. Remove from pan and place on warm serving platter in low oven.

4. Return sauté pan to stove on medium heat, add shallots, and sauté ¹/₂ minute; deglaze pan with Marsala or dry white wine, and stir in Brown Sauce. Taste to adjust seasoning.

5. Place cooked veal back in sauce for less than a minute. Remove toothpicks. Arrange veal and sauce on heated serving platter or individual plates, and serve at once.

Serve with fresh spinach, sautéed zucchini, or Italian green beans.

Serves 1 for dinner or 2 for luncheon.

---

* Sliced and flattened breast of turkey or chicken makes a good substitute for veal if high quality veal is unobtainable.

Two Basic Sauces
Deux Sauces Mères

Béchamel Sauce
Basic White Sauce

Sauce Béchamel
Sauce Blanche

3 tablespoons butter
3 tablespoons flour (level)
2 cups milk, half and half, or *cream*
½ cup white stock (fond blanc)
  (optional)

Pinch nutmeg
¼ teaspoon salt or to taste
⅛ teaspoon freshly ground white
  pepper or to taste

1. To make *blond roux* use equal parts butter and flour: in heavy saucepan or double boiler melt butter and stir in flour with a whisk. Let roux cook slowly without coloring for 4–5 minutes to remove the taste of uncooked flour.

2. Heat milk or cream just below boiling point, then slowly pour into roux, stirring with a whisk to prevent lumps. The amount of milk or cream used depends on thickness required for sauce. *Fond blanc* can be added to increase flavor. Season to taste with nutmeg, salt, and pepper.

3. Cook for 15 minutes in saucepan on low heat or in double boiler. More liquid can be added, if sauce becomes too thick.

4. If not using right away, float a little butter on top and cover with plastic wrap. Refrigerate.

Makes approximately 2 cups.

USES: Generally used as a base for compound sauces such as *Sauce Mornay* (p. 52) and *Sauce Soubise* (p. 55). It is combined with cooked vegetables such as spinach and mushrooms. One tablespoon gives thickness to a cream sauce, if *Sauce Suprême* is not on hand. Also used to cover cauliflower, salsify, carrots, and other vegetables such as peas, leeks, Brussels sprouts, corn, pearl onions, and celery for gratinéeing.

Velouté Sauce
Basic Ivory Sauce

Sauce Velouté
Sauce Ivoire

2 tablespoons butter
3 tablespoons flour
2 cups white stock (fond blanc)
A few grinds fresh nutmeg
¼ teaspoon salt, or to taste

Freshly ground pepper to taste
½ teaspoon Glace de Viande *(p. 40)*,
(optional)
2 egg yolks (optional)

1. In a heavy saucepan or double boiler melt the butter, stir in flour with a whisk, and cook without coloring for several minutes to remove taste of uncooked flour.
2. Heat *fond blanc;* slowly pour into roux using whisk to prevent lumps. Season to taste with nutmeg, salt, and freshly ground pepper. *Glace de Viande* is added to intensify flavor, if desired.
3. Cook for about ½ hour in saucepan on low heat or in double boiler. If sauce becomes too thick, more liquid can be added to the finished Velouté Sauce to give more lightness and more color if dish covered with sauce is put under a broiler. However, do not boil the sauce at this stage—it would cause curdling.

Makes approximately 2 cups.

Use for white meat such as poultry and veal. To use this sauce for fish, substitute fish stock *(fond de poisson)* for *fond blanc* and substitute *glace de poisson,* if available, for *Glace de Viande.*

Compound Sauces
Sauces Composées

Mornay Sauce

Sauce Mornay

This sauce is used to glaze dishes such as Artichaut Florentine *(p. 259)*, Gnocchi Parisienne *(p. 82), Eggs Florentine (p. 130), or Veal Prince Orloff (p. 219). It is also used to glaze vegetables such as cauliflower, broccoli, asparagus, salsify, heart of palm, and braised endive. Reserve some of the grated cheese to sprinkle on top of sauce, or add more cheese over sauce before glazing.*

2 cups Sauce Béchamel *(p. 51)*
¼ cup grated Gruyère cheese
¼ cup grated Parmesan cheese
2 egg yolks

¼ cup heavy cream, whipped
A few grinds fresh nutmeg
Salt and pepper to taste

1. Make *Sauce Béchamel* in a double boiler or heavy saucepan. Keep warm. When ready to use, stir in grated cheese.
2. Finish sauce by stirring in egg yolks mixed with whipped cream. If egg yolks are omitted, *Sauce Mornay* will not brown well under the grill or broiler.
3. Add nutmeg, salt, and pepper to taste.

Makes 2¾ cups.

Suprême Sauce (Cream Sauce)   *Sauce Suprême*

Some chefs finish this sauce with egg yolks. However, if the sauce stands too long or boils, egg yolks will form little yellow specks; so I do not recommend it.

1 quart chicken stock
½ cup mushroom stems or
   trimmings
2 cups chicken Sauce Velouté
   (p. 52)
2 cups heavy cream

Salt and freshly ground white pepper
   to taste
1–2 tablespoons butter

1. In a heavy saucepan cook chicken stock and mushroom stems or trimmings until reduced to about half the original amount. I do not use whole mushrooms because a large amount of mushrooms will discolor the sauce.
2. Add *Sauce Velouté* and reduce again to two thirds the amount.
3. Slowly pour in cream while stirring constantly. Add salt and white pepper to taste, and cook on low heat until the sauce coats the back of a spoon.
4. Strain sauce and swirl in a little butter on top to prevent crust from forming.

Makes 1 quart.

   Use for chicken and veal dishes such as Veal Calvados, for creamy mushroom and vegetable dishes, or to give a thickness to sauces.

White Wine Sauce   *Sauce Vin Blanc*

*2 cups Sauce Velouté (p. 52) made
    with fish stock (p. 21)*
½ cup Fumet de Poisson (p. 22)
*¼ cup white wine: Chardonnay,
    Chablis, Sauvignon, or Fumé Blanc*

½ cup heavy cream
A few drops lemon juice

1. Put *Sauce Velouté, Fumet de Poisson,* and wine in a heavy saucepan and reduce by half over medium high heat.
2. Finish sauce on low heat by stirring in cream and lemon juice. Serve with quenelles, terrine of fish, or broiled, steamed, or poached fish.

Makes approximately 2 cups; serves 6–8.

Champagne Sauce   *Sauce Champagne*
                                     Sauce Champenoise

Any dry white sparkling wine made by the méthode Champenoise *may be substituted for French Champagne.*

*1 recipe Sauce Vin Blanc (p. 54) made
    with Champagne*

1–2 tablespoons Champagne

Prepare *Sauce Vin Blanc* and, just before serving, stir in 1–2 tablespoons of Champagne to lend an effervescent quality. Do not cook further or the bubbles will deflate. The wine will give a little extra acidity to the sauce, which is pleasant. If acidity is not desired, sauce can be recooked.

Serve with braised salmon (p. 176), trout, petrale, and rex sole (p. 180); broiled steamed, poached, or fried fish such as halibut or turbot. Sauce can be served as a mirror on the plate with sautéed fish placed on top.

How to Glaze Fish with White Wine Sauce

*2 pounds fish with skin and bones or
    1 pound fish fillets, such as halibut,
    flounder, petrale sole, codfish,
    turbot from the English Channel;
    also fresh salmon*
*Braising liquid reduced to a thick
    syrup*

1 cup White Wine Sauce (p. 54)
*2 tablespoons Hollandaise Sauce
    (p. 58)*
1 tablespoon whipped cream

1. Braise fish just until lightly cooked. Remove fish with skimmer, drain, and place on ovenproof plate or platter.

2. Make sauce by combining White Wine Sauce, Hollandaise Sauce, reduced braising liquid, and whipped cream on low heat.

3. Pour over cooked fish and glaze under broiler. Watch carefully, as sauce burns very easily.

   Hollandaise, and sauces with hollandaise as an ingredient, will curdle, if poured over fish about to be heated in the oven. Do *not reheat* fish or meat in the sauce, either—it can only be poured over the warm fish when ready to serve at table.

Serves 3–4.

NOTE: To determine amount of fish to serve, figure 3–4 ounces boned fish for one person as a main course; 8–10 ounces fish with bones for one person as a main course. (Fifty to sixty percent of weight of fish is lost when skin and bones are removed.)

Onion Cream Sauce   *Sauce Soubise*

1 pound onions, sliced very thin or chopped
2–3 tablespoons butter
2 cups Sauce Béchamel *(p. 51)*
Pinch sugar
Pinch salt and freshly ground white pepper

½ cup light or heavy cream
¼–½ cup stock from meat, chicken, or fish dish for which sauce is prepared (optional)

1. Parboil onions for 5 minutes, drain, and pat dry.

2. Sauté onions in butter without coloring until soft. Stir in *Sauce Béchamel,* sugar, salt, and white pepper. Simmer about ½ hour in heavy pan or double boiler. Strain through fine sieve or quickly purée in food processor.

3. Reheat sauce in heavy pan and stir in cream—amount depends on consistency required. Taste to correct seasoning. Stock or sauce from meat can be added.

   Serve on top of vegetables such as steamed broccoli; with fish, lamb, veal, and chicken dishes. This is used in preparing Veal Prince Orloff

(p. 219) and in Bread Crumb Sauce for roast grouse by adding a small amount of fresh bread crumbs to *Sauce Soubise.*

Makes approximately 1 quart; 1–2 tablespoons served per person as a topping.

White Chaud-Froid Sauce   *Sauce Chaud-Froid Blanche*

The words chaud-froid *mean hot to cold. Cooked warm poultry or meat is chilled and covered with the opaque sauce, which often has clear aspic applied as a glaze on top. Chaud-Froid de Volaille is a fancy dish served on buffet tables. It can be made with whole poached or baked chicken, cut-up chicken, or poached chicken breasts. If the cooked chicken is cut up, the skin is removed, the bones are removed from the legs, and the pieces are trimmed to be fairly uniform. Each piece of chilled chicken is covered with chaud-froid sauce, decorated with thin slices of truffle or pieces of truffle made into designs, and glazed with clear aspic. The serving dish is lined with clear aspic, the chicken pieces are arranged on top, and aspic cut-outs are placed on the border. Hard boiled eggs can be presented in this way. Black olives may be substituted for truffles. To decorate fish or a fish terrine with chaud-froid sauce,* fumet de poisson *(fish stock) is used instead of chicken stock,* fond blanc, *or* Consommé Clair.

1½ cups Sauce Velouté (p. 52)
1 cup Consommé Clair (p. 6) or concentrated chicken stock
½ cup heavy cream
1 tablespoon unflavored gelatin (approximately, if needed)

1–2 tablespoons sherry or Madeira used to soften gelatin or add for flavor

1. Pour *Sauce Velouté* in a heavy porcelain-lined or stainless steel pot. Begin reducing the sauce while whisking in the consommé or stock. Whisk in about 3 tablespoons of the heavy cream. Reduce to about two thirds the original amount.

2. Strain sauce and, off heat, add remaining heavy cream. When sauce has reached room temperature, test consistency by putting a layer on a plate and refrigerate. If it does not gel enough, reheat the sauce, adding a little gelatin to dissolve in the sauce. Chill until it is thick enough to coat chicken, hard boiled eggs, or other cold food.

Makes 3 cups.

Brown Chaud-Froid Sauce   *Sauce Chaud-Froid Brune*

2 or 3 cups Brown Sauce or Demi-
Glace (p. 39)
2 or 3 tablespoons Glace de Viande
(p. 40) and ½ cup juices from the
pan in which meat was cooked

1 or 2 tablespoons Madeira, port, or
sherry
1 tablespoon gelatin
(approximately)
Salt and freshly ground pepper

1. In a heavy saucepan put Brown Sauce, *Glace de Viande,* and degreased, strained sauce in which meat was cooked or about ½ cup water. Reduce to about one third the original amount while stirring. Add Madeira, port, or sherry. Taste for seasoning.

2. Test sauce as explained for White Chaud-Froid Sauce. If sauce does not gel sufficiently, dissolve plain gelatin in water and add a little at a time to the warmed up sauce. Meat or chops must be cold before applying chilled sauce. Several layers should be applied before the decoration, refrigerating meat between applications. Chill platter, put layer of sauce on before arranging decorated meat. Keep refrigerated until ready to serve.

    This sauce is used for meat such as beef and lamb or game such as venison, grouse, quail, duck.

Makes approximately 3 cups.

Genevoise Sauce   *Sauce Genevoise*

Originally called Sauce Génoise *by Carême, the name of this sauce was changed to* Genevoise *by Reculet and then Gouffé.* Genevoise *means "of Geneva," a city more noted for gin than red wine, which is essential in the composition of the sauce. The incorrect name has prevailed.*

1 medium carrot
1 small onion
2 parsley stems
4 tablespoons butter or oil
1 sprig thyme
½ bay leaf
2½-pound head of salmon
(preferred) or fish bones and head
of red snapper, turbot, or halibut
Coarsely ground pepper to taste

7 cups red wine, such as Bordeaux,
Cabernet Sauvignon, Burgundy, or
Pinot Noir
2¼ cups Brown Sauce (p. 39)
2¼ cups fish stock
1 tablespoon anchovy paste or
1 anchovy put through a sieve or
*in a blender with a little sauce **

5 ounces (1¼ sticks) butter

* 1 tablespoon Bordelaise Sauce can be substituted for anchovy paste.

1. Make a fine *mirepoix* (p. 39) with carrots, onion, and parsley stems. Sauté in butter or oil with thyme and bay leaf until lightly browned. Add cut-up salmon head or fish bones, cover, and simmer for 15 minutes.
2. Drain off butter, add 4½ cups of the red wine, and reduce by one half. Add the Brown Sauce, and simmer for 10–15 minutes on medium heat, skimming constantly. Strain into another pot. Remove all fat from surface.
3. Add remaining 2½ cups red wine and the fish stock. Simmer, skimming often until reduced to desired thickness.
4. Put through a fine strainer and finish with anchovy paste and about 5 ounces butter stirred in with a whisk.

    Serve with salmon, trout, or white fish such as turbot, sole, flounder, monkfish, or angler.

Makes 1½ pints to 1 quart.

Butter and Egg Sauce
Sauce au Beurre aux Oeufs

Hollandaise Sauce   *Sauce Hollandaise*

BLENDER/FOOD PROCESSOR METHOD:
4 egg yolks
⅛ teaspoon freshly ground white pepper
4 tablespoons very hot water

1¾ cups warm clarified butter, unsalted (p. 66)
2–3 tablespoons fresh lemon juice
Salt to taste*

1. Place egg yolks and white pepper in blender or food processor. Cover and process briefly, or blend at low speed for 1 minute. Add very hot water slowly with motor running, then add warm clarified butter in a thin stream. (If necessary, increase speed of blender to make sauce thicken—it should be just thick enough to coat the food.)
2. Add lemon juice a little at a time, tasting for correct amount and mixing briefly. Add a little salt, if required. Transfer to a warm container, and place in warm spot on stove until ready to serve.
3. Leftover Hollandaise can be refrigerated for several days and reheated in a double boiler. If it curdles, add about 1 tablespoon *cold* water. Always use

---

* I found that if half salted and half unsalted butter is used, it is not necessary to add any more salt.

opposite temperature to correct this condition—*hot* against *cold* or vice versa. Serve with vegetables such as broccoli, cauliflower, asparagus, artichokes; broiled or poached fish such as salmon, sole, whitefish, broiled mackerel or bluefish.

Makes approximately 2¼ cups. Recipe can be halved.

Use for leftover *Sauce Hollandaise:* Stir in small amounts of chopped herbs such as tarragon, basil, parsley, chervil, or chives. Refrigerate until chilled enough to roll the size of a half dollar; wrap in foil. Freeze and cut off as needed to serve like maître d'hôtel butter.

Sauces That Are Variations of *Sauce Hollandaise*

Mousseline Sauce

Sauce Mousseline or
Sauce Chantilly

½ cup heavy cream, whipped   *1 cup* Sauce Hollandaise

Fold cold whipped cream into room temperature Hollandaise just before serving. Taste to adjust seasoning. Use for vegetables such as steamed asparagus and for poached fish and poached eggs.

Mustard Sauce

Sauce Moutarde

1 tablespoon mustard, Dijon style   *1 cup* Sauce Hollandaise
1 tablespoon white wine

Stir and fold mustard mixed with white wine in *Sauce Hollandaise* just before serving. Serve with broiled steak, broiled or poached fish.

Maltese Sauce

Sauce Maltaise

3–4 tablespoons fresh orange juice,   *½ teaspoon finely grated orange rind*
*   preferably blood or Seville oranges,*   *2 cups* Sauce Hollandaise
*   if available*

59

1. Reduce orange juice and grated orange rind on medium heat until they make a paste.
2. Make Hollandaise and keep warm. Fold reduction of orange juice into freshly made *Sauce Hollandaise*.

    Serve with poached cauliflower, steamed or poached asparagus, artichokes, or broccoli.

Butter and Egg Sauce with Tarragon
Sauce au Beurre et aux Oeufs avec l'Estragon

Béarnaise Sauce   # *Sauce Béarnaise*

HANDMADE METHOD:
1 tablespoon chopped shallots
1 tablespoon chopped fresh tarragon
or 1½ teaspoons dried
1 tablespoon chopped fresh chervil or
1½ teaspoons dried
4 tablespoons white wine vinegar
4 tablespoons dry white wine
Pinch salt

Pinch crushed white pepper
4 egg yolks
1¾ cups warm clarified butter, made
from 1 pound unsalted butter
½ teaspoon chervil
½ teaspoon tarragon
Pinch cayenne
A few drops lemon juice

1. Put first seven ingredients in heavy saucepan and reduce on medium heat to 2 tablespoons. Cool slightly.
2. Put egg yolks in mixing bowl—make sure that bowl will not move. Whisk yolks until light with 1 tablespoon water and cooled mixture from Step 1.
3. Place bowl over simmering water, whisk yolks until thick and creamy, and gradually beat in clarified butter (p. 66), a few drops at first, increasing to a thin stream, the same way Hollandaise Sauce is made. Whisk until thick. Strain sauce to remove crushed pepper, if preferred.
4. Steep the chopped chervil and tarragon in boiling water. Add to Béarnaise Sauce with a pinch of cayenne and a few drops of lemon juice.

    Keep Béarnaise Sauce warm on side of stove. Do not allow to get too warm, which will cause it to separate. If it does, whisk in 1 tablespoon cold water.

    Serve with grilled and sautéed meats: *Tournedos Henri IV* (p. 223); broiled, grilled, or baked fish: *Loup en Croute* (p. 200).

Makes 2½ cups.

SAUCES

BLENDER/FOOD PROCESSOR METHOD:

1 tablespoon finely chopped shallots
1 tablespoon chopped fresh chervil or
  1½ teaspoons dried
1 tablespoon chopped fresh tarragon
  or 1½ teaspoons dried
1 black or white peppercorn, crushed
4 tablespoons tarragon-flavored
  white wine vinegar, warmed

4 egg yolks
1¾ cups warm clarified butter
  (p. 66)
4 sprigs parsley, stems removed,
  chopped
No salt is needed if salted butter is
  used; otherwise, add salt to taste

1. Combine shallots, chervil, tarragon, pepper, and vinegar in small saucepan and cook on high heat until reduced by half, or slightly less.

2. Put egg yolks in blender or food processor, run for about 30 seconds on low speed for blender; or process briefly, using steel blade to mix well. With machine still running, add warm tarragon vinegar mixture to thickened sauce in bowl of machine. This cooks the eggs slightly. Blend at high speed for about 5 seconds to mix.

3. With machine still running, add warm clarified butter in a very thin, slow stream.

4. Keep warm on side of stove until ready to serve. Béarnaise Sauce is always served lukewarm as overheating will cause it to curdle. Stir in chopped parsley just before serving. Salt if necessary.

Makes approximately 2¼ cups, and can be halved, if desired.

Leftover Béarnaise can be spooned onto foil, rolled up like sausage (carefully!) and frozen to be sliced into pats and placed on broiled steaks or lamb chops just before serving.

Paloise Sauce   *Sauce Paloise*

This sauce is the same as *Sauce Béarnaise,* but substitute 6–8 mint leaves, finely chopped, for the tarragon leaves. Serve with lamb.

61

Oil and Egg Sauce
Sauce à l'Huile aux Oeufs

Mayonnaise Sauce   *Sauce Mayonnaise*

I learned that mayonnaise will keep for weeks under refrigeration like commercial mayonnaise if whole eggs are used in the blender or processor. When mayonnaise is made by hand using only egg yolks, it will probably curdle under refrigeration in about 24 hours.

This recipe can be doubled, but it will be difficult to control or push down the mayonnaise in a standard blender. If the new, larger-sized food processor is used, then it is possible to double the recipe.

BLENDER/FOOD PROCESSOR METHOD:
1 tablespoon wine vinegar (white or red may be used)
1 cup salad oil or half olive oil and half salad oil
1 whole egg, at room temperature

½ teaspoon salt
1 teaspoon prepared mustard (Dijon or French's Pure Prepared Mustard)
⅛ teaspoon white pepper

The secret to making a smooth, thick *liaison* is to have ingredients at room temperature and to add the oil very, very slowly in a thin trickle.

1. Put vinegar in a small saucepan, ready to be brought to the boil after the oil is incorporated. Measure the oil into a suitable jug with a pouring spout.

2. Put egg, salt, mustard, and pepper into blender, or use food processor fitted with steel blade. Cover and blend well.

3. With motor running, slowly add oil through opening in cover. Sauce will become very thick. (If using blender, scrape down sides of container after stopping motor.)

4. Bring vinegar to the boil and quickly add to mayonnaise, mixing at high speed until just incorporated. (The boiling vinegar preserves mayonnaise for storage in refrigerator.)

Makes 1¼ cups.

Compound Oil and Egg Sauces
Sauces à l'Huile aux Oeufs Composés

Green Sauce   *Sauce Verte*

2 spinach leaves
2 bunches watercress
1/2 teaspoon dried tarragon or
   6 leaves fresh
2 sprigs parsley

1 teaspoon dried chervil or a few
   leaves fresh
2–3 cups homemade mayonnaise
Salt for green vegetables and herbs

1. Clean spinach and watercress, removing stems. In a saucepan put just enough water to reach ¼ inch up the sides. Add a pinch of salt and bring water to a boil.

2. Add spinach and watercress; 2 seconds later add fresh or dried herbs, blanching all about 1 minute or until they turn a bright green.

3. Drain, cool under cold running water, drain again, and squeeze out liquid in towel. Chop very fine by hand or in processor. Fold into freshly made mayonnaise.

   Serve with cold poached salmon (p. 175) or any type of cold fish such as striped bass, also called rockfish. Used to make Eggs Stuffed with *Sauce Verte* (p. 137).

Makes 2–3 cups; serves 4–6.

Watercress Sauce   *Sauce Cresson*

1 large bunch watercress
1/2 teaspoon green peppercorns
1 cup homemade mayonnaise
1/2 teaspoon lemon juice

4 tablespoons whipped cream or *sour*
   cream
Salt to taste

1. Wash watercress and cut off thick stems and remove leaves from small stems; dip in pan of boiling water for 1 second. Pour into strainer; cool off under cold running water immediately. Drain, and dry leaves on paper towels.

2. Crush green peppercorns with the back of a knife. In a mixing bowl put mayonnaise, crushed green peppercorns folded in with lemon juice,

63

whipped cream, watercress leaves, and salt to taste.

Serve with Terrine of Trout (p. 98), Mousse of Salmon (p. 99), with seafood and green salad, cold poultry, and meat dishes.

Makes approximately 1½ cups.

Mayonnaise Vincent   *Sauce Mayonnaise Vincent*

¼ cup spinach leaves
¼ cup watercress leaves, stems
   removed
2 tablespoons lemon juice
2 cups homemade mayonnaise

1 tablespoon coarsely chopped capers
1 tablespoon chopped or snipped
   chives
1 tablespoon chopped chervil or dill

1. Wash and blanch spinach and watercress leaves in small amount boiling water for less than a minute. Drain and pat dry. Purée leaves with lemon juice in blender or processor.
2. In mixing bowl put fresh mayonnaise, fold in puréed spinach and watercress, chopped capers, chives, and chervil or dill. Chill at least 2 hours.
   Serve with cold trout, salmon, shellfish.

Makes approximately 2½–3 cups.

Butter Sauces
Sauces au Beurre

White Butter Sauce   *Sauce Beurre Blanc*

Beurre Blanc *has been called the sauce of the Old Lady Clémence from Le Pays Nantais near the Loire River, where* Brochet Beurre Blanc *was a specialty.*

1 teaspoon finely chopped shallots
2 tablespoons white wine vinegar
6 tablespoons Muscadet wine from
   Loire River Valley or Chardonnay
   or Chenin Blanc
4 tablespoons heavy cream
*½ pound (2 sticks) butter, unsalted,**
   at room temperature

Salt and freshly ground pepper to
   taste
Use non-aluminum pot: sauteuse—
   pot with slanting sides, or russe—
   pot with straight sides

* To avoid oversalting, use half salted butter and half sweet—it will not be necessary to add more salt.

1. Put finely chopped shallots, white wine vinegar, and white wine in a sauce-pan; reduce on high heat by one half.

2. On low heat add cream and bring to a boil. Cut butter into ½-inch pieces, and add piece by piece, stirring constantly in a circular motion with a whisk or wooden spoon. Sauce should coat spoon lightly. It is not as heavy as a cream sauce, but is an emulsion which is supposed to be fluffy or frothy.

3. When *Sauce Beurre Blanc* is finished, it can be spun in a blender to homogenize. Run machine for 1 minute, adding a little more heavy cream, if desired. Sauce will become more velvety. If the *Sauce Beurre Blanc* should curdle from cooling, reheat slowly, then put in blender with a little cold water and run machine until correct consistency is regained. As mentioned before, always use opposite temperature to correct curdling—cold against hot and vice versa.

4. Leftover sauce may be chilled, wrapped in foil in the shape of a roll and frozen, to be served with broiled fish.

   Sauce can be made 1 hour ahead, but no earlier.

   Serve with sautéed, broiled, poached fish; mousses and terrines of fish.

Makes 2–3 cups; serves 4.

White Butter Sauce with Herbs   *Beurre Blanc aux Fines Herbes*

1 recipe Sauce Beurre Blanc *(see recipe above)*
1 tablespoon chopped fresh tarragon or 1 tablespoon chopped fresh basil or 1 tablespoon chopped fresh chives

1 tablespoon chopped fresh parsley

Make *Sauce Beurre Blanc* and add chopped fresh herbs, using either one herb or a combination of herbs.

65

Butter Sauce   *Beurre Monté*

1–2 tablespoons lemon juice
4–6 tablespoons water
6–8 ounces (1½–2 sticks) butter,
  unsalted or salted, firm, just at
  room temperature

Salt and white pepper to taste

In a saucepan bring water and lemon juice to a boil. On heat, whisk in firm butter 1 tablespoon at a time into boiling water. Butter can also be swirled into pan while holding onto the handle. Swirl or whisk last tablespoons of butter off heat, as butter should not melt. Sauce should be opaque and have consistency of very light cream. When properly made, sauce does not separate.

Serve in sauceboat or on platter or plate with poached, steamed or grilled fish and with vegetables.

This sauce turns into clarified butter if it is reheated and the water becomes evaporated.

Makes 1½–2 cups.

Clarified Butter   *Beurre Clarifié*

Warm clarified butter is used when making Hollandaise Sauce and its variations and when preparing delicate cakes such as Gâteau Génoise. *Clarified butter should also be kept on hand for sautéing meat, fish, and poultry, as it can be heated without burning to a much higher temperature than unclarified butter. Unsalted or sweet butter is preferred, particularly when baking, as the taste is far more delicate. It is, however, more perishable and should be kept well wrapped in the refrigerator or freezer. Unsalted butter also contains less water than salted butter, which keeps longer because of the salt it contains.*

1. Slowly melt butter on low heat in a heavy pan or in a *bain-marie*. After butter has melted, it will look as clear as olive oil, and milk solids will have sunk to the bottom of pan.
2. Skim off white froth on top of melted butter, and discard. Carefully pour butter into another container, leaving white milk solids behind in pan. To be sure that butter is completely clear, it can be strained through a cheesecloth.

Clarified butter will keep for weeks without developing an off flavor if kept airtight—it is the soured milk solids that cause butter to go rancid.

Since oil can be heated to quite high temperatures without smoking or burning, a mixture of half oil and half unclarified butter can be used for sautéing. This combination prevents butter from burning.

Flavored Butters
Beurres Composés

Green Butter   *Beurre Montpellier* or *Beurre Vert*

*6 sprigs watercress, thick stems
   removed*
6 sprigs chervil, stems removed
6 sprigs parsley, thick stems removed
6 leaves tarragon

2 leaves basil
6 stalks chives, cut up
2 leaves spinach
*½ pound (2 sticks) unsalted butter,
   at room temperature*

1. Blanch all herbs together in boiling water for less than a minute. Drain and squeeze out moisture.
2. Put in a blender or food processor, chop, and add unsalted butter. Butter will turn green. Store in refrigerator or freeze.

Makes 1½ cups; serves 8.

Uses: (a) As a variation of *Sauce Beurre Blanc* (p. 64) for poached fish, and with Terrine of Trout (p. 98), use *Sauce Beurre Vert* made with green butter; (b) As little pats for broiled fish, steak, or veal.

Pimento Butter   *Beurre de Piment*

*1 small can pimentos, drained, or 2
   fresh red bell peppers, roasted,
   skinned, seeded, and juiced
   (p. 14)*

*½ pound (2 sticks) unsalted butter,
   at room temperature*

Purée pimentos in blender or processor. Add butter. Butter will turn reddish. Refrigerate.

Makes approximately 1½–2 cups.

Use to make *Sauce Beurre Rouge* for poached, broiled, or sautéed fish.

67

Two Contemporary Sauces Using Oil
Deux Sauces Contemporaines à l'Huile

Sauce of Virgin Olive Oil and Tomato   *Sauce Vièrge*

½ cup extra virgin olive oil
1 ripe tomato, peeled, seeded, and
    diced
1 sprig parsley, without stem,
    chopped
1 sprig chervil, chopped

Pinch chopped fresh tarragon
1 clove garlic
½ teaspoon crushed coriander seeds
Juice of ½ lemon
Salt and freshly ground pepper to
    taste
Fresh tomato juice (optional)

1. About 1 hour before needed, combine olive oil, tomato, herbs, coriander seeds, lemon juice, salt and pepper in blender or food processor. Mix briefly until amalgamated (sauce will form into a salmon-pink liaison); taste and adjust seasoning if necessary.

2. Pour into warmed bowl and set this in another container such as a saucepan half filled with hot water. Put in warm spot, such as beside stove. Flavors will develop on standing. Sauce should be served lukewarm, not hot, as heat would cause it to separate. Thin sauce with tomato juice, if desired.

   Serve with *Saumon à la Moutarde de Meaux* (p. 188) or most broiled, steamed, or poached fish.

Makes 1 cup; serves 4. Recipe can be doubled.

Fresh Tomato Sauce   *Sauce Tomate Frais*
in Style of Gazpacho   *à la Façon Gazpacho*

1 clove garlic, peeled
2 sprigs parsley (Italian), stems
    removed
½ small red onion or Bermuda
    onion, peeled
¼ red or green bell pepper or Fresno
    pepper, peeled, seeded, and sliced
½ large cucumber, peeled
10–12 fresh tomatoes, peeled and cut
    in quarters (Italian style are good)

Salt and freshly ground pepper to
    taste
Juice of ½–1 lemon, or to taste
2–3 tablespoons olive oil (high
    quality)
¼–½ cup tomato juice, or to taste, to
    thin sauce
A few grains cayenne, if desired

68

1. Put the garlic, parsley, onion, and bell or Fresno pepper slices in bowl of processor fitted with steel blade and process until almost puréed. Add cucumber and process until puréed.
2. Add peeled and quartered tomatoes, salt to taste (about ¼ teaspoon) and process until puréed. Add freshly squeezed lemon juice, tasting at the same time to get right amount so that it does not overpower the tomato flavor but softens the bitterness of the raw vegetables. Add olive oil to blend with purée.
3. Add just enough tomato juice to create sauce consistency. Carefully add a little ground pepper and cayenne, if needed. Refrigerate until completely chilled, or overnight.

    Serve warm with Seafood Ravioli (p. 165) or broiled or steamed fish.

Makes about 4 cups.

NOTE: To make Gazpacho Soup (Spanish Iced Soup) from this recipe, add 2 or more cups of tomato juice to puréed gazpacho sauce. Refrigerate overnight. Serve cold gazpacho with the following condiments in separate dishes: cubed garlic croutons made from sourdough French bread, diced cucumber, tomato, bell pepper, and cut green onions.

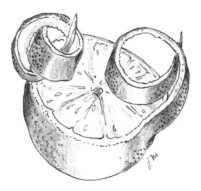

Chapter Three

CREAM PUFF PASTE

Swans, Crowns, Eclairs, Puffs, Potato Balls, and Gnocchi, All Designed from *Pâte à Choux*

For my first lesson on pastry *(la pâtisserie)* I have chosen *pâte à choux,* cream puff pastry, for it will be an instant success if it is measured, mixed, beaten, and baked properly. It can be made in 10–15 minutes, if all the ingredients and utensils are conveniently situated and organized. *Pâte à choux* does not have to rest or be chilled like other French doughs: it is usually shaped and baked as soon as it is made. It is also the only dough that is cooked twice, with the exception of *pâte à génoise,* which is beaten over simmering water before folding in sifted flour. It is very easy to disregard the fact that these delicate pastries were named for their resemblance to the irregular round appearance of cabbage.

This is also the first time I am giving the instructions which are to be followed throughout the five chapters on pastry making:

1. Always sift flour before measuring to aerate it and remove any extraneous matter.
2. Bring large-sized eggs to room temperature before incorporating in doughs, batters, and for meringues in order to create more volume.
3. Always make sure heavy cream is well chilled before whipping.
4. Measurements by weight are more accurate than by volume. This explains why flour, sugar, butter, grated cheese, and nuts are often given in weight.

A note of warning when making *pâte à choux*: Watch that correct amount of water does not boil away when butter is added. The casein (protein in milk) in butter could cause the mixture to foam and boil over. Also, if the batter seems slightly stiff when testing it by dropping dough from a wooden spoon held in the air, an extra egg or two can be beaten in. Although the light puffiness of the baked *choux* are due to the large number of eggs beaten in, they are created by steam from the water in the egg whites, which evaporates during baking, thus putting pressure on the protein walls of the puffs. When baked properly, cream puffs should be crisp outside and soft inside. It is a mistake to scoop out soft cooked dough—*choux* would contain too much

72

filling when piping in pastry or whipped cream. There should be a balance between the soft inside and filling.

In my role of *le chef pâtissier* I can fashion "in a flash" whatever designs are required for the occasion with *pâte à choux*—swans, crowns, horseshoes, "nuns," parts of the structure of *gâteaux.* Using a ½-inch round tube and a ¹⁄₁₆-inch tube inserted in two large pastry bags, parts of two swans (p. 77) appear on the pastry sheets. With a ¾-inch tube fitted in a pastry bag, a crown of three rings is shaped for a *Paris-Brest* (p. 76). A classic pastry, *La Religieuse* (p. 155), has a structure of choux, éclairs, and rings ("doughnuts") filled with *Crème Pâtissière* (p. 286). Although not commonly seen today, *La Religieuse* is elegant on a buffet table as a centerpiece.

Usually served as a hot hors d'oeuvre, *Gougère Bourguignonne,* a Burgundian cheese pastry, is made from *pâte à choux* with the sugar omitted, milk substituted for water, and Gruyère cheese added to the dough after it is formed. Soufflé fritters and mushroom fritters *(beignets de champignons)* are also hors d'oeuvres belonging to the same family of dough. See how prolific this *pâte* is: Very tiny puffs *(profiteroles)* are shaped in the size of large peas, baked and served as a garnish in consommé; dumplings *(Gnocchi Parisienne,* p. 82) are formed; they are a "make ahead" first course, and are also related to two Italian gnocchi dishes (pp. 84 and 85).

Here is the opportune moment to explain the distinction between the words *pâte* and *pâté* by unearthing their derivation—it appears they both come from the Greek word "paste" and the early Latin word "pasta" meaning a mixture of flour and water or a mixture of pounded meat or fish. *Pâte,* meaning dough, has no accent, while *pâté* means a meat or fish dish enclosed in pastry and baked in the oven. *Pâte à pâté* means a dough made to encase a ground meat filling. The words *pâtissier* and pastry come from the same root.

The Pastes
Les Pâtes

Cream Puff Paste   *La Pâte à Choux*

7 ounces butter (1¾ sticks), cut up
2 cups water
Pinch salt
1 teaspoon sugar (too much sugar
  inhibits rising)
2 cups flour
7–8 large eggs

¼ cup slivered almonds (optional)
1 egg beaten with 1 teaspoon water
  for glazing
Heavy pot, 4½ inches deep and 8
  inches in diameter (approximate
  measurements)

1. Combine butter, water, salt, and sugar in a heavy non-aluminum pot and bring to the boil. As soon as butter is melted, remove from the heat. Water should not be boiled away.

2. Using a wooden spoon, add flour all at once and stir briskly. Return pot to heat and continue stirring rapidly until all the flour is absorbed and the mixture leaves the sides of the pan. It should have the consistency of mashed potatoes. This will take less than 1 minute. Let dough cool for another minute.

3. Off the heat, add the eggs, one at a time, stirring and beating vigorously with a flat wooden spatula. (The batter can be put in the bowl of an electric mixer and eggs incorporated with beaters.) Batter must have consistency of heavy cream sauce—it should barely drop from a wooden spatula held in the air. If batter is too thick, another egg can be beaten in.

4. Shape into puffs or *choux* using a pastry bag or two tablespoons dipped in cold water, about 3 inches wide and 1½ inches high, placing them on a greased pastry sheet about 2 inches apart.

5. Brush with egg wash, being careful not to let any drip down the sides (this prevents puffs from rising). Sprinkle with slivered or sliced almonds if desired, pressing them down lightly. Bake at 375-400 degrees for 25 minutes. (Baking time depends on size of puffs.) Do not open oven door while puffs are rising or they may collapse, never to rise again.

6. When dough is baked sufficiently, it should be crisp on the outside. Let puffs dry out for 5 minutes, or up to ½ hour to prevent collapsing, in a turned-off oven, after making a small slit in each to let steam escape. Puffs will become soft on the outside after a short time, even if stored in a tin; *choux* are best eaten the same day they are baked. They can be frozen.

Makes 24 large puffs, 3 inches in diameter, or 136 (approximate amount) small puffs *(profiteroles)* 1 inch in diameter. Recipe can be halved.

NOTE: Pea-sized *choux* puffs are used as a garnish for *consommé;* 1-inch puffs are used for hors d'oeuvres when filled with savory creamed mixtures, caviar, small oysters; petit fours when filled with pastry cream. Large puffs are used for dessert, filled with flavored whipped cream, ice cream, fresh fruit.

Five Pastries Made with *Pâte à Choux*
Cinq Sortes de Pâtissières avec Pâte à Choux

Eclairs

1. Fill a pastry bag fitted with a ½-inch round tube with *pâte à choux* to make elongated strips of dough 2 inches long and ½ inch wide *or* use a 1-inch round tube to make éclairs 3½ inches long and 1 inch wide on a pastry sheet, lightly buttered. Tops may be brushed with a glaze of 1 beaten egg mixed with 1 teaspoon water.
2. Bake in 375-degree oven for 15–20 minutes or until lightly browned and crisp on outside. Dry out in turned-off oven for 5 minutes or as long as ½ hour to prevent collapsing. Cool on rack.
3. To fill, make two small holes underneath, and use pastry bag fitted with ¼-inch round tube, to insert *Crème Pâtissière* (p. 286) or *Crème Chantilly* (p. 79). Chill.
4. Glaze with Fondant Icing (p. 299).

Halved recipe makes approximately 30 medium-sized éclairs (3½ x 1-inch wide) *and* 60 small éclairs (2 x ½-inch wide).

Pistachios   *Choux à la Pistaches*

1. Make same length as éclairs but shape like horseshoes or crescents. For *petits fours* use pastry bag fitted with ¼-inch tube to make tiny pastries.
2. Bake, fill with *Crème Pâtissière* (p. 286) tinted slightly with turquoise food coloring, and decorate with Fondant Icing (p. 299) colored green.

Halved recipe makes 24 crescents (3½ x 1-inch wide).   75

Small Cream Puffs   *Profiteroles*

1. Make small puffs ½–1 inch in diameter; bake in 375-degree oven until done, about 15 minutes.
2. To fill *profiteroles* do *not* remove tops—make a small cut across each top and fill with *Crème Pâtissière* (p. 286) or *Crème Chantilly* (p. 79) and chill in refrigerator. If filling with ice cream, do so just before serving and pour Chocolate Sauce (p. 80) over top. If filled with pastry cream, decorate with Fondant Icing (p. 299).

Halved recipe makes 65 small *choux* 1 inch in diameter.

Cream Puff Ring   *Paris-Brest*

This is a crown-shaped pastry made from three rings—two become the base, with a smaller ring placed on top. The same pastry can be designed in a long rectangle.

1 recipe Pâte à Choux *or cream puff dough (p. 74)*
1 egg, beaten, for glaze
2–3 tablespoons slivered almonds

*1 recipe Praline Pastry Cream (*Crème Chibouste, *p. 289)*
Confectioners' sugar
Pastry bag fitted with ¾-inch round tube

1. Butter and flour a baking sheet. Fill pastry bag fitted with ¾-inch tube and pipe two circles of *Pâte à Choux* about 7 inches in diameter, one circle inside the other, onto baking sheet. Pipe a third circle 5½ inches in diameter on top of two base rings. It is important to have bottom rings touching in order to keep third or top ring from falling down between lower rings.

2. Glaze top with beaten egg and sprinkle with slivered almonds. Bake in 375-degree oven about 20 minutes or until lightly browned and the ring tests done. Dry in turned-off oven for 5–10 minutes. If pastry begins to fall from contact with air, return to turned-off oven 5 more minutes. Pastries will become soft again in several hours. As soon as pastry is cold, it may be frozen.

3. After rings are cooled, cut off top ¼ inch thick. Fill with pastry cream (can use pastry bag fitted with star tube and make two layers), put top back on, and sprinkle confectioners' sugar over top and sides. Refrigerate until ready to serve.

Serves 8–10.

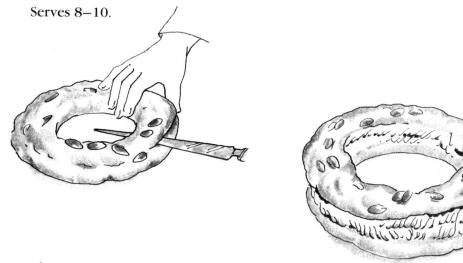

The Swan   *Le Cygne*

Choux *puffs are not supposed to be rock hard on the outside and hollow within. The charm of these ephemeral little pastries is the contrast of the crisp outer surface, the "web" of soft cooked dough within, and the filling. To be at their best, they should be made within hours of eating and assembled at the last possible moment.*

½ recipe Pâte à Choux or cream puff dough (p. 74)
1 egg beaten with 1 teaspoon cold water for glaze
1 cup heavy cream
1 teaspoon vanilla extract or 1 tablespoon Grand Marnier or 1 tablespoon Cognac

2 tablespoons confectioners' sugar plus confectioners' sugar for decoration
Pastry bag with ½-inch-thick tube (No. 10) and ¹⁄₁₆-inch tube (No. 3) or parchment paper for cone

77

1. To make heads and necks of swans: Form fifteen 3-inch-high "question marks" with choux paste on a greased baking sheet, using a pastry bag fitted with a ¹⁄₁₆-inch plain tube or a parchment paper cone. Add an extra blob for head, tailing it off for the beak. Brush with egg wash (1 egg beaten with 1 teaspoon water) and bake at 375 degrees for 5–10 minutes.

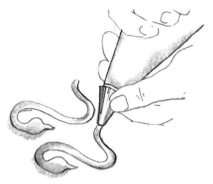

2. To make bodies: Form fifteen 3-inch-long teardrop shapes on a separate greased baking sheet, leaving 2 inches of space between each for expansion, using a pastry bag with a ½-inch tube or 2 tablespoons. Brush with egg wash and bake at 400 degrees for 25 minutes. Do not open oven door during baking time, or the puffs may fall. Make a little slit in each baked puff to allow steam to escape, and cool on a rack in turned-off oven.

3. Whip 1 cup heavy cream, flavoring with vanilla, Grand Marnier, or Cognac.
4. To assemble swans: Cut one third off top of each "body" and slice this in two lengthwise for the wings. Fill body cavity with flavored whipped cream

sweetened with 2 tablespoons confectioners' sugar, using a pastry bag and a star tube. Insert "wings" at an angle, and place "head and neck" in position. Sift confectioners' sugar over completed swans.

Makes 15 swans.

One Simple Pastry Filling, Sauce, and Icing
Une Crème, Sauce, et Glaçage pour Garnir

Sweetened Whipped Cream   *Crème Chantilly*

2 cups heavy cream, chilled   1 teaspoon vanilla
4–6 tablespoons confectioners' sugar

1. Chill stainless steel or ceramic mixing bowl and beaters before using to whip chilled heavy cream. Then, whip cream, starting at low speed, increasing speed until cream starts to thicken. (Whipped cream without sugar is called *crème fouettée*. It can be flavored with coffee extract, praline paste, lemon essence, Amaretto, and Grand Marnier, to name a few flavors.)

2. Beat in confectioners' sugar 1 tablespoon at a time until cream holds its shape. Do not overbeat, which will ruin its soft, fluffy consistency.

3. Stir in flavoring and refrigerate until ready to use.

4. A new method is to add Italian Meringue (p. 347) for more fluffiness and less richness to unsweetened, partially whipped cream.

    Most heavy cream is half whipped (lightly whipped) for folding into mousses and other cream desserts; if fully whipped, the action of subsequent folding will not give a smooth texture.

5. To develop more volume in whipped cream, a copper bowl is used with a

chilled balloon whisk. Copper bowl should be cleaned first with lemon juice or vinegar and salt, rinsed with water, and turned upside down to drain.

Makes 4 cups.

NOTE: Egg whites will also develop greater volume if they are beaten with a balloon whisk in a copper bowl, except that they must be at room temperature. A balloon whisk with a wooden handle has more grip than one with metal. A narrow whisk *(fouet)* is recommended for making pastry cream to avoid bubbles.

Simple Chocolate Sauce   *Sauce au Chocolat Simple*

This sauce is very quick and easy to make, pours well, and has a pleasing bittersweet flavor, in contrast to most chocolate sauces, which contain butter or cream.

4 ounces semi-sweet chocolate, cut up
¼ cup cold water
2 teaspoons coffee extract or instant espresso

1 tablespoon rum or Cognac (optional)

Place chocolate, cold water, and coffee flavoring in top of double boiler over simmering water. Let chocolate melt and stir just enough to combine. Add rum or Cognac if used, and serve immediately.
Serve over ice cream, *Profiteroles* (p. 76), or plain poached pears.

Makes approximately 1 cup; serves 4.

Basic Glacé Icing   *Glaçage à l'Eau*
Sugar Glaze or Plain Icing

1½ cups confectioners' sugar
1–2 tablespoons water or other liquid flavoring (rum or liqueur)

1. Sift sugar into a pot. Moisten with the liquid. Warm just enough to melt the sugar.

2. Spread quickly over pastry, cake, or cookies.

This method is only recommended for use in an emergency. If rum or a flavoring with liqueur is used instead of water, it will stay on the cake better. It will not have the shiny texture of fondant icing.

Makes ½ cup.

Five Hot Dishes Using *Pâte à Choux*
Cinq Façons de se Servir
de Pâte à Choux

Dauphine Potatoes
Pommes de Terre Dauphine

2 large Idaho potatoes or *other
baking potatoes*
Salt and pepper to taste
Pinch nutmeg
1 egg yolk

1 tablespoon butter
¼ recipe Pâte à Choux, *1⅛ cups,
unsweetened (p. 74)*
*Oil for deep frying, 3 inches deep in
pot*

1. Wash and dry potatoes. Puncture with a fork to relieve internal pressure and bake in a 350-degree oven for 45–60 minutes, or until tender.

2. While still hot, slice off tops, scoop out pulp, and dry this in a medium hot oven for about 30 minutes. Put through a ricer or sieve and season with salt, pepper, and nutmeg to taste. Two *large* baking potatoes make about 2 cups riced potato.

3. Beat 1 egg yolk into riced potato, using a wooden spoon, and stir in 1 tablespoon butter.

4. Combine one third of the unsweetened *Pâte à Choux* with two thirds of the mashed potatoes. Taste to correct seasoning. Lighter potato balls are made from the proportion of one half potato mixture to one half *Pâte à Choux*.

5. Form tablespoon-sized balls using two tablespoons. Drop them into oil heated to 300–325 degrees. Deep fry for about 6–7 minutes; potato balls will puff up and turn by themselves during frying process. Drain on paper towels and serve immediately as a garnish on dinner plates.

Makes about 20–24 depending on the proportion of *pâte à choux*.

| Potatoes Lorette | *Pommes de Terre Lorette* |

Made with the same recipe as Dauphine Potatoes, except that the mixture is piped, using a ½-inch tube, into a cigar shape and deep fried.

Potatoes Chamonix   *Pommes de Terre Chamonix*

| *½ cup grated Gruyère* or *Emmentaler cheese* | *1½ tablespoons chopped chives*
2 cups Dauphine potato batter |

Combine above ingredients and deep fry as for Dauphine Potatoes (p. 81). Serve as soon as possible.

Makes 25 potato balls.

Dumplings   *Gnocchi Parisienne*

Gnocchi can be prepared one day ahead, then put in the oven just before serving. Serve as a first course, or use to garnish a roast served on a silver platter. Gnocchi can serve as the starch on a dinner plate with green vegetables and a meat or poultry dish.

| *2½ cups* Pâte à Choux *dough made with milk (p. 74)* | *½ cup grated Parmesan cheese*
5–6 cups Tomato Sauce (p. 41) |

1. Add grated cheese to *Pâte à Choux* dough, which should be warm.
2. Form gnocchi with pastry bag using ½–¾-inch tube. Have large pot of simmering salted water ready. Break off 1½-inch cork-shaped pieces with a knife as they come out of the tube so that they will fall into the water.
3. Poach about 8 at a time until gnocchi rise to the surface and are firm. Cooking time is about 10 minutes. Drain on paper towels.

Makes 68–70 gnocchi; serves 8–10.

Uses: Serve as an hors d'oeuvre, 4–5 to a person, or as a garnish with the main course. For a first course, serve 6 to a person with ½ cup tomato sauce to 1 serving.

Dumplings with Mornay Sauce   *Gnocchi au Gratin*

1 cup Mornay Sauce (p. 52)
12 Gnocchi Parisienne (p. 82)

2 tablespoons grated Parmesan
*   cheese*
1–2 tablespoons butter

1. Butter shallow ovenproof gratinée dish and line dish with most of the Mornay Sauce.
2. Place cooked and drained gnocchi on top. Cover with more sauce, sprinkle Parmesan cheese on top, and dot with butter.
3. Place in 425-degree oven until heated through and top is browned.
4. Gnocchi can be served in individual gratin dishes. They can be wrapped in wax paper and stored in refrigerator with or without sauce.

Serves 2 for a first course.

Three Kinds of Gnocchi　　　　　*Trois Sortes de Gnocchi*

1. *Gnocchi Parisienne* or *Gnocchi au Gratin,* made with *pâte à choux.*
2. *Gnocchi à la Romana*—semolina flour is used in place of white flour.
3. *Gnocchi à la Piémontaise* or *Gnocchi de Pommes de Terre*—potato purée is used with eggs and ground meat or chicken.

Semolina Dumplings à la Romana　　*Gnocchi à la Romana*

1 quart milk
3 tablespoons butter
6 ounces (1 cup) semolina flour
　(coarse, granular variety)
2 large whole eggs
2 large egg yolks

Salt, pepper, and nutmeg to taste
4–6 ounces (1–1½ sticks) unsalted
　butter, melted
4–6 ounces (approximately 1½
　cups) Gruyère cheese, grated, or half
　Romano, grated, and half Gruyère

1. Using a heavy saucepan, bring the milk and butter to a boil. On medium heat stir semolina into boiling liquid until it becomes thick like mashed potatoes.
2. Remove pot from stove and stir in whole eggs, one at a time; then add yolks. Add salt, pepper, and nutmeg to taste.
3. Line a jelly roll pan with foil or parchment paper (pan can be oiled, instead) and spread mixture out to about ¼ inch thick. Let cool in refrigerator for 1 hour before turning out on a marble slab or cutting board. Cut into 1½-inch squares or *losanges,* which do not leave any waste. A round cutter can also be used.
4. Dip cut pieces in melted butter, then coat with grated cheese. Arrange in individual ovenproof gratinée dishes and cook in 350-degree oven about 7–10 minutes until lightly browned. Dishes can be put under a hot broiler for 30 seconds, if more browning is desired.

Serves 10–12. Recipe can be halved.

Potato Dumplings à la Piémontese

Gnocchi à la Piémontese
Gnocchi de Pommes de Terre

1½ pounds potatoes, Idaho or red Bee
4½ ounces (1 cup less 2 tablespoons)
* flour*
2 eggs
Salt and pepper to taste

2 tablespoons butter
6 ounces (approximately 1½ cups)
* Parmesan cheese or Gruyère,*
* grated, or half of each, combined*

1. Boil or steam potatoes in their skins until done, peel while hot, and put through a food mill or potato ricer, or mash in a food processor.

2. Mix mashed potatoes and flour in a mixing bowl; beat eggs slightly and add, stirring with a wooden spoon. Season with salt and pepper. When ready to cook, flour hands lightly and roll potato mixture into small balls the size of large walnuts; flatten slightly.

3. In several quarts of simmering water, add a little salt, and poach 4 or 5 gnocchi at a time for about 20 minutes. When they rise to the top of the water, it does not mean they are done. Taste to be certain. Remove with a slotted spoon and drain on a towel for a few minutes.

4. Serve immediately with grated cheese and a little butter sprinkled over the gnocchi; or arrange in layers in a gratinée dish, sprinkle with cheese and butter, and just before ready to serve, heat in a 350-degree oven until lightly browned.

   Serve as a first course or as a side dish with the main course. Gnocchi can also be served with a light meat sauce or tomato sauce.

Makes 18–20 gnocchi; serves 4–6.

Using the Metric System Without Fear

For cooks who are timid about converting metric measurements to the American system of weights and measures, a simple way of converting recipes where exact measurements are not so important is to use the following calculations:

1 pound *(livre)* is approximately 500 grams (½ kilogram)

1 quart is approximately 1 liter (100 centiliters)

1 quart of water or clear liquid weighs 2 pounds

Here is my recipe for *pâte à choux,* which I use in the restaurant to make 60–68 large *choux:*

1 liter of water	=	1 quart
500 grams butter	=	1 pound
500 grams flour	=	1 pound
16–18 eggs		
Pinch salt		
Pinch sugar		

My reason for presenting this recipe is to explain that cooks can substitute American measurements estimated above (1 quart for 1 liter and 1 pound for 500 grams) which will not affect the consistency of the dough. For in making the substitutions, slightly less water, butter, and flour will be used, proportions not significantly changed to make any difference.

An explanation of metric measurements and equivalent measures is included for reference in the appendix. Here are some commonly used:

1 egg	=	50 grams or 1½ ounces
2 tablespoons	=	1 ounce = 28.34 grams
1 tablespoon sugar	=	15 grams
2 tablespoons gelatin	=	28–29 grams
1 tablespoon unflavored Knox gelatin	=	14 grams (1 package)

Chapter Four

"HORS D'OEUVRE VARIÉS" and LES ENTRÉES (First Courses)

Terrines of Seafood, *Pâtés,* and Mousses; *Les Salades* Served Alone and as Accompaniments

Although *les hors d'oeuvre* are first on the menu, they are not first on the curriculum of cooking schools, for learning basic techniques and acquiring experience in cuisine come first. The term *hors d'oeuvre* means literally "outside the work"—they are not considered a part of the meal, just a prelude. In France, they are served in the home at lunch and dinner, where the thrifty housewife can use her leftover vegetables and meats to make appetizers eaten with a fork and served attractively at the table. In America, home of the cocktail party, hors d'oeuvres are usually bite-sized morsels eaten while standing in the reception or banquet room of a hotel or restaurant or in the living room of a home before the dinner is served. The cook and menu planner should always remember that hors d'oeuvres are meant to excite their guests' appetites for the meal which is anticipated, not to surfeit it. Also, appetizers should not contain the same food that will be featured in the dinner to follow, but should suggest the high quality of the rest of the menu for the occasion.

A broad classification of hors d'oeuvres, often stated as hot *(chaud)* and cold *(froid)* is a deceptive simplification, for all the chef's resources or armamentaria are exerted to produce elegant formal hors d'oeuvres as well as informal ones. Cooks will want to become familiar with saucemaking, *pâtisserie, boulangerie,* meat, poultry, and fish cookery, as well as the art of garnishing before they can produce the tiny cases to be filled with tempting *salpicons,* mixtures of cooked meat, poultry, and fish in thick spicy sauces. Tiny individual pastry shells of *pâte brisée* are called *tartelettes* if round, *barquettes* if oval, *bouchées* if made from *pâte feuilletée,* and *profiteroles* when made from *pâte à choux.* Little crustades carved out of bread, real shells or ovenproof pottery facsimiles are filled with seafood just as small *crêpes* are filled with sauced vegetable or meat mixtures. *Petits brioches* are baked in tiny molds, their tops removed to serve as a cover after they are filled with a *salpicon. Cassolettes (casserolettes),* meaning casseroles, are baked *tartelettes* of *pâte brisée* or *pâte feuilletée* with a handle made of the same dough. (A French casserole is a fairly deep pot with a handle.)

For chefs who do not have the patience for these tiny individual preparations, there are pie-sized quiches, loaf-type *pâtés,* and terrines of veal, fish, pork, poultry, liver, or game which can be baked in advance, displayed on the buffet table, and sliced for service. They are garnished inside with marinated strips of meat and truffles, if available. *Galantines* (p. 206) serve large groups and represent a type of hors d'oeuvre served with knife and fork.

In a class by themselves are the *canapés,* artistically garnished bite-sized gems, hot or cold, served on trays. They are usually open-faced "sandwiches" made of bread or puff pastry—the day-old bread (*pain de mie* or brioche) may be toasted or fried and cut into small rounds, diamonds, crescents, or oblongs spread with compound butters, plain sweet butter, cream cheese or mayonnaise. The tops may be brushed with aspic, decorated using a pastry bag fitted with a tube, and feature smoked salmon or trout, *pâté,* caviar, fine ham, tongue, cheese, mushrooms, or hard boiled eggs to name some food-stuffs. Chefs are free to create designs that reflect the spirit of their time. Canapés are served with aperitifs, cocktails, or on a buffet table. If guests are seated at tables, a small selection of canapés might be served on individual plates. In France, canapés were eaten before dinner while sitting in the drawing room. This explains the derivation of the French word *canapé,* meaning sofa or couch, on which guests sat to enjoy the first serving of food morsels.

A nonpareil group of uncooked hors d'oeuvres demands experience to procure as well as discriminating taste to select and savor. They are fresh *foie de canard, foie gras d'oie,* steak tartare, black caviar from sturgeon (p. 96) or the cheaper domestic varieties such as golden whitefish caviar. Light or dark red salmon caviar are also very acceptable. Not to be excluded are fresh oysters (Bélon, Portuguese, Long Island Blue Points, Pigeon Point, tiny Olympia served in saki cups with wine vinegar and chopped shallot sauce); Dungeness crab, Alaska king crab, snow crab found only in Alaska, soft shell crabs, blue crab from the Chesapeake Bay, stone crabs from Florida; Maine lobster (the true *homard*), spiny lobster *(langouste)* from California, tiny Pacific and Maine shrimp, Little Neck and Cherrystone clams. Carefully selected fruits—seedless table grapes, tropical and exotic fruits—and vegetables trimmed in fancy styles serve as decorations for a buffet table and are enjoyed as hors d'oeuvres at the same time.

Cooked hors d'oeuvres reflect the influence of international cuisine, which has enlarged the choice: tempura, sushi or a sushi bar from Japan; steamed shao-mai dumplings or fried won tons from China; satays from the Far East Pacific islands and miniature kebabs from the Middle East; Italian Bagna Cauda and Fritto Misto; Swiss Fondue; Greek filo triangles (tiropetes); Indian curry sauce and samosas; Scandinavian smorgasbord; Russian blini.

To compose a tray or cart of colorful and tempting *Hors d'Oeuvre Variés,* the chef selects from a specific group of foods, each served in an individual white porcelain or glass dish called a *ravier.* They are rectangular or square, 4–6 inches wide and ½–1 inch high. To assist in making a balanced display of *Hors d'Oeuvre Variés,* five main qualities are found to exist:

1. Raw vegetables *(les crudités):* cucumber, radish, red and white cabbage, fennel, red and green bell peppers, celery root, celery hearts, thin green beans, carrots, tomatoes, cauliflower, broccoli.
2. Salty products *(les salaisons):* caviar, olives, pickles, anchovies, herrings, gravlax, smoked salmon, trout, sturgeon, eels (all salted and smoked).
3. Dried, cured, and cooked meats *(charcuterie):* salami type of sausage, cured ham usually smoked such as Talmadge from Georgia or American-made prosciutto, *pâtés,* terrines, galantines, salads from cooked meat or poultry (pp. 123–124), smoked quail, turkey, poussin, *confit de canard* (p. 245), smoked beef *(viande de grisons).*
4. Cooked vegetable salads *(légumes en salade):* to supply a soft and smooth element—potato salad, rice salad, beans (white and green), beets, stuffed eggs (pp. 135–137).
    Vegetables cooked in oil *(légumes à la Grecque):* artichokes (p. 95), celery, mushrooms, zucchini, leeks (p. 95), pearl onions.
5. Fresh fish *(les poissons frais):* prawns; oysters; mussels; sea, bay, or calico scallops; lobster in sauce; poached salmon (p. 175); crayfish; lump crabmeat; small claw from Maryland and the West Coast; Dungeness and stone crab; ceviche with squid; or whitefish.

Certain hors d'oeuvres lend themselves to the position of a first course if served in larger amounts—terrines of fish (pp. 98, 101, and 102) and meats, *Rillettes de Saumon* (p. 94), *Huîtres à Ma Façon* (p. 93), Mousseline of Scallops and Salmon (p. 192), Scallops in Pastry Shells (p. 92), Chicken Liver Pâté (p. 104), *Les Oeufs Farcis au Foie de Volaille* (p. 105).

Three terrines in Chapter 4 and two in Chapter 7 are made of seafood and are more perishable than those prepared from meat, poultry, or game. They do not benefit from ripening, as do the latter; they are best served the same day they are baked or within the next couple of days. Fish terrines will keep longer if the refrigerator is not opened too often to let in warm air. Freshly cooked and cooled *pâtés* can be covered with pork, duck, or goose fat to prolong their conservation.

Today inventive chefs make terrines of vegetables *(terrine de légumes)* which also must be served soon after they are baked and chilled—three or more different vegetables are placed in layers of contrasting colors, some are puréed, others parboiled, sliced in various shapes or diced, and flavored with herbs. Aspic, eggs, ground chicken or fish often solidify the loaf shape, and they are served with vegetable sauces. A chef in Bordeaux, France, has created a fruit loaf for dessert served with fresh raspberry sauce. It is composed of fresh peaches, strawberries, and raspberries in a Bavarian cream.

So now the definition of a terrine, meaning earthenware pan, includes vegetables and fruits as well as meat, poultry, liver or fish forcemeat baked without a crust. The term *pâté* traditionally meant forcemeat baked in a crust served hot or cold, but it is often used for forcemeat that has been cooked before it is placed in a mold and served chilled. An example of the latter is *Pâté Foies de Volaille* (p. 104). To avoid confusion, *pâté en croute,* used to label ground meat or poultry baked in a crust, is a more certain term. There are freestanding *pâtés en croute;* however, when baked in a mold, the *pâté* is easier to remove if the mold is hinged. A round hinged tin mold, a *tourtière,* may be used for a *tourte*—a deep, layered pastry of uncooked fish, chicken, vegetables, or partially cooked meat enclosed in puff pastry or *pâte brisée* with a sealed top of the same dough. An opening in the top allows steam to escape while baking. *Pâte à tourte* is also made as a double-crust pie, similar to an American pie.

One will not want to lavish too much attention on the introduction to the luncheon or dinner: the other courses will take the greater time and effort.

Gruyère Cream   *Crème de Gruyère*

8 egg yolks
12 ounces (3 cups) Gruyère cheese or
   Parmesan cheese, grated
2 ounces (¹/₂ cup less 2 tablespoons)
   flour

1 quart milk
1 cup (2 sticks) butter
Salt and pepper to taste
Pinch nutmeg

1. In a large heavy pot mix egg yolks, cheese, and flour. Stir in milk on low heat.
2. Bring to a boil stirring constantly, and boil for 5 minutes. Remove from heat.
3. Add butter, salt, pepper, and nutmeg. Chill. This *crème* is excellent in small *choux,* and even better in *bouchées* (puff pastry shells) or *barquettes* served for hors d'oeuvres or canapés.

Makes approximately 7 cups.

Scallops in Pastry Shells

Coquilles Saint-Jacques Grandmère

1½ pounds scallops
1 large shallot, finely chopped
1½ cups dry white wine
1 tablespoon butter
Juice of 1 lemon
1 egg yolk
4 tablespoons cream

Salt and pepper to taste
¼ teaspoon chopped thyme
4 tablespoons grated Gruyère cheese
4 baked pastry shells of Pâte
  Feuilletée *(p. 307)* or Pâte Brisée
  (p. 141)

1. Wash and drain scallops. Cut in fairly uniform pieces. Put in saucepan with finely chopped shallot, wine, butter, and lemon juice, and simmer just until done (about 5 minutes depending on size of shallots). Gentle poaching draws out juices and prevents scallops from becoming tough.

2. Drain scallops and keep warm. Reduce sauce to about ¾ cup, beat egg yolk with cream, add to sauce off heat and season with salt and pepper. Stir in thyme. Place scallops in pastry shells, cover with sauce, sprinkle over grated cheese and dot with a little butter. Put shells on a tray and brown under broiler just until light in color.

    Serve as a first-course dish, or tiny shells may be filled with scallop mixture and served as an hors d'oeuvre.

Serves 4.

To make a shell *(coquille)* **with pastry dough:**
1. Take 2 shells of uniform size; butter inside of one and outside of the other. Roll *pâte feuilletée* or *pâte brisée* to ¼-inch thickness. Line shell buttered on inside with dough, pressing in carefully. Trim and place buttered bottom of other shell on top.
2. Put a weight on concave or top shell and bake in 375-degree oven about 20 minutes or until done. Unmold.

Oysters in My Style

Huîtres à Ma Façon

12 oysters in the shell, unopened
(medium sized, such as
Bluepoints)
1 teaspoon chopped shallots or green
onion
1 tablespoon dry white wine, dry
Alsatian, Gewürztraminer, or
California Chardonnay
1 teaspoon chopped parsley

2 cloves garlic, chopped
1/4 cup butter, at room temperature
Salt to taste
1/8 teaspoon freshly ground black
pepper
1 tablespoon fresh bread crumbs
1 tablespoon grated Swiss cheese
(Gruyère)

1. Open oysters, leaving in shell. Arrange in a large baking pan.

2. In a saucepan simmer shallots with the wine until liquid is almost evaporated. Let cool to room temperature. Add to shallots chopped parsley,
   garlic, butter, salt, pepper, bread crumbs, and cheese. Mix with a spatula
   to make a paste. Spread mixture over oysters.

3. Place in a preheated 400-degree oven and bake for about 8 minutes. Arrange baked oysters on individual plates.

Serve 4–6 to a person for an appetizer; serve 2 to a person as a canapé.

Fried Whitebait

Friture de Petits Poissons

1–2 pounds anchovies, whitebait,
small perch, blue gill, Rex sole, or
fillet of flat fish, cut in sticks
1 cup beer or milk with 1/2 teaspoon
yeast dissolved in 1/4 cup of the
(warmed) milk

Pinch cayenne pepper
1 cup flour
Salt and pepper to taste
Vegetable oil or hydrogenated
shortening for deep frying
1 bunch fresh parsley

1. Soak fish in beer or milk with a pinch of cayenne pepper for 5–10 minutes
   or 30 minutes longer.

2. Put 1/4 cup flour and some salt and pepper in a paper bag, add about six
   fish, shake bag to coat fish, and remove fish to a plate. Continue coating
   fish with flour in small batches to prevent mushiness, adding more flour
   as needed.

3. In small batches, deep fry in vegetable oil or shortening heated to 350–
   375 degrees. When light brown and crispy, drain fish on paper towels and

keep warm until ready to serve on a tray covered with a white napkin or use paper doilies.

4. Wash and dry parsley, deep fry a quarter bunch at a time, drain on paper towel, and serve on tray with small fish.

One pound of fish serves 5–6 as hors d'oeuvres for cocktails or serve with aperitifs.

Potted Salmon   *Rillettes de Saumon*

Rillettes *originated in Le Mans or Tours, France, where they were made primarily with pork. They are now made with rabbit, goose, duck, venison, and fish such as whitefish with smoked sturgeon, or fresh and smoked salmon as stated in this recipe.*

10 ounces salmon, fresh fillet without bones, or 16 ounces salmon steak
1½ quarts Court Bouillon (p. 174)
3½ ounces salmon, smoked, cut in small dice
1 egg yolk
4 ounces (1 stick) unsalted butter, soft room temperature or creamed

1 tablespoon olive oil
1 lemon, grated peel only
Salt and pepper to taste (but consider salt in smoked salmon)
1 cup heavy cream, lightly whipped
Croutons—thinly sliced toast

1. Poach salmon in Court Bouillon about 2–3 minutes if ½ inch thick, 3–4 minutes if 1 inch thick. Drain. If steaks are used, remove skin and use needlenose pliers to remove bones. Mash while warm with fork and mix with diced smoked salmon. Let cool.

2. Put egg yolk in a bowl; blend with butter, oil, grated lemon peel, partially whipped cream, salt and pepper to taste. Gently fold in the salmon. Put in an attractive terrine, or form into a roll using foil to wrap it in.

3. Refrigerate overnight to let the lemon and olive oil develop flavor of the dish.

    Serve as an hors d'oeuvre with toast or as an appetizer or first course on a bed of lettuce with croutons.

Makes approximately 3½ cups; serves 18–20 as a dish for a buffet.

Little Artichokes à la Grecque   *Petits Artichauts à la Grecque*

2 or 3 dozen tender, very small
  artichokes
12 small onions
1/2 cup olive oil
1 cup stock (optional)
1 teaspoon peppercorns

1 teaspoon coriander seeds
1 bouquet garni
Juice of 1 lemon or 2 tablespoons
  wine vinegar
Pinch salt

1. Cut off about 1 inch from tops of artichokes, pull off some outside leaves, trim stems, and rub with lemon, or put in acidulated water. Blanch onions to remove outside skin.

2. Put enough water in a saucepan to cover artichokes, add all other ingredients, and boil for 10 minutes. Add artichokes, cover, and simmer until done, testing with a fork. They should be tender in about 25 minutes.

3. Let cool, put in jar with lid or covered bowl, keep in refrigerator until ready to serve. Keep artichokes in their liquid. Serve as an hors d'oeuvre in *raviers,* rectangular china dishes used for that purpose. Also used as an ingredient in salads.

Serves 8–12.

Leeks Vinaigrette   *Poireaux Vinaigrette*

12 small leeks
1 bay leaf
Salt and pepper to taste
1–2 tablespoons chopped parsley

1/2 cup Sauce Vinaigrette,
  approximately (p. 111)
2 hard boiled eggs, sliced for garnish

1. Trim leeks, removing roots, any blemished outside leaves; cut off most of green tops and reserve to use in stock. Slice leeks in half lengthwise and soak in cold water to remove sand.

2. In wide saucepan place leeks flat in boiling water, just enough to cover leeks. Add bay leaf, salt and pepper to taste, and simmer, covered, until they are tender but still firm. Drain and cool.

3. Arrange in gratin dish, cover with vinaigrette dressing, sprinkle chopped parsley on top. Marinate in refrigerator until ready to serve. Garnish with sliced or quartered hard boiled eggs.

    Serve with tray of cold *hors d'oeuvre variés.*

Serves 4–6.

Jellied Trout in White Wine   *Truite en Gelée au Vin Blanc*

8–10 trout, 8–10 ounces each (whole
  fish)
Salt and pepper to taste
Court Bouillon (p. 174), enough to
  cover fish
2 egg whites and shells
  (approximately)

2 tablespoons gelatin, unflavored
Tarragon leaves, blanched
Lemon slices
Sprigs of watercress, dill, or fennel
  tops or julienned yellow or red bell
  peppers for garnish

1. Clean trout and season with salt and pepper.

2. Place trout in *cool* Court Bouillon and *simmer,* covered, until fish tests done (pp. 168–170). If Court Bouillon is simmered very slowly, it might not get cloudy and would not need clarification. In that case, reduce one half, soften gelatin in warm water, and dissolve in hot Court Bouillon. Cool until it starts to set.

3. If a fancier presentation is desired and Court Bouillon appears cloudy, clarify it according to instructions in "How to Clarify Stock to Make *Consommé Clair*" (p. 7), omitting ground meat.

4. Remove skin from one side of trout only and arrange on long platter, skinned side up. Apply 1–2 layers of aspic, decorate with tarragon leaves, and continue to coat with aspic layers, chilling fish after each layer. Four layers should be sufficient. Decorate platter with lemon slices and herb bouquets or julienned peppers.

   Serve with *Mayonnaise Vincent* (p. 64), *Sauce Verte* (p. 63), or *Sauce Cresson* (p. 63). Serve for a cold buffet dish or a first course.

Serves 8.

Colored Jewels from the Sea

Caviar has been called "the most elegant egg of all" and "the costliest snack in the world." Traditionally, fresh caviar is the unfertilized eggs or roe of three varieties of sturgeon. The three top varieties of fresh caviar are: *Beluga,* large gray eggs which set the standard for all caviar; *Osetra,* medium grain with a golden brown cast; and *Sevruga,* the smallest grain, black in color. The grains should be unbroken and glisten, with very little scent. The word Mallossal means the caviar has been lightly salted. Vacuum packed caviar is not desirable because it has been heavily salted. *Pajusnaya* or *Pausnaya,* pressed caviar, is a mixture of damaged eggs from the three kinds of caviar.

The taste of caviar can be appreciated best with the least condiments. The sturgeon of the slightly salty, blue-green, landlocked Caspian Sea produces the most coveted caviar in the world. The large Beluga sturgeon, which provide the top quality caviar, need twelve to fourteen years to mature. Iran has set up a sturgeon spawning farm which is expected to double their caviar production. The female sturgeon are caught as they swim upriver to spawn. They are then induced to lay eggs at the farm in controlled conditions, which ensures four million young sturgeons being released into rivers flowing into the Caspian Sea. However, poachers are a serious threat that could bring about the extinction of the species in that sea. It has been reported that the food of kings has now become, in Iran, available to the proletarians. Due to the war between Iran and Iraq at the present time, the latter sentence of this report may no longer be valid.

New varieties of domestic caviars have recently appeared on the market: golden whitefish caviar, a natural limpid gold color and a little smaller egg than sevruga, comes from the Great Lakes; trout roe, an amber yellow; Oregon Pacific sturgeon, shiny black caviar; Atlantic sturgeon, which is available in larger quantities than from Pacific sturgeon; and Pacific Northwest and Alaska salmon, whose color can be light orange to bright red, one of the largest roes prepared as caviar.

Eggs Stuffed with Caviar   *Les Oeufs Farcis au Caviar*

6 hard boiled eggs, chilled*
12 tablespoons caviar, kept on ice
1–2 tablespoons finely chopped
  parsley

Parsley sprigs
2 lemons, cut in wedges

1. Peel hard boiled eggs and cut in half lengthwise. Remove yolks and reserve. Cut a small slice from underside of each egg to keep them steady and upright.
2. Cover whites and refrigerate until ready to serve. Then, fill with selected caviar. Sieve enough of the yolks to decorate the edges of the stuffed egg whites. Mix sieved yolks with chopped parsley and place around edges of egg whites.
3. Place stuffed eggs on a platter decorated with parsley sprigs and lemon wedges.

Serves 12 for hors d'oeuvres.

* I prefer brown eggs because the yolks are a deeper yellow color. Hardcooked quail eggs may be used, also.

Caviar with Deviled Eggs

Caviar aux Oeufs à la Diable

6 hard boiled eggs, chilled
2½ teaspoons lemon juice
2½ tablespoons mayonnaise or sour cream

Salt and pepper to taste
2 teaspoons caviar
Parsley sprigs or watercress sprays

1. Shell cold hard boiled eggs. Cut in half lengthwise and remove yolks. Mash yolks to a paste, add lemon juice, and mayonnaise or sour cream. Season with salt and pepper to taste.

2. Fill whites with prepared yolks, leaving some hollowed-out space at the top of yolks. Put about a quarter of a teaspoon of caviar on top of each egg. Arrange on a platter decorated with parsley sprigs or watercress.

Serves 12 for hors d'oeuvres.

Terrine of Trout

Terrine de Truite

¼ cup Essence of Trout (p. 196) prepared from reserved trout trimmings
¾ cup milk
2½ ounces (3 slices) white sandwich bread, crusts removed, cut into ½ inch dice
9 ounces fresh trout fillets cut from 4 medium trout—bones, skin, and heads reserved
1 egg
⅓ cup heavy cream, lightly whipped

1 tablespoon chopped truffles (optional)
1 tablespoon pistachio nuts, shelled and peeled, or pine nuts
Salt and white pepper to taste
Freshly grated nutmeg to taste
1 tablespoon butter for mold
Oval terrine, porcelain or Pyrex, 6½ x 4½ x 3 inches deep, measured from inside (terrine does not have to be filled)

1. Prepare Essence of Trout.

2. Bring milk to boil in a heavy, non-aluminum saucepan, add prepared bread, and stir with a wooden spoon until thick and smooth, about 1 minute. (This mixture is known as a *panade*.) Let cool.

3. Using a meat grinder fitted with a fine blade, grind trout meat with cooled *panade*.

4. Transfer mixture to a food processor fitted with a steel blade. Add egg and process for 30 seconds. Add Essence of Trout and process for 1 second. Add lightly whipped cream, truffles if used, pistachios, salt, pepper, and nutmeg. Process for 1 second—overblending could cause mixture to curdle. Stir gently with a wooden spoon before filling mold.

5. In order to check seasoning, poach a tablespoon or two of trout mixture in barely simmering water. It should have a delicate flavor of trout; the use of salt should not be evident.

6. Coat terrine with butter, spoon in trout mixture, and set it in a baking pan. Add enough boiling water to come halfway up sides of terrine, cover loosely with foil, and bake at 350 degrees for 45 minutes. Test with a toothpick—if it comes out clean, the terrine is ready. Cool on a rack before refrigerating for 24 hours to let flavors mellow. Unmold and coat with Chaud-Froid Sauce (p. 56) or serve from terrine. In either case, serve with Watercress Sauce (*Sauce Cresson,* p. 63), *Sauce Verte* (p. 63), or *Mayonnaise Vincent* (p. 64).

Serves 8–10 for a first course.

To make a larger Terrine of Trout to serve 20 people, use a long rectangular ovenproof terrine or an ordinary bread loaf pan 8½ × 4½ × 3 inches deep measured from the inside, and increase the ingredients as follows:

½ cup Essence of Trout (p. 196)
1 cup milk
4 ounces (5 slices) white sandwich
  bread, crusts removed, cubed
2 pounds fresh trout fillets cut from 8
  medium trout (reserve skin, bones,
  and heads for Essence of Trout) *
2 egg whites

2 cups heavy cream, lightly whipped
2 tablespoons chopped truffles
  (optional)
2 tablespoons pistachio nuts, shelled
  and peeled
Salt and white pepper to taste
Freshly grated nutmeg to taste
2 tablespoons butter for terrine

* 2 fillets = 8 ounces; their trimmings = 7 ounces—40–50% weight of trout is lost from trimming skin, bones, and heads.

Salmon Mousse   *Mousse de Saumon*

1¼ pounds fillet of fresh salmon,
  skinned and boned
4 egg yolks
3 cups heavy cream
A few grinds fresh nutmeg
Salt and freshly ground pepper to
  taste
Truffles or pitted black olives, sliced,
  for center

Butter and flour for mold
2-quart mold, rectangular or half
  moon shape
Parchment paper to line mold and to
  cover top (optional)
1 quart clear aspic to coat mousse
3½–4 cups fish stock for aspic,
  clarified, if necessary (p. 21)
1–2 tablespoons plain gelatin

99

1. Grind salmon fillets in meat grinder using fine blade. Purée ground salmon for a few seconds in processor fitted with steel blade.
2. Working quickly, add egg yolks to salmon purée and pour cream in through feed tube with machine running. Season with nutmeg, salt, and pepper to taste.
3. In advance, butter and flour mold; or butter mold and line with parchment paper, if desired. Fill mold halfway with salmon mousse, place a row of sliced truffles or black olives in center, and fill to top with rest of mousse. Cut parchment paper to correct size to cover top, butter it, place on top of mousse, and put aluminum foil over parchment. Place in *bain-marie* and bake in a 350-degree oven for 45–55 minutes or until done. Test by pressing on top and inserting a knife in center.
4. Let cool at least 10 hours or overnight before applying aspic in thin layers. Half of the aspic may be used for decorations.
5. This mousse or *pâté* can be served without aspic, or it may be covered with thinly sliced cucumbers resembling scales of fish, which keep top moist for a buffet.

    Serve with thin toast for an hors d'oeuvre or with warm Lobster Sauce (p. 199) or Sorrel Sauce (p. 254) for a first course.

Serves 12–14 for a first course.

NOTE: *Consommé à la Madrilène* (p. 9) with added gelatin can be used to coat a mousse or *pâté*. One tablespoon of plain gelatin will jell 2 cups of liquid. Test consommé to determine how much gelatin will be required to dissolve in heated consommé. (Canned *Consommé Madrilène* is available)

When using gelatin in mousses, remember that if the main ingredient is already cooked before making the mousse, it is necessary to add gelatin. If the main ingredient, such as fish, is uncooked, the natural gelatin of the fish with the binding power of the eggs are enough to coagulate the mixture to allow for unmolding after the mousse or *pâté* is cooked and chilled.

Terrine of Sole   *Terrine de Sole*

2 pounds fresh fillet of sole*
  (4½ pounds before skinning and
  boning as 60% of fish is lost)
2 egg whites
½ quart fish stock reduced to ½ cup
A few grinds nutmeg
Salt and freshly ground white pepper
  to taste

1 quart heavy cream
Carrot rounds, asparagus pieces, or
  cut string beans, steamed, to
  arrange in center of terrine
Butter and flour or *parchment paper*
  to line buttered mold
2-quart rectangular mold
Foil to cover top of mold

1. Put sole fillets through meat grinder using fine blade.

2. Put ground sole in bowl of processor fitted with steel blade and purée a few seconds. Mix in egg whites quickly, add reduced fish stock, freshly ground nutmeg, salt, and white pepper to taste. Pour in heavy cream with machine running. Do not overprocess.

3. Butter and flour or line mold with parchment paper, fill halfway with fish mixture, arrange steamed cut and dried vegetables in center. Fill terrine to top with rest of sole mixture. Cut parchment paper to cover top of mold, butter it, place on top with foil over paper. Place in *bain-marie* and bake in 350-degree oven for 30 minutes or until done.

   Can be served warm from the terrine with *Sauce Vin Blanc* (p. 54), *Sauce Nantua* (p. 199), or *Sauce Tomate* (p. 41). Served cold it must be chilled at least 10 hours before unmolding, and can be served with *Sauce Cresson* or *Mayonnaise* (pp. 62 and 63), *Sauce Vièrge* (p. 68), or *Mayonnaise Vincent* (p. 64). Terrine will keep 4–5 days under refrigeration.

Serves 24 as hot or cold appetizer; serves 16 as a warm fish course.

If bowl of processor is too small to hold full amount of fish mixture, process fish and egg whites first. Then remove half of mixture to large mixing bowl, and add 1 pint heavy cream to remainder in processor and process quickly. Transfer this to separate mixing bowl. Repeat with other half by putting back in processor and adding rest of cream. Blend two batches in one bowl. Do not omit seasoning.

* Dover or petrale sole, halibut or flounder can be used for this terrine. However, English or lemon sole are not recommended, as they lack enough texture or substance.

Terrine of Sole and Salmon in Three Colors

Terrine de Sole et Saumon au Trois Couleurs

½ recipe Mousse of Salmon—use darker colored salmon (p. 99) (makes 3 pounds total)
1 recipe Terrine of Sole (see preceding recipe)
1 tablespoon chopped basil
1 tablespoon finely chopped spinach or watercress

1 teaspoon finely chopped tarragon
2 quart rectangular mold (aluminum, Pyrex, Corning ware)
Butter and parchment paper to line mold

1. Prepare Mousse of Salmon through Step 2 and set aside.

2. Prepare Terrine of Sole through Step 2 and divide into one-third and two-third amounts in separate bowls. Flavor and color the smaller amount with finely chopped herbs. If green color is too light, add more chopped herbs.

3. Butter a 9 × 5 × 3-inch terrine, lining long side (9-inch) with parchment paper. Spread bottom and sides with ½ inch thick layer of plain white sole mixture, reserving one quarter for top of terrine.

4. Place orange salmon mixture in large pastry bag (without tube). Place green herb flavored sole mixture in second large pastry bag.

5. Pipe a salmon pink stripe along bottom of lined terrine, next to side. Follow with a green stripe right next to it. Repeat with another salmon pink and another green stripe to cover bottom of terrine. Reverse procedure, covering salmon pink stripes with green, and green with pink, to form a checkerboard pattern. When terrine is filled ½ inch from top, cover with remainder of white sole mixture using a small spoon. Smooth top with a spatula.

6. Cover top with piece of buttered parchment cut same size as terrine. Place sheet of foil over parchment. Place in *bain-marie*—a baking pan filled with enough hot water to reach halfway up sides of terrine. Bake at 350 degrees for 40 minutes or until terrine tests done by pressing finger on top for firmness and inserting knife in center to check if it comes out clean.

7. Allow to cool before unmolding—refrigerate for several hours before unmolding. When terrine is sliced, it will reveal checkerboard pattern within.

   Serve as a first course with *Sauce Vièrge* (p. 68), *Sauce Mayonnaise* (p. 62), or *Cresson* (p. 63).

Serves 34–36 as an appetizer cut in ¼-inch slices; serves 16–18 as a main luncheon course cut in ½-inch slices.

NOTE: Bake any leftover mixture in timbale molds for individual servings. Terrine may be served warm with *Sauce Beurre Blanc* (p. 64) or *Beurre Rouge* (p. 67). Serve cold terrine with cool Sorrel Sauce (p. 254) or one of cold sauces made with mayonnaise (pp. 112–113).

How to Sauté Forcefed Goose and Duck Liver for a First Course or Salad

1. Usually the forcefed livers are sold with the membrane removed. If there are any veins, they should be removed along with membrane. Slice liver ¼ inch thick or just a little thicker, if desired. Sauté in a dry pan or with a little butter on medium heat for ½ minute on each side. Fattened goose liver is composed of so much fat that it will melt very easily, as does butter. While still pink, remove liver to warm plate, pour fat from pan, and deglaze with raspberry, honey or sherry vinegar, or sherry wine. Pour this sauce over liver.

2. If serving sautéed liver without a salad, prior to deglazing, sauté it in a pan with a little goose or duck fat—precooked corn kernels or julienned vegetables or mushrooms (shiitake, oyster, *trompette de la morte,* porcini, inoke). Deglaze pan as described in Step 1 and serve vegetables on same plate with foie gras. Sliced fresh truffles may be added as a garnish.

103

3. To make a salad with fresh sautéed duck or goose liver, arrange butter or leaf lettuce or *mâche* (also called corn salad) on individual plates with liver, and pour deglazed juices (Step 1) over all. Or make the same salad using endive and radicchio, two lettuces with contrasting colors.

4. Duck or goose fat can be substituted for olive or vegetable oil when making a sauce for a salad. Endive leaves may be sautéed separately in the fat.

Chicken Liver Pâté *Pâté Foies de Volaille*

This pâté *may be made with fresh duck livers. Chicken and duck livers should be soaked in milk for 24 hours to remove the bitterness acquired sometimes by contact with the gall bladder. If any green is left after removal of gall bladder, be sure to remove it from liver before soaking in milk.*

*½ pound (2 sticks) unsalted butter,
  just at room temperature
1 pound chicken livers
¼ small onion, minced
½ clove garlic, minced*

*⅛ teaspoon basil
2 tablespoons Cognac or brandy
½ teaspoon salt, or to taste
¼ teaspoon freshly ground pepper
One-quart terrine or mold*

1. In a heavy skillet melt ¼ pound of the butter on medium high heat. Add the chicken livers, previously cleaned and dried, and sauté quickly, turning often until brown on the outside but still quite pink inside.

2. Cool in same pan, partly covered, turning livers several times to prevent darkening.

3. As soon as butter starts to congeal, put livers and cooked butter with juices in food processor fitted with steel blade. Add minced onion and garlic. Process liver for about a minute, then add remaining butter, crushed basil, Cognac, salt, and freshly ground pepper. Blend until smooth and taste to correct seasoning.

4. Spoon *pâté* into mold, smoothing top with spatula. If *pâté* is to be un-molded, line terrine with foil or parchment paper. Cover and refrigerate overnight. The consistency of this chicken liver pâté is similar to a *mousse au foie gras.*

   Serve for hors d'oeuvres, canapés, or a first-course dish with a salad of radicchio and endive in vinaigrette on the side. Also serve thin toast or tiny brioche (p. 317) sliced and toasted for an hors d'oeuvre or first course.

Serves 12. Recipe can be doubled to serve 30–40 for an hors d'oeuvre.

NOTE: Chicken Liver Pâté may be molded by hand into the shape of a clay chicken, or spooned into a buttered mold resembling a chicken. When it is unmolded from a rectangular terrine, the top can be decorated with hard boiled chopped egg white and yolk. Chopped chives may be added.

Eggs Stuffed with Chicken Livers   *Les Oeufs Farcis au Foie de Volaille*

4 hard boiled eggs
6 chicken livers (approximately)
2–3 tablespoons butter for filling,
  softened

2–3 tablespoons dry Duxelles
  (p. 274)
Salt and pepper to taste
Parsley sprigs for garnish

1. Peel cold hard boiled eggs; cut in half lengthwise. Sieve yolks or put in bowl of food processor to purée with cooked chicken livers.

2. Sauté livers on medium heat with a little butter. Remove from heat when still pink inside. Let cool a little. Put in food processor with yolks, purée, adding softened butter, and season to taste. Add dry *Duxelles*.

3. Fill whites and arrange on platter with parsley sprigs. Leftover filling can be served as a *pâté* in a bowl.

Serves 8 as an hors d'oeuvre.

VARIATION: Stuff with mousse of foie gras or canned mousse of pork and foie gras, or substitute chicken liver in this recipe for fresh duck liver which has been soaked in milk for 24 hours. Hard boiled eggs may also be stuffed with Chicken Liver Pâté (p. 104). Quail eggs, hard cooked, can substitute for large eggs.

Quenelles of Pheasant   *Quenelles de Faisan*

1 large pheasant, about 3 pounds

MARINADE:
⅛ cup Armagnac or *Cognac*
Pinch thyme
1 bay leaf

½ teaspoon green peppercorns
1 shallot, peeled
1 clove of garlic, peeled

PANADE:
½ cup milk
1½ ounces (3 tablespoons) butter

2 ounces (7 tablespoons) flour
2 egg yolks

105

REMAINING INGREDIENTS FOR QUENELLES:
2 eggs
1½ cups heavy cream
2 tablespoons fresh chopped truffles
Pinch nutmeg

Salt and pepper to taste
2 quarts chicken stock
Truffle Sauce (Sauce Périgourdine,
p. 44) or Bordelaise Sauce (p. 42)
or Cream Sauce (Sauce Suprême,
p. 53).

1. Bone and skin the pheasant. There should be about 1¼ pounds of meat. Combine ingredients of marinade and place meat in the mixture. Refrigerate overnight.

2. The next day, remove and discard garlic, shallot, and bay leaf from marinade. Using the fine blade on a meat grinder, grind the meat with the rest of the marinade ingredients. Refrigerate for 1–2 hours, as the meat will get warm when ground. It must be very cold, which is the secret of any quenelle.

3. To make the panade, combine the milk and butter in a saucepan and bring to a boil. Add the flour and stir over low heat with a wooden spoon until mixture does not stick to either the sides of the pan or the spoon. (This process is called drying the panade.) Remove from heat, let cool for 2 minutes, and beat in egg yolks one at a time. Allow to cool, and then refrigerate, covered.

4. In bowl of food processor, combine panade, ground pheasant, and eggs. Process for 1 minute and, with motor running, slowly add the cream. Process for 1 minute more; do not overmix. Transfer to a large bowl and stir in the truffles. Season to taste with nutmeg, salt, and pepper. Refrigerate for 2–3 hours.

5. Butter a large sauté pan or roasting pan. Mold quenelle mixture into ovals between the bowls of 2 tablespoons and place in pan. Add cold chicken stock to pan. Slowly, bring to simmering point, and poach quenelles for 6–7 minutes. Do not let boil. Quenelles can be kept in the chicken stock under refrigeration for several days or used immediately.

6. To serve, place desired number of quenelles in a shallow baking dish and cover with one of the three sauces chosen by the cook. Heat for 6–7 minutes in 350-degree oven.

Makes approximately 30 quenelles; serve 2 per person as an appetizer.

Introduction to Salads Served as a First Course, a Side Dish, or Main Course for Luncheon

The classification of salads has not remained as it was in the past. The conventional headings were Plain Uncooked and Cooked Salads *(Salades Simples),* Mixed Vegetable Salads *(Salades Composées)* in vinaigrette or mayonnaise, Vegetables Molded in Aspic, and Composed Salads that feature hot or cold meats, poultry, or seafood. Salad dressings *(assaisonnements),* garnishes, types of greens, and ideas on how to mix salads have expanded due to a profusion of new garden products and varieties of mustard, vinegar, and oil. Produce unseen and almost unknown before the advent of air freight now appears in markets. From New Zealand come tamarillo, a tomato that must be skinned, to use as a fruit or vegetable; pepino, a small yellowish green tree melon; passion fruit with a hard dark purple shell concealing a sweet sauce-like gooey fruit; and the translucent green fruit of the kiwi, which is sliced like a banana after being peeled, revealing similar tiny, soft black seeds. Kiwi, now grown in California, are called kiwi fans or clusters when one piece of fruit is as large as three single kiwis, similar to super-sized strawberries with stems. Mangoes and papayas are as plentiful as pineapples arriving from Hawaii. Fresh seedless grapes flown from Chile in winter and spring brighten our tables, whereas Fuyu and Hachiya persimmons are grown in the states.

Other exotic fruits which California growers have adopted are Asian pears with the crunch of apples and the juice of pears, cherimoyas (native of Peru and Ecuador with a green skin and white creamy pulp), and carambola or star fruit with a sour flavor similar to lemons originally from the East Indies. Is there any doubt left that chefs are inspired to create fanciful salads with such an array?

Even European lettuces are now grown in small quantities to add color and new flavors—the Italian rose-and-white-veined *radicchio trevisano* and a green, jagged-edged leaf lettuce, arugula or roquette; and *mâche,* also called lamb's lettuce or corn salad, originally from France. The salad lover is fortunate in that a salad made of far-flung produce often can be as enticing as any dish and at the same time contain little fat and more nutrients than most other courses. Salads do not demand of the chef as many prepared-ahead stocks, sauces, butters, and stovetop or oven cooking. Usually the more spontaneously applied and the fresher the ingredients, the better the salad. Salads do not have to fall out of favor in winter when there are warm salads composed of duck or chicken breast and mango, for instance; sliced beef or lamb salad; shellfish salads (p. 76); or spinach (p. 118).

Two varieties of duck (Muscovy and Moulard) and *foie de canard* recently produced in America have joined cooked quail or squab to make individual warm or cold first-course or luncheon salads. They may be decorated with radicchio, chicory, endive, and oak leaf lettuces, for example, with sautéed wild mushrooms such as chanterelles or morels or cultivated ones. Medium rare duck breast *(magret de canard)* becomes part of a "fantasy" salad served with locally cultivated shiitake, tree oyster or enoki mushrooms. The slender white, nail-like enoki mushrooms add a unique shape but little flavor compared to porcini, cêpes, chanterelles, and morels, dried or fresh, which are a welcome change from the ubiquitous cultivated white mushrooms. I explain how to make forcefed duck or goose liver salad with sauce on page 103.

Salads newly classified, with examples, are:

1. First Courses and the Classics: *Champignons, Courgettes,* or *Artichauts à la Grecque; Salade Niçoise,* raw spinach salad *(Epinards Crus en Salade),* potato salad *(Pommes de Terre en Salade),* raw vegetables with dip *(Crudités en Fondue), Salade Foie de Canard Frais* or *Foie Gras Chaud de Canard; Salade aux Fruits à la Japonaise, Salade Russe,* hot or cold pasta primavera, warm or cold seafood salads of steamed scallops, lobster, or crayfish; Cobb Salad, Caesar Salad, *Carpaccio all'Italiana* (marinated raw beef salad).

    When quantities are increased in first-course salads, they become a luncheon dish. In even larger quantities most salads can become buffet salads.

2. Main Courses: Pasta salads with vegetables, cheese, seafood, or meats; *Salade de Boeuf à la Parisienne,* salad of squab, chicken, turkey; salad of breast of duck (rare), pheasant or partridge; cold shrimp salad, Crab Louis.

3. Third-Course Salads Served After the Main Course or as Side Dishes: Green salad with hot or cold California goat cheese or *chèvre* from France such as Montrachet, Boucheron, or Crotin de Chavignol; mixed lettuces with herbs in vinaigrette served with or without sliced Gruyère or a variety of Brie; various slaws made of cabbage, beets, or carrots; marinated green bean, potato, or artichoke salads.

4. International Salads: Greek salad with feta cheese, hot German potato salad, Scandinavian cucumber salad, Tunisian orange salad, Lebanese Tabbouleh or Bulgur wheat salad, Chinese chicken salad, American raw mushroom salad, Sicilian caponata, French celeriac rémoulade, Early

American wilted lettuce salad, Andalusian or gazpacho salad, Mexican guacamole salad, Italian-style fresh pasta salad with red and green peppers and anchovies.

5. Dessert Salads: Fresh fruits marinated in liqueurs served with ice cream or sorbets.

Americans' predilection for fresh lettuces arranged with assorted food-stuffs has raised the position of salads to their highest level of all time. As early as 1926 when *A Book of Salads,* also titled *The Edgewater Beach Hotel Salad Book,* by Arnold Shircliffe was published with more than eight hundred salad and dressing recipes, salads were recognized to have been improved in the American kitchen. Mr. Shircliffe writes in his foreword:

> America has never been given credit for any advancement in the culinary field. So right here and now, for the edification of all, we claim for America the credit of assembling, blending, and bringing to perfection this health-giving item, the salad.

He also gave women credit for the evolution of salads due to their demands that salads be served at club luncheons, which was long before men adopted salads to their diet. However, the first sentence of my quote would no longer be valid today, for America has come of age in every component of the culinary world. The colored illustrations in *A Book of Salads* seem out-moded in their meticulous arrangement of ingredients to create a rigid form: Panama salad has a pineapple slice for a base with orange and grapefruit segments fitted precisely together in a melon shape; Fan Salad has "alligator" pear, grapefruit, and orange segments, and red and green pepper strips arranged in a procession on endive with cream cheese piped around the edges; and Poinsettia Salad is a tomato slit five times from top to stem end to make petals which are folded back to place an asparagus spear in the center of each petal. A little rosette of whipped cream or cream cheese is piped at each opening between the petals with chopped green peppers and egg yolk sprinkled on the center. Contemporary salads are more free form, reflecting the styles of modern art. Also the salad has to blend with the wine for a dinner party, as discussed in Chapter 13 on "Choosing Wines for Menus" (p. 375).

Another custom followed early in this century was to name salads after opera stars—Galli-Curci, Mary Garden, Jenny Lind; operas—*Tosca, Aïda, Mikado, Figaro, Parsifal;* or well-known personalities—William Penn, Charles Lamb, Queen Victoria. Contemporary salads are less likely to be named for celebrities.

The custom in restaurants is for the chef to start the cold salad in the kitchen with the maitre d' assembling and finishing the tossed salad in the dining room. Warm salads, of which there are a growing number, are prepared by the chef in the kitchen.

Let us leave the lettuce and review the two ingredients that are the mainstay of the vinaigrette, oil and vinegar. The finest olive oil is "extra virgin." This means not only that it is produced from the best ripe fruit, produced cold without heat, pressed using physical not chemical means, but also that it must have less than 1.5% acidity. Fine virgin olive oil must have less than 3% acidity, and virgin not more than 4%. Olive oil is imported from France, Italy, Spain, and Greece, and it is also made in the U.S.A. Vegetable or nut oils can be used for dressings or mixed with olive oil to adjust the flavor —walnut, hazelnut, almond, and sesame seed oil provide a strong nutty flavor which requires a temperate use. Vegetable oils are made from soybeans, corn, safflower seeds, cottonseeds, or sunflower seeds. Peanut oil should be included with the less expensive and milder tasting oils.

The word vinegar comes from the French *vin aigre,* meaning sour wine. Its strength comes from the amount of acetic acid it contains. The finest vinegars to use for salad come from white, red, and rice wine, and sherry and Champagne. Distilled vinegar made from cereal grains and cider vinegar made from apple juice are used for pickling and other cooking processes. The most prestigious food store in Paris carries no less than eighteen separate flavors of bottled vinegars. The flavors are garlic, cider vinegar with honey, lemon vinegar, shallot, herbs of Provence, mint, muscat, blueberry, raspberry, green peppercorn, peach, four red fruits (in one vinegar to season mushroom salad and Swiss potato salad), thyme, tarragon, Xeres, ending with strawberry, cherry, black currant, and red currant (to perfume fruits and green salads, used in moderation). Not to be omitted are flowers, the rose and violet to name two, and citrus fruit used to make vinegar. Vinegar can be made using any kind of berries or cherries in the following way—use one basket red raspberries to one quart plain white or red wine vinegar, heat to boiling point, and pour over fruit. Put in a glass container and keep in a dark place for one month. Herbs, such as tarragon, plus spices, garlic, and shallots can be macerated in wine vinegar, but do *not* heat.

An old Spanish proverb still bears repeating, for it uncovers the hidden drama that exists in the preparation of simple or composed salads: "Four persons make a salad—a spendthrift for the oil, a miser for the vinegar, a counselor for the salt, and a madman to stir them up." Let this old saying be a warning to the salad maker that a precarious balance exists in mixing the basic ingredients for the dressing.

Dressings
Assaisonnements

Vinaigrette with Variations   *Sauce Vinaigrette de Différentes Façons*

*Suggested proportions for ingredients of **Basic Vinaigrette**:*

*2 tablespoons white or red wine
   vinegar or fresh lemon juice
6 tablespoons olive oil (top quality
   or virgin grade)
Salt and freshly ground pepper to
   taste*

*1 teaspoon prepared French style
   mustard (optional) added to 1 cup
   vinaigrette makes a stronger
   dressing without adding more
   vinegar. One-half teaspoon dried
   mustard can replace prepared type.*

VINAIGRETTE VARIATIONS—proportions based on ½ cup (approximately) basic vinaigrette. Individual taste can vary proportions:

1. **With mustard:** One teaspoon prepared mustard or ½ teaspoon dry mustard.

2. **With garlic:** Salad bowl can be rubbed with garlic clove, or clove can be placed in salad dressing jar. The French method is to rub several cubes of dried bread with the cut end of fresh garlic, toss with the salad, and remove before serving. The bread cubes are called *chapons*.

3. **With Roquefort:** Two tablespoons crumbled Roquefort or blue cheese.

4. **With anchovy:** Two fillets of boned, finely chopped, or sieved anchovies. Omit salt in basic vinaigrette.

5. **With egg yolk:** Two hard boiled egg yolks rubbed through a sieve.

6. **With tarragon:** Two teaspoons fresh chopped tarragon or use tarragon vinegar in basic vinaigrette.

7. **With herbs:** One teaspoon (approximate amount) finely chopped fresh parsley, chives, chervil, and tarragon. Instead of mixing herbs in dressing, they can be sprinkled into the mixed greens. The salad is then called *Salade aux Fines Herbes.*

8. **With watercress:** Two tablespoons finely chopped egg yolks and 2 tablespoons finely chopped watercress leaves, also called *Sauce Cressonière.*

9. **With wine:** Substitute dry red or white wine or Champagne for half of the vinegar.

10. **With curry:** Add ½ teaspoon curry powder and 2 teaspoons minced shallots. Use with stronger flavored greens.

111

11. **With cream:** Substitute cream (fresh heavy cream or commercial sour cream) for the olive oil and use about 1 tablespoon vinegar according to individual taste.

Mayonnaise:

Mayonnaise (p. 62) is used particularly for *salades composées* or combination salads. Since mayonnaise is very rich, it should be used with discretion and can be thinned with cream or water. It can be flavored to taste with prepared mustard; a pinch of cayenne; chopped chives; mixed green herbs such as chopped parsley, tarragon, chervil; watercress; spinach; Worcestershire sauce; vinaigrette; lemon juice; tomato purée.

MAYONNAISE VARIATIONS—made with 1 cup:
1. **With anchovy:** One or 2 boned, mashed anchovies or anchovy fillets.
2. **With curry powder:** One teaspoon curry powder and 2 teaspoons chopped chives.
3. **With tarragon:** One-quarter cup chopped tarragon.
4. **With herbs:** One teaspoon each chopped parsley, chives, chervil, tarragon, oregano, or marjoram.
5. **With Roquefort:** One cup mashed Roquefort, 1 cup sour cream, and 4 drops Tabasco sauce.
6. **With watercress:** One quarter cup chopped watercress (see *Sauce Verte,* p. 63, and *Sauce Cresson,* p. 63).

COLD SAUCES—made with 1 cup Mayonnaise:
1. **Niçoise Sauce *(Sauce Niçoise):*** Two tablespoons tomato purée, 2 tablespoons chopped pimentoes, a few leaves fresh tarragon.
2. **Collioure Sauce *(Sauce Collioure):*** One teaspoon anchovy paste, ¼ teaspoon chopped parsley, pinch finely minced garlic.
3. **Tartare Sauce *(Sauce Tartare):*** One tablespoon chopped capers, 1 tablespoon chopped cornichons, and 1 teaspoon chopped chives. Serve with fish. I consider this sauce about the same as *Sauce Rémoulade.*
4. **Rémoulade Sauce *(Sauce Rémoulade):*** One teaspoon Dijon mustard, 2 teaspoons chopped gherkins, 2 teaspoons capers, 2 teaspoons chopped parsley, ½ teaspoon each chervil and tarragon steeped in boiling water and drained, and ½ teaspoon anchovy paste. Use for cold meat, poultry, and fish salads as well as hors d'oeuvres, first courses, and main courses.

5. **La Varenne Sauce** *(Sauce La Varenne):* One-third cup *duxelles* cooked in oil, and ½ teaspoon each parsley and chervil blanched in boiling water and drained. Use for hors d'oeuvres, eggs, fish, and salads.

6. **Russian Sauce** *(Sauce Russe):* Cooked coral and tomalley of 1 lobster mixed with 1 tablespoon caviar, rubbed through a fine sieve to make a purée; 1 teaspoon prepared mustard; 1 teaspoon finely chopped chives or parsley is optional. One tablespoon Vodka may be added. Use for cold shellfish and salad.

7. **Mousquetaire Sauce** *(Sauce Mousquetaire)*—ingredients for *2* cups Mayonnaise: Cook 2 tablespoons finely chopped shallots in ½ cup dry white wine until the liquid is almost all reduced; add 1 tablespoon meat glaze, stir to dissolve, and let cool. Slowly beat this mixture into 2 cups Mayonnaise. Season with a few grains cayenne pepper. Use for cold meats and vegetables.

GARNISHES

1. Many foods used for *garniture* are also ingredients in salads. Some of the best known ones are: hard boiled eggs (halved, quartered, or chopped), cornichons or gherkins, truffles, cooked beets (cut into rounds or julienned), radishes, black or green olives, anchovies, shrimp, watercress, peeled tomatoes (cut in thin slices or quartered), capers, celery, scallions, nuts.

2. *Herbs* are also considered a garnish. Fresh herbs should be washed, dried, their leaves stripped of stems, chopped fine (as an ingredient in salad and salad dressing) or left whole. Some of the most popular herbs are moss-curled and fern-leaved parsley *(persil);* sweet marjoram and pot or wild marjoram *(marjolaine);* chervil *(chervil frisé);* chives *(ciboulette);* dill; small young leaves of sorrel; tarragon *(estragon);* sweet and bush basil *(basilic)*—dwarf *(piccolo),* green small-leaved, lettuce-leaved, curled leaf, large purple sweet, or compact; common thyme *(thymus vulgaris),* golden lemon and silver thyme; rosemary *(romarin)* used sparingly; sweet fennel *(fenouil)* and Florence fennel *(Finnocchio);* summer and winter savory *(sarriette);* spearmint *(menthe);* black and white mustard seed and powder *(moutarde);* coriander or cilantro, leaf and seed; blue-flowered borage *(bourrache);* angelica *(angélique);* sage *(sauge):* common garden variety *Salvia officinalis.*

3. *Spices* used in salad are ground: cayenne (use sparingly), cloves, curry powder, ginger, nutmeg, paprika, white and black pepper.

SALAD GREENS

Characteristics and flavors of fresh lettuce and greens: *Bibb or limestone* (very delicate in flavor and texture—use little vinegar in dressing), a miniature head considered the finest of all lettuce; *Boston or butterhead,* larger than bibb, mild and tender; *Chicory or curly endive,* spreads out, has stronger flavor than more delicate-textured, bland Boston lettuce; *Escarole,* broad curly leaves which fan out, texture is tougher to the bite; *Iceberg,* round, light green head, most popular, less nutritional value, outside leaves form cups for holding salad ingredients; *Romaine* or *Cos,* long, deep green leaves used for garnish and prized for its piquant flavor; *Leaf* lettuce or *Loosehead,* light green to red, a curly-edged or oak leaf shape, a variety called Australian is fairly common; *Spinach; Sorrel* or sour grass, small, younger leaves can be used in salad (however, as it contains oxalic acid, it should be used in moderation); *Watercress,* remove thicker stems, leaves have slightly bitter flavor (store bunch with stems in water in refrigerator covered loosely with plastic bag); *Endive (Belgian),* bleached white by wrapping leaves and growing in dark place: long, narrow head of tightly pointed waxy leaves almost devoid of mineral salts, chlorophyll, and vitamins; *Field lettuce* or *Lamb's Tongue,* small spears on delicate stems, scarce; *Cabbage,* pale green or purple-red leaves, shredded finely; *Chinese Cabbage; Dandelion Greens,* tender young stalks; *Scallions;* green tops of *Shallots; Fennel,* feathery leaves on stalks of fennel bulb. *Radicchio, arugula,* and *mâche* are described in Introduction to Salads (p.107).

HOW TO ASSEMBLE A GREEN SALAD

1. Lettuce should be washed quickly in cold water using a *panier à salade* (wire basket) to hold the leaves. Drain lettuce and dry between two towels, being careful not to bruise the leaves. I recommend a high quality plastic spin-dryer using centrifugal force.

2. Do not *cut* lettuce leaves; they should be torn into large bite-size pieces. If the salad bowl—wood, plastic, or glass—is chilled, it will retain the coldness of the ingredients.

3. Different varieties of lettuce mixed in the same salad add color and subtle flavors along with chopped, fresh herbs *(fines herbes),* which should be added last.

4. High quality olive oil, extra virgin olive oil, and good wine vinegar make the best dressing. Fresh lemon juice can be substituted for the vinegar or for half the amount. Since lemon juice is nature's most delicate and perfumed acid, it does not interfere with wine when salad is served at a

special wine dinner. Olive oil gives a fruity smoothness to the salad, while lemon juice or wine vinegar add the needed tang or zip. Sherry wine vinegar and Balsamic vinegar are special wine vinegars (p. 110).

5. When applying dressing it is useful to know that *water repels oil,* and *oil repels vinegar.* For a sharper flavor, pour vinegar on first, oil last. For a more delicate flavor, pour oils on first because it coats the leaves, allowing other seasonings to cling also. For exact measurements, it is best to mix the dressing in a jar or the empty salad bowl. Do not pour or mix dressing with salad greens until ready to serve. If the dressing is put on ahead of time, it will cause the lettuce to become soggy, as the vinegar will eat into the connective tissues, and the salt will absorb the water content of the leaves.

Crayfish Salad with Chicory and Raddichio

Salade d'Ecrivisses aux Chicorée et Salade de Trevise

1 pound live crayfish in shells, uncooked (12–16 crayfish to a pound), or blue shrimp from Hawaii

Court Bouillon (p. 174)
1 head chicory lettuce
1 head radicchio (salade de trevise)

VINAIGRETTE:
1 teaspoon Pommery Mustard
1 tablespoon Xeres vinegar
Pinch salt
Freshly ground pepper to taste

3 tablespoons hazelnut oil
2 tablespoons fresh whipped cream
1 teaspoon lemon juice

1. Cook live crayfish in a large pot of Court Bouillon, covered, for 2 minutes. Remove meat from tail. Serve lukewarm or at room temperature.

2. Wash chicory, removing green part of leaves. Use only the white part. Dry lettuce in lettuce spinner. Wash radicchio, dry, and arrange like petals of a flower on edge of each salad plate. Prepare vinaigrette dressing.

3. Toss chicory with vinaigrette. Mix in crayfish tails and arrange in center of salad plate. More dressing may be made and added to lettuce, if desired.

Serves 4 as a first course for dinner or main course luncheon dish.

Warm Scallop Salad Carlo

Salade Tiède de Calico Carlo

On March 30, 1984, a friend who is a chef made this salad in my kitchen on the same day his wife gave birth to a boy they named Carlo. From this union of a Cuban mother and an Italian father was born an American boy.

LETTUCE WITH DRESSING:

1 small head chicory lettuce (chicorée salade) or 1 head radicchio, lamb lettuce (mâche), and endive	*1 tablespoon olive oil*
	Juice of 1 lemon
	Salt and freshly ground pepper to taste
1 small tomato	

SAUTÉED SCALLOPS AND SAUCE:

1 tablespoon olive oil	*1 tablespoon Xeres vinegar (sherry vinegar)*
1 pound calico scallops	
1 clove garlic, chopped	*1 tablespoon Brown Sauce (p. 39)*
1 tablespoon chopped parsley	*Salt and pepper to taste*

1. Wash and spin dry lettuce. Peel, seed, and dice fresh tomato. In a salad bowl place lettuce and tomato. Toss with olive oil and lemon juice. Season with salt and pepper and place in center of individual salad plates warmed to room temperature.

2. In a skillet on low heat pour 1 tablespoon olive oil; sauté scallops for 1 minute without raising heat. Add chopped garlic and parsley, sauté a few seconds, deglaze pan with vinegar, and finish with the Brown Sauce, bringing almost to a boil. Remove scallops, place around salad, bring sauce to a quick boil, add salt and freshly ground pepper to taste, and pour over scallops.

Serves 4.

Artichokes Narcisse

Artichauts Narcisse

1 pound Maine shrimp or Pacific baby shrimp, cooked	*8 artichoke bottoms, fresh (preferably) or canned—2–2¼ inches wide when trimmed (3 inches diameter, 3½ inches high when raw)*
1 tablespoon catsup	
1 tablespoon Vodka	
2–3 drops Worcestershire sauce	
2–3 drops Tabasco sauce	*6–8 radishes, pink or red, sliced*
½ cup Sauce Mayonnaise (p. 62)	*1 hard boiled egg yolk, chopped*
Salt and pepper to taste	*2 tomatoes, sliced*
Shredded lettuce	*½ cup Vinaigrette dressing (p. 111)*

116

1. Marinate shrimp with the catsup, Vodka, Worcestershire sauce, and Tabasco for 30 minutes. Add mayonnaise, salt, and pepper to taste.

2. On salad plates arrange a bed of shredded lettuce. Place an artichoke bottom in the center; fill with a heaping mound of shrimp. Arrange sliced radishes around shrimp between artichoke top and filling to resemble the leaves of an artichoke. Sprinkle center with chopped egg yolk.

3. Place thinly sliced tomatoes around edge of plate near lettuce. Pour about 1 tablespoon of Vinaigrette over top of decorated artichoke bottom. Serve immediately.

Serves 8 as an appetizer. If a larger artichoke is used, it makes an attractive luncheon dish. Recipe can be halved.

Lettuce Salad with Fresh Herbs and Sautéed Chicken

Thanks to Chef Michel LeBorgne of the New England Culinary Institute for the general idea of this recipe.

1 head red leaf lettuce　　　　　　　*¼ cup finely chopped shallots*
2 heads butter lettuce　　　　　　　*Salt and pepper to taste*
⅓ cup olive oil　　　　　　　　　　*⅓ cup red or white wine vinegar*
2 whole chicken breasts, skinned,
　boned, and cut in ¾-inch cubes*

DRESSING:
1 teaspoon finely chopped garlic　　*4 tablespoons wine vinegar*
1 tablespoon Dijon mustard　　　　*½ cup olive oil*
Salt and pepper to taste

FRESH HERBS:
1 teaspoon coarsely chopped　　　　*½ cup finely snipped chives*
　tarragon leaves or ¼ teaspoon　　*½ cup coarsely chopped basil leaves*
　dried
⅓ cup finely chopped parsley　　　　*1½ cups julienned mushrooms*

1. Wash lettuce and dry in a salad spinner. Break leaves in half and refrigerate in a plastic bag. Make dressing in a jar or in the salad bowl.

2. In a large skillet or wok heat 3½ tablespoons oil until very hot; add chicken cubes, chopped shallots, and stir-fry until chicken starts to brown. Season with salt and pepper to taste; pour in vinegar on high heat and stir until

---

* Duck can be substituted for chicken; if so, leave on the skin and cook until it is crispy.　　　**117**

vinegar is almost evaporated. Remove pan from heat. Put lettuce in salad bowl, toss with dressing, sprinkle herbs on lettuce, and add chicken with shallots.

3. Quickly sauté julienned mushrooms in same pan with remaining oil for about 1 minute. Add to salad bowl and lightly toss. Serve at once.

Serves 6 as an appetizer and 4 as a main-course luncheon dish.

Spinach Salad   *Salade aux Epinards*

2 bunches fresh spinach
6–8 tablespoons olive oil
2–4 tablespoons lemon juice
1 clove garlic, minced

Grated rind of 1 lemon
Salt and freshly ground pepper to taste
Croutons sautéed in garlic butter (optional)

1. Wash spinach, removing stalks and central vein. Drain and pat dry with towels. Tear large leaves into edible-size pieces.
2. In a saucepan large enough to hold the spinach, heat olive oil and lemon juice on medium heat. Add the minced garlic and grated lemon rind.
3. Toss spinach leaves in the saucepan, coating all the leaves. Season with salt and pepper and correct liquid ingredients, if necessary.
4. Warm a large glass salad bowl or platter. Place spinach salad in center and garnish with croutons.

Serves 4–6.

VARIATION: Spinach Salad with Bacon *(lardon)*—sauté bacon strips, remove from pan, and drain on paper towel; pour off some of the fat, add some olive oil, and wilt spinach in sauté pan. Serve salad with seasonings in bowl or on plates with bacon pieces.

Alice Salad   *Salade Alice*

4 Golden Delicious apples
Half a lemon to prevent apples from discoloring
½ cup diced celery

½ cup diced banana
¾ cup sour cream
Salt and pepper to taste

1. Slice ½ inch from top of each apple, rub with cut lemon half, and reserve. Scoop out insides of apples, leaving a shell of ⅛-inch thickness. (Use a curved serrated grapefruit knife first, then a small spoon.) Rub inside of apples with lemon. Dice scooped out apple meat.

2. Mix diced apple, celery, and banana with sour cream, adding salt and pepper to taste. Fill apples with this mixture and put the tops in place.

Serves 4 as an appetizer or first course at a luncheon.

Eve Salad   *Salade Eve*

Both this salad and Salade Alice *make attractive first courses at a luncheon.*

4 Golden or Red Delicious apples
1 diced banana
½ cup diced pineapple
3 tablespoons walnut halves
¾ cup heavy cream

½ cup lemon juice or mild white wine vinegar
Salt and pepper to taste
8 small Belgian endive leaves or watercress sprigs

1. Prepare in the same way as *Salade Alice,* tossing the fruit in a dressing made of 3 parts heavy cream to 1 part lemon juice or vinegar.

2. Tops of apples may be decorated with 2 small Belgian endive leaves (make a small hole in top of apple) or decorate with a sprig of watercress.

Serves 4.

Fresh Fruit Salad with Grapes   *Salade Véronique*

1 cup Lime and Oil Dressing for fruit salad (see below)
1 bunch romaine lettuce
½ head chicory lettuce
2–3 large navel oranges

1 ripe avocado pear, chilled, or 1 large red apple
Lemon juice
1–2 bunches (2 cups) fresh seedless green or red grapes or both

1. Mix salad dressing. Fresh lemon juice can substitute for the fresh lime juice.

2. Wash and dry lettuces. Peel oranges, removing most of the white pith. Slice in ¼-inch thick slices.

3. Peel and slice chilled avocado pear. Sprinkle with lemon juice. Or, if apple is used, do not peel. Cut into wedges and sprinkle with lemon juice.

119

4. Line four chilled salad plates with romaine leaves. Alternate slices of orange and avocado, or arrange orange slices on top of lettuce and place apple wedges on either side of oranges. Place ½ cup grapes on top. Decorate with pieces of chicory. Pour ¼ cup salad dressing on each salad.

Serves 4 for a luncheon dish.

LIME AND OIL DRESSING FOR SALAD WITH FRUIT:
- *⅓ cup fresh lime juice (fresh lemon juice can be substituted)*
- *½ cup olive oil or salad oil*
- *¼ teaspoon salt*
- *2 tablespoons honey*
- *Freshly ground pepper to taste*

SOUR CREAM DRESSING FOR OTHER FRUIT SALADS:
- *1 tablespoon honey*
- *2 tablespoons lemon juice*
- *1 teaspoon grated orange rind*
- *¼ teaspoon salt*
- *1 cup dairy sour cream or unflavored yogurt*

Tomatoes Stuffed with Guacamole   *Tomates Farcies au Guacamole*

- *4 large tomatoes*
- *2 tablespoons finely chopped onion*
- *1 small clove garlic, finely chopped or minced*
- *½ tomato, peeled, seeded, and chopped (optional)*
- *1 canned or fresh Serrano chili pepper (light green color) or 1 canned Jalapeño pepper, rinsed and chopped*

- *2 ripe avocados, chilled*
- *½ teaspoon salt, or to taste*
- *1½–2 tablespoons fresh lemon or lime juice, or to taste*
- *2 sprigs cilantro (Chinese parsley), chopped (optional)*
- *Lettuce leaves for garnish*

1. Cut tops of tomatoes, reserving tops, and scoop out seeds and tomato pulp. Tomato pulp and strained juice can be added in a small amount to mashed avocado. In that case the ½ tomato listed in the ingredients should not be used. Turn tomatoes upside down to drain. Chill in refrigerator.

2. To make guacamole in food processor: Put onion, garlic, and chili pepper in bowl using steel blade and run just long enough to mince. Peel chilled avocados,* put fruit in bowl of food processor and run just long enough to mash. Avocado should not be made into a purée. Remove mixture from bowl, add about ¼ cup chopped tomato, season to taste with salt, lemon or lime juice, and stir in chopped cilantro, if desired. Chill guacamole until ready to fill chilled tomatoes.

* Instead of peeling avocado, it can be cut in half, seed removed, and pulp scooped out with a teaspoon.

3. Fill tomatoes just before serving and place lids on to cover half of filling. Serve on lettuce leaves.

Serves 4 as a first course or salad course dish. To use for hors d'oeuvres, substitute tiny tomatoes or Italian-style tomatoes.

Artichoke Stuffed with Crab Meat Salad

Salade Artichaut Farci au Crabe

4 large artichokes
1½ cups crab meat or shrimp, freshly cooked and chilled
½ cup finely chopped celery
2 tablespoons chopped chives
½ cup mayonnaise
Salt, pepper, and nutmeg, used sparingly

Romaine or iceberg lettuce leaves or both
8 tomato wedges, 4 lemon wedges, and watercress or parsley sprigs for garnish

1. Prepare and cook large artichokes (p. 256). Drain and remove chokes. Chill.

2. Mix prepared crab meat with celery, chives, mayonnaise, salt, pepper, and nutmeg to taste.

3. Fill artichokes with mixture; arrange on bed of lettuce on individual plates decorated with tomato wedges, lemon wedges or slices, and sprigs of watercress or parsley.

Serves 4 as an appetizer or luncheon dish.

NOTE: As an hors d'oeuvre, use tiny artichoke bottoms filled with crab or shrimp mixture.

Avocado Stuffed with Crab Meat and Lobster

Salade d'Avocat Farcie aux Crabe et d'Homard

4 ripe avocados, chilled
Lemon juice
2 cups crab meat, preferably fresh
    (approximate amount)
1 cup diced lobster meat
1 medium tomato, peeled, seeded,
    and chopped
1 teaspoon chopped chives
1 teaspoon chopped fresh tarragon or
    ½ teaspoon dried

2 tablespoons chili sauce
½ cup mayonnaise
Salt and pepper to taste
2 tablespoons chopped parsley
Thin tomato slices and ripe olive
    slices for garnish
Lemon wedges
Lettuce leaves

1. Cut cold, ripe avocados in half, remove seeds, and sprinkle with a little lemon juice.

2. Mix crab and lobster meat with remaining ingredients. Fill avocados with seafood salad. Place on individual plates lined with a bed of lettuce. Decorate top of salad with thin slice of tomato topped with slice of black olive; arrange lemon wedges dipped in chopped parsley on plate.

Serves 4 as first course on dinner menu or as main course for luncheon menu.

NOTE: Other cold, cooked fish can substitute for either crab or lobster, such as shrimp, prawns, salmon, or tuna. *Sauce Rémoulade* (p. 112) or *Sauce La Varenne* (p. 113) can be used instead of the ingredients listed above.

Belgian Endive Salad with Apples and Walnuts

Salade d'Endives aux Pommes et Noix

1 cup mayonnaise (p. 62)
6 Belgian endive
3 red apples, preferably Red Delicious
    or Gravenstein

¾ cup coarsely chopped walnuts

1. Make mayonnaise using ¼ cup walnut oil and ¾ cup olive or vegetable oil.

2. Remove cone from bottom end of endive and remove any damaged outside leaves. Cut several endive into ½-inch rounds and the rest of the endive heads into lengthwise strips.

3. Do not peel apples so that the color will contrast with the white endive. Cut apples into cubes just before serving.

4. Put cut endive, cubed apples, and chopped walnuts in a salad bowl. Mix together and toss with mayonnaise just before serving.

Serves 6 as a side dish or appetizer.

Belgian Endive and Mushroom Salad

Salade d'Endives et de Champignons

8 Belgian endive
10 mushrooms, fresh white or *enoki, optional amount*
Lemon juice

1–2 bunches watercress
Sauce Vinaigrette (p. 111) or *a variation*

1. Slice endive in half lengthwise, clean mushrooms, and slice both thinly; sprinkle with lemon juice. Wash watercress, drain, and remove thick stems.

2. Arrange on individual salad plates, pour dressing over; or cut endive in smaller pieces, toss all ingredients together in a salad bowl, and mix in dressing. Serve at once.

Serves 4–6 as a side dish.

Cold Duck Salad

Salade de Canard Froid

A Chinese barbecued duck from a Chinese vendor may be used for this salad.

4–5 pound roast duck with crisp skin (p. 242)
2 bunches fresh asparagus or *green beans* (haricots verts)
1 cup Vinaigrette dressing (p. 111) using raspberry vinegar or sherry wine vinegar ("Jerez" from Spain) and hazelnut oil, if available

1 1/2 pounds fresh mushrooms
Lemon juice
1/2–1 pound fresh cooked foie gras (foie gras frais) or *foie gras in a tin*

1. Have ready a roast or barbecued duck. A crisp skin comes from basting with soy sauce and honey. Cut meat into large chunks, and detach skin so that duck will show on salad plate. Bring meat to room temperature.

2. Steam asparagus by tying in bunches and standing upright in vegetable

123

steamer, or steam green beans. Stop cooking as soon as tips are tender and asparagus is still green. Drain and marinate in Vinaigrette dressing.

3. Clean fresh mushrooms, but do not soak in water, which removes flavor. Rinse and pat dry. Remove stems and cut into ¼-inch slices. Sprinkle with lemon juice. Marinate in Vinaigrette.

4. Assemble salad just before it is time to serve: Place slice of chilled foie gras in center of plate. Arrange a circle of mushrooms around the foie gras. Place slices of duck meat, about four to a plate, next to the sliced mushrooms. Place duck skin at an angle on meat.

5. Place asparagus spears or green beans around edge of plate and over top of mushrooms on plate.

Serves 4–6 as a first-course or main-course luncheon dish.

Beef Salad   *Salade de Boeuf à la Parisienne*

Serve as a luncheon dish in the patio or as a summer salad for a picnic.

Romaine or butter lettuce leaves	*SALAD DRESSING:*
1 pound leftover boiled beef, thinly sliced, about 1½–2 inches long	*1 teaspoon French mustard*
4 large potatoes, boiled and thinly sliced	*1 teaspoon chopped capers*
1 tomato, cut in quarters	*2 teaspoons finely minced shallots*
2 pickles or pickled gherkins, sliced	*1 teaspoon finely chopped parsley*
1 hard boiled egg, quartered	*¼ teaspoon salt*
1 bouquet watercress for decoration	*Freshly ground pepper to taste*
	½ teaspoon chopped tarragon
	2 tablespoons wine vinegar (tarragon vinegar optional)
	6 tablespoons olive oil

Prepare salad dressing. Place lettuce leaves on a platter. Arrange alternate layers of thinly sliced beef and potatoes and cover with salad dressing. Garnish platter with tomato, pickles, and egg quarters interspersed with watercress. Beef and potatoes can marinate in dressing for several hours, if desired, before arranging on platter or individual plates.

Serves 4.

NOTE: Leftover cooked brisket, short ribs of beef, or beef shank can be substituted.

124

Chapter Five

EGGS

Les Oeufs Are Evaluated, Stuffed, and
Turned into Filled Omelets

For my class I will prepare eggs in different styles, which are all quickly done. As to the inimitable omelet, I do not recommend adding water to the beaten eggs, which, however, would increase their volume. Adding cream increases the fat content. The eggs should be at room temperature, and they should be slightly beaten with a thin wire whisk, which gives better texture to the omelet. Although most fillings for omelets are simple, they should be prepared before starting to cook the eggs. For example, the mushrooms should be sautéed in advance for a mushroom omelet, reserving a few cooked, sliced mushrooms to decorate the top *(Omelette aux Champignons,* p. 134). The true French *omelette* is creamy in the center, described as *baveuse* by the French. To serve it correctly, remember the saying, "You can wait for an omelet, but the omelet will not wait for you." It will become tough as it gets cold.

There are three classifications: *omelette garnie*—vegetables used as a garnish; *omelette fourrée*—a filled omelet, of which there are more than five hundred varieties; *omelette sucrée*—a sweet omelet, made with jam, sugar, or fruits. Omelettes are unrivaled as a last minute dish for breakfast or lunch, for the ingredients are usually on hand. Not only is very little advanced preparation required, but also a thrifty cook will delight in such an attractive way to use leftovers.

It has been established that there are about eight basic ways to prepare eggs, resulting in hundreds of different dishes.

The Eight Basic Ways to Cook Eggs:

1. Soft boiled *(oeufs à la coque* and *oeufs mollets)*
   Hard boiled *(oeufs durs)*
   Stuffed *(oeufs farcis)*
2. Poached *(oeufs pochés)*
   Hot dish or cold covered with aspic *(oeufs pochés en gelée)*
3. Scrambled *(oeufs brouillés)*
4. Plain fried *(oeufs sautés ou poêlés)*
5. Deep fried *(oeufs frits)*

6. In casserole *(oeufs en cocotte):* a cocotte set in shallow pan of hot water, covered, until white sets
In a mold *(oeufs moulés)*

7. Shirred *(oeufs sur le plat, oeufs au miroir):* baked or broiled in shallow ramekin

8. Omelets *(omelettes)*

Countless variations have developed from the above methods. The following facts have been gathered to answer questions about the freshness, storage, and characteristics of eggs:

Eggs keep best at a temperature below 40 degrees F., where they will keep for about two months. Store round end up, as the egg cartons in which they are packed keep the yolk suspended properly in the white. Spoilage is retarded if the less perishable white protects the yolk. The paper carton also prevents eggs from absorbing refrigerator odors, as the porous shells of eggs absorb odors easily. To test for freshness, place an egg in a horizontal position in a bowl of cold water—if it stays there, it is fresh; but if it turns on end—vertically—it is stale. It is easier to separate eggs when they are cold, for the yolks break easily when warm. They can warm up after they are separated, for it is best to cook with eggs at 70–75 degrees F.

Ways to use eggs in soups and sauces: If eggs are added to hot mixtures such as a soup, a small amount of the hot soup must be added to the yolks first to warm them and prevent curdling before they are mixed into the pot of soup. Eggs should not be heated above 170 degrees or they will scramble. In Step 3 of "How to Glaze Fish with White Wine Sauce" (p. 54) I warn against heating fish in the oven that are covered with a sauce containing hollandaise. Warm egg sauces like hollandaise or sabayon are raw, since they are only heated to 125–130 degrees F., which prevents curdling. Mayonnaise and some butter creams also contain raw egg yolks, which demands that they be kept under refrigeration—eggs become spoiled by bacteria if allowed to become too warm.

Although this statement is repetitious, it is not out of place to explain that hollandaise sauce can only be made in a stainless steel or porcelain-coated pot, or a glass or china bowl because the egg yolks contain sulfur and the lemon juice acid.

Egg yolks behave like whole eggs when beaten with sugar—they turn very light in color and "make the ribbon" *(faire un ruban).*

Egg whites are able to increase their volume seven times when beaten in a clean bowl. A pinch of salt or cream of tartar acts as a stabilizer. Step 5 of Sweetened Whipped Cream (p. 79) tells how to beat egg whites in a copper bowl.

Two Unusual Ways to Cook Eggs:

Broiled egg: Fry egg and trim white edges. Wrap in a piece of prosciutto, secure with toothpick, put on grill or hibachi, and broil for a few seconds until prosciutto is hot.

Eggs en brochette: With a skewer puncture a hole in each end of raw egg, blow on one end to make raw egg come out the other end into a bowl. Season egg with salt, pepper, snipped chives, or finely diced shrimp and scramble lightly. Put scrambled egg in a pastry bag using a small tube and fill hollow egg shell. Push skewer through filled egg shell. One skewer can hold three to four eggs. Put on grill, turning often, for a minute or two.

These recipes would be amusing for a picnic or outdoor brunch.

The Six Ways Raw Eggs Function in Cooking:

1. Thickening agent (yolks only) for soups, sauces, and custards. Binding for ground meat, fish, sauces, doughs.
2. Leavening agent or raising agent for cakes, cookies, meringues, soufflés, omelets, quick breads, pastries *(pâte à choux)*. Whites are beaten separately to lighten soufflés, cheesecakes, pies, mousses, omelets. Egg whites are added separately to lighten quenelles and mousselines.
3. Coating agent for croquettes, fritters, fish sticks, cutlets.
4. Glazing agent for pastries and bread as well as adding golden color to foods and dishes.
5. Emulsifying agent in oil-based sauces such as mayonnaise and butter-based sauces such as hollandaise and béarnaise sauce.
6. The whites are used to clarify soup stocks. Wine makers also use egg whites to clarify red wine.

Eight Ways to Prepare Eggs
Huit Façons de Préparé les Oeufs

Eggs should always be at room temperature in order to judge the cooking time correctly. Remove from refrigerator several hours before using.

Hard Boiled Eggs/*Oeufs Durs*

1. Use an enamel or stainless steel pot the correct size for the number of eggs to be boiled. To prevent the shells from cracking, the oval end of the

egg can be pierced with the Hoffritz Egg Piercer or wrapped in a piece of aluminum foil.

2. Cover the eggs with simmering water. Boiling water will make them tough; starting eggs in boiling water will help center the yolks, however. Cook 8–10 minutes depending on the size of the eggs. As soon as they are done, place in a bowl of cold water.

Poached Eggs/*Oeufs Pochés*

1. Use a fairly shallow saucepan, the size depending on the number of eggs to be poached at one time.
2. The poaching liquid proportions are:
   1 quart of water
   1 tablespoon vinegar—wine vinegar can be used; do not use any salt
   Bring the water to a boil, then lower the temperature to a simmer.
3. If the egg is broken into a shallow saucer, it will be easier to lower into the simmering water by tilting the saucer to let the egg gently slip in. Check to be sure the egg does not stick to the bottom of the pot.
4. Poach for a minimum of 3 minutes depending on the size of the egg. Lift out with a slotted spoon or a skimmer. Dip in cold water to rinse off the vinegar, and trim the ragged edges with a knife.
5. If the poached eggs are not to be used right away, place in a bowl of cold water with a little salt. Refrigerate. To reheat, place the eggs in a bowl of hot water for 2 minutes.

Eggs Benedict   *Les Oeufs Poché Bénédictine*

1. Butter an English muffin and toast it lightly.
2. Poach two eggs in advance and keep warm.
3. Sauté one thin piece of cooked ham in a little butter.
4. Make Hollandaise Sauce (p. 58) in advance.
5. To assemble, place the slice of ham on toasted English muffin, arrange two poached eggs on top of ham, pour Hollandaise Sauce on top to cover the eggs. Garnish with a slice of truffle or black olive.

   Serves 1.

Deep Fat Fried Eggs/*Oeufs Frits*

1. Use a deep pot of very hot oil or an electric deep fat fryer. Temperature of oil should be 350 degrees. Be careful of spattering!
2. Lower a raw egg in the hot oil, rolling with a wooden spatula for ½ minute to gather the white around the yolk. Fry less than 1 minute. Drain on a paper towel. Sprinkle a little salt on the cooked egg.
3. Deep fry some sprigs of dried parsley to serve on the plate with the fried egg.

Shirred Eggs/*Oeufs sur le Plat*

Eggs Florentine   *Les Oeufs à la Florentine*

1. Use a gratinée dish. Butter it lightly.
2. Line with a layer of cooked spinach.
3. Place one or two poached eggs on top of the spinach.
4. Cover with Mornay Sauce (p. 52); sprinkle grated Swiss or Parmesan cheese and melted butter on top.
5. Glaze under the broiler until lightly browned, or brown in a high oven. Ingredients should be warm before glazing.

Serves 1.

VARIATION: When served without a bed of spinach this dish is known as Eggs Mornay—the ovenproof dish may be lined with a crouton or Mornay Sauce and poached eggs covered with Mornay Sauce sprinkled with bread crumbs.

Baked Eggs in Ramekins/*Oeufs en Cocotte*

Eggs Jeannette in Cocotte   *Les Oeufs en Cocotte à la Jeannette*

1. Use a small porcelain baking dish with a tight-fitting lid called a cocotte or ramekin *(ramequin)*.
2. Butter the inside of the cocotte.
3. Line with a layer of Chicken Quenelle mixture (p. 11).
4. Break an egg on top. Season with salt and pepper.
5. Put on the lid and place the cocotte in a *bain-marie*. Cook in a 350-degree oven for 5–6 minutes.
6. When cooked, remove the top and pour a ring of Velouté Sauce (p. 52) around the egg.
7. Garnish with asparagus tips.

   Serves 1.

Omelets/*Omelettes*

Basic Omelet   *Omelette au naturel*

1. Use a heavy iron skillet about 10 inches in diameter for a three-egg omelet. A fairly long handle is helpful. A heavy aluminum pan lined with Teflon prevents sticking.
2. Beat eggs slightly with a fork or thin wire whisk. Do *not* add any water. One tablespoon of cream is optional.
3. Put 1 tablespoon butter in omelet pan on high heat. Tilt pan to coat surface with melted butter. As soon as butter begins to foam and sizzle, pour eggs into pan. Stir with tines of fork held flat (or parallel) while shaking pan back and forth on burner. Start to roll congealed eggs to one side of pan as soon as underside is colored. Off heat shake pan to roll omelet over to brown other side for a few seconds if desired. It should be moist on the inside. Omelet can be shaped with a towel.
4. Turn over onto a warm serving dish—a hot dish would cause omelet to become overcooked. Serve immediately.

How to Fill an Omelet

1. Freshly prepared or leftover vegetables can be used: tomatoes, spinach, asparagus, or mushrooms, to name a few. Cut-up cooked chicken with cream sauce is another filling.
2. One to two tablespoons of filling is sufficient for a two-egg omelet to fill before folding or rolling. Some omelets can be filled just after they are made by cutting a slit in the top.

Dessert Omelet   *Omelette Sucrée*

One tablespoon of jam will fill a two-egg omelet. A sweet omelet requires a *little* sugar beaten in the eggs with a pinch of salt. The jam should be warmed before being added to the cooked omelet. After folding omelet, place on a warm dish and sprinkle with sugar.

Mousseline Omelet   *Omelette Mousseline*

This is half omelet and half soufflé because the eggs are separated, beaten separately, and the whites are folded into the yolks and cooked on a low fire *without* stirring. After it has risen, it can be folded once, or browned in a moderate oven.

Omelets with Fillings/*Omelettes Fourées*

The following variations call for 2–3 large eggs and 1 tablespoon butter for the omelet pan. Freshly chopped parsley should be on hand for a garnish as well as an ingredient. Salt eggs to taste.

Sorrel Omelet *(Omelette à l'Oseille):* Finely shred 1 cup washed sorrel. In a saucepan heat butter, add sorrel, and sauté until soft, then add to beaten eggs. *Or* shredded, tender, young leaves of sorrel, 1 chopped scallion, ⅛ teaspoon dried chervil are added to beaten eggs.

Cheese Omelet *(Omelette au Fromage):* Several tablespoons grated Parmesan, Gruyère, Camembert, or Roquefort added to beaten eggs.

Omelet Duxelles *(Omelette à la Duxelles):* Make *Duxelles* (p. 274). Dice about 2 teaspoons cooked ham, sauté in butter with 2 tablespoons *duxelles.* Fold into cooked omelet; surround with *Demi-Glace* flavored with *Sauce Tomate.*

Crouton Omelet *(Omelette aux Croutons):* Fry several tablespoons bread cubes in butter; add to beaten eggs. Sour dough type bread, slightly dried out, has better flavor than ordinary white bread.

Omelet Chasseur *(Omelette Chasseur):* Slice thin 2 or 3 chicken livers and 2 mushrooms; sauté in butter, reserving some of the filling for topping the omelet; add several tablespoons *Demi-Glace* to pan, and keep warm. Beat eggs, make omelet, and spread with mixture before rolling. Put sliced liver, mushrooms, and chopped parsley on top. Surround with *Sauce Chasseur.*

Provençal Omelet *(Omelette Niçoise, Omelette à la Provençale):* Peel, seed, chop tomato; mix with 1 teaspoon chopped parsley and ½ teaspoon minced garlic; add to beaten eggs.

Herb Omelet *(Omelette aux Fines Herbes):* Finely chop 1 tablespoon mixed herbs, usually parsley, chives, chervil, and tarragon; add to beaten eggs. Amount of herbs can vary to one's taste as well as the variety. Basil, thyme, or oregano are not classic choices but can be used.

Filled Vegetable Omelets/*Omelettes Fourrées aux Légumes*

French name for each vegetable omelet is that for all French dishes using the particular vegetable:

Brussels Sprouts Omelet *(Omelette Bruxelloise):* Very small Brussels sprouts sautéed in butter, folded in cooked omelet.

Cauliflower Omelet *(Omelette Du Barry):* Small heads of cauliflower, steamed (sautéed in butter, optional), folded into cooked omelet. Sprinkle with chopped parsley. Coat with *Sauce Mornay,* sprinkle with Parmesan cheese, brown under broiler.

Spinach Omelet *(Omelette Florentine):* Cooked spinach (water removed) mixed with cream, folded into beaten eggs or spread over cooked omelet before folding. Sprinkle with chopped parsley on top. Coat with *Sauce Mornay,* some grated Parmesan cheese, brown under broiler.

Asparagus Omelet *(Omelette Argenteuil):* Steamed or sautéed asparagus tips added to beaten eggs. Surround finished omelet with *Sauce Suprême.*

Eggplant Omelet *(Omelette Aubergines):* Dice a few tablespoons of eggplant and sauté with a slice of eggplant for garnish. Add diced eggplant to beaten eggs, cook, garnish with eggplant slice and chopped parsley. Surround with *Demi-Glace* sauce.

Onion Omelet *(Omelette Lyonnaise):* Mince and sauté 3 or 4 tablespoons onions until lightly browned. Mix into beaten eggs with 1 teaspoon chopped parsley.

Carrot Omelet *(Omelette Crécy):* Shred some cooked carrots, add to beaten eggs, or fill cooked omelet with highly seasoned, cooked puréed carrots.

Potato Omelet *(Omelette Parmentier):* Dice a small potato; sauté in butter until tender and brown. Season with salt and pepper; add to beaten eggs. Garnish with cooked ham or sausage.

Green Pea Omelet *(Omelette Clamart; Saint Germain* also signifies use of peas in French): *Petit pois* cooked with onion and lettuce, folded into cooked omelet; make slit in top for about a tablespoon of cooked peas.

Chive Omelet *(Omelette Ciboulette):* Cut several tablespoons fresh chives into small pieces. Add to beaten eggs.

Mushroom Omelet *(Omelette aux Champignons, Forestière*—French word signifies use of mushrooms): Slice 2 or 3 tablespoons fresh mushrooms; sauté on high heat in butter and oil. Reserve enough slices to garnish omelet. Beat eggs, and add cooked mushroom slices. Sprinkle chopped parsley on top with reserved mushroom slices.

Artichoke Omelet *(Omelette aux Artichauts):* Slice thinly an artichoke bottom. If not previously cooked, sauté in butter until tender. Add to beaten eggs. Very thin slices of cooked potato can also be added. Garnish with slices of cooked artichoke on top.

Scrambled Eggs/*Oeufs Brouillés*

Eggs in the Shell with Smoked Salmon

Les Oeufs à la Coque au Saumon Fumé

2 brown eggs (shells are stronger, making them easier to cut)
1 teaspoon butter
1 teaspoon finely chopped onion
8 capers, chopped
1 tablespoon sour cream

1–1½ ounces smoked salmon, chopped
Pinch freshly ground pepper
Salt to taste
Bread fingers, toasted
2 egg holders
Egg cutter

1. Cut top off pointed end of eggs with egg cutter. Pour eggs into top of double boiler. Clean bottoms and tops of egg shells by washing out with cool water. Turn upside down to dry.

2. Melt butter in top of double boiler. Beat with eggs and scramble over boiling water in the double boiler. Add chopped onion, capers, sour cream, smoked salmon, and salt and pepper. Remove from heat. Fill egg shells with mixture, put on top, and serve eggs in their holders. Serve with toasted small bread fingers.

Serves 2 as an appetizer or first course.

VARIATION: To make Eggs in the Shell with Caviar: Omit the smoked salmon, scramble the eggs with 1 teaspoon butter, and add finely chopped onion, chopped capers, sour cream, and salt and pepper to taste. Fill egg shells and place 1 teaspoon caviar, any variety, on top as a garnish. Cover with egg shell tops.

Stuffed Eggs/*Oeufs Farcis*

Quail and Chicken Eggs Stuffed with Foie Gras Mousse — *Les Oeufs Lucullus*

Visualize a group of penguins (pengouins) *made of hard boiled eggs placed on a large mirror to simulate a frozen lake with ice carvings for mountains, glaciers, and igloos; I created this for a Château Pétrus Dinner in 1975.*

3-ounce can foie gras or 1 fresh goose liver poached in port	Salt and pepper to taste
2½ ounces (4½ tablespoons) unsalted butter, softened	12 large hard boiled eggs, chilled
¼ cup heavy cream	12 hard boiled quail eggs, chilled
1 tablespoon port	Black olives for decorating penguins
Dash of paprika	Miniature aspic cutters
	Clear, light aspic for decorating penguins

1. If using canned goose liver, remove any fat and put through a sieve, if necessary. Otherwise, trim fresh goose liver, cook, and remove membrane and veins. Purée in processor fitted with steel blade.

2. In a mixing bowl, cream softened butter and blend with foie gras. Whip cream and fold into mousse with the port, paprika, and salt and pepper to taste.

3. Peel chilled hard boiled eggs; cut about a ¼-inch piece of white from flat end of large eggs and reserve for penguins' caps. Remove yolk from cut

135

end, stuff with mousse, and stand egg on stuffed end. Peel quail eggs. Attach quail egg for head to other end of large egg, using a toothpick with a frill top to attach heads and cap (made from large egg). Using miniature aspic cutters cut black olives into shapes of flippers, beaks, eyes, and buttons. Cut eye with round tube, then use miniature cutter to make oval shape out of circle. Attach by dipping cut olive shapes into clear aspic. Put on caps and let thin clear aspic drop down penguins. Refrigerate after first and second coats or layers. A third coat may be necessary. Refrigerate again.

Serves 12 for a buffet or appetizer.

Eggs may be stuffed with Salmon Mousse (p. 99) or tinned mousse of pork and foie gras (less expensive); if so, name of dish would be changed.

Eggs Stuffed with Sorrel   *Les Oeufs Farcis à l'Oseille*

6 hard boiled eggs
½ cup sorrel chiffonade
5 tablespoons sour cream
3 tablespoons cream cheese, softened

2 tablespoons spinach, cooked,
   squeezed dry, and chopped
Salt and pepper to taste

1. Cut eggs in half lengthwise. Remove yolks and place whites on a serving plate. Put yolks in blender or bowl of food processor fitted with steel blade.

136

2. Add the sorrel, sour cream, cream cheese, and spinach to yolks and blend. Taste for seasoning. Put in a bowl and chill for 30 minutes to 1 hour.

3. Spoon mixture into egg whites or use a pastry bag with a star tube.

Serves 6 for hors d'oeuvres.

Eggs Stuffed with Mushrooms

Les Oeufs Farcis au Champignons

6–8 medium mushrooms, cultivated or mixed with other variety such as shiitake
4 tablespoons butter, softened
6 hard boiled eggs

Juice of ¹/₂ lemon
1 tablespoon finely chopped fresh dill or 1 teaspoon dried
Salt and pepper
Tiny dill sprigs

1. Mince mushrooms in food processor using steel blade. Heat 1 tablespoon of the butter on medium high heat and cook mushrooms, stirring until all liquid has evaporated. Cool.

2. Peel, halve, and remove yolk from eggs. Put yolks through a sieve *or* in bowl of food processor, mash, and mix with remaining ingredients. Stuff the halved egg whites. Garnish with dill sprigs.

Serves 6 for hors d'oeuvre.

Eggs Stuffed with *Sauce Verte*

Les Oeufs Farcis au Sauce Verte

Remove yolks from cold, halved hard boiled eggs. Mix sieved yolks with enough *Sauce Verte* (p. 63) to get a good consistency, and fill whites. Decorate platter with sprigs of watercress or parsley, or julienned red bell peppers.

Serve on a buffet table or for hors d'oeuvres.

Chapter Six

PIE and PASTRY DOUGH

Pâte Brisée for Quiches;
Pâte Sucrée and *Sablée* for *Tartes* and
Cookies;
Pâte à Crêpes; Pâte à Nouille

I start my class on *pâte brisée*, the next dough after *pâte à choux*, by answering the question of a student cook: "How do you make a quiche?" The fastest answer is to make a small *tartelette:* Line a 5-inch pie tin with *pâte brisée*, bake it blind (*cuire à blanc*—line pan with a paper muffin cup and fill with dried beans) for 10 minutes, remove muffin cup, sprinkle grated cheese on the bottom, pour in a beaten egg mixed with enough cream to fill pan two thirds full, add salt, pepper, and nutmeg, and bake in a 350-degree oven for about 20 minutes. *Voilà!* You have a cheese tartlet ready to be turned out of its pan to eat. Quiches baked with this dough in 9-inch pans should be turned out to prevent pastry from becoming soggy. Quiches are baked the same way as caramel custards in a 350-degree oven to prevent holes from forming in the custard and to prevent the filling from becoming watery. Also, a higher temperature causes the quiche to puff up, which might spoil the texture. American Swiss cheese should not be used because it is apt to create water on the bottom, nor should milk be substituted for cream because it, too, causes water to develop.

As soon as *le pâtissier* has successfully made *pâte à choux* and *pâte brisée,* the student chef's dream of making *Gâteau Saint-Honoré* and *La Religieuse* is possible, as these classics require both doughs. The former was named after St. Honoré, the patron saint of bakers *(les boulangers).* The patron saint of pastry cooks *(les pâtissiers)* is Saint Michel.

Pâte brisée, used for pies, fruit tarts, pastries, and croustades or cases, is made with varying proportions of flour, eggs, butter, and water. I have labeled two different recipes for this dough No. 1 and No. 2; both make three 9-inch pie shells and can be cut in half or in thirds. No. 1 requires a little more skill to make, as it contains 3 eggs, large or medium sized, in contrast to recipe No. 2, which uses 2 eggs with ½ cup cold water. (The latter is easier to halve because of the even number of eggs—2 cups flour, 5 ounces butter or 10 tablespoons, 1 egg, ¼ cup cold water, and a pinch of salt.) If the cook has had little previous practice, the dough can be made in a bowl, rather than on a pastry board. Proportions for one 9-inch pie shell are given for recipe No. 1 on page 143. Dough No. 2 was the one I used for my demonstrations when I toured the country, and it is preferred for the liquid fillings of quiches and pumpkin pies.

Doughs can be made sturdier by using more butter or lard (*corps gras* —literal translation is body fat). This is the substance which gives moisture to dough when it is cold as in a *pâté en croute* or a *tourte*. *Saindoux,* animal fat from pork, is still used today in France. So, if a recipe calls for shortening, *pâte au saindoux* is a substitute dough. *Corps gras* stands for any kind of animal or vegetable fat added to flour to make dough. In England veal and ham pie is made with pork fat pastry.

When a pastry requires extra sweetness, I usually choose one of three sweet doughs, which are lighter and have a cookie-like consistency. My *pâte sucrée* is a very delicate dough which is easier to handle for the novice if it is rolled out between two pieces of plastic wrap and the instructions are followed exactly. *Pâte Sucrée* with Almonds is a little sturdier dough to work with. *Pâte à Sablée,* another pastry and cookie dough, is more *friable* (crumbly) than other sweet doughs due to a slightly larger amount of butter, and is baked blind without "pie pellets," as the dough is too soft to support their weight. To keep the edges from getting too brown, I cover them with a strip of foil as described on page 143. My Tart with Juicy Summer Fruits is made with a special cake-like dough for fruit tarts called *Pâte à Tarte à Spatule ou Corne pour Fruits Frais* (p. 153).

The Pastes
Les Pâtes

Pastry and Pie Dough No. 1   *Pâte Brisée* No. 1

1 pound (3½ cups) all purpose flour
8 ounces (2 sticks) unsalted butter,
  firm room temperature

3 eggs
½ teaspoon salt

1. Sift flour onto wood, plastic, or marble pastry board. Make a well in center of flour; cut butter in 1 inch cubes and put in center. Break eggs on top of butter. Add salt. Squeeze ingredients together lightly with palms of hands to form a mass as quickly as possible.

2. Using palm and heel of hand, press or "smear" dough in a forward direction, which is called *fraisage. Do not work or knead* dough, which will

141

cause it to shrink when baking! Form dough into a loaf shape, from which it is easier to cut portions of dough. (Clean dough from hands with flour, which can be absorbed in the dough.)

3. Enclose dough in plastic wrap and let rest in refrigerator for a minimum of 1–2 hours before rolling out. It will keep in refrigerator for several days or may be frozen either in "loaf" form or rolled out and placed in pie pans.

    Pâte brisée can be made in an electric mixer using a flat beater *(palette)* or dough hook. All ingredients are put in bowl at once and mixed until dough is formed, at which time it is fraisaged lightly. Then it must be refrigerated for 24 hours.

4. When ready to line pie pan, cut off one third of the dough. Sprinkle a little flour on pastry board, place chilled dough on top, and hit with a rolling pin to soften dough a little. Roll from center to form a circle about 12 inches in diameter and about ⅛ inch thick. Lift and turn dough over to prevent it from sticking to pastry board. If it should become too warm, and therefore sticky, chill dough briefly. When dough is rolled out into a 12 inch circle, roll it up onto a floured rolling pin, center over buttered pie pan, and unroll so that it falls evenly over pan. Push dough against sides and bottom of pan using a small wad of extra dough as a pad. Trim dough about ½ inch beyond edge of rim and crimp edges, using thumb and forefinger or a pastry crimper.

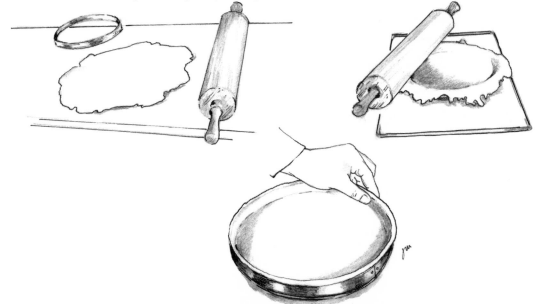

5. Prick bottom and sides of dough with a sharp-tined fork, cover, and chill for at least 30 minutes.

6. To bake *blind,* cover dough with a sheet of aluminum foil or crumpled parchment paper (crushed in fist for more flexibility) and fill with dried beans, raw rice, or aluminum "pie pellets" which will prevent pastry from puffing up in oven. Bake at 375 degrees for 10–15 minutes. Remove aluminum foil with beans and bake for a further 5 minutes to firm up bottom of pastry. It will be light in color at this stage. Cool on rack, then fill as desired and complete baking process.

Makes three 9-inch pie shells.

> **Proportions for one 9-inch pie shell:**
> 5 ounces (1 cup) flour
> 2⅔ ounces (approximately 4¾ tablespoons) butter
> 1 egg
> Pinch salt

NOTE: When baking blind in tartlet pans, use a paper muffin cup or foil on top of dough to hold beans or pellets, and bake for only 10 minutes. Remove foil and pellets, and bake 5 minutes more to cook bottom of crust.

Pastry and Pie Dough No. 2   *Pâte Brisée No. 2*

4 cups all purpose flour
1¼ cups (2½ sticks) unsalted butter,
  firm room temperature

½–1 teaspoon salt
2 eggs
½ cup cold water

1. Sift flour onto pastry board, make a well in center of flour, cut butter in ½–1-inch cubes, add salt, and quickly mix butter with flour, forming a rough mass.

2. Beat eggs slightly, mix cold water with eggs, and stir or mix into flour and butter. *Fraisage,* pushing dough forward several times until it forms a loaf. Do not overwork dough! Continue with Step 3 for Pastry and Pie Dough No. 1.

Makes three 9-inch pie shells.

Proportions for one 9-inch pie shell:

1⅓ cups flour
⅓ cup plus 2 tablespoons butter, firm room temperature
⅓ teaspoon salt
1 large egg
⅙ cup cold water

Proportions for ½ recipe:

2 cups flour
⅝ cup (10 tablespoons) butter, firm room temperature
¼–½ teaspoon salt
1 large egg
¼ cup cold water

Quiche of Bacon, Ham, and Cheese   *Quiche Lorraine*

*5 strips lean bacon, undercooked,
    Canadian bacon, or pancetta*
*9-inch, partially baked pie shell (Pâte
    Brisée No. 1 or No. 2, p. 141 or
    143)*
*½ cup diced or shredded Gruyère
    cheese*
*¼ cup diced or julienned ham (mild
    Danish type or Prosciutto)*

4 eggs
*1½ cups heavy cream or half and
    half*
*Salt and freshly ground white pepper
    to taste*
Pinch nutmeg

1. Sauté bacon briefly until slightly crisp and drain on paper towels. Cut in 1 inch squares and scatter over bottom of pie shell. Arrange cheese and ham over bacon.
2. Beat eggs with whisk or electric beater until mixed, add cream, and beat slightly. Add salt, pepper, and nutmeg to taste. (If available, do this in a bowl with a pour spout.) Eggs, cream, and seasonings also can be mixed in a blender on high speed.
3. Pour half of liquid into pie shell over bacon, ham, and cheese. Place quiche on oven rack in 350-degree oven and carefully add remaining cream and egg mixture. Fill pie shell a little more than three quarters full.
4. Bake about 30 minutes until top is light brown and custard is set. Place quiche on cooling rack for several minutes, then use a metal spatula to turn quiche out of pan. Serve warm.

Serves 10–12 for an hors d'oeuvre; 6–8 for a first course.

NOTE: Unless extra-deep quiche pans with removable bottoms are on hand, it is better to use a pie pan for this recipe to accommodate more filling.

VARIATION: To make Smoked Sturgeon Quiche, omit bacon, ham, and cheese and add 8 ounces smoked sturgeon, seasonings, and 1½ cups heavy cream.

Cheese Tartlets   *Tartelettes au Fromage*

3 large eggs
1 cup heavy cream or *half and half*
Salt and freshly ground white pepper
 to taste
Pinch nutmeg
1 cup shredded Gruyère cheese or
 crumbled Roquefort cheese

1 tablespoon chopped chives and
 ¼ cup smothered onions
 (optional)
4 partially baked tartlet shells—
 4½ inches wide and 1 inch deep
 (use two thirds Pâte Brisée *recipe,*
 No. 1 or No. 2, p. 141 or 143)

1. Beat eggs with whisk or electric beaters until well mixed. Stir in cream, optional chives and smothered onions, and add salt, pepper, and nutmeg to taste.

2. Sprinkle about ¼ cup shredded Gruyère on bottom of each partially baked pie shell and fill almost to top or three quarters full with ½ cup egg-cream mixture. Place on baking sheet and bake in a 350-degree oven until custard starts to brown on top and tests done, about 20 minutes.

3. Remove from oven, place on cooling rack, and after 5 minutes turn out of pans, inserting a small metal spatula between pastry and pan. If left to cool in pans, pastry would become soft underneath. Serve warm.

Serves 4–6 for a first course; serves 12 for an hors d'oeuvre.

NOTE: American metal pie pans were used here, but smaller French quiche and *tartelette* pans with and without removable bottoms are better for hors d'oeuvres.

Leek Tart   *Quiche aux Poireaux*

4 cups sliced leeks, white part and
 some green
3–4 tablespoons butter
A few grinds nutmeg
Salt and freshly ground white pepper
4 eggs

1½ cups heavy cream
½ cup grated Gruyère cheese
One 9-inch pie shell, partially baked
 (p. 143)—use pie pan or extra-
 deep quiche pan

145

1. Sauté leeks in 3 tablespoons butter for about 10 minutes, uncovered, with nutmeg, salt, and pepper to taste. Stir often on medium low heat without browning. As soon as leeks are cooked, remove from heat and cool slightly.

2. Beat eggs in electric mixer or with hand held beater. Mix in the cream, leeks, and ¼ cup of the Gruyère. Pour into partially baked pie shell and sprinkle remaining Gruyère on surface. Bake in a preheated 350-degree oven for about 30 minutes or until custard tests done and is lightly browned on top.

Serves 12 for an hors d'oeuvre; serves 8 as a first course.

Smoked Salmon Quiche   *Quiche au Saumon Fumé*

¾ pound (1½ cups) lightly salted smoked salmon (such as Nova Scotia salmon)
4 whole eggs
2 cups heavy cream or part half and half
1 tablespoon minced parsley or 1 teaspoon chopped dill

Salt and white pepper to taste
A few grinds nutmeg
One 9-inch pie shell, partially baked (p. 143)
1½ teaspoons butter for top (optional)

1. Slice smoked salmon very thin and cut into 1½-inch pieces. Pieces of leftover salmon may also be used.

2. Beat eggs until mixed with a whisk or electric beater; add the smoked salmon, cream, chopped parsley or dill, nutmeg, salt, and freshly ground white pepper to taste. Pour half of mixture into partially baked pie shell and place on partially pulled out rack in center of preheated 350-degree oven. Finish filling pie shell on rack in oven by pouring rest of mixture from a pitcher. Dot with butter.

3. Bake for about 30 minutes or until quiche tests done. Cool on rack. Serve lukewarm or chilled.

Serves 12–14 for an hors d'oeuvre; serves 6–8 for a first course.

Sorrel Quiche
Quiche à l'Oseille

1 pound sorrel, washed, deveined,
  and drained
4 tablespoons butter
1½ cups thinly sliced red or sweet
  Spanish onions

4 eggs
1½ cups heavy cream
Salt and pepper to taste
One 9-inch pie shell, partially baked
  (p. 143)

1. Sauté sorrel in 2 tablespoons butter until liquid has evaporated and sorrel becomes purée-like.

2. In a low sided, heavy pan sauté sliced onions in remaining butter, covered, until onions are transparent and almost puréed without browning. Stir occasionally.

3. In a large bowl, mix onions and sorrel and let cool to lukewarm. Beat eggs until well mixed, beat in cream, and add salt and pepper sparingly. Stir liquid mixture into sorrel and onions. Pour into pie or quiche shell and bake in a 350–375-degree oven until top is lightly brown and the custard is set, about 30–40 minutes. Serve warm.

Serves 10–12 for an hors d'oeuvre; serves 6–8 for a first course.

VARIATIONS: If acidity of sorrel is objectionable, ½ pound spinach can be substituted to make a Spinach Quiche. A Zucchini Quiche requires 2 small sliced zucchini sautéed in a little olive oil with several tablespoons of chopped or thinly sliced onion.

Sweetened Short Pastry Dough
Pâte Sucrée

½ pound (2 sticks) sweet butter, at
  room temperature
½ pound (1⅞ cups) confectioners'
  sugar
3 eggs, medium or large

1 teaspoon vanilla extract
Pinch salt
Pinch baking powder
1 pound (3½ cups) all purpose flour

1. Start with room temperature butter placed in bowl of electric mixer fitted with the *flat* beater. (Do not use mixer with beaters. Dough can be made by hand.) Cream butter and sugar, then mix eggs in one by one. Add vanilla.

2. Mix baking power and salt into flour, then mix in dough until just blended.

147

Refrigerate overnight. Do *not* work this dough, which would cause it to become too hard.

Makes 4 circles approximately 9½ inches in diameter.

NOTE: After dough is rolled out (see pages 141–143) and arranged in baking pan, it has to rest in refrigerator for 20 minutes or longer. *Pâte Sucrée* will keep 15 days under refrigeration or can be frozen in sections.

Pâte Sucrée with Almonds   *Pâte Sucrée avec Amandes*

14 ounces (3½ sticks) sweet butter, just at room temperature, plus 1½ ounces (3 tablespoons) salted butter, just at room temperature
7 ounces (1¼ cups) confectioners' sugar

Grated peel of 1 lemon (no pith)
5 yolks
Dash vanilla extract
7 ounces (2 cups) almonds, finely ground
1 pound (3½ cups) flour

1. In electric mixer with flat beater blend sweet and salted butter. Cream sugar and butter and add grated lemon peel. Mix in eggs, one by one, and add dash of vanilla. This dough can also be made by hand (p. 141).

2. Incorporate ground almonds and flour just until blended. Do *not* overmix, and do *not* use *fraisage*. (*Note:* Peeled whole or sliced almonds can be ground in processor, being careful not to overprocess, in meat grinder using fine blade, or they can be purchased already ground.)

3. Refrigerate overnight. Keeps several weeks in refrigerator or can be frozen.
   This dough is more fragile than *Pâte Sucrée* without almonds (above). After rolling out to fit tart pan, refrigerate pastry shell for 10 minutes before filling and baking. An easy way to roll dough is to place it between two sheets of plastic wrap.

Makes 4 circles approximately 8–9 inches in diameter.

VARIATION: This dough makes excellent cookies and does not have to be rested or chilled: Pinch off small pieces and roll lightly into ¾-inch balls. Place on heavy cookie sheet and flatten slightly with floured wooden cookie press, or roll in chopped almonds and flatten slightly with two fingers. Refrigerate for 10 minutes, then bake in 350-degree oven for 10 minutes. Cool on wire rack. For rolled and cut cookies, use dough when thoroughly chilled. Roll about ¼ inch thick between two sheets of wax paper.

Makes approximately 120 round cookies, 2–2½ inches wide.

Sweetened Tart Pastry Dough   *Pâte à Sablée*

10 ounces (2½ sticks) unsalted
  butter
10 ounces (approximately 1½ cups)
  sugar
1 egg yolk

2 whole eggs
A few drops vanilla extract or lemon
  juice
10 ounces (2 cups) flour
½ teaspoon baking powder

1. Cream butter and sugar.
2. Incorporate egg yolk and eggs, one at a time, and flavoring. Add flour mixed with ½ teaspoon baking powder. *Do not overmix.*
3. Chill for at least 3 hours, or overnight.
4. When ready to use, divide into three sections with a knife and work with only one section at a time, refrigerating the rest. If making 1 *tarte,* cut off one third of dough. Roll out on a heavily floured board, using a floured rolling pin, and line tart pan.
5. If baking blind or unfilled tart shells, do not use dried beans or metal pellets, as the dough is too soft. Bake at 350 degrees. Should the edges brown too quickly, cut out a "donut" of foil and lay on top to cover borders of tart. I use it for fruit tarts.

Makes three 8-inch *tartes.*

VARIATION: To make cookies, roll dough out ⅛ inch thick, a section at a time, on a heavily floured board, using a floured rolling pin. Cut into 4-inch rounds with a crinkle-edged cutter and transfer to ungreased baking sheet. Cut each round into four fan-shaped pieces, separating them slightly. Bake at 350 degrees for about 10 minutes until cookies start to brown at edges. Cool on a rack and store airtight.

Makes about 120 fan cookies.

Lemon Soufflé Tart   *Tarte Soufflée aux Citrons*

8 eggs, separated
8 ounces (1¼ cups) sugar
Grated peel of 1 lemon
1 cup freshly squeezed lemon juice
½ cup heavy cream

1 teaspoon cornstarch
2 prepared tart shells of Pâte Sucrée
  (p. 147), 8½ inches diameter,
  1¾ inches high
Confectioners' sugar (optional)

149

1. Beat egg yolks and 5 ounces (¾ cup) sugar in bowl of electric beater for 4 minutes, or until mixture forms a slowly-dissolving ribbon when beaters are lifted.
2. Add grated lemon peel, lemon juice, and cream. Cook in double boiler, whisking constantly as for *Sauce Hollandaise*. After 6–7 minutes mixture will thicken.
3. Beat egg whites to soft peak stage, add remaining 3 ounces (½ cup less 1 tablespoon) sugar blended with cornstarch in a slow stream. Continue beating until a stiff meringue is formed. Fold into yolk mixture.
4. Pour into prepared tart shells and bake at 325 degrees for 15–20 minutes. Shells can be prebaked, in which case bake with lemon filling for only 10 minutes. Serve at room temperature.

Serves 6–8. Recipe can be cut in half.

NOTE: Confectioners' sugar may be dusted over tarts. The light, foamy filling contrasts beautifully with the rich pastry shell, and does not fall when cooled.

Lemon Tart   *Tarte aux Citrons*

6 large whole eggs
4 egg yolks
14 ounces (approximately 2 cups)
  sugar
8 ounces (2 sticks) unsalted butter,
  creamed
Juice and grated rind of 6 lemons

Dash vanilla extract
1 prepared tart shell of Pâte Sucrée
  (p. 147), 9½ inches diameter,
  1⅜ inches high
Confectioners' sugar for top

1. In double boiler or large bowl set over simmering water, beat eggs and yolks with sugar until mixture is thick and reaches 100 degrees. Remove from heat and continue beating until mixture is cold and forms a slowly dissolving ribbon from a lifted beater.
2. Whisk together room temperature creamed butter and lemon juice. If necessary, put in double boiler and stir until creamy. Fold into egg and sugar mixture and add grated lemon rind and vanilla.
3. Pour filling into tart shell, pouring to top of rim to prevent dough from slipping down during baking. Bake at 325 degrees for 15–20 minutes until filling is set and pastry is cooked. Unmold and cool tart on cake rack to prevent pastry from becoming soggy.
   Dust with confectioners' sugar before serving.

Serves 10–12.

> **How to Make Tart Shell Using a Ring:**
>
> Cover a pastry sheet with parchment paper. Place metal pastry ring 9½ inches in diameter on parchment. Roll out chilled dough and arrange on ring, pressing down inside to form a shell. Trim excess even with top of rim. Dough on bottom, sides, and top should be same thickness. With a piece of dough or towel push dough in all corners to remove any empty space. Chill 1 hour.
>
> Pour in filling to top of dough-lined rim, which prevents dough from slipping down during baking.

Lemon Tart with Orange   *Tarte aux Citrons et à l'Orange*

Pâte Sucrée (p. 147) to fit 12-inch shallow flan pan with removable fluted ring:
1½ cups all purpose flour
¼ cup sugar

FILLING:
4 large eggs
1¼ cups sugar
¾ cup plus 2 tablespoons lemon juice
⅔ cup orange juice

1 stick plus 1 tablespoon unsalted butter, chilled
1 small egg, lightly beaten

Grated rind of 3 lemons
½ cup heavy cream
3 tablespoons sweet butter, softened
Confectioners' sugar for top

1. Sift together flour and sugar. Cut *cold* butter into bits. Blend butter and egg into flour following directions for *Pâte Brisée* (p. 141). If necessary, add 1–2 tablespoons water while forming dough into a ball. *Fraiser* with the heel of the hand for a few seconds to distribute the butter evenly. Re-form into a ball. Dust lightly with flour, wrap in plastic wrap, and refrigerate for at least 1 hour or overnight, which is better.

2. After dough has been chilled, roll out into ⅛-inch thick round on a floured board or marble surface. Draping dough over rolling pin, arrange it into 12-inch shallow flan pan. Press dough firmly into pan, trimming excess. Prick bottom of dough with a fork and chill in refrigerator for 1 hour.

3. To make filling, beat eggs until light; add sugar until mixture makes a ribbon. Transfer to heavy enameled or stainless steel saucepan. Add lemon

151

juice, orange juice, and grated rind of lemons; cook on medium low heat, stirring with a whisk until mixture is thick. Do not allow to simmer.

4. Remove pan from heat and stir in ½ cup heavy cream and 3 tablespoons softened sweet butter. Transfer filling to a small bowl. Fill a large bowl with ice and set in it the small bowl; stir occasionally until it is cool.

5. Pour filling into *tarte* shell and bake in upper third of 325-degree oven for 25 minutes or until set. Let tart cool on rack. Sprinkle confectioners' sugar on top before serving.

Serves 12.

Linzer Torte

Linzer Tarte
Tarte Linzer

This is an Austrian raspberry tart with a spiced soft pastry shell. The pastry is made in much the same way as pâte sucrée *or* sablée.

10 ounces (2½ sticks) unsalted butter
10 ounces (1¼ cups) sugar
2 large eggs
1 egg yolk
10 ounces (2 cups) flour

½ teaspoon cinnamon
2 ounces (½ cup) hazelnuts, ground
1½ cups raspberry jam (approximately)
Confectioners' sugar

1. Cream butter and sugar, then incorporate one egg at a time and the egg yolk. Do not overmix!

152

2. Sift flour and cinnamon together, add to batter. Stir in ground hazelnuts and refrigerate dough at least 2 hours. (Dough will keep for several days, or can be frozen.)

3. For each 9 x 1½-inch tart (it is best to use pans with loose bottoms) use half of the dough. Roll out two thirds to line pan; reserve the other third for a lattice top. (If dough is too soft to roll, simply pat into place with fingers.) Spread with about ¾ cup raspberry jam. Roll out remaining third of dough and cut into ⅓-inch wide strips, or roll into thin ropes by hand. Arrange in lattice pattern on top of jam, and around edge of pan (see illustration opposite).

4. Bake in 375-degree oven for 25–30 minutes. Pastry will rise somewhat and turn golden. When cool, dust with confectioners' sugar.

Makes two 9-inch tarts.

Tart with Juicy Summer Fruits   *Tarte aux Fruits Frais de Saison*

*9 ounces (2 sticks plus
    2 tablespoons) unsalted butter
12 ounces (about 1¾ cups) sugar
5 eggs
1 tablespoon cream
Dash vanilla extract
1 pound (3½ cups) flour
½ teaspoon baking powder
Pinch salt*

*2 baskets (12 ounces each)
    blueberries, blackberries, or
    boysenberries*
1–2 tablespoons sugar for berries
    (optional)
2 tablespoons Kirsch
Confectioners' sugar (optional)
Two 10–10½-inch cake pans,
    buttered and floured*

1. Cream butter and sugar together.

2. Add eggs one by one, beating well, and stir in cream and vanilla.

3. Fold in flour, baking powder, and salt.

4. Spread batter into two 10½-inch cake pans with a spatula, and arrange fruit on top of dough. (If fruit is very acid, sprinkle with a little sugar.)

5. Bake in a 375-degree oven for 25–30 minutes. Dough will rise up around fruit, become slightly crisp at the edges, and turn light golden. It should remain somewhat soft in the center.

* Peeled and quartered ripe peaches may replace berries.

6. To unmold, quickly turn tarts face down on a cake rack, then reverse onto a second cake rack so that tarts are right side up. Sprinkle with Kirsch and let cool. Tarts may be sprinkled with confectioners' sugar before serving, if desired.

Makes two 10½-inch tarts. Recipe can be halved to make one 10½-inch tart.

NOTE: This special dough for fresh fruit tarts is called *Pâte à Tarte à Spatule ou Corne.*

Saint Honoré Pastry   *Gâteau Saint-Honoré*

One 10-inch diameter x ⅛-inch thick circle of Pâte Brisée *(p. 141)* or Pâte Sucrée *(p. 147)*
½ recipe Pâte à Choux *dough (p. 74)*
1 egg for glazing Pâte à Choux

2 cups Crème Chantilly *(p. 79)* or Crème Pâtissière *(p. 286)*
1 cup Caramelized Sugar *(p. 156)*
1 recipe Crème Chibouste *(p. 288)*

1. Place circle of pastry dough on greased baking sheet lined with greased heavy paper. Prick with a fork to prevent rising.
2. Put *Pâte à Choux* dough in a pastry bag fitted with plain ½-inch tube and form a rim just inside edge of pastry circle, first brushing edge of pastry with water so that *chou* paste will stick. Brush *chou* rim with egg glaze. (If less *Crème Chibouste* is desired for center of assembled *gâteau,* pipe another circle or spiral of chou paste in center of pastry to fill more space.)
3. Bake *Saint-Honoré* shell at 400 degrees for 10 minutes, then lower oven heat to 350 degrees for a further 30 minutes or until *chou* rim is puffed and pastry base is golden brown. Allow to cool thoroughly before filling.
4. Form 12 small *choux* the size of ping pong balls. Brush with egg glaze and bake in 350-degree oven for 30 minutes. Make a small slit in the bottom of each puff to allow steam to escape, and dry out for 10 minutes in turned off oven. Allow to cool completely.
5. To assemble *Gâteau Saint-Honoré:*
   a. Fill small choux with *Crème Chantilly* or *Crème Pâtissière* from underneath,* and dip tops in Caramelized Sugar. Secure to rim of shell at equal intervals, like a crown, with a little caramel.
   b. Fill pastry bag with *Crème Chibouste* and pipe a continuous spiral of cream in center of shell, forming a dome.

Serves 8–10.

* Push tip of pastry tube into base of puff, then fill.

The Nun

La Religieuse

This classical presentation is not as difficult to prepare as it may sound! It is advisable to make éclairs the day before, so that they dry out thoroughly and do not collapse when the dessert is assembled. The pastry base, Crème Pâtissière, *and* Fondant *can also be prepared the day before, leaving only the final assembly of this creation to be made. This pastry makes a centerpiece on a buffet table for a special party such as a christening or a first communion. It may be flanked by two plates of small frosted éclairs of coffee and chocolate.*

½ recipe Pâte à Choux *(p. 74)*
Pâte Brisée *(p. 141) or* Pâte Sucrée *(p. 147) for 8-inch quiche pan*
Crème Pâtissière *(p. 286)*
Fondant *(p. 299), 1 cup each coffee-flavored and chocolate-flavored*

Sucre Caramel *(p. 156)*
Crème Chantilly *(p. 79)*
10-ounce soda bottle
12–14 inch pastry bag
⅝-inch plain pastry tube

1. Make eight 5-inch éclairs, one 3½-inch diameter "doughnut," one 2½-inch diameter "doughnut," and one 1½-inch round puff from a half recipe of *Pâte à Choux* paste, using a ⅝-inch plain pastry tube. Bake (without an egg wash) in the usual way.

2. Line an 8 inch individual-size quiche pan with *Pâte Brisée* or *Pâte Sucrée* and bake blind.

3. To assemble: Using a pastry tube or the point of a knife, punch two holes in bottom of each éclair. Fill a pastry bag (tube inserted) with *Crème Pâtissière* and fill éclairs. Repeat with "doughnuts" or crowns and the round puff. Frost four of the éclairs, large crown and round puff with coffee-flavored *Fondant;* frost other four éclairs and smaller crown with chocolate-flavored *Fondant.* Allow to dry.

Oil a small soda bottle, and set it in the middle of the baked pastry shell (see illustration, p. 156)—this will be removed later. Prepare *Sucre Caramel* and dip the underside of each end of an éclair in it. Rest one end against the edge of the pastry base, the other end against the oiled soda bottle. (The *Caramel* for the top end should be toward one side, and it is

155

advisable to trim the éclairs if necessary to make them all the same height. Put trimmed end at the bottom where it won't show.) Repeat with rest of éclairs, alternating coffee and chocolate colors, forming a complete circle. Remove the soda bottle, fix the large crown, the smaller crown, and the round puff in place with a little *Caramel,* and complete *La Religieuse* by decorating with *Crème Chantilly,* using a pastry bag and a star tube (see illustration above). The *Crème Chantilly* can be added just before serving.

Serves 8—10.

Caramelized Sugar   *Sucre Caramel*

1 cup granulated sugar   ***Sugar thermometer***
2 tablespoons water
Small heavy saucepan or poêlon, *a*
   sugar pot made of unlined heavy
   copper

1. Cook sugar and water on medium high heat without stirring until it comes to a boil and turns a reddish brown color. Shake pan occasionally while sugar is boiling. Use brush dipped in cold water to remove sugar crystals from sides of pan.

2. As soon as sugar has turned the correct color (320 degrees F. on a sugar thermometer), remove from stove and place pot in a pan of cold water to stop the cooking. That will prevent caramelized sugar from turning too brown.

3. Melt caramelized sugar on low heat when it becomes solidified.

NOTE: There are many other uses for caramelized sugar. Some of them include:
    Caramel coated nuts to serve for candy
    For making praline paste
    For lining molds for custards
    As a sauce or flavoring for desserts
    For making spun sugar (*Cheveux d'Ange*, p. 343)
    As a glaze for pastries and fruits
    For assembling *Croquembouche* and *Gâteau Saint-Honoré*
    For glazing *choux*

Basic Pancakes   *Pâte à Crêpes*

Pâte à Crêpes *was such a fashionable dough at one time that it may have fallen out of favor from too much familiarity. Interest can be revived with fresh ideas for fillings, sauces, and unusual ways to arrange the crêpes, such as a* Gâteau de Crêpes, *a quiche of crêpes, for* entrées en chemise, *or as liners for dessert molds. Crêpes readily turn into triangles, envelopes, cigar shapes, and rolls. Friends still remember how I entertained audiences in department stores by making two crêpes at the same time, the one juggling act for which French chefs are noted. I brought equal astonishment to people when I flipped my quiches out of the pie pan right side up as soon as they were baked. The dough I used then is the same one in this cookbook,* Pâte Brisée *No. 2. It must have aroused further astonishment to see the former Executive Chef of the White House bring forth from the blender batters that produced* Crêpes Normandy, Quiche Lorraine, *and sauces that formerly were fit for a president.*

In the 1960s the blender was the new machine with which every kitchen was equipped, while at this time it is the food processor. I did adapt a number of dishes for the blender; but, of course, now the processor can take over most of those preparations, just one of its many accomplishments (p. 250).

Even if only one crêpe is made at a time, there will still be several stacks before long, as they cook less than a minute on the first side and less than a half minute on the second side. Overcooking causes toughness. The sugar in the batter helps color the crêpes, and the butter improves the flavor and texture.

HANDMADE/MIXER METHOD:
5 eggs
2 cups milk
1 tablespoon sugar
Pinch salt
1 teaspoon vanilla extract
1½ cups flour, sifted
2 tablespoons salted browned butter
   (beurre noisette)

1 or 2 small iron pans (poêle à crêpes), 7½ inches in diameter, or similar sized pan with long handle, used only for crêpes and cleaned only with salt

1. Using an electric mixer on medium speed or a whisk, beat together eggs, milk, sugar, salt, and vanilla for about 1 minute. Fold in flour. Pass through a chinois to remove any unmixed pieces of egg. The batter should be thick enough to coat a spoon and can be used right away because the flour is blended in last.

2. Heat butter in a sauté pan until it just turns brown, and whisk into batter while still hot. No extra butter is needed for the pan while cooking crêpes because of the *beurre noisette.*

3. Heat a crêpe pan, grease with a piece of cheesecloth dipped in butter, stir batter, and pour in about 2 tablespoons crêpe batter, tilting pan to cover bottom. Pour any excess back in bowl. On medium heat cook for about 1 minute until lightly browned, turn over with a spatula, and cook for about ½ minute. Put on a plate with second cooked side up, which makes them easier to fold later.

4. Arrange crêpes in small stacks, wrap in plastic wrap or waxed paper, and cover with foil, if not using right away. They may be refrigerated for 4 or 5 days or frozen.

Makes approximately 30–40 crêpes. Recipe can be cut in half.

If crêpes are to be used for an entrée, a pinch of sugar in the batter is enough for coloring; *not* 1 tablespoon.

Some fillings: cottage cheese or ricotta cheese, sour cream, and sugar; whipped cream flavored with Cointreau and sugar; *Crème Pâtissière* (p. 286), with confectioners' sugar on top.

BLENDER METHOD FOR CRÊPES:
3 large eggs
Pinch salt
1½ tablespoons sugar
½ teaspoon vanilla extract

1½ cups milk
1 cup flour
2 tablespoons browned butter
   (beurre noisette)

1. Place eggs, salt, sugar, and vanilla in blender container. Cover and run on low speed for 5 seconds.

2. Add milk slowly through the cap opening while running on low speed.

3. Add flour on low speed using a funnel, if necessary, or a tablespoon to hold flour.

4. Brown butter in crêpe pan and add slowly to other ingredients with machine running. This batter can be used right away. Pour into a bowl or pitcher and stir occasionally while making crêpes.

Makes 25–30 crêpes.

NOTE: This recipe can also be made in processor using steel blade.

Suzette Butter for *Crêpes Suzette*

BLENDER METHOD:

2 oranges, including peel
2 strips lemon peel, 1 inch long x ½ inch wide
⅔ cup sugar

⅔ cup butter, at room temperature
6 tablespoons orange Curaçao liqueur
2–4 tablespoons brandy or *Cognac*

1. Use vegetable peeler to remove orange part of peel without any of the white pith.

2. Squeeze juice of 2 oranges or make ½ cup orange juice. Place orange juice, orange peel, and lemon peel in blender container. Cover and run on low speed until the peel is chopped.

3. Add sugar, butter, and 4 tablespoons of the Curaçao. Cover and blend on high speed until mixed.

4. Spoon about ½ cup Suzette butter into a heated large chafing dish or a shallow skillet. Melt on medium heat. Dip one crêpe at a time in sauce, heating both sides. Fold in half with brown side up and fold again into quarters, placing each crêpe overlapping on side of pan. Add more sauce as needed.

5. Spoon 2 tablespoons brandy and 2 tablespoons liqueur over crêpes. Flame, using a match, and baste with sauce to keep flame burning. Tip pan to get more sauce.

Makes enough sauce for 12 crêpes.

Suzette Butter for *Crêpes Suzette* Made in Sauté Pan

1 tablespoon sugar
1 orange: cut peel in ½-inch strips with white pith removed
1 lemon: cut peel in ½-inch strips with white pith removed
2 tablespoons butter

Juice of 2 oranges
Juice of ½ lemon
2–3 tablespoons Cointreau
½ cup Grand Marnier (approximately)
¼ cup Cognac (approximately)

1. Use a large, heavy sauté pan. Sprinkle enough sugar to cover bottom of pan, and add orange and lemon peel. Caramelize sugar on high heat. Run fork around pan to hasten caramelizing process. Remove from fire as soon as caramelized. Add the butter and the orange and lemon juice.
2. Pour in Cointreau and ¼ cup Grand Marnier. Remove orange and lemon peel. The sauce should be golden brown.
3. Put saucepan back on low heat to prevent alcohol from igniting prematurely, and start dipping one crêpe at a time, second cooked side up, rolling it around in sauce until covered. Next, fold in half, top side up, then fold again. Continue with each crêpe, placing them overlapping on the side of a heatproof serving dish.
4. Add rest of the Grand Marnier and the Cognac. Flame, while continuing to spoon sauce over crêpes in order to glaze them. Continuous shaking of pan will keep flame from going out.
5. Using a chafing dish or burner, bring crêpes to table, sprinkle with more sugar, and flame again in front of dinner guests.

This amount of sauce is enough for serving 8 crêpes. Two or 3 crêpes are usually served to 1 person.

Apples Normandy   *Pommes à la Normande*

FILLING FOR CREPES:
2 tablespoons butter
2 large tart apples, peeled, cored, and diced into ¼-inch cubes
⅛ teaspoon cinnamon

2 tablespoons brown sugar
¼ cup corn syrup
¼ cup Calvados brandy (heated)
10 crêpes

1. In a large sauté pan or chafing dish, heat butter until light brown. Add prepared apples, cover, and cook until just tender and brown. Stir to prevent burning. Sprinkle cinnamon and brown sugar over apples, and steam for 1 minute.

2. Place 1 tablespoon cooked apples in each warmed crêpe, roll up, and place around side of pan.
3. Pour syrup and brandy into pan with crêpes, flame, and baste crêpes with sauce. More sauce may be required.

Serves 4.

Other fillings for crêpes:

a. Peel bananas, cut in ¼-inch slices, dip in flour, and sauté like apples. Flame with dark rum. Bananas can be sliced lengthwise before sautéing.
b. Slice fresh strawberries; flame with Kirschwasser or Grand Marnier.

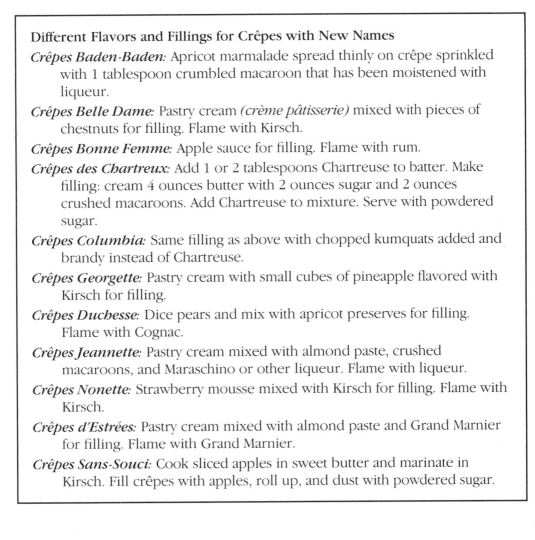

Different Flavors and Fillings for Crêpes with New Names

Crêpes Baden-Baden: Apricot marmalade spread thinly on crêpe sprinkled with 1 tablespoon crumbled macaroon that has been moistened with liqueur.

Crêpes Belle Dame: Pastry cream *(crème pâtisserie)* mixed with pieces of chestnuts for filling. Flame with Kirsch.

Crêpes Bonne Femme: Apple sauce for filling. Flame with rum.

Crêpes des Chartreux: Add 1 or 2 tablespoons Chartreuse to batter. Make filling: cream 4 ounces butter with 2 ounces sugar and 2 ounces crushed macaroons. Add Chartreuse to mixture. Serve with powdered sugar.

Crêpes Columbia: Same filling as above with chopped kumquats added and brandy instead of Chartreuse.

Crêpes Georgette: Pastry cream with small cubes of pineapple flavored with Kirsch for filling.

Crêpes Duchesse: Dice pears and mix with apricot preserves for filling. Flame with Cognac.

Crêpes Jeannette: Pastry cream mixed with almond paste, crushed macaroons, and Maraschino or other liqueur. Flame with liqueur.

Crêpes Nonette: Strawberry mousse mixed with Kirsch for filling. Flame with Kirsch.

Crêpes d'Estrées: Pastry cream mixed with almond paste and Grand Marnier for filling. Flame with Grand Marnier.

Crêpes Sans-Souci: Cook sliced apples in sweet butter and marinate in Kirsch. Fill crêpes with apples, roll up, and dust with powdered sugar.

Noodle and Pasta Dough—the Italian Connection

The only characteristic noodle dough *(pâte à nouille)* has in common with the pastry doughs in Chapter 6 is that it is unleavened. The differences are:

1. Pasta or noodle dough has no butter, although sometimes a tablespoon of oil is used, but not in the recipe for ravioli (p. 163).
2. It depends for its moisture on a number of extra large whole eggs.
3. All purpose unbleached flour is preferred as it has more body or texture than all purpose bleached flour.
4. After the eggs are incorporated, the dough is kneaded until it becomes shiny and pliable, about 10 minutes.
5. It then rests about 1 hour at room temperature to be kneaded and rolled out in a pasta machine. The final kneading and rolling can be done by hand with an Italian pasta pin (30 inches long by 1½ inches diameter) or a ball bearing pin; but this is not necessary, as a machine is easier to use.

Contrary to its reputation, pasta is not more difficult to make than most other doughs. It is worth the effort to have the gratification of serving freshly made noodles or ravioli to family and friends. Pasta is high in energy-producing carbohydrates and low in fat, two dietary requirements. The sauces should be chosen according to the freshest ingredients of the season. Perhaps pasta owes its present popularity to the variety and color it lends to meals through its use of different vegetable purées in the pasta itself and the endless combinations of all categories of food for the sauces. We do know that our third president, Thomas Jefferson, was responsible for bringing pasta to this country after his ambassadorship abroad. Jefferson, America's first Renaissance man, was a great connoisseur of food and wine in the 1700s.

Ravioli is one of the main groups of pasta. It has to be formed as soon as it is rolled out in the same way as do lasagne and stricchetti (bows or butterflies). Ravioli and agnolotti are usually square shaped, while tortellini di Bologna are in circles of 1½ inches, twisted into a navel shape; anellini of Parma are semicircular; and cappelletti di Romagna are cut into 3-inch circles, filled and formed into "hat" shapes.

One method of grouping pasta is:

1. String pasta (round) used for boiling, such as spaghetti, spaghettini.
2. Tubular forms used for boiling and baking, such as rigatoni.

3. Envelopes of stuffed pasta, such as ravioli, agnolotti, tortellini, cannelloni, lumache, manicotti.

4. Ribbon or flat pasta, such as noodles, lasagne, fettuccine.

5. Fancy shapes of pasta, such as wheels, stars, butterflies, snails, little ears, shapes as tiny as peppercorns like lentine or occhiolini.

Noodle Dough   *Pâte à Nouille*

This noodle or pasta dough can be made by hand, in a mixer, or food processor. Directions for making by hand are given in Noodle Dough or Pasta for Ravioli (below). Even though ingredients and proportions are different, the method is the same.

In France, I used a laminoir *for kneading and rolling out dough and a* coupeur de pâte à nouille *to cut noodles in different sizes. The Italian pasta machine combines* le laminoir *and* le coupeur.

2 pounds flour (1 kilo = 2.2 pounds = 35 ounces)
10–11 large eggs
2 tablespoons olive oil
Pinch salt

RECIPE CUT IN HALF:
1 pound flour
6 large eggs
1 tablespoon olive oil
Pinch salt

Noodle Dough or Pasta for Ravioli   *Pâte à Nouille pour Ravioli*

Uncooked ravioli may be frozen on baking sheet in single rows, and then stored in sealed containers in freezer until ready to use. Do not thaw out before cooking. If frozen, they will take a little longer to cook. To prevent freshly made ravioli from sticking together, they may be frozen for a matter of minutes or hours, or they can be sprinkled with cornmeal and covered with plastic wrap or a towel for an hour before cooking.

1½ cups unbleached all purpose flour, unsifted
2 extra large eggs
Hand-cranked or electric pasta machine for kneading and rolling dough

Scalloped cutting wheel
Ravioli filling of fresh crab, shrimp, or lobster (p. 165)

1. Place 1½ cups flour on pastry board. Make a well. Break eggs into the well,

163

and beat with a fork. Start incorporating flour from inner edge of well, using fork to mix flour with eggs.

2. As soon as a thick paste is formed (dough starts to form), use fingers dipped in flour to make a ball with dough. Start to knead dough, incorporating remaining flour gradually until dough is no longer sticky, about 10 minutes, and until a finger imprint disappears slowly. Wrap dough in plastic wrap and let rest 1–2 hours at room temperature. Any remaining flour should be sieved and reused in Step 3.

3. Use a pasta machine to knead and roll out dough after it has rested. Cut dough in half, set machine on widest opening (which is the lowest number), dust each piece of dough lightly with flour, and separately run through machine. Working with two pieces of dough, one after the other, dip one side of dough in flour lightly, fold in three, floured side inward, straightening edges to be as square as possible and pressing folded dough together with side of hand. Continue to knead in this fashion until dough is smooth and pliable; each piece will be about 12 inches long. When right consistency is reached, fold one more time without dusting with flour, and run through at widest setting.

4. Start thinning dough by running it through machine, changing setting each time until it has reached the thinnest setting. If dough becomes too long to handle, cut in half. Cover unused strips with cloth or plastic wrap to prevent them from drying out. Dough is now ready to be made into noodles or other pasta.

5. To make ravioli, place one strip of 5-inch wide pasta on floured board or towel, place 1 teaspoon of cool or chilled filling at 2-inch intervals in two rows, and cover with another strip of pasta, pressing around filling with side of finger or hand to press out any air trapped in between the pasta. If strips are narrower, it may be easier to put single row of filling on lower half of strip, folding upper half over filling on lower half of strip. In either case, press around filling to remove air. Using scalloped cutting wheel, cut into 1½–2-inch squares. If dough should become a little dry, seal edges with a little water before cutting.

6. To cook ravioli, bring a large pot with approximately 5 quarts of water to a boil, add salt, and cook about 10–12 ravioli at a time for 5 minutes or until *al dente* (firm to the bite). Serve as a first course with *Sauce Vièrge* (p. 68), Lobster Sauce (p. 199), or Tomato Sauce in the Style of Gazpacho (p. 68).

Makes approximately 40 ravioli. Pasta recipe can be doubled. Serve 5–6 to a person.

Seafood Filling for Ravioli

Farce de Poisson pour Ravioli

*1 combined tablespoon chopped
  onion and shallot*
1 tablespoon butter
½ cup shrimp, lobster, or *crab,
  cooked and cut into small dice*
¼ cup dry vermouth
*2 tablespoons spinach, cooked and
  chopped*
1 egg, beaten

2 tablespoons fine bread crumbs
½ teaspoon herbs: basil or *oregano
  or half of each*
Salt and pepper to taste
Pinch nutmeg (optional)
Fresh ravioli dough (p. 163)
Parmesan or *Emmentaler, freshly
  grated, served separately*

1. Simmer chopped onion and shallot in butter until soft, add cut up seafood, and simmer with vermouth for about 15 minutes.

2. Put mixture in bowl of processor fitted with steel blade and process quickly with spinach, beaten egg, bread crumbs, herbs, and seasonings. Cool or chill in refrigerator before making teaspoon-sized balls to fill ravioli (p. 163). Ravioli can also be made in 3–4-inch squares, each filled with 1 tablespoon of stuffing mixture. Serve ravioli with a separate bowl of grated cheese. Sauces are suggested in above recipe.

Fills about 40 ravioli.

Pasta Prepared Ahead of Time

Pâte Alimentaire Préparé à l'Avance

Certain types of pasta can be prepared ahead of time and sauced at the last moment without loss of quality if the following technique is employed.

*½ pound dried or fresh pasta:
  spaghetti, noodles, shells, risi,
  fettuccine,* or *capellini*

2 tablespoons olive oil
2 tablespoons butter
Salt to taste

1. Use large pot of boiling water to cook dried or fresh pasta. If cooking dried spaghetti, add about ½ teaspoon oil to lightly salted water and do not cut spaghetti. Stir at beginning of boiling to prevent strands from sticking together.

2. Start testing for doneness by biting a strand after the first 7 minutes—fresh pasta will cook in half that time. As soon as pasta is *al dente,* drain, place in a large dish, and add 2 tablespoons olive oil. Mix lightly, cover with plastic wrap and refrigerate until required. Bring to room temperature before reheating.

3. When ready to reheat *(chauffante)* and serve, heat the butter and ¼ cup water in a large skillet. The water prevents the butter from being absorbed by the pasta. Toss pasta in skillet for 30 seconds, then toss with desired sauce—mushroom, seafood, fresh herbs with butter, or fresh vegetables.

4. Rinse any leftover seasoned spaghetti and drain, leaving a little water to cling to pasta for reheating later.

Serves 4 as a light first course.

Noodles Gourmande   *Les Nouilles Gourmandes*

*½ pound noodles: fettucine or
   tagliatelle*
1 tablespoon butter
2 shallots, finely chopped
1 cup chicken broth
½ cup heavy cream

1 cup sour cream
4 ounces goose liver pâté, *diced*
1 tablespoon chopped truffles
Salt and pepper to taste
*2 tablespoons finely snipped fresh
   chives*

1. Cook noodles in boiling salted water until just tender, and drain.

2. In a large saucepan melt butter and add chopped shallots. Cook for a few minutes until shallots are soft but not browned. Pour in broth and cook for 3 minutes on high heat. Add heavy cream and sour cream and bring to a boil. Remove from heat and stir in *pâté* and truffles.

3. Gently stir hot cooked noodles into mixture in saucepan, along with finely snipped chives.

Serves 4–5 as an appetizer.

Chapter Seven

SEAFOOD

Les Poissons Are Poached, Braised,
Steamed, Sautéed;
Puréed for Quenelles and Ground for
Sausages

W hile I enjoy many kinds of cuisine, I must admit that I've always been especially fond of seafood—both the preparation and serving of fish. Their great variety and fine flavor probably account for this partiality.

Although authorities claim there are twenty-five thousand to thirty thousand species of fish, the edible varieties run only into the hundreds. Excluding shellfish, there are either round or flat, fresh water or salt water fish. Seafood dishes require little extra salt, as fish have already acquired salt from the sea. Since the fish has much less fibrous connective tissue than meat, it should not be overcooked, so test for doneness early.

I always keep a supply of fresh salmon in my walk-in refrigerator. This explains why I have given more space in this book to salmon than to any other species. To poach a salmon correctly, the basic poaching liquid, court bouillon (p. 174), must be prepared first and allowed to cool before the fish is placed in the liquid. If the liquid were boiling, the skin of the fish would break and the fibers or muscles would toughen. Many different fish are prepared this way. One of them is sole, which is the centerpiece of one of my favorite dishes, Sole *à la Nage* (p. 175): I place the fish in the cooled poaching liquid and arrange citrus fruit or vegetables in a pattern in the shallow baking dish. For scallops *à la nage,* instead of citrus fruit, sometimes I place thinly sliced, notched carrots in the poaching liquid floating with thinly sliced onion rings. The liquid is then simmered. I served the cooked garnishes on the dinner plate with the fish.

All the other cooking methods besides poaching are successful for cooking fish. These include sautéeing, braising, steaming, and cooking *en papillote* (see page 186). In light of possible health problems, I am not too enthusiastic about charcoal grilling, but I will give a few instructions:

Whole fish to be broiled may be seasoned inside with basil, tarragon, dill or fennel. The skin on the back is slashed to let the heat penetrate in such fish as porgy *(daurade),* mackerel, herring, or trout. Thin fish can be lightly dusted with flour first, while other fish are rubbed with vegetable oil and seasoned. Grease and preheat the rack of broiler pan. The fish should not be too close to the coals, about 6 inches away, basted often, and turned just once. It may not be necessary to turn fish at all, if started on a very hot receptacle. Fish sticks, fillets, and steaks broil well.

When fish is to be grilled, the coals should have turned gray and the flames should have died down. Fish can be supported in a hinged grill made of tinned steel with or without legs. These are made in various sizes, and must be oiled and preheated before fish are enclosed. Dried fennel stalks and rosemary are two herbs used to flavor fish. Baste frequently with oil or butter.

The gas grill and spit roaster have become increasingly popular today for both restaurants and home use. Mexican mesquite charcoal gives a very intense heat and cooks quickly. With any grill, do not start cooking until the flames have died down and the charcoal is reduced to a white ash. Some sauces to serve with fish are: flavored butter (p. 67), *Beurre Monté* (p. 66), *Sauce Verte* (p. 63), *Sauce Hollandaise* or *Mousseline* (pp. 58 and 59).

It is easier to stuff and serve a fish such as a sole or trout with its bones removed. *Le chef poissonnier* uses a special knife made of flexible steel called a *"filet de sole"* knife. This French knife is 6½ to 7 inches long, but if not available a sharp boning knife can be used. To bone a flat fish, make a cut or seam across the center of the side with the eyes facing up. Using the *filet de sole* knife, scrape the bones away from the flesh on either side of the backbone. Cut the bones loose with a scissors. Break the backbone into several pieces before removing. Fish stock can be made with the bones and heads. Place stuffing in cut side and cook with that side up. Although fish tastes better with the bones left in, it is easier to stuff when boned, as I stated above. Dover sole, flown to the United States from Europe, is more easily boned because its flesh is firmer than that of the Petrale and English sole found on the West Coast. Quenelles, mousses, or soufflés make fancy stuffings for fish. In Step 3 of *Gratin d'Ecrevisses aux Mousseline de Truite* I offer a method for preparing trout mousse that is much simpler and faster to prepare than Trout and Salmon Quenelles (pp. 196 and 189).

When selecting fish at the market, it is best to buy a whole fish. Look for an odorless fish with bright eyes and firm skin. Someone at the market or the cook can then fillet or cut it into steaks. Fish that are just caught have a protective coat or film like mucous on their skin which lasts for several hours. Large fish stay fresh longer than small ones; whole fish, after they are gutted, are less subject to contamination than fillets. Fresh fish and shellfish have a semitransparent look. In order not to overcook them, watch for the change in the flesh from translucent to opaque or intransparent. Sometimes, it takes only seconds for shrimp and scallops to turn opaque.

The fish that inspired European chefs to create great dishes was sole. It has a unique fillet of fine texture and delicate flavor. This flatfish, with a small mouth and little eyes set closer together, was named for its resemblance to the sole of a foot.* Unlike flounder, which are round in shape, sole are more elliptical and have thicker flesh. An expert can identify the true English sole by the ease with which the skin can be separated from the flesh. Dover sole received its name from the port of Dover, where the catch was landed a century ago and rushed to Billingsgate Market in London. Later fish dealers created new names for other flatfish, not as highly prized as sole, to help them sell, such as witch flounder, which was marketed as *gray sole*. Today, the authentic sole can be found in the United States, where it arrives by air freight from England, France, Holland, and Scandinavia.

* The following quotation gives a more accurate meaning to the name of sole *(Solea solea)*: "The name *Solea* is from the Greek, 'as the Greeks considered it would form a fit sandal for an ocean nymph.' " (Day) from *North Atlantic Seafood* by Alan Davidson (New York: Viking Press, 1980), p. 158.

Identification and Habitats of Sole, Flounder, and Other Flatfish †

Dover sole: Common sole of Europe found from Mediterranean to Denmark, Pacific flounder found from California to Alaska, weight 10 pounds; deepwater flatfish *called* Dover sole.

English sole: Small Pacific flounder found from northern Mexico to Alaska. Their fillets are attractive, but fish would not pass the sole test of the skin separating easily from flesh.

Lemon sole: French market name is *sole limande*. U.S. market name for a winter flounder over 3 pounds.

Winter flounder: Most abundant and popular eastern flatfish. The bay fish weigh 1–2 pounds; "sea flounders" can weigh 5 pounds.

Petrale sole: Large Pacific flounder found from Mexican border to Alaska—ranked first among Pacific flatfishes.

Rex sole: Small Pacific flounder found from southern California to Bering Sea. Delicate and of fine texture.

American plaice: Flounder marketed as dab, sand dab—found on both sides of Atlantic. French names in cuisine: *Carrelet* or *Plie*.

European flounder: Plaice found from Barents Sea to Bay of Biscay.

Summer flounder: "Fluke," 3–5 pounds found in U.S. from Maine to South Carolina.

Atlantic halibut: Largest flatfish (also a flounder), reaches weight of 600–700 pounds, length of 9 feet. Chicken halibut, under 10 pounds are the most

---

† Some of this information is from *The Encyclopedia of Fish Cookery*, A. J. McClane and Arie de Zanger (New York: Holt, Rinehart & Winston, 1977), pp. 251, 357–65.

popular. One of the largest of edible fish. Found from New Jersey to Greenland and northern European coast to English Channel. *Flétan* is French name.

California halibut: Left-eye flounder family, weight to 60 pounds; usually 4–12 pounds.

Pacific halibut: Meat superior to California halibut, fish is similar to Atlantic halibut. Main source is from Alaska.

Brill or *barbue:* European flatfish, related to turbot, more oval in shape than turbot. Found from Mediterranean to North Sea up to Bergen, Norway, and into the Baltic.

Turbot: Common name for several Pacific flounders. European flatfish equal or superior to sole, can weigh up to 60 pounds; turbot and halibut used interchangeably in recipes.

Turbotin: Small or "chicken" turbot.

French *raie:* 8–10 pounds, skate is closely related, common or flapper skate of Europe considered best for food; big skate and California skate best species on Pacific coast. Smooth butterfly ray and winter skate used on East coast.

Saint-Pierre or John Dory: Oval, flat, thick skinned, large spines on back, flesh similar to turbot and sole; common in Mediterranean, eastern Atlantic. Saint-Pierre is the patron saint of fishermen.

Some flatfish that may be interchanged in recipes are turbot and halibut, flounder, and fillet of sole. The following list describes the amounts of fish I serve on individual plates and the size of fish I buy for my restaurant:

Serve whole fish 12–14 ounces* to 1 person
Serve fillet of Dover sole 14–16 ounces to 1–2 persons
Serve fillet of Dover sole 16–20 ounces to 2–4 persons
Serve fillet of Turbot 6–8 ounces to 1 person
Serve whole lobster 1–1½ pounds (broiled, poached, or for sauce) for 1 person

For the kitchen I prefer to buy:

Turbot: 12–14 pounds
Turbotin: 4–6 pounds
Salmon: 12 pounds
Lobster: 1–1½ pounds for 1 person
Lobster: 2–3 pounds or larger for *médaillons*

* Approximately 30–40% of fish is lost in bones, skin, and head.

The Regal Salmon

Salmon has been crowned the king of fish, with its skin colored a regal silver and its flesh a soft orange. It not only has more meat than other fish, but it is the most tender and firm with the least bones. Salmon has enough natural oil to maintain moistness even if slightly overcooked. It lends itself to all cooking techniques: whole fish, fillets, and steaks are poached; steaks and *paillardes* are grilled; whole stuffed fish are baked; steaks or fillets are braised; whole salmon is smoked, then sliced very thin; large or small fillets are pickled (gravlax), made into a pie (coulibiac), into hash (tweed kettle), ground to make mousses and quenelles, and canned; served cold in aspic and salad; skewered for *brochettes de saumon*. Salmon roe makes superior light and dark red caviar. Finnish salmon soup, salmon tartare, and *Rillettes de Saumon* (p. 94) are produced from the flesh.

In California, we have fresh salmon almost the entire year. They are caught by California fishermen from May through October. From November to April we receive salmon from Oregon and Washington State caught by the Northwest Indians, the only people allowed by the government to catch salmon at that time of the year. I learned from years of experience that when the salmon is returning to spawn in the river, it is more oily, so it may be necessary to add more egg when making quenelles without a panade (p. 189). If quenelles are made with a panade, it may be necessary to add more flour. A panade is composed of a liquid—milk, water, or stock—heated and combined with flour or bread to add body to quenelles (p. 196) or terrines.

The way to remove the bones from a cooled, poached whole salmon is to remove the skin and thin layer of dark meat, the muscle; and depending on the size of the fish, cut top fillet into sections, removing with a large spatula. Remove the large backbone, and carefully replace the fillets in their original shape. Do not try to remove the skin of the side on which the fish is resting. To decorate, cover with *Sauce Chaud-Froid Blanche* (p. 56), thin cucumber, zucchini, or lemon slices.

Fresh salmon continues to be in the markets year-round, with Norway now supplying us in the early spring months when it might otherwise have been more scarce. That helps to explain why I have included thirteen recipes for the king of fish in Chapters 4, 6, 7, and 9:

Salmon *à la Nage* for a *darne* (center cut) or fillets (p. 175)
Poached Whole Salmon (p. 175)
Quenelles de Saumon (p. 189)
Saumon en Papillote (p. 186)
Saumon à l'Oseille (p. 178)

Mousse de Saumon (p. 99)
Mousseline of Scallops and Salmon (p. 192)
Terrine of Sole and Salmon in Three Colors (p. 102)
Salmon Soufflé with Zucchini, Green and Red
   Peppers, and Dry Vermouth (p. 178)
Smoked Salmon Quiche (p. 146)
Eggs in the Shell with Smoked Salmon (p. 134)
Fillet of Salmon with Whole Grain Mustard (p. 188)
Potted Salmon (p. 94)

The five species of salmon in North America* are the *Chinook* (king), first to appear in abundance in May, the most desirable of marine game fish from southern California to Alaska and Japan, weighing up to one hundred pounds; the connoisseur's fish. Rare white kings are even more succulent than deep pink ones.† The *Coho* (silver salmon, salmon trout), caught from Mexico to Alaska to Japan; *Pink* (humpback salmon), common to the west coast, smallest of five species; *Sockeye* (red or blueback salmon), whose red color does not fade in cooking and which can survive transportation better than other species—habitat from southern Oregon to northwestern Alaska and Asia; *Chum* (dog or fall salmon), found from southern California to northwestern Alaska and Asia, best fishing areas from Washington to British Columbia.

In the ice-free water of the fiords of the west coast of Norway, salmon are successfully bred in hatcheries that are controlled by the Norwegian government. There, the young fish are raised until they are six months old, then transferred to net pens near the shore and fed on ground fish and shrimp for two years, at which time they are harvested. This aquaculture produces unblemished, deep red firm-textured salmon, which are scooped into ice water tanks and flown abroad within twenty-four hours of their catch.**

*James J. Squire, Jr., and Susan E. Smith, *Anglers' Guide to the United States Pacific Coast* (Seattle, WA: U.S. Dept. of Commerce, November 1977), pp. 103–04.

† Susan Herrmann Loomis, "Savoring Seattle's Salmon," *The New York Times,* 29 July 1984, Travel section.

** Isaac Cronin and Paul Johnson, "Salmon Thrive in Norway Waters," Los Angeles *Times,* 14 February 1985, part VIII, p. 20.

Court Bouillon for Fish and Shellfish Made with White Wine

Court Bouillon au Vin Blanc

1 onion, sliced
1 carrot, sliced
2 sprigs parsley
1 bay leaf
1 sprig thyme or ¼ teaspoon dried

6 peppercorns, cracked
Salt to taste
2 cups dry white wine: Chardonnay, Muscadet, or Chablis
1 quart water or light fish stock

1. Place all ingredients in a large pot, bring to a boil, and simmer for 20 minutes. Let cool before poaching salmon, sole, turbot or other kind of fish or shellfish such as *écrivisses* (crayfish).
2. Amounts of ingredients and liquids are based on size of fish.

Makes 1½ quarts.

Court Bouillon with Lemon Juice or Vinegar

Court Bouillon au Citron ou Vinaigre

1 onion, sliced
1 carrot, sliced
2 sprigs parsley
1 bouquet garni (p. 6)
A few peppercorns

Salt to taste
¼ cup wine vinegar or juice of 1 lemon
1 quart water or light fish stock

Place all ingredients in a large pot, bring to a boil, and simmer for 20 minutes. Let cool before poaching fish. Water should be barely shimmering *(frissonner),* to prevent fish flesh from toughening.

Makes 1 quart plus ¼ cup.

Poached Fish
Poissons Pochés

Fish *à la Nage*   *Poissons à la Nage*

Almost any kind of fish can be poached in a court bouillon made with white
*wine: sole, halibut, turbot, flounder, trout, herring, or mackerel, to name a
few. This is also true of shellfish: scallops,* langouste *or lobster, crayfish, shrimps.
I do not recommend poaching with red wine, which discolors the court bouillon. However, salmon, sole, and eel can be* braised *with red wine. Turbot,*
darne *of 1 pound, takes 15–20 minutes to poach, while crayfish takes 2
minutes. Flatfish should be barely covered with liquid and simmered for 6–7
minutes with lid on and a sprig of thyme and 1/2 bay leaf added.*

6–10 ounce center cut (darne), *with
   bones,* or *fillet of salmon*
Court Bouillon (p. 174) to cover fish
*1 lemon, unpeeled, notched, and
   sliced*

1 orange, unpeeled, cut in wedges
Parsley sprigs
Salt and pepper to taste

1. Place fish in oval copper or stainless steel ovenproof pan. Cover with
   cooled Court Bouillon; place sliced lemon, orange wedges, and parsley
   sprigs around fish arranged in one layer.
2. Cover with aluminum foil, and poach on top of stove for 10 minutes or
   until done. Be careful to ensure liquid simmers, not boils! Fish may be
   poached ahead of time. Serve garnishes with fish. Serve with *Beurre Vert*
   (p. 67), *Sauce Beurre Blanc* (p. 64), *Sauce Hollandaise* (p. 58), *Sauce
   Mousseline* (p. 59), or *Sauce Vièrge* (p. 68). A sauce can be made of court
   bouillon with a small amount of butter swirled in. Serve with a green
   vegetable.

Serves 2 for a first course and 1 person for a main course.

How to Poach a Whole Salmon

7–8 pounds fresh salmon
*5–6 quarts Court Bouillon (p. 174);
   add water if more liquid needed*
Black olive for decorating
*Sliced cucumbers for decorating
   (optional)*

Sliced lemons for garnish
1 bunch parsley
Cheesecloth
Heavy aluminum foil (optional)
Fish poacher or larger roaster

175

1. Fish poacher requires a rack for lifting out fish and a lid, or large rectangular roaster can be used with heavy foil for a rack. Wrap fish in cheesecloth, place on rack in poacher, cover with cooled Court Bouillon and simmer until done, covered. Do not boil! If pan is too large for oven, place on two burners on stovetop.

2. Test early for doneness in order not to overcook salmon. One way is to insert a pointed knife through flesh in center of fish to spinal bone. If bone moves easily, it is done; or, test flesh by pressure—it should be slightly set. Instant thermometer should register 140 degrees when inserted in thickest section.

3. Let cool in Court Bouillon. Salmon can be left in a cool room overnight. The cooking liquid will be gelatinous.* Lift fish out carefully, unwrap, drain, peel off top skin, remove fins and dark part of salmon meat, which is muscle hemoglobin. This thin layer of dark meat is removed because it has a bitter taste; then the orange color of salmon is revealed.

4. To decorate: Remove the eye and replace with small black olive. Place notched round cucumber slices on top of fish to look like scales. Place slices of lemon around outside of platter. Sprinkle with chopped parsley.

5. Start serving salmon from the tail. Since this section is smaller, it will be more well done. Serve cold fish with *Sauce Verte* (p. 63), or Mayonnaise Vincent (p. 64).

Serves 10–12 for a first course.

* The Court Bouillon with gelatinous liquid drained from fish can be boiled down and used for aspic, fish sauces, or frozen. It will be necessary to add plain gelatin to reduced Court Bouillon.

Braised Fish
Poissons Braisés

Sole Bréval

METHOD A:

Butter for gratinée dish
1–2 tablespoons butter
2 shallots, chopped
4–6 fillets of sole (3 ounces each) or
*   fillets of salmon (4 ounces each)*
6–8 mushrooms, sliced
1–2 tomatoes, sliced

½–1 cup dry white wine: Chablis,
*   Chardonnay, or Chenin Blanc*
½–1 cup Court Bouillon (p. 174)
*   (optional)*
2–3 tablespoons heavy cream
Salt and pepper to taste
2 tablespoons chopped parsley
Parchment paper

1. Butter a large oval ovenproof gratinée dish with or without handles. Place 2 tablespoons butter and chopped shallots on bottom of dish with fish fillets on top in one layer. Arrange sliced mushrooms around fish and sliced tomatoes on top of fish. Add white wine or white wine and Court Bouillon to cover halfway up side of fish. Place a piece of buttered parchment paper on top. Cover loosely to allow steam to escape.

2. Place in 350-degree oven for 5–8 minutes or until fish tests done by pressing for firmness. Baste several times during braising.

3. As soon as fish is cooked, blend cream and salt and pepper into cooking liquid and serve garnishes in gratinée dish with chopped parsley on top of fish.

Serve 1 fillet to a person for an appetizer and 2 fillets to a person for a main course dish.

METHOD B:

Ingredients and cooking steps are the same, but sauce is finished differently with 1–2 tablespoons beurre manié *or 1–2 tablespoons* Sauce Hollandaise *(p. 58).*

1. Remove cooked fish and garnishes with skimmer, drain, and place on serving plate or platter. Keep warm in low oven.

2. Pour braising liquid from gratinée pan into a heavy pot, reduce to about one half the amount, and thicken sauce by stirring in 1–2 tablespoons *beurre manié* or *Sauce Hollandaise.* Add salt and pepper to taste. Pour over fish, sprinkle chopped parsley on top, and serve immediately.

METHOD C FOR FINISHING SAUCE OF SOLE BREVAL DISH:

1 egg yolk to make Sauce Sabayon
2 tablespoons heavy cream, whipped
1/2–3/4 cup reduced braising liquid of
  fish

In a heavy non-aluminum pot whisk egg yolk with 1 tablespoon water and stir in the whipped cream. Stir with whisk until partially thickened, then stir in fish liquid reduction. Place fish on heavy platter or plates, pour sauce over fish, and glaze under broiler for a few seconds.

Serves 4–6 for a first course.

Braised Salmon with Sorrel

Saumon à l'Oseille

1 cup dry white wine, such as Chenin Blanc
1 cup dry vermouth
2 shallots, minced
1–2 tablespoons butter
1–2 drops lemon juice

Salt and pepper to taste
32 sorrel leaves, washed, stems and veins removed, and shredded
6 salmon fillets, 6 ounces each, or *Rockfish fillets*
1 cup heavy cream

1. In shallow ovenproof pan large enough to hold fillets in single layer combine wine, vermouth, shallots, butter, lemon juice, salt, pepper, and shredded sorrel. Place salmon fillets on top. Cover and simmer on top of stove or in 325-degree oven until fish is cooked, about 7 minutes.

2. Remove salmon to warm serving platter and place in warm oven. Pour juice from serving platter into cooking pan and reduce liquid to one half.

3. On low heat slowly add cream and cook until sauce thickens. Spoon over salmon and serve immediately.

Serves 4–6.

NOTE: If fresh sorrel is not available, it can be obtained preserved in jars.

Salmon Soufflé with Zucchini, Green and Red Peppers, and Dry Vermouth

Soufflé de Saumon aux Courgettes, Piments Rouge et Vert, et Vermouth

MARINADE FOR FISH MOUSSE:
1 tablespoon olive oil
Pinch fresh tarragon, parsley, and green peppercorns

3 ounces scallops
2 ounces sole

REMAINING INGREDIENTS FOR MOUSSE:
2 egg yolks
Salt, pepper, and nutmeg to taste
1/2–3/4 cup heavy cream
2 egg whites

18 ounces salmon fillets, trimmed, skinned, and boned
3–4 small zucchini, thinly sliced and blanched

GARNISH FOR SAUCE:
1 tablespoon butter
1/2 tablespoon chopped onion
1 tablespoon peeled and chopped green bell pepper
1 tablespoon peeled and chopped red

bell pepper or *1/2 of 7-ounce can pimentos*
1 medium tomato, peeled, seeded, and diced

BRAISING LIQUID AND SAUCE:

1 tablespoon chopped shallots
1 cup dry vermouth or dry white
  wine

1 cup fish stock
4–6 ounces (8–10 tablespoons)
  butter

1. Marinate scallops and sole with olive oil and herbs for 5 hours or overnight. After fish is marinated, grind in a meat grinder, then purée in a food processor using steel blade. Add to mixture in processor 2 egg yolks, salt, pepper, and nutmeg, and as much heavy cream as needed. Remove to a mixing bowl.

2. Whip 2 egg whites until firm. Fold into fish mousse. Refrigerate until needed.

3. Cut prepared salmon into ten pieces of the same size (1½–2 ounces); salt and pepper fillets on top just before covering with 1 heaping tablespoon of mousse.

4. After covering fillets with fish mousse, placed sliced and blanched zucchini on top of each one to resemble scales of fish. In this step, you can arrange fish in a casserole as directed in Step 6, without liquid. Recipe can be prepared 2 hours ahead at this point and refrigerated. Remove from refrigerator ½ hour prior to cooking.

5. To make garnish, simmer chopped onion in 1 tablespoon butter until transparent; add prepared peppers and tomato. Cook until *al dente* and set aside.

6. Butter a low-sided ovenproof casserole or gratinée dish. Place half of the chopped shallots on the bottom; then arrange prepared fillets in dish and pour in ½ cup vermouth and ½ cup fish stock, or just enough liquid to braise without floating the fish fillets. Cover with buttered parchment paper and bake in 400-degree oven for 5 minutes. Remove juice from baking pan, reserve, and keep fish warm in *low* oven, or place fish on serving platter and keep warm.

7. In a skillet, sauté remaining shallots in a little butter for 2 minutes. Add remaining ½ cup vermouth, juice from baking pan, and ½ cup fish stock; reduce to concentrate flavors. Finish sauce by whipping in butter as for a *beurre blanc.* Strain sauce over garnish of cooked onion, peppers, and tomato. Pour around fish, served hot on individual plates or serving platter.

Serves 10–12 as an appetizer or first course.

Braised Trout Stuffed with Sorrel   *Truites à l'Oseille*

2 large trout or 6 small trout, whole
  but not cleaned
1½ pounds sorrel, washed, deveined,
  and chopped
4 tablespoons butter
  (approximately)
1 medium onion, chopped, or
  3 shallots, finely chopped

½ cup dry white wine (Chardonnay)
½ cup fish stock or Court Bouillon
  (p. 174) (approximately)
6 tablespoons heavy cream
Salt and pepper
Parchment paper

1. Slit top of fish with a sharp knife on either side of backbone to separate
   fillets, being careful not to cut skin of the fish belly. Use scissors to clip out
   backbone from head and about an inch from tail. Clean out fish, wash, and
   dry.

2. Prepare sorrel and make a purée—sauté in a few tablespoons of butter,
   salt, and pepper until sorrel "melts."

3. Season fish cavities with salt, pepper, and put in about ½ teaspoon butter.
   Fill with puréed sorrel. Put a little butter on top of fish and wrap each fish
   in parchment paper. Put a layer of chopped onions or shallots on bottom
   of shallow baking or gratin dish. Place fish belly down in dish, pour wine
   and Court Bouillon three quarters way up side of dish. Bake uncovered in
   a 375-degree oven for about 10 minutes depending on size of fish.

4. Remove fish, unwrap, remove skin, put on warm serving platter, and place
   in warm oven. Reduce cooking liquid to about one half. Stir in cream, salt,
   and pepper to taste and cook 2 or 3 minutes. Pour some over fish and
   serve rest in sauceboat.

Serves 6.

Sautéed Fish
Poissons Sautés

Rex Sole with Sorrel Sauce   *Sole à l'Oseille*

3 tablespoons each butter and oil
2–3 shallots, minced
32 sorrel leaves, cleaned and
  shredded
1 cup dry white wine, such as Chenin
  Blanc
1 cup vermouth

1 cup heavy cream
3 rex sole, whole, or fillets of petrale
  or Dover sole
Salt and pepper to taste
¼ cup milk
3 tablespoons flour

180

1. In an 8–10 inch sauté pan, heat 1 tablespoon *each* butter and oil, add minced shallots and simmer for 2 minutes. Add sorrel and sauté for several more minutes.

2. In same pan simmer white wine and vermouth for about 15 minutes or until reduced over one half. Taste to correct seasoning. Finish sauce, a few minutes before fish is ready to serve, by stirring in cream and simmering until sauce is thickened.

3. Clean fish with damp towel, season with salt and pepper, dip in milk and coat lightly with flour. In heavy sauté pan heat several tablespoons butter and oil and simmer fish for about 5 minutes covered loosely with a lid. Turn fish once halfway through cooking time, being careful not to break skin.

4. Remove whole rex sole from sauté pan and place on cutting board. Using a sharp knife, remove about ¼ inch of flesh from each side of edge of fish. Carefully cut off fillet from each side of backbone. Use a spatula to lift off fillets. Remove backbone and reassemble sole.

5. Place in a warm serving dish and pour sauce over fish.

Serves 3.

NOTE: Neither sliced lemon or chopped parsley are needed for this dish, as the sorrel gives both the sour flavor and the green color.

The sauce can be made ahead, adjusting the amount of wine and cream to the number of fish cooked. The fish should not be sautéed ahead of time.

Fillet of salmon and whole trout may be cooked by the same method.

Abalone with Scallops Flamed with Calvados

Abalone aux Coquilles Saint-Jacques Flambée Calvados

Calamari steaks made from large squid make an acceptable and far less expensive substitute for abalone. Fresh squid is also easier to obtain.

This creation won an award in a Calvados contest!

6 bay scallops or 3 large sea scallops, sliced
Juice of 1 lime

Salt and freshly ground pepper to taste

GARNITURE:

2 small leeks, sliced in half lengthwise, cut into fine sections, and julienned at one end (like a scallion brush)

1 carrot, cut in half lengthwise, core trimmed away, cut into 5 sections

2 ounces (4 tablespoons) sweet butter

2 tablespoons dry vermouth

1 Golden Delicious apple, peeled and cored

2 ounces Calvados

Two 2-ounce slices of fresh abalone, trimmed and pounded (reserve trimmings)

Flour for dusting

2 tablespoons heavy cream

1. Marinate sliced scallops in lime juice and pinch of salt.

2. Prepare *fumet* with abalone trimmings and scraps from vegetables—simmer for about 20 minutes. Gently poach vegetable garniture in enough water to cover and 1 tablespoon butter. Cook until vegetables are tender, about 7–8 minutes, remove with slotted spoon, and reserve in a warm place. Add this vegetable broth and vermouth to *fumet* and reduce to ¼ cup liquid.

3. Cut apple in half, and with a small scoop make 12 small balls. Make v-shaped cuts in top surface of other half to give a crown effect, working from center to outer edge. Sauté gently in 1 tablespoon butter, and add apple balls when nearly done. Flame with 1 tablespoon Calvados and keep warm.

4. Dust abalone with flour and sauté very quickly on each side (about 30 seconds). Do the same with scallops. Place abalone in center of plate and surround with 5 scallops, reserving the last one.

5. Deglaze pan with half of remaining Calvados, add *fumet* and cream. Bring to a boil, strain, whisk in remaining butter and season to taste with salt and freshly ground pepper. Add apple balls and pour sauce around abalone.

6. Place leek "fans" and carrot sections between each scallop. Place apple crown on top of abalone. Put last scallop slice inside cored apple crown to form a well. Pour in heated Calvados and flame at table or on serving table in dining room.

    Serve as a main course for a luncheon or dinner. A smaller portion can be served as a first course for a dinner. Serve with steamed rice or pasta such as noodles or plain or buttered spaghetti.

Serves 1.

Sea Scallops with Orange and Saffron

Coquilles Saint-Jacques à l'Orange et Safran

*1 pound fresh sea scallops
(approximately 16 pieces to a
pound)*
1 orange
1 tomato, skinned, seeded, and diced
½ teaspoon saffron threads

1 teaspoon butter
1 small shallot, chopped
2 tablespoons dry white wine
¼ cup cream
2 tablespoons chopped parsley
Salt and pepper to taste

1. Slice each scallop in thirds or ¼ inch thick. Place in a bowl.

2. Grate orange skin, being careful not to include the white pith, which is bitter. Squeeze juice and pour into bowl with scallops. Add grated peel, diced tomatoes, saffron, salt, and pepper. Marinate for 3–4 hours or longer in refrigerator.

3. Strain scallops—reserve marinade. Put butter and shallots in sauté pan, add scallops, and sauté for 1 minute—be careful not to overcook to retain flavor and tenderness. Remove scallops, add white wine, marinade for scallops, and cream. Reduce by one half.

4. Return scallops to pan, bring to a boil, and transfer immediately to serving dish. Sprinkle with parsley.

Serves 4 as an appetizer or first course.

Steamed Fish
Poissons Cuisson à la Vapeur

Steamed Fish   *Poissons Cuisson à la Vapeur*

*½ quart Court Bouillon (p. 174), if
    using pot 6 inches in diameter**
*Spices for Court Bouillon: choice of
    whole black, green, or pink
    peppercorns, mixed, or use just one
    kind; Szechuan pepper; few grinds
    nutmeg*
*1 pound salmon (center cut), cut
    into 4-ounce steaks, or other whole
    fish, fillets, or steaks*
Salt and pepper to taste
*Herbs: choice of fresh basil,
    marjoram, thyme, dill, fennel,
    tarragon, coriander*
*Chopped scallions to season fish
    (optional)*

Fresh ginger, slivered (optional)
Lemons, quartered
*Large pot fitted with perforated metal
    tray or steamer basket and tight
    lid, or fish poacher (poissonnière)
    with rack raised 1–2 inches above
    steaming liquid*
*Aluminum foil to cover top of fish if
    lid is not tight enough*
Cheesecloth to wrap whole fish

1. Steaming preserves natural juices of fish, prevents shrinking and drying out. It is similar to poaching, except fish must be 1–2 inches above court bouillon or other liquid. Before placing rack with fish inside pot, bring court bouillon to a boil and let cook for a few minutes with spices.

2. Prepare fish by seasoning with salt and pepper, sprinkling herbs, scallions, and ginger (if desired) inside. Wrap whole fish in cheesecloth to facilitate removal. Place on oiled rack, put in steamer, cover with tight lid, and maintain steady temperature of steaming liquid. Fish tests done in same way as poached fish—10 minutes per inch of thickest part of whole fish measured with a ruler perpendicular to table, or according to translucence of flesh, or looseness of bones.

    Serve with *Sauce Hollandaise* (p. 58), *Sauce Vièrge* (p. 68), melted butter *(beurre fondu)* or Butter Sauce *(Beurre Monté,* p. 66), or Flavored Butter (p. 67), and quartered lemons. Serve with boiled potatoes and green vegetables such as sugar snap peas or Spinach in Cream (p. 278).

Serves 4.

* The amount of fish determines size of pot and quantity of Court Bouillon.

Steamed Crustaceans and Mollusks

Crustacés et Mollusques à la Vapeur

In the area around Chesapeake Bay, I found that the local people use beer instead of court bouillon for steaming shellfish.

The quantity of each shellfish serves 2.
Choose from:
1 dozen oysters
1½ pounds mussels
2 dozen clams
2 lobsters, 1–1¼ pounds each
16–20 crayfish
1 large hard shell crab or 6 soft shell
  blue crabs
16–20 Hawaiian shrimp (6–8 to a
  pound) or 16 medium shrimp

½ cup Court Bouillon (p. 174) or
  liquid for pot 6 inches in diameter
  without a rack*
Spices for Court Bouillon: mixed
  peppercorns, nutmeg
Beer (instead of Court Bouillon) for
  blue crab from Chesapeake Bay
  and Baltimore
Unsalted butter
Large pot for steaming with tight
  fitting lid

1. Scrub and rinse oysters, mussels, or clams under running water. Soak mussels and clams in salted water for 2–3 hours or longer to reject sand.

2. I prefer to steam both crustaceans and mollusks without a rack, in a small amount of Court Bouillon in order to have a full-flavored juice from which to make a sauce. I reduce the juice as required and whisk in enough sweet butter to make a light sauce. The fruit of the sea has natural salt, eliminating the need for added salt.

3. Steam mussels with 2 tablespoons of Court Bouillon on low heat, covered, until they open. Use this liquid plus any mussel juices for sauce. Discard any mussels or clams that do not open. Steam oysters just long enough to be able to insert a knife into the shell to open.

Serves 2.

* The size of pot and amount of liquid is determined by the amount of seafood.

Landlubbers' Clambake

Steaming in an oven or on a grill requires a good supply of fresh seaweed. Scrub and soak clams or oysters first. Place seaweed on bottom of large pot or use foil. Place oysters or clams on top of seaweed, cover with more seaweed, place foil on top and cover pot with tight lid; or close foil package securely. Steam until shells open. Discard any mollusks that do not open. Serve with melted butter, unsalted, as the fruit of the sea has its own salt. A butter sauce may be made with juice from pot or foil.

The landlubbers' clambake prepared in the kitchen is a substitute party for the New England clambake held on the beach with participants gathering seaweed, driftwood, and rocks to fill the hole for the fire.

Salmon in a Paper Case   *Saumon en Papillote*

2 shallots, minced
8 mushrooms, sliced
2 tomatoes, peeled, seeded, and diced
1 cup dry white wine, Sauvignon
   Blanc or Chenin Blanc
Salt and pepper to taste
4 salmon fillets, 4–6 ounces each

1 cup heavy cream
4 sheets cooking parchment,
   approximately 15 inches square
   (lightweight foil can be used if
   parchment paper is not available)
Butter for parchment paper
Egg white for sealing edges

1. Combine shallots, mushrooms, tomatoes, white wine, salt, and pepper in a shallow pan. Bring to the boil, lower heat, place salmon fillets on top of vegetables, and cover. Simmer on top of stove until fish is half done—about 1 minute.

2. Drain salmon thoroughly and reserve.

3. Boil sauce until reduced by half. Add cream and stir. Continue cooking until mixture is again reduced by half.

4. Fold sheets of cooking parchment in half. Cut each into a half heart shape, as large as the paper allows. Open out into full heart shape and butter lightly. Place thoroughly drained salmon fillet on one half of heart. Top with one quarter of the sauce and fold other half of paper over contents. Brush edges of paper with egg white to seal, then complete the seal by folding and crimping the two edges together all the way round. Secure the point of the heart with an upward twist of the paper. Repeat with the other three salmon fillets.

5. Shortly before serving, place packages on a baking sheet and bake at 375 degrees for 3–4 minutes or until paper starts to brown. Slide onto warm dinner plates and serve in the parchment. (Each diner makes a large semicircular slit in the paper, which releases the fine aroma and allows access to the contents.)

186   Serves 4.

NOTE: This recipe can be prepared an hour ahead through Step 4. The method of cooking can be used for other varieties of whole fish, fish fillets, tender cuts of veal or lamb, and chicken breast. Be sure to cut a parchment heart large enough to enclose the filling with enough extra space to puff up while baking. Entrées baked *en papillote* retain all the flavor of the juices and do not become dry.

Fried Fish
Poissons Frits

Fried Fish Sticks

Filets de Poissons Frits en Goujons ou Goujonnettes

Flatfish are preferred, but fried fish sticks can be made with striped bass, sea bass, salmon cut against the grain.

The name Goujonnette *comes from a tiny fish called a Goujon found in the lakes and rivers of Europe. Fried small fish are called Friture de Petits Poissons (p. 93).*

1 pound fillet of tender flatfish: sole, turbot, flounder	*½ cup flour*
5 slices American white sandwich bread, trimmed	*2 whole eggs*
¼ cup beer or milk with ½ teaspoon granulated yeast dissolved in the (warmed) milk	*Salt and pepper to taste*
	1 bunch fresh parsley, trimmed of thick stems
	Vegetable oil for frying
	Lemon slices

1. Cut fish fillets into ½–¾-inch wide strips about 4 inches long. Dry well. Trim crusts off fresh sandwich bread, put in container of blender or processor to make crumbs. Store crumbs in refrigerator.

2. Arrange four separate shallow pans in row on counter containing: a) milk or beer (helps flour to stick to fish); b) flour; c) whole egg mixed with salt, pepper, and a little oil; and d) bread crumbs, which will not burn like flour.

   This coating is called *à l'anglaise* or *panure à l'anglaise, paner* meaning to bread. (Fish can be fried using only first two ingredients.)

3. Dip fish strips in each of the four ingredients in order given in Step 2. Drain off extra egg before dipping in bread crumbs. Roll strips in hands *(buissant)* before deep-frying in oil heated to 360–380 degrees. Fry about six sticks at a time.

187

4. Fry for about 1–2 minutes, using slotted spoon to remove. Drain on paper towels. After fish is cooked, fry parsley for a few seconds to serve as garnish. Fry a handful at a time—parsley will become crisp quickly.

   Serve as a luncheon dish or first course with *Sauce Tartare* (p. 112), *Sauce Tomate* (p. 41), or *Sauce Beurre Blanc* (p. 64) and lemon slices.

Serves 4–6.

Broiled Fish
Poissons Grillés

# Fillet of Salmon with Whole Grain Mustard	# *Paillarde de Saumon à la Moutarde de Meaux*

This appetizer or first-course dish with its contrasting sauces is very quick and easy to prepare.

For the restaurant I usually buy a 12-pound salmon. For the home kitchen a 4–6 inch center cut of fresh salmon can be sliced ¼ inch thick with the grain, which is very pronounced in salmon flesh.

Serve with thin sliced pumpernickel or bread of cook's own choice, or with finger sandwiches spread with butter.

The word paillarde *means flat—the procedure in Step 1 can be applied to veal and breast of chicken, which are flattened to be broiled or grilled.*

2½ ounce slice of salmon fillet, 4 x 4 x ¼-inch thick	*2 tablespoons whipped cream*
1 teaspoon moutarde de meaux *(whole grain mustard)*	*1 tablespoon white wine*
	Salt and pepper to taste
	Sauce Vièrge *(p. 68)*

1. Put salmon fillet (see illustration below) between two pieces of plastic wrap, flatten with a pounder to ⅛ inch thick, and center on a large, sturdy dinner plate.

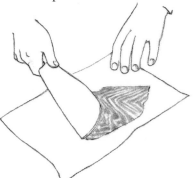 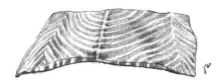

2. Combine mustard, whipped cream, wine, salt, and pepper and brush this mixture over entire surface of salmon.

3. Place under preheated broiler for 30 seconds, by which time fish will be cooked and the sauce very lightly browned.

4. Surround salmon with *Sauce Vièrge* and serve at once.

Serves 1.

NOTE: How to grill and broil fish is discussed in Introduction (p. 168).

Quenelles

Salmon Quenelles   *Quenelles de Saumon*

*10 ounces fresh salmon, skinned and
  boned,* or *14 ounces whole fish*
2 whole eggs
*3 ounces (6 tablespoons) heavy
  cream*
Pinch nutmeg

Salt and pepper to taste
*3 ounces (6 tablespoons) unsalted
  butter at room temperature*
*Large shallow pot about 4 inches
  high and 10 inches wide*

1. Grind skinned and boned salmon in meat grinder using fine blade or in processor fitted with steel blade. Then pass through a sieve, if necessary.

2. Put ground, strained salmon in blender container or bowl of processor and beat in eggs, one at a time, until mixture is creamy. Quickly add cream, nutmeg, salt, and pepper to taste. Do not overmix!

3. Using a wire whisk, beat room temperature butter to consistency of cold cream—this process is called *beurre en pommade*. Fold butter into quenelle mixture in processor or by hand.

4 Chill mixture for 5–6 hours or overnight. Form into sausage shaped morsels using 2 tablespoons dipped in cold water.

5. Poach in large pan of *simmering* water for about 10 minutes. Do not crowd pan. Quenelles sink to bottom of pan at first, rising to top as they are poaching. Test for doneness.

6. Quenelles will keep in cooking liquid under refrigeration for 5–6 days. If they are warmed up in cooking liquid, *do not boil!* A better method of reheating is to have quenelles covered with the light sauce in which they are to be served. Since quenelles expand when reheated, use a light sauce. Two quenelles require 1 cup sauce.

189

Serve with light Béchamel Sauce (p. 51), Nantua Sauce (p. 199), or White Wine Sauce (p. 54).

Makes about 14 quenelles when shaped with tablespoons.

NOTE: Fresh petrale or sole or red snapper can be substituted for salmon.

Quenelles of Turbot and Avocado
Quenelles de Turbot et Avocat

Small-sized quenelles of turbot and avocado can be used as a garnish with baked or poached fish dishes; they are an attractive pastel green color.

½ *pound fresh turbot* or *fluke, skinned and boned*
1–2 *ripe avocados, chilled*
4 *egg whites*

A few grinds nutmeg
Salt and white pepper to taste
¼ *cup heavy cream*

1. Chop fish and process lightly in food processor. Remove and set aside. Halve chilled avocado and scoop out enough flesh to measure 1½ cups. Purée quickly in processor, add fish and process until just mixed.
2. Quickly add egg whites through feed tube of processor, being careful not to overprocess.
3. Season with nutmeg, salt, and white pepper to taste. Add heavy cream with machine running.
4. Chill for 1 hour or more until ready to shape. Form into neat ovals using two spoons—dessert spoons for first-course-sized quenelles; coffee spoons for quenelles to be used as a garnish. Or use oval ice cream mold size of an egg. Poach in simmering water for 8–10 minutes. (Note: Forming quenelles quickly takes practice. Some home cooks find it easier to butter a non-stick skillet, carefully add the formed quenelles one by one, and then fill the pan with simmering water, pouring it gently down one side of the pan. Then poach as usual.) Serve with White Wine Sauce (p. 54) or Lobster Sauce (p. 199).

Makes 24 first-course quenelles.

Mousselines and Terrines of Seafood

Mousseline of Scallops

Mousseline Saint-Jacques, René Verdon

16 ounces fresh scallops, calico
  (Florida), bay, or sea scallops
1 whole egg
1 egg white
¾–1 quart heavy cream
½ tablespoon chopped truffles
  (optional)
A few grinds nutmeg

Salt and freshly ground white pepper
  to taste
1 ounce (2 tablespoons) butter,
  melted, for molds
8–10 small metal molds (oval
  shape) or ramequins, 2 inches deep
  and 3 inches in diameter

GARNISH:
1 bunch (1 pound) fresh spinach,
  shredded
1 bunch watercress, shredded

1 tablespoon butter
Sauce Beurre Blanc (p. 64)

1. Grind scallops in meat grinder using fine blade. Chill ½ hour in refrigerator. (Processor can be used, but it is not preferred.)

2. Place ground scallops, eggs, salt, pepper, and nutmeg in bowl of food processor fitted with steel blade and process for 1 minute only.

3. Pour cream through feed tube of processor, run for 3 seconds or just until blended. Overprocessing can cause mixture to get buttery. Fold chopped truffles, if using, in mousseline with a spatula and taste to correct seasoning.

4. Butter molds, spoon in mixture filling almost to top of mold. Place molds in a large rectangular pan (bain-marie), fill 1 inch high with hot water, cover with aluminum foil pierced with about 1 dozen holes to allow steam to escape, and bake in 350-degree oven for 30 minutes. Mousselines should bake slowly like a caramel custard; oven temperature should not be any higher than 350 degrees. Press tops to test for doneness. If solid, remove from oven and place on rack.

5. Sauté spinach and watercress in butter for 1 minute.

6. When ready to serve, place circle of spinach and watercress same size as mold on each warm plate. Unmold mousseline on top of garnish. Pour *Sauce Beurre Blanc* around each scallop mousseline and serve immediately.

Serves 8–10 as a first course.

Mousseline of Scallops and Salmon

Mousseline aux Coquilles Saint-Jacques et Saumon

*1 recipe Mousseline of Scallops
(see preceding recipe)*
8 ounces fresh salmon fillet
1 whole egg
1 egg yolk
*Salt and freshly ground pepper to
taste*

GARNISH:
*1 bunch fresh spinach, washed and
shredded*
1 bunch watercress, shredded

1 pint heavy cream
*16–18 small oval metal molds or
ramekins*
*Pastry bag, 1-inch round tip
(optional)*
*1 ounce (2 tablespoons) butter,
melted, for molds*

1½ teaspoons butter
Sauce Beurre Blanc (p. 64)

1. Prepare Mousseline of Scallops mixture at same time as salmon is prepared. Grind salmon in meat grinder using fine blade (can grind salmon after scallops without washing grinder). Cool in refrigerator for 30 minutes.

2. Without washing bowl of processor after using for scallops, put in ground salmon, 1 whole egg, 1 yolk, salt and pepper to taste, and process for 1 minute. Pour cream in a stream through feed tube until blended—about 3 seconds.

3. Butter molds; fill molds half full with scallop mousseline. Fill pastry bag with the salmon mixture and pipe it into center of scallop mixture until mold is filled to top.

4. Bang molds to even the tops before putting in low-sided rectangular pan filled 1 inch high with hot water; cover with foil pierced with small holes to allow steam to escape. Bake in 350-degree oven for ½ hour. Mousselines should bake slowly like a caramel custard, as too high a temperature would cause them to disintegrate. If a single large mold is used, bake 45 minutes to 1 hour.* Mousselines are done if tops are solid when pressed. Remove from *bain-marie* and put on rack.

5. Sauté shredded spinach and watercress in butter for 1 minute. When ready to serve, arrange bed of spinach and watercress on warm plates same size as mold. Unmold each mousseline on top of garnish. Pour *Sauce Beurre Blanc* around and serve immediately.

* This recipe will make two molds of 1½ quarts each—round (charlotte mold or soufflé ramekin), square, or rectangular. All should be 3 inches high or it will fill one 3-quart mold 3 inches high.

Can serve cold with *Sauce Cresson* (p. 63), *Sauce Verte* (p. 63), *Sauce Tomate* (p. 41), or a Fresh Tomato Sauce in Style of Gazpacho (p. 68). To reheat chilled mousselines: put in *bain-marie* in slow oven (325–350 degrees) for 15 minutes.

Serves 16–18 as a first-course dinner dish or main-course luncheon dish.

Seafood Sausage   *Cervelas aux Fruits de Mer*

1 pound onions
2 tablespoons butter
  (approximately)
2 pounds white calamari or *squid*
4 pounds fillet of sole
1 pound fresh, uncooked crab meat
  (removed from shell) or *1 pound*
  uncooked shrimp or *prawns,*
  shelled*
6 whole eggs, beaten slightly

1 quart heavy cream
1½ teaspoons salt (approximately—
  more may be needed)
½ teaspoon pepper (approximately—
  more may be needed)
Dash nutmeg
1 large truffle, chopped (optional)
¼ pound Bochwurst casings
  (approximate)
1 bunch parsley for garnish

1. Chop onions; sauté in skillet with butter until transparent. To clean calamari peel off speckled membrane from hood and pull out transparent, sword-shaped shell from inside. Then pull body with tentacles from hood. Wash well, removing all contents of hood. Dice squid, and sauté with onions, adding 1 tablespoon water. Cover and cook until dry. Remove from heat.

2. Put sole, crab, and/or prawns through a meat grinder using medium-sized blade. Place in large mixing bowl, stir in beaten eggs and cream. Add cooked calamari, salt, pepper, nutmeg, and truffle (if used).

3. Prepare sausage casings ahead (see p. 194). Use a funnel or sausage stuffing horn or pastry bag to stuff sausage mixture into casing. I usually use a sausage stuffing horn, which is an attachment of an electric mixer or electric meat grinder, to form the *cervelas*. Twist and tie sausages or *cervelas* into size you prefer. Tie with white string.

   Makes 35–40 sausages about 4 inches long and 1 inch wide when made from pork casings. If beef casings are used, recipe will make about 24 *cervelas* or sausages, for they are about 1½ inches thick.

4. Poach in large pot of barely simmering water (185 degrees F.) for 15–20 minutes. Sausages will keep under refrigeration for 5 or 6 days in a container covered with a damp towel.

* Both crab and prawns as well as about ½ pound fresh fillet of salmon may be included.   **193**

5. To serve, bring to room temperature and sauté in butter and oil as you would cook blood sausage, bochwurst, or frankfurters. Brown slowly so that they will not burst. Decorate serving platter with parsley and carved vegetables, or slice in 4 or 5 pieces on plate for individual serving with mirror of sauce on bottom of plate.

Several sauces to serve with seafood sausage are *Sauce Beurre Blanc* (p. 64), Lobster Sauce *(Sauce Homard à l'Anglaise,* p. 199), or *Sauce Vin Blanc* (p. 54).

Makes 35–40 sausages if using pork casings (24 sausages if using beef casings); serve 1 per person as an appetizer.

ABOUT SAUSAGE CASINGS:

There are fresh skins and salted skins. There are pork, beef, and lamb casings (or skins) made from the cleaned intestines of those animals. Soak casings preserved in salt in cold water for 24 hours or overnight. Add a dash of vinegar to the water. Before filling, rinse inside of casing with cold water. Sausage casings can be purchased from a butcher who makes his own sausage.

The Roving Trout

Flesh color ranges from white to brilliant red, depending on the diet in the waters the trout inhabits. Where trout (family *Salmonidae*) feed on crayfish or shrimp or red copepod in mountain lakes of the west, the flesh will be a deeper color.

By law, all trout in United States restaurants are from hatcheries, with the exception of lake trout and steelhead. Some of the best tasting species are:

Pink-fleshed brook trout *(Salvelinus fontinalis)* of central Labrador and Quebec
Crimson-meated rainbows *(Salmo gairdneri)* of southern Chile and Argentina
Fresh-run steelhead from Oregon's Rogue River
Native cutthroat trout *(Salmo clarki)* of the Rocky Mountains
Golden trout *(Salmo aguabonita)* of Sierra Nevada Mountains
Brown trout *(Salmo trutta)* from Iceland and Norway
Salmon or sea trout, also called *truite saumonée* or *omble chevalier,* live in both salt and fresh water all over Europe.*

---

* A. J. McClane and Arie de Zanger, *The Encyclopedia of Fish* (New York: Holt, Rinehart & Winston, 1977), pp. 410–22.

Trout are the most universally cultured fish for the commerical market. Domestic propagation began in the fourteenth century when Dom Ichon, a French monk, discovered that trout eggs could be artificially impregnated. In 1852 the first public-owned trout hatchery was begun in France. In 1864, Seth Green built a hatchery in Mumford, New York. He started with native Eastern brook trout, then hardier rainbow trout of the West Coast. In 1886, Von Behr of Germany sent the first brown trout to America. By the beginning of the twentieth century, rainbow trout was shipped throughout the world.

Boning and Skinning a Trout
(***Désosser and Dépouiller une Truite***)

1. Using a sharp knife or scissors, cut off sharp fins along backbone and belly.

2. Lay fish on its side and make a diagonal cut below head and behind gills halfway through fish—in other words, do not cut its head off. Next make a slit along length of fish where back fins had projected.

   Almost parallel with the table, scrape along backbone to free flesh. Make a shallow cut just above tail and lift fillet free. Turn trout over and repeat on other side, leaving head and tail attached by the backbone. Reserve these trimmings for fish stock.

3. To skin fillets, hold tail end securely between thumb and forefinger, flesh side of trout uppermost, and scrape knife blade against skin. The fillet will "curl" away from skin in one piece. Repeat with other fillet, and check both for tiny bones along edges, using a finger to locate—run a knife under small bones to remove tiny bones with a little flesh.

   This method can be used for any round fish, such as mackerel, salmon, rockfish or sea bass, snapper. Use a needlenose pliers to remove remaining bones from *truite saumonée* and *saumon*.

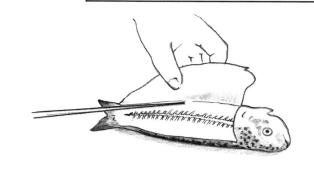
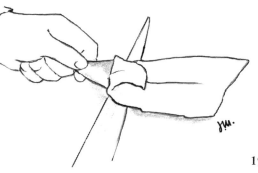

Trout Quenelles *Quenelles de Truite*

PANADE:
1 cup milk
3 ounces (6 tablespoons) butter
4½ ounces (1 cup less 2 tablespoons)
* flour*
4 egg yolks

5 trout, 8–10 inches each, after
* boning and skinning (reserve*
* heads, skin, and bones for Essence*
* of Trout)*
¼–½ cup Essence of Trout (see
* below), chilled*

3 egg whites
1 pint heavy cream
Salt and white pepper to taste
Nutmeg to taste

1. To make panade, bring milk and butter to boiling point, stir in flour all at once, and beat well. Off the heat, beat in egg yolks one by one. Allow to cool.
2. Using fine blade of meat grinder, grind trout meat with panade.
3. Transfer to bowl of food processor, fitted with steel blade. Add chilled Essence of Trout, egg whites one at a time, cream, and seasonings. Be careful not to overprocess. Chill several hours or overnight.
4. Shape and poach in fish stock as explained in Steps 4 and 5 for Salmon Quenelles (p. 189).
5. Trout quenelles can be refrigerated for 2 or 3 days if placed on a damp towel and covered with plastic wrap, or they can be frozen. (Thaw in refrigerator before heating in sauce.)
6. To serve, cover with sauce of your choice, such as *Sauce Vin Blanc* (p. 54), light *Sauce Béchamel* (p. 51), or *Sauce Nantua* (p. 199), and heat in 375-degree oven for about 10 minutes. Quenelles will puff up.

Makes 20 large or 30 medium quenelles; serves 10 as a first course.

Essence or Extract of Trout *Essence ou Extrait de Truite*

3 tablespoons butter
1 large shallot
1 large rib celery, cut up
1 large carrot, cut up
1 large onion, halved

Heads, skin, and bones of 4 trout
1 bay leaf
8 black peppercorns
1 cup dry white wine, such as
* Chardonnay or Chablis*

1. In a heavy saucepan, melt butter, add a layer of vegetables, then fish bones and seasonings. Cover with 3 cups water.

2. Steam, covered, for about 20 minutes. Mixture should simmer slowly.

3. Add wine, and simmer until liquid is reduced by half. Strain through dampened cheesecloth and reduce to 1 cup. Refrigerate. (Can be frozen.)

Makes 1¼ cups.

Crayfish au Gratin with Trout Mousse

Gratin d'Ecrevisses aux Mousseline de Truite

12 crayfish (écrevisses), *about
    1 pound—Red Claw* (Patte Rouge)
    are best for flesh
1 quart Court Bouillon (p. 174)
½ cup Crayfish Butter (Beurre
    d'Écrevisses, *see following recipe*)
1 medium trout
1 egg white

½ cup heavy cream
*Salt and freshly ground pepper to
    taste*
Pinch nutmeg
*1¼ cups Sauce Hollandaise (p. 58)
    made with Crayfish Butter*
1 tablespoon Cognac

1. Clean crayfish thoroughly, removing intestines, extreme end of which is found under middle of tail where it is pulled out. Otherwise, crayfish may have a bitter taste.

2. Simmer crayfish in Court Bouillon for 2 minutes only. Remove meat from tails to serve on finished platter. Reserve 3–4 shells to decorate plates, and save rest of shells to make crayfish butter. Crayfish butter must be made in advance.

3. To make trout mousse, remove skin and bones of trout, which will leave 3 ounces of flesh. In a blender or food processor grind trout, then blend with egg white, cream, salt, pepper, and nutmeg. Pass through a sieve, if mixture is not fine enough. In a small baking dish, bake mousse for 2–3 minutes in a 350-degree oven.

4. Make *Sauce Hollandaise*, cutting recipe in half and using ½ cup melted Crayfish Butter, which is automatically clarified.

5. To reheat crayfish tails, simmer in butter for 2 minutes. Remove from heat and flame with Cognac.

6. To assemble: On a round ovenproof platter place crayfish tails in center, surround with a circle of mousseline of trout, spoon *Sauce Hollandaise*

197

over crayfish tails, and glaze under broiler just until it begins to brown. Watch carefully! Arrange 3 reserved whole crayfish shells on outer rim of platter.

Serves 3 for a first course.

Crayfish Butter   *Beurre d'Ecrevisses*

Crayfish butter is always available in my freezer, for I make it whenever I have a good supply of crayfish shells reserved for that purpose. It is a simple but time-consuming process. So home cooks may wish to prepare it in advance before it is actually required.

1 pound crayfish shells
½ carrot
½ onion
2 shallots
1 rib celery

1¼ pounds (5 sticks) unsalted butter
½ bay leaf
Pinch thyme
¼ cup Cognac

1. Save shells of *écrevisses* or crayfish after removing meat from previous recipe. Pound shells in mortar and pestle, or grind in food processor using steel blade.

2. Make a *brunoise* with carrot, onion, shallots, and celery by cutting into small dice about ⅛ inch across. Simmer in 4 tablespoons butter in a covered pan until soft, about 10 minutes.

3. Add pounded shells to *brunoise* of vegetables and flame with Cognac. Place in double boiler or *bain-marie* with bay leaf, thyme, and the pound of butter. Let butter melt slowly. Simmer for about 3 hours.

4. Line a strainer with cheesecloth and set over a bowl of ice. Pour butter into strainer. After butter has solidified on ice, dry it with a cloth and put in a container. Store in refrigerator or freeze. It is used as an enrichment in seafood sauces.

   Shrimp and lobster shells are used to make *Beurre de Crevettes* and *Beurre de Homard. Beurre de Crabe* is made with crab shells in the same way as *Beurre d'Ecrevisses.*

Makes approximately 2 cups.

Two Seafood Sauces
Deux Sauces pour Poissons

Nantua Sauce   *Sauce Nantua*

1 cup Béchamel Sauce (p. 51)   *1 tablespoon heavy cream*
¼ cup cream   *Pinch cayenne pepper*
3 tablespoons Crayfish Butter   *Dash of brandy or Cognac*
  (p. 198), or shrimp or lobster butter

1. Make Béchamel Sauce, add cream, and reduce by one third.
2. Soften Crayfish Butter, whisk in sauce and add cayenne, brandy or Cognac.
    Serve with quenelles of salmon or trout; blend with pasta.

This sauce is a substitute for the classic *Sauce Nantua,* as explained at the conclusion of the recipe for Lobster Bisque (p. 25).

Serves 4.

Lobster Sauce   *Sauce Homard à l'Anglaise*

These two sauces are quick to make when crayfish or lobster butter have been made ahead and are frozen. The classic sauce for lobster is on page 26 of recipe for Lobster Bisque.

1 cup Béchamel Sauce (p. 51)   *Pinch cayenne pepper*
*2 tablespoons Lobster Butter (*Beurre   *2 tablespoons diced lobster meat*
  de Homard, *p. 198)*
½ teaspoon anchovy paste

Make Béchamel Sauce, add Lobster Butter, anchovy paste, and cayenne pepper. Taste to correct seasoning. Stir lobster meat in at last minute to prevent toughness.

Serve with Seafood Sausage (p. 193), Quenelles of Turbot and Avocado (p. 190); blend with pasta.

Makes 1 ¼ cups; serves 4.

Bass in Puff Pastry

Loup en Croute

3 pounds puff pastry (Pâte Feuilletée,
  p. 307)
1 striped bass, 6 pounds

(approximate weight), or *a whole
salmon can be substituted for
striped bass*

MARINADE:
1 teaspoon chopped fresh tarragon
1 teaspoon chopped fresh chervil

¼ cup Cognac
Salt and pepper to taste

MOUSSE:
½ pound raw prawns, shelled
1 egg white or 1 whole egg
1 cup heavy cream

Salt and pepper to taste
Pinch nutmeg
1 tablespoon Cognac

1 egg yolk for glaze

1. Make *Pâte Feuilletée* in advance. Marinate fish with Cognac, herbs, salt, and pepper for 1 hour.

2. Prepare mousse by grinding raw prawns in food processor or blender. Purée while adding egg white or whole egg. Beat in cream with wooden spoon, placing mixing bowl over ice. Add seasonings and Cognac.

3. Roll *Pâte Feuilletée* into two thin sheets large enough to encase whole fish. Place fish on top of one sheet of pastry and cover with mousse. Place second piece of pastry over mousse. Seal edges with cold water.

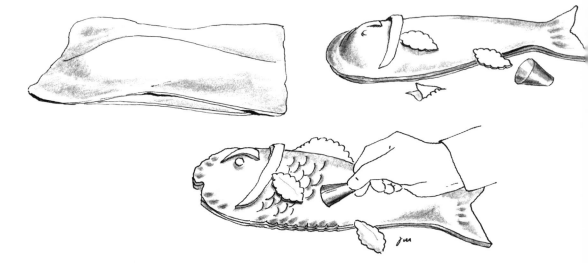

4. Decorate pastry to resemble scales, gills, head, and tail of fish. Glaze with egg yolk mixed with 1 teaspoon water. Bake in 350-degree oven for 45 minutes to 1 hour.

    Serve with *Sauce Béarnaise* (p. 60), *Sauce Choron,* or *Sauce Beurre Blanc* (p. 64).

Serves 10 for main course, 15–18 for hors d'oeuvres.

Chapter Eight

MEATS and POULTRY

Les Viandes Are Stewed and Braised; *Les Volailles*—Chicken, Turkey, Pheasant, *Poussin*—Are Roasted, Boned, Stuffed, and Braised

In moving from *le chef poissonnier* to *le chef rotisseur* and *grillardin* (handler of roasting and broiling), we go to the world of meat and poultry *(la viande et la volaille)*. The produce I prepared in advance for the techniques and recipes demonstrates the method of *mise en place* (p. xvi): the club steak to be larded (see p. 210) has been trimmed of excess fat, the plump chicken to be trussed has been cleaned, and the vegetables pared as if they grew that way.

I start with the veal for *Blanquette de Veau,* since it has to cook 1½ hours. In advance, cut up the breast, shank, or shoulder in 1½-inch cubes. Next, blanch the veal to remove any impurities, especially when it is to be served in a cream sauce. To blanch: cover veal with cold water, bring it just to a boil, instantly drain in a colander, and rinse under cold water. The same treatment should be used for boiled beef and sweetbreads *(ris de veau).* However, it is not necessary to blanch veal cutlets or the veal used in the preparation of Veal Chasseur, a stew made with stewed tomatoes, fresh mushrooms, white wine, tarragon, and Brown Sauce. *Sauce Chasseur* (p. 48) is especially appropriate for white meat such as poultry and veal, although it is used for lamb and other meat. The word *chasseur* means hunter or huntsman.

Chapter 2 dealt mainly with sautéed beef and veal dishes. In this chapter duck, turkey, chicken, veal, lamb, rabbit, and beef are roasted, stewed, braised, and poached. To compare sautéing with the latter methods, it is easy to decide which is faster; for to sauté is akin to the Chinese style of stir-frying. It is well known that tougher cuts of meat require slower and longer cooking times. Line drawings or charts of beef, lamb, and veal show the location of various cuts of meat. These locations explain their degree of tenderness. The tenderest meat, which is muscle, lies along the backbone and is called the loin. The muscles least used by the animal are the tenderest; these include the ribs as well as the loin. The tough cuts are from the shoulders, legs, and lower belly. Tender cuts are cooked with dry heat (broiling, roasting, pan broiling), whereas the tougher cuts are cooked with moist heat (braising or poaching slowly in a large amount of liquid).

When shopping for meat and poultry the cook soon learns how to detect freshness and quality. Observing the color is one of the best ways, especially for veal: the most tender veal is a pinkish white because it is milk fed, while the darker pink veal is grass fed. Veal fed on grass is more like baby beef. Beef that is corn fed has a richer flavor than grain fed beef, which has yellower fat. The color of fresh, correctly aged beef should be bright red. Brownish red means it has been exposed to air. Old beef, also, is a dark purplish red, while young beef is always brighter in color. Young spring lamb is a light rose color, in contrast to older lamb, which has a darker tint. Freshness can be judged by the fat of lamb: if the fat is dry, it is old; if it is moist and firm, it is fresh. Poultry should have glistening, clear, creamy white skin without any brown or dry spots. The skin color is influenced by their feed. A fresh smell to the meat and firmness to the touch are other important ways to judge freshness.

Prime and Choice are the only two grades of meat that can be aged—stored for 2 to 6 weeks at a temperature between 34 and 38 degrees F. Veal is never aged. Organ meats—sweetbreads, brains, liver, and kidneys—are very perishable. So is ground meat, which should be used as soon as possible. When meat and poultry are stored in the refrigerator, they should be wrapped loosely in butcher paper to keep the surface dry.

Chefs' tasks are not so far removed from the butcher's trade when it comes to boning meat and poultry and grinding meat for stuffing. Partially or completely boned birds present a more elaborate main course dish. Ever since I opened my restaurant, I have had *Globi de Volaille* on the menu. It requires some skill to bone (p. 230) in order to make the chicken half, shaped like a pear and stuffed, stand on the plate. *Poussin à l'Alsacienne* is a recipe I devised when California poussins came on the market a short time ago. It is a little simpler to bone than the *globi,* for it is supported by a parchment paper case, made by hand, to act as a baking dish for each bird (p. 232). The most advanced preparation is the *Dodine de Faisan* (p. 237), which is boned similarly to the *globi* up to the step that disconnects the breast from the leg. The two marinations for this dish are responsible for the 48 hours it takes to complete.

A *dodine* is actually a small *ballottine,* which is a boned, stuffed bird or piece of meat or fish braised in stock and wine and served hot. A Dodine of Pheasant, which is served cold, is a different dish; briefly, the stuffed bird is wrapped in a towel and cooked in a heavy stock which includes gelatinous pigs or calves feet.

My Dodine of Chicken *(Dodine de Poulet)* serves four persons—it is made from a whole breast and stuffed with a mousse of veal and spinach (or mousse of veal and lobster or crayfish) served with a sauce of half cream and half lobster sauce. It is served sliced on a platter, garnished with watercress and a vegetable. My similar preparation for duck consists of the leg stuffed with ground veal or lean pork and mushrooms, called a *jambonette.* I cook it

205

like a confit, covered with duck fat, and present this dish for one person served with wild rice and a green vegetable. The knob end of the leg is covered with a frill, and watercress garnishes the plate, with a notched lemon slice.

To help differentiate the meaning of the two words, *ballottine* and *galantine,* it may help to note that the word *ballottine* begins with the same letter as the word *braising*—which is the cooking process used for a ballottine. A galantine is usually made from a large bird such as a whole chicken, turkey, duck, etc. The bird is boned, stuffed, rolled, and tied into a cylindrical shape, wrapped in a cloth, completely covered with liquid such as water, wine, and stock, and poached with the lid on. After the galantine is cooked, it is cooled in the poaching liquid, unwrapped, and decorated with its own aspic or *Chaud-Froid Sauce* (p. 57). These two cooking methods produce excellent buffet dishes for a large party or a first course for a dinner.

Internal Temperatures for Roast Meat

The instant meat thermometer, one that is inserted in the meat for testing toward the end of roasting time, removes the guesswork from determining the degree of doneness. When the thermometer is inserted, it should never touch the bone of the meat or rest in fat. This aid is only 5 inches long and has a range of 0–220 degrees F. Based on the type used in laboratories, this thermometer is so sensitive it registers in less than a minute. If the roast is brought to room temperature before putting it in the oven, it is easier to gauge the cooking time. I recommend roasting in a 350–375-degree oven unless otherwise stated.

INTERNAL TEMPERATURE:

Veal *(le veau)*	160–165 degrees	medium (pink in center)
Veal	170 degrees	well done
Lamb *(l'agneau)*	130–140 degrees	rare
Lamb	145 degrees	medium rare
Beef *(le boeuf)*	130–140 degrees	rare
Beef	160 degrees	medium
Beef	170 degrees	well done
Pork *(le porc)*	170 degrees	well done
Lamb	170 degrees	well done

Roasts may be removed from the oven when they reach an internal temperature 5–10 degrees lower than the chart recommends, as the meat continues to cook while it "sets" or rests *(reposser)*. However, it is not advisable to remove *very* rare roasts ahead of time—they will not have enough internal heat to continue cooking. To prevent meat from cooking further after removal from the oven, elevate it from any juices by tilting the pan. Roasts should not be carved as soon as they are removed from the oven. Allow the juices to congeal or "set" for 15–20 minutes. The larger the roast, the more setting time is required.

Roast Fillet of Beef *(Filet de Boeuf Rôti)* should be cooked faster at a higher temperature in order to keep it from drying out. Roast in a 450-degree oven, which will require about 35–40 minutes cooking time for a 4–6-pound fillet. Let it rest 10–15 minutes before carving into ½-inch thick slices.

Internal Temperature:

Beef, fillet or tenderloin	120 degrees	very rare
Beef, tenderloin or fillet	130 degrees	rare
Beef, prime ribs	120 degrees	rare
Beef, strip roast	140 degrees	medium rare

The New York strip or sirloin strip *(contre filet rôti)* can weigh from 12–18 pounds. Average roasting time is 60–65 minutes to 1 hour and 15 minutes in a 375–400-degree oven.

My Method for Slicing Braised or Roasted Meats

Here are a couple of reasons for starting to slice from the smaller end of the roast. First, the more well done meat at the smaller end will *not* continue to cook; and second, the rarer meat at the thicker end will continue to cook and stay warm at the same time. (Slice whole poached fish the same way.)

The Best Way to Use Flour When Stewing or Braising Beef and Other Meat

For as long as I can remember I was taught to brown flour separately for stewed or braised beef, lamb, venison, or wild boar. Coating stew beef, *Boeuf à la Mode* or *Boeuf Bourguignonne,* with flour before it is browned and seared will cause flour to burn, marring the taste of the sauce. There are three ways to brown the flour without this result, using the proportion of 1 to 2 tablespoons flour to 1 quart stock and wine, to be added *after* flour is browned:

1. Sprinkle flour over and around browned roast on stovetop or in the oven, stirring over heat until the flour is browned, about 10 minutes;

2. Remove browned meat, pour out the fat, discard any burned particles which might give a bitter taste, and brown flour on medium heat. Return meat to pan, add amount of stock and wine required for a ragout or braised beef; cook in a 300–325-degree oven or simmer on top of stove.

3. Flour can be browned without using any fat if several tablespoons of it are put on a pastry sheet in a 350–375-degree oven and turned with a

207

spatula occasionally until it acquires a light brown color. Of course, add it to pan with browned meat.

Since flour is meant to thicken the sauce, it will have plenty of time to cook this way, and it will give a more brilliant color to the finished sauce, in contrast to a *beurre manié* added after the sauce is reduced, which makes the sauce cloudy, as I stated in Step 8 of Brown Sauce (p. 39). In the Introduction to Sauces (Chapter 2), I mentioned that I do not ever use flour when making a sauce for roasts with the natural juices and stock made from the bones of the lamb for roast leg of lamb or extra beef bones for prime rib of beef. If a different sauce is used, the name of the dish is changed. The same technique is used for sirloin of beef, roast squab, quail, turkey, or chicken. I might add a little cornstarch to give a slight sheen and firmness to the sauce. *Au contraire,* I do use flour for a giblet sauce as suggested in Step 5 of "How to Roast a Turkey."

Salt and the Preparation of Vegetables, Meats, and Other Dishes

The role salt plays in preparing vegetables is contradictory, in a sense. On the one hand, a small amount of salt in the cooking water, about ½ teaspoon, will help maintain the green color of green vegetables such as string beans, broccoli, spinach.

On the other hand, salt will draw out the water in vegetables:

1. Tomatoes to be stuffed will reject their juice when cut in half, salted, and turned upside down.
2. Cucumbers become more digestible if they are sliced, salted, and allowed to drain.
3. Eggplant and zucchini, sliced and sprinkled with salt, will lose most of their water in about ½ hour while they drain in a colander.

Meat should never be salted in advance, as the salt will draw out the blood. Just before serving the meat, when it is arranged on the plate, add a little salt to bring out the flavor. When preparing any dish such as a terrine, mousse, or timbale, it is better to add the salt at the end of the preparation, because the only way to correct a mixture with too much salt is to make a second unsalted batch to add to the first oversalted one.

Marinades for Meat and Game
Marinades des Viandes et Gibiers

Uncooked Marinade   *Marinade Cru*

3 cups red or *white wine*
½ cup red or *white wine vinegar*
1 cup olive oil
1 large onion, sliced
1 large carrot, sliced
2 cloves garlic, peeled or crushed
1 celery rib, sliced
1–2 sprigs parsley
1 teaspoon green peppercorns or
  6–8 black peppercorns

1 bay leaf
*2 sprigs fresh thyme or ½ teaspoon
  dried*
6 crushed juniper berries (Genièvre)
  *and 6 coriander seeds added for
  venison and lamb*
Salt and pepper for seasoning meat

1. Amount of liquid is determined by size of roast or amount of stew beef. Correct proportions of wine, vinegar, and oil are stated in list of ingredients. Marinade should just cover meat to keep air out. Ingredients can be mixed together and poured over meat, or added separately, as the oil will rise to the top. Use a deep enough bowl for the meat so that it is completely covered.

2. Length of time meat is marinated depends on the variety, cut of meat, and how it is to be used. Anywhere from 18–48 hours is suggested, during which time meat should be refrigerated. Turn meat several times. Leave at room temperature only 6–8 hours. Vegetables placed on top of meat will impart flavor.

3. Dry white wine is used in place of red wine when it is required in the sauce, for example, to prepare Sauerbraten.

4. Dry meat well before cooking.

TWO OTHER UNCOOKED MARINADES:

Unsweetened papaya juice tenderizes meat.
Onion and garlic juice mixed with olive oil and water to equal ½ cup marinade for 1 pound of lamb. Turn often.

Cooked Marinade for Meat   *Marinade Cuite*

*Ingredients same as Uncooked
    Marinade (see preceding recipe)
    except—*

*Wider choice of herbs for Step 2:
    rosemary, mint, marjoram, ginger,
    basil, coriander,* or *cilantro
Spices for Step 2—a few cloves, 1/8
    teaspoon cracked pepper*

Sauté aromatic vegetables—sliced onions, carrot, celery, and crushed garlic —in a little oil until brown. Then simmer with remaining ingredients for ½ hour. Let cool. Meat will keep longer in cooked marinade. Always store marinade with or without meat in a non-aluminum pan in refrigerator. This marinade gives a venison taste.

Use for fillet of venison or beef; rack, leg, or loin of lamb; sirloin of beef; beef stew; or loin of pork, which will develop a wild boar flavor.

1. Cooked marinade keeps longer than one that is not cooked. It can be reused as long as it is boiled again, strained, and reboiled once a week. When reheating marinade, add an appropriate amount of wine and vinegar. When cooked marinade is reduced, it can be used for sauce or as an ingredient in a meat sauce.

2. Any cut of meat that is aged and cannot be used right away will keep under refrigeration better if it is marinated in uncooked or cooked marinade completely covered to exclude air. Meat must be turned over every day in wine, vinegar, and oil marinade. Use a container just large enough to hold meat comfortably. Do not use salt! Use cracked pepper, bay leaf, cloves, and herbs. Dry meat well before cooking.

3. Cubed meat or poultry for shish kebab does not have to be completely covered with marinade containing oil and lemon juice instead of wine vinegar. Meat has to be turned occasionally.

4. Steak that has *not* been marinated can acquire an herb flavor by making a little brush with sprigs of rosemary, thyme, and a bay leaf to dip in oil and baste steak while it is being broiled or barbecued.

    Fresh or dried rosemary, thyme, bay leaves, and juniper berries can be tossed on coals before and during barbecuing.

Larding
Larder

Larding is used for meat lacking in fat. It adds fat and flavor to the inside of the meat muscle. Fresh pork fat is best, which should be cut into lardoons or strips from a rectangular slab. It should be kept cool and placed skin side downwards to cut into the size strips required for the meat.

The lardoons *(lardons)* are inserted into the meat by a larding needle *(lardoir)* or a larding spike with a wooden handle.

Fat from salt pork or bacon can be used after it is parboiled.

Other ingredients used for larding to give flavor, but not to add fat, are anchovies, ham strips, and marinated veal. Strips of fat can be used at the same time as anchovies, ham strips, or marinated veal. When meat is sliced, the inserted lardons give color and a marbelized appearance.

How to Truss a Bird of Any Variety
Brider or *Trousser*

Trussing maintains the attractive shape of the bird until it is ready to be carved. It also keeps the legs and wings from drying out.

1. Thread a French trussing needle with strong, white string. Tie string to eye of needle. Fold tip of each wing under large wing bone, akimbo style, to make the wing flat.

2. Lift up the two legs. Starting from the right and leaving some string hanging from the puncture, run the trussing needle through the back of upper right thigh (second joint), through the body of chicken, and out through the back of the left thigh. Continuing with the same needle and thread, go through back of arm of left wing, through neck skin and middle of back, on through back of large bone of second wing. You are now on the same side where string is waiting to be tied tightly together with end of string left in needle. Tie.

3. Thread trussing needle again. Leave 3 or 4 inches of string at entry. From right side put needle through tail piece, run needle through lower end of left leg, then through lower end of right leg where string left at entry is met. Pull strings tight and tie. This also closes cavity of chicken.

How to Bard the Bird
Barde

1. It is necessary to bard partridge, pheasant, squab, pigeon, and guinea hen to protect the breast which is the driest part.

2. It is best to use a thin sheet of fresh pork back-fat. It can be pounded thinner between two sheets of waxed paper. Drape over the breast, or tie on. Salt pork or bacon can be used if they are pounded first, then simmered in water for about 5 minutes.

3. In order to brown the skin, the bard should be removed from the breast before the bird is through cooking.

211

How to Slide Truffle Under the Skin
Truffer

Place sliced truffle under the skin of the poultry using your finger to push the slices under the lower part of the skin of the breast. Do not put slices at the top of the breast where they might fall out.

How to Bone a Bird
Désosser

METHOD A: The procedure—boning the bird with back skin cut—is similar for turkey, chicken, poussin, duck, squab, quail, and pheasant. The smaller the bird, the softer the bones.

1. Use a sharp boning knife *(couteau à désosser)*. A scissors is also useful to have. Place bird breast side up. Remove neck if not done by butcher. Remove wing at second joint.
2. Turn chicken over and slit chicken down backbone. Start scraping meat away from backbone by pushing knife against bone. Repeat on other side.
3. Find the ball joint of both thighs and disconnect. Use same procedure for ball joint of shoulder. Scrape the meat from the large bone of the wing and remove bone.
4. Scrape meat away from the breastbone and disconnect the keel of the breastbone by cutting along the soft cartilage. This releases the carcass but does not cut the skin of the front of the bird.
5. Scrape meat away from thighbone and remove. To remove drumstick, disconnect tendons with knife. Scrape away meat.
6. Leg bones can now be removed, if desired. You may leave tip of the drumstick bone by cutting bone halfway down with scissors.

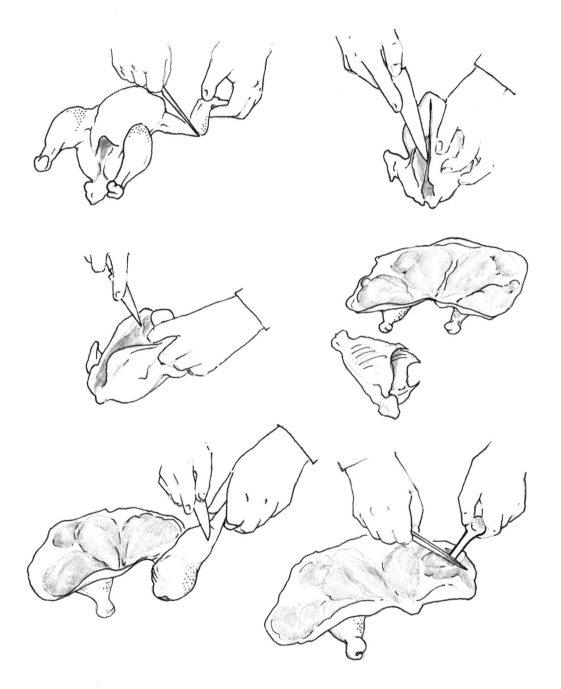

METHOD B: How to bone a squab *(pigeonneau)*, poussin, or a game bird *(gibier)* without cutting the skin.

1. Snap each thighbone out of socket by putting one thumb on thigh, other on bird's body close to hip joint, and exerting pressure.

2. Working with bird breast side up, push skin back from neck and locate wishbone with fingers. Scrape meat away from wishbone with fingers and a sharp knife, and remove.

3. Pushing back both skin and flesh, locate wing bone joints. Cut cartilage to separate bones from carcass. Scraping with knife tip, free wing bones from carcass.

4. Turn back skin and flesh to expose the ribcage and backbone, working around skeleton to free it.

5. Cut tendons and hip joints to free thighbones. Detach carcass from tail. Scrape back flesh from thighbones and detach them at leg joints.

6. Pull out carcass, leaving leg and wing bones intact, with the bird turned inside out. Turn bird right side out. Bird is now ready for stuffing and re-forming into its original shape.

How to Carve a Turkey at the Table
Découper

1. Let turkey rest 20 minutes before carving. Place on a large sturdy platter or carving board *(planche à découper)*. Use sharp carving knife and have sharpener at hand. A carving fork helps to hold the bird or roast steady.

2. Remove the leg and thigh first. Find the joint connecting the drumstick to the thigh and sever the drumstick. Next, sever the joint that connects the thigh to the backbone and carve into uniform slices parallel to the bone.

3. Make a horizontal cut deep into the breast where the wing is attached. Find the joint where the wing is attached and remove the wing. The large section of the wing can be carved also, or place the wings on either side of the serving platter.

4. Now the carver *(le trancheur)* is ready to carve the breast into thin slices: Place carving knife a little below "keel" of breast bone and slice to the cut made before removing the wing. The slices should fall away from the turkey. Slice just enough for the first serving. Arrange dark and white meat slices on warm serving platter decorated with parsley.

How to Roast a Turkey
Dindonneau Rôti

Roast turkey is almost as popular in France during the holiday season as it is in the United States. But the preparation techniques differ at least to some extent, for turkey is stuffed and roasted in France in a different traditional style than is used here.

1. In France the stuffing sometimes consists of chestnuts *(marrons)* and chipolata, very small link sausages. Cognac is sprinkled inside the turkey before it is trussed (p. 211).

2. The neck and gizzard are roasted in the pan around the bird. Use a deep roaster to hold steam coming from juices and vegetables. Place sliced carrots, onions, and celery in roasting pan after turkey is half cooked—they create steam to keep turkey moist. An American touch is fresh rosemary, basil, sage, and thyme scattered with vegetables and stuffed in the neck.

3. Roast turkey first quarter of cooking time on one side, second quarter of cooking time on other side, third quarter of cooking time breast down, fourth quarter of cooking time breast side up or on the back. If breast starts to get too brown, cover with foil.

4. Roast 15-pound turkey 3 hours in 350-degree oven. Roast 25-pound turkey 5 hours in 350-degree oven. An instant thermometer inserted in thickest part of thigh without touching any bone should register 180–185 degrees when turkey is done.

5. To make the sauce: Remove turkey when it tests done and skin is well browned; let it rest 20 minutes on a warm platter to give juices a chance to settle. Remove juices from platter before carving. Degrease pan juices and strain out vegetables. Deglaze *(déglacer)* pan with Madeira wine. Peel and chop roasted gizzard to add to sauce, if desired. Cornstarch diluted with stock, water or wine can be used to thicken sauce. Giblet sauce can also be thickened with Brown Sauce (p. 39) or a *beurre manié.* Taste to correct seasoning. Serve in sauceboat.

6. To carve turkey: Remove trussing strings. Decorate platter with watercress and preserved or fresh fruit for presentation at table. Have ready a separate platter to arrange turkey slices, wing, and leg bones. Start carving by turning turkey on one side, first removing wing and then the leg. Breast meat can be sliced in long thin slices or as suggested in "How to Carve a Turkey at the Table" (above). Serve with a purée of yams or *Gratin de Pommes de Terre Dauphinoise* (p. 269) and a green vegetable.

215

Old-Fashioned *Blanquette* of Veal   *Blanquette de Veau à l'Ancienne*

2 pounds veal from breast, shank, or
shoulder, cut into 1½-inch cubes
3–4 cups white veal stock or *water*
1 tablespoon flour to make a blanc—
mix flour with ¼ cup water to add
to veal cooking liquid to keep veal
white
1 carrot, sliced
1 onion, stuck with 2 cloves
1 celery rib, sliced

FOR VELOUTÉ SAUCE:
2 tablespoons butter
2 tablespoons flour
1 cup sauce strained from the
reduced veal poaching liquid
¼–½ cup cream

Bouquet garni—parsley, thyme, bay
leaf tied with a string (wrap in
green stalk of leek)
½ teaspoon salt
12–16 small mushrooms, poached in
a little water, salt, and lemon juice
for 1 minute
12–16 small onions, poached for 5
minutes and peeled, saving
cooking liquid

2 egg yolks
¼ teaspoon salt
⅛ teaspoon white pepper
Pinch nutmeg
2–3 teaspoons lemon juice

1. Blanch veal as described in Introduction (p. 204). This is a white stew so that the veal is *not* seared first, that is, not browned in hot oil.
2. Cover veal with water or white stock, add *le blanc,* aromatic vegetables, *bouquet garni,* and salt. Simmer, covered, for 1½–2 hours until veal is tender. The stew can be simmered on a burner or in a 300-degree oven in a heavy casserole.
3. Remove cooked veal cubes to a saucepan. Add to the veal the blanched mushrooms and tiny onions with half of their cooking liquid.
4. Reduce veal poaching liquid in casserole by half.
5. Use a heavy saucepan or double boiler for the Velouté Sauce. Use a whisk to make a roux with the butter and flour. Cook 7 minutes. Strain 1 cup of reduced sauce from the veal into the roux, stirring to thicken. Add more veal stock and cream if sauce is too thick.
6. Mix egg yolks with a little cream before adding to the sauce. Add salt, pepper, nutmeg, and lemon juice. Pour over veal and *simmer,* not boil, for 2 or 3 minutes. Serve with steamed rice.

Serves 6–8.

NOTE: This sauce will curdle if *Blanquette de Veau* is boiled again as a leftover dish.

Old-Fashioned Veal Fricassée *Fricassée de Veau à l'Ancienne*

This recipe should be learned by contrasting the method of cooking a brown stew with that of Blanquette de Veau à l'Ancienne, *a white stew.*

2 pounds shoulder or breast of veal,
  cut into 1½–2-inch cubes
3 tablespoons butter (approximate
  amount)
1 carrot, sliced
1 leek, sliced
1 medium onion, sliced
1 rib celery, sliced
3 tablespoons flour (approximately)
3 or 4 cups fond blanc or *white veal
  stock*
1 cup dry white wine: Chablis,
  Macon, White Burgundy, or Grave

1 bouquet garni *(see preceding
  recipe)*
Onions and mushrooms (see
  preceding recipe)
2 egg yolks
½–1 cup heavy cream
Salt and pepper to taste (white
  pepper preferred)
Pinch nutmeg
1 teaspoon lemon juice
  (approximately)
1½ tablespoons chopped parsley or
  chopped chives

1. Blanch veal, dry carefully, and sauté in butter in heavy casserole or skillet until browned. (Do not use aluminum, as it will darken egg-enriched sauce.) Remove veal. In same pan lightly sauté sliced carrot, leek, onion, and celery. Add the flour slowly with a little more butter, if necessary, stirring to make a white roux.

2. Return veal to casserole, add enough stock to just cover veal and the wine, and bring to the simmer, shaking pan to blend roux with stock and wine. Add *bouquet garni,* cover tightly, and simmer slowly on top of stove or in a 300–325-degree oven for 1½ hours or until tender.

3. Ten minutes before cooking is completed, add 16 poached, small, white onions and the stock in which they were simmered. Add 16 mushroom caps which have been cleaned and kept white in lemon water.

4. When veal is cooked, remove and put in a warm oven. Remove *bouquet garni.* Skim fat from sauce, reduce on high heat until it coats a spoon, and remove from burner. Beat 2 egg yolks with ½ cup heavy cream or more, blend in a little of the sauce from stew (this prevents curdling), and pour this mixture into casserole, blending and stirring with wooden spoon. Be careful not to crush onions and mushrooms. Return to fire and stir until sauce *almost* reaches boiling point. Do *not* allow to boil.

5. Correct seasoning with salt, white pepper, a few drops of fresh lemon juice, and nutmeg. Return veal to pot, mixing it in sauce until it is hot. Serve *Fricassée* in heated deep dish. Sprinkle with parsley or chives.

Serves 6.

Veal Chop Trianon   *Côtes de Veau Trianon*

1 cup mushrooms
½ cup cooked ham
¼ cup truffles
½ cup grated Gruyère cheese
3 tablespoons butter
2 cups sour cream
*4 veal rib chops or veal cutlet from
    leg, 1 inch thick, 3 inches long,
    8 ounces each*

Salt and pepper to taste
*½ cup dry white wine, such as
    Chardonnay*
½ cup Brown Sauce (p. 39)

1. Cut mushrooms, ham, and truffles into slivers or fine julienne slices. Heat 1 tablespoon butter in pan and sauté mushrooms for 2–3 minutes until dry. Add slivered ham and truffles. Off heat, mix in 1 cup sour cream and ½ cup grated cheese. Let mixture cool in order to congeal—refrigerate for several hours.

2. Make slit through center of veal chop without separating from bone. If cutlet has no bone, be careful to leave two cut halves attached. Place waxed paper over each cut section; using a metal pounder *(batte),* pound to flatten veal to ¼ inch thickness without breaking veal.

3. Lightly salt and pepper veal, and place stuffing inside veal. In heavy sauté pan heat 2 tablespoons butter and sauté stuffed veal chops for 5 minutes on each side or until done.

4. Remove veal to warm serving platter and place in warm oven. Deglaze pan with dry white wine on medium heat; add Brown Sauce and 1 cup sour cream on medium heat, stirring to make a cream sauce. Taste to correct seasoning. Pour around veal and serve.

    Serve with braised endive, celery, salsify, or steamed asparagus.

Serves 4.

Veal Cutlets Chasseur   *Escalopes de Veau Chasseur*

2 tablespoons butter
2 tablespoons oil
*2 veal cutlets, each ½ inch thick—rib
    chops, loin chops, or veal from leg*

*6 mushrooms, sliced fairly thin or
    quartered*
½–¾ cup Sauce Chasseur (p. 48)
1 tablespoon finely chopped parsley

1. Heat butter and oil in heavy sauté pan, brown cutlets on each side, with

pan partially covered, sautéing for about 6 minutes. Remove from pan, place on warm serving platter, and keep warm in low oven.

2. A few minutes earlier or simultaneously, sauté mushrooms briefly in separate pan.

3. Heat *Sauce Chasseur* in same pan used to sauté veal, or quickly make sauce using ingredients listed in recipe for sauce (p. 48).

4. Pour sauce around veal and decorate tops of cutlets with sliced mushrooms and parsley.

     Serve with noodles and a green vegetable such as Spinach in Cream (p. 278).

Serves 2.

Veal Prince Orloff   *Veau Prince Orloff*

This elaborate dish not only gives the cook an opportunity to make basic preparations given in this cookbook, but it can be assembled ahead of time for a party of 8–10.

4–5 pound leg of veal, boned, rolled,
   and tied
Salt and pepper
2–3 tablespoons butter and oil
2 carrots, sliced
1 onion, sliced
Veal bones from roast, cracked
2 cups white stock
1 cup dry white wine
1 bouquet garni
2 cups dry Duxelles (p. 274)

2 cups Sauce Soubise *(p. 55)*
3–4 cups Sauce Mornay *(p. 52)*
1 tablespoon each grated Gruyère
   and Parmesan
1 tablespoon butter
Braised or steamed vegetables to
   garnish platter: choice of endive,
   artichokes, or *asparagus, trimmed*
Roast potatoes
Heavy casserole with tight lid

1. Wipe veal roast with damp towel, season with salt and pepper, and brown in butter and oil on medium-high heat in heavy casserole. Brown sliced carrots and onion with veal.

2. Add veal bones, stock, and white wine to cover half of veal, *bouquet garni* and braise in 325-degree oven, with lid on, for approximately 2 hours. Baste occasionally, and use instant thermometer to test for doneness. When it registers a little below 160 degrees, veal will be pink inside—remove

and tilt roast on platter to prevent further cooking in its own juice. Let cool before slicing. Pour pink juice into sauce.

3. Degrease, strain, and reduce braising liquid to serve around roast or in sauceboat.

4. Dry Duxelles and *Sauce Soubise* or onion purée can be made a day ahead of time and *Sauce Mornay* earlier in the day. Béchamel sauce for *Soubise* should be thick.

5. If roast was cooked ahead and chilled, slice in ¼ inch slices, keep in same shape of roast, and bring to room temperature before heating assembled dish.

   To assemble: Use a heatproof gratinée dish for roast or a platter, reconstruct roast in original shape, placing duxelles between each slice, *Soubise* purée on top of assembled veal, and cover all with *Sauce Mornay*. Sprinkle top with grated Parmesan and Gruyère and dot with butter. Heat in 350-degree oven for 15–20 minutes or until heated through. Put under broiler to glaze *(glaçer)* top.

6. Place braised or steamed vegetables around roast, if served on a platter. Otherwise, serve vegetables in separate dish. Pour some reheated sauce around roast, serve rest of sauce in a sauceboat.

Serves 10.

NOTE: I use a saddle of veal with bones when I prepare this dish in my restaurant. It usually weighs around 8–10 pounds and serves about 10–12. The saddle is not boned, but it is trimmed so that it can be carved easily.

Veal Chop with Sorrel Sauce   *Côte de Veau à l'Oseille*

1 veal steak or chop, boned,
  6–8 ounces
Salt and pepper to taste
Flour for dredging
1½ tablespoons butter or half butter
  and half oil

1 teaspoon minced shallots
1 tablespoon dry white wine
6 or more sorrel leaves, stems and
  veins removed, shredded
¼ cup heavy cream

1. Salt and pepper veal, and dredge lightly with flour. Do this just before cooking, or coating will become soggy. (Veal needs this coating to keep moisture inside meat.)

2. Heat butter in a heavy skillet and sauté veal until done, partially covered, about 10 minutes, turning once halfway through cooking time.

3. Remove meat and keep warm on serving platter in low oven.

4. In same skillet, simmer minced shallots for several minutes, deglaze pan with white wine, and add shredded sorrel. Cook for 2 minutes, then add cream. Reduce sauce on medium heat until thick enough to coat veal, about 3 minutes.

5. Spoon sauce over veal and serve immediately.

Serves 1.

VARIATION: Veal Chop with Chives is done the same way, using 2 tablespoons chopped chives.

Chicken Breast with Sorrel Sauce   *Suprême de Volaille à l'Oseille*

Substitute 1 chicken breast for veal chop (have butcher leave large wing bone on, remove rib bones).

Proceed as directed for Veal Chop with Sorrel Sauce, browning chicken first and then cooking for about 10 minutes in partially covered pan. Cooking time depends on size of chicken breast.

Serves 1.

Noisettes of Lamb with Yogurt   *Noisettes d'Agneau au Yogourt*

An excellent summer dish.

MARINADE FOR LAMB:
½ onion
1 clove garlic

8 noisettes of lamb, 1½ inch thick, boned and trimmed loin of lamb (carré d'agneau ou selle d'agneau)
2 cucumbers, peeled
2 tablespoons olive oil
¼ cup lamb or veal stock

1 tablespoon olive oil and ¼ cup water

3 tablespoons chopped chives
6–8 ounces plain yogurt
6 mint leaves, chopped
Salt and pepper to taste
Mandoline to cut cucumbers or a grater

221

1. To make marinade for lamb: Squeeze together onion and garlic to get their juices using a vegetable juicer, or purée in a food processor with ¼ cup water. Strain and discard solids. Add olive oil and water to make ½ cup of marinade. Marinate lamb noisettes 24–48 hours (no longer), turning occasionally.

2. Using *mandoline,* cut peeled cucumbers as thin and in as long pieces as possible.

3. Season with salt and pepper and sauté noisettes in skillet with olive oil until cooked rare, about 1½ minutes on each side. Keep warm. Remove; degrease and deglaze pan with lamb stock and half of chives.

4. Have pan of boiling water ready to dip in cucumbers just long enough to warm up and serve crisp-tender.

5. Heat yogurt just long enough to take the chill out. It will curdle if overheated.

6. To serve: Arrange individual plates with a border of yogurt, sprinkle mint over yogurt. Place noisette in center of plate, add the shredded cucumbers on top of yogurt around lamb, then pour pan sauce around lamb. Sprinkle rest of chopped chives on top of lamb.

Serves 4.

Lamb Chops Champvallon · *Côtelettes de Mouton Champvallon*

2 large onions, sliced thin
4 tablespoons butter and oil
  (half butter, half oil)
2–3 pounds potatoes, peeled, sliced
  thin (new red potatoes preferred)
4 lamb chops, preferably shoulder
  chops, 1 inch thick

1 cup stock
Salt and pepper to taste
2 cloves garlic, peeled
Bouquet garni—sprig parsley, thyme,
  and bay leaf

1. In a large sauté pan, sauté thinly sliced onions in 2 tablespoons butter and oil until lightly browned. Remove onions with slotted spoon, brown thinly sliced new potatoes, adding more butter and oil if necessary. Remove potatoes and sauté chops, turning several times until meat is seared inside. Pour fat from pan, and deglaze with stock.

2. Butter a shallow baking dish, and put layer of potatoes on bottom, then a layer of onions, the chops, and finish with layer of onions and potatoes on

top. Salt and pepper each layer. Add stock to go halfway up sides of casserole. Intersperse garlic and *bouquet garni.* Do not cover!

3. Braise in a 350-degree oven for 40 minutes or until done.

A green salad would be appropriate to serve after this homey, family kind of dish, a variation of *Pommes de Terre Boulangère* (p. 270).

Serves 3–4.

Tournedos Henry IV   *Tournedos Henri IV*

4 artichoke bottoms, cooked and
 trimmed
8 tablespoons Sauce Béarnaise
 (p. 60)
4–6 potato sticks, cut about 3 inches
 long with 1-inch square or cubed
 ends*

Oil for frying potatoes
4 tournedos or filet mignon, about
 1½ inches thick
4 croutons, sautéed in clarified
 butter, same size as tournedos
1 bunch fresh watercress bouquet to
 serve on plate

1. Prepare in advance artichoke bottoms (p. 256) and the *Sauce Béarnaise.* Fry the potatoes in a heavy skillet.

2. Broil tournedos until medium rare. Place crouton on warm plate, set tournedos on crouton, then the artichoke on top of tournedos and spoon Béarnaise sauce into artichoke bottom. Garnish with watercress bouquet.

Serves 4.

NOTE: If 4–6 Tournedos Henry IV are served, arrange fried potatoes in center of platter with beef and artichokes alternating in a circle or oval (depending on shape of platter) around potatoes. Watercress bouquets should alternate with circle of beef and artichoke bottoms filled with *Sauce Béarnaise.*

* Not only did *Sauce Béarnaise* receive its name from the capital of Provence, Béarn, the home of King Henry IV, but this style of potatoes, called *Pommes Pont-Neuf,* was named from a bridge built in Paris by Henry IV. The potatoes resemble the piles used in construction of the bridge.

Tournedos Louis XV

Recipe is the same as Tournedos Henry IV except that *Pommes de Terre Soufflées* (p. 262) are used instead of *Pommes Pont-Neuf.*

Tournedos Chasseur

Cook tournedos as described for Steak Bordelaise (p. 42). Fried croutons to put tournedos on are optional.

Remove sautéed tournedos from pan, keep in warm oven, and prepare *Sauce Chasseur* as described on page 48 with optional addition of 2 tablespoons brandy added before the wine, and a teaspoon of tarragon and chervil with the chopped parsley.

Filet Mignon with Raisins in Black Peppercorn Sauce

Tournedos Vigneronne

1 tablespoon seedless dark raisins
1 tablespoon Cognac
1 tablespoon crushed black
*   peppercorns or green peppercorns*
Salt to taste
2 tournedos (filet mignons), well
*   trimmed, about 6 ounces each*

1 tablespoon butter for sautéing
*   croutons*
2 croutons cut same size as the meat
½ tablespoon butter
½ tablespoon olive oil
½ cup Brown Sauce (p. 39)
1 tablespoon heavy cream (optional)

1. Macerate the raisins in the Cognac for 1 hour. Press the crushed peppercorns and salt into both sides of the steaks.

2. Sauté croutons in butter (or brown in the oven without butter) to make toast. Keep warm.

3. Heat the butter and oil in a heavy skillet. Sauté tournedos for about 2½ minutes on each side for medium rare meat. Remove from pan and keep warm.

4. Deglaze pan with Cognac and raisin mixture, being careful as it will ignite. Stir in Brown Sauce, reduce for a few seconds, and add heavy cream, if desired.

5. Place steaks on top of toasted croutons, pour sauce over steaks, and serve at once. Plain cooked spinach (p. 271) may be substituted for croutons.

Serves 2

Hunter's Chicken   *Poulet Chasseur*

3 tablespoons butter
3 tablespoons oil (olive oil preferred)
2 chickens, 3 pounds each, cut up
Salt and pepper
3–4 tablespoons flour
3–4 shallots, chopped
1–2 cloves garlic, minced
1½–2 pounds fresh mushrooms,
   sliced and chopped

1½–2 cups dry white wine, such as
   Chardonnay
4 tomatoes, peeled, seeded, and
   chopped
4 tablespoons tomato sauce
6 tablespoons Brown Sauce (p. 39)
1–2 tablespoons chopped parsley
¼ teaspoon chopped tarragon and
   chervil

1. Heat butter and oil in a large, heavy, deep pan *(braisière)*. Season chicken with salt and pepper, and coat lightly with flour. Sauté on medium heat so that the flour does not burn. Chicken will brown lightly in about 10 minutes. Cover and sauté for another 10 minutes. Remove chicken and keep in warm oven.

2. Put shallots and mushrooms in same pan, and cook for a few minutes. Add garlic and white wine; cook until it is reduced by two thirds. Add tomatoes, tomato sauce, and Brown Sauce. Return chicken to saucepan and cook slowly for another 5–10 minutes. Remove fat from sauce by dipping spoon over surface of sauce before adding parsley and herbs. Correct seasoning.

Serves 6–8.

Breast of Chicken Chasseur   *Suprême de Volaille Chasseur*

4 chicken breasts or fillets
Salt and pepper to taste
2 tablespoons flour
4 tablespoons butter or half oil and
   half butter
2 shallots, minced
1 clove garlic, minced
½ pound mushrooms, fresh or dried
   morels (morilles)

2–3 tablespoons Cognac
½ cup dry white wine, a Chardonnay,
   or red or white Burgundy
2 tablespoons tomato sauce or purée
1 cup Brown Sauce (p. 39)
2 tablespoons Glace de Viande
   (p. 40) (optional)
2 teaspoons chopped parsley
4 croutons, buttered

1. Season chicken fillets with salt and pepper. Lightly coat with flour. Heat butter in a heavy skillet on medium high heat, and brown chicken for about 10 minutes; finish cooking in about another 10 minutes (with cover ajar) on medium low heat to prevent flour from burning.

225

2. Remove chicken, keep warm in low oven, and sauté shallots, garlic, and sliced mushrooms in same pan for about 3 minutes. Deglaze pan with Cognac and white wine, reduce slightly, then add tomato sauce, Brown Sauce, *Glace de Viande,* if using, and chopped parsley. Stir sauce on medium low heat until it thickens. Taste to adjust seasoning.

3. Place chicken breasts on croutons, arrange on warm serving platter, and cover with sauce.

   Serve with steamed rice and plain steamed vegetables.

Serves 3–4.

White House Chicken   *Poularde Maison Blanche*

4 cups chicken stock (fond blanc de volaille)

CHICKEN VELOUTÉ SAUCE:
4 ounces (1 stick) butter
½ cup flour

4 cups chicken stock

32 mushroom caps, small size
Juice of ½ lemon for acidulated water
3 tablespoons butter for sautéing
1 tablespoon chopped onion
2 cups rice, rinsed
½ cup golden raisins

Salt and pepper to taste
2 chickens, 3–3½ pounds each
6 shallots
6 mushroom stems
4 parsley sprigs
1½ cups Champagne
1 pint heavy cream

1. Make chicken stock ahead of time using method under *Consommé Clair* (p. 6), omitting beef bones, beef, and cooking a shorter length of time. Make Chicken Velouté Sauce (p. 52) with the butter, flour, and 4 cups chicken stock.

2. Clean mushrooms caps, parboil in acidulated water with 1 tablespoon butter for several minutes, drain, and keep warm in a slow oven.

3. Sauté chopped onion in 2 tablespoons butter until soft, add the rice and raisins. Mix well, pour in 4 cups hot chicken stock, salt to taste, and bring to a boil. Transfer to a casserole with a cover and bake in 350-degree oven for 18 minutes or until done. Dot with butter.

4. Truss chickens (p. 211), season with salt and pepper, rub skin with butter or oil, and roast, half the time on one side, then turn and finish roasting other side in a 350-degree oven for 25 minutes. Remove pan from oven

and add shallots, mushroom stems, and parsley sprigs. Roast breast side up for 30 minutes more. Take chickens out of pan, remove strings, and keep warm in low oven.

5. Skim fat from pan, deglaze pan juices with a little of the Champagne, strain, and pour into a heavy saucepan on top of stove. Add remaining Champagne, reduce sauce by about two thirds, stir in *Sauce Velouté* slowly, using a whisk, and lastly add the cream. Simmer for about 15 minutes.

6. On a warm serving platter arrange the cooked rice in a layer, and place chickens on top surrounded with the mushrooms. Pour the Champagne sauce over the chicken and rice.

  Serve with fresh vegetables of cook's choice.

Serves 8.

Chicken in Fleurie Wine   *Poulet au Vin de Fleurie*

1 chicken, 3 pounds, cut up
2–5 tablespoons butter
Salt and pepper to taste
2 tablespoons finely chopped shallots
2 tablespoons Cognac or brandy
1 bottle Fleurie wine*
4 sprigs parsley
1 bay leaf
Pinch thyme
12 small onions, peeled and
 blanched (blanchir)

3 slices salt pork, cut in ½-inch
 pieces, blanched
12 small mushroom caps
Pinch sugar
1 tablespoon beurre manié *or*
 cornstarch or several tablespoons
 Brown Sauce (p. 39)
4 slices white bread, cut in heart
 shape and sautéed in butter

1. In a large, heavy casserole brown chicken pieces on all sides in 2 to 4 tablespoons of the butter. Salt and pepper chicken; sprinkle with chopped shallots. Pour off any excess butter. Warm Cognac and flame chicken.

2. Add the red wine, parsley, bay leaf and thyme; cover and simmer on stovetop for about 35 minutes or until chicken is done. Chicken can be braised in 350-degree oven, if preferred. White meat can be removed before dark meat is cooked.

---

* A different wine can be used, such as a Zinfandel or Pinot Noir. If so, the name of the dish is changed to Chicken in Zinfandel Wine, for example.

227

3. Before cooking chicken or during that time, peel and blanch onions and salt pork. Drain onions. Sauté mushroom caps, onions, and salt pork in butter blended with a pinch of sugar to give vegetables a glaze. Just before chicken is done, garnish a warm serving platter with the vegetables.

4. Remove chicken to warm serving platter. Keep warm.

5. Degrease and reduce sauce to concentrate the flavors before adding 1–2 tablespoons *beurre manié* in small pieces, stirring with a wooden spoon; or stir in cornstarch diluted with water, or several tablespoons Brown Sauce. Taste to correct seasoning.

6. Pour sauce around chicken and vegetables on platter and decorate edges with heart-shaped bread sautéed in butter.

Serves 4.

Chicken Breasts Stuffed with Cheese

Suprêmes de Volaille Farcies aux Fromages

STUFFING:
¾ cup grated Gruyère cheese
2 ounces (¼ cup) Roquefort cheese
1½ teaspoons unsalted butter

2 whole chicken breasts, weighing about ¾ pounds each
Salt and pepper to taste
2 teaspoons Dijon-style mustard (approximately)

1 large egg
1 tablespoon vegetable oil
1 cup all purpose flour
1 cup fresh bread crumbs
¼ cup Clarified Butter (p. 66)
Sauce Madère *(p. 43)*

1. Bring Gruyère, Roquefort, and butter to room temperature. Cream together in a bowl. Spread mixture into a 12-inch strip on wax paper. Using the paper as a guide, roll cheese mixture into a log, and chill for 1 hour.

2. Skin, bone, and halve the chicken breasts. Flatten between 2 sheets of wax paper until they are ¼ inch thick. Season both sides with salt and pepper and spread on the mustard.

3. After the cheese log has been chilled sufficiently, quarter it crosswise. Put one piece in the center of each breast half, and enclose it completely in the chicken. Put chicken on a plate and chill it, covered, for 1 hour.

4. Beat egg lightly with 1 tablespoon vegetable oil. Put egg, flour, and bread crumbs in separate pans. Roll each chicken breast—first, in flour, shaking

off excess; next, in egg mixture, letting excess drip off; and lastly, in bread crumbs. Chill breasts on plate for 1 hour.

5. Using a heavy skillet or sauté pan, sear chilled chicken breasts in Clarified Butter on moderately high heat for 2 minutes, or until they are golden. Transfer with a slotted spoon or spatula to a baking pan; bake in a 325-degree oven for 10 minutes or until cooked.

6. Transfer chicken to heated platter and serve with *Sauce Madére,* which can be made in pan in which chicken was sautéed—deglaze with ½ cup Madeira wine, reduce, add Brown Sauce, and taste for seasoning.

Serve with fresh pasta or Dauphine Potatoes (p. 81) and green vegetables.

Serves 4.

NOTE: 1 cup goat cheese *(chèvre)* with herbs can be used in place of Gruyère and Roquefort cheeses.

Pear-Shaped Chicken with Pink Peppercorns

Globi de Volaille au Poivre Rose

2 chickens, 1¼–1½ pounds each, or
  2 poussins or *2 Rock Cornish hens*

MARINADE:
¼ cup Cognac
Pinch thyme

1 small bay leaf, crushed
Salt to taste

STUFFING:
1 slice white bread, crusts removed
½ cup heavy cream
½ teaspoon pink peppercorns from Ile de la Réunion or *substitute green peppercorns from Madagascar (do not use pink peppercorns from South America)*

½ cup finely ground raw veal, chicken, or *white meat of turkey*
5–6 shiitake mushrooms or morilles, *diced*
Pinch nutmeg
Salt and pepper to taste

SAUCE:
¼ cup Cognac
1 cup fond blanc or fond brun *(veal* or *beef stock)*
½ cup heavy cream
½ teaspoon pink peppercorns

1–2 tablespoons butter, melted, to brush on globi
Frills, white or pastel-colored, to cover end of leg bones

229

1. Bone chickens or poussins as directed below to make two globi from each chicken. Marinate chickens for 1 hour in Cognac, thyme, bay leaf, and salt to taste.

2. Prepare stuffing by soaking bread in the cream. Crush ½ teaspoon pink peppercorns, put in mixing bowl with ground veal or chicken, diced shiitake mushrooms, soaked bread with the cream, nutmeg, salt, and pepper to taste. Put several tablespoons stuffing in pocket of each leg as directed (p. 231), form in pear shape, and with leg bone standing up, place in greased baking pan. Brush *globi* with melted butter. Bake in a 350-degree oven for 30–40 minutes or until chicken is cooked through. Baste occasionally.

3. Remove chicken, place on warm platter, and keep warm while preparing sauce.

4. Remove fat from baking pan, put pan on burner, deglaze with ¼ cup Cognac, and flame while liquid is still hot. When flame dies down, add stock to pan, and strain into a saucepot. Stir in cream and pink peppercorns, bring to a boil, and continue boiling until sauce is thickened. Taste to correct seasoning.

5. To serve: Place white or pastel-colored frill on knob end of *globi,* place on warm dinner plate and surround with sauce. Serve with fluted mushrooms, parboiled, and sautéed vegetables such as green beans, carrots, zucchini, salsify, or potatoes trimmed into large olive shapes.

Serves 4.

How to make a frill by hand:

Cut thin white or pastel-colored paper into a strip 2¾ inches wide and 5 inches long. Fold in half. Using a table as a guide, place 1 inch of closed edge of folded paper over edge of table. Using a weight to hold paper in place, cut ¼-inch spaces in folded edge. After paper is cut, reverse it to get fluffiness. Roll up on a pencil or thin stick, staggering the frills. Fasten in place with Scotch tape.

Boning one chicken will produce two *globi:*

1. Begin boning chicken by cutting down along breast bone, scraping along the bones to keep meat intact.

2. Disjoint wing and continue boning along wishbone.

3. Turn chicken over and cut along backbone, carving out the meat from the

bone including the oyster. Disjoint the thigh and continue to remove entire half of chicken with skin intact.

4. Cut off wing at first joint, leaving only shoulder bone attached. Scrape meat off this remaining wing bone to remove bone, leaving meat and skin attached to the half chicken.

5. Remove thigh bone, leaving meat attached to chicken half. Cut around the knob end of leg, releasing skin and tendons. Press leg meat and skin firmly toward thigh so that 1½–2 inches of leg bone is exposed. Cut away nob from end of leg bone (see illustration below).

6. Repeat with second half of chicken. Salt and pepper chicken. Place filling, 2 heaping tablespoons, inside and push into pocket made by boned leg. Fold breast flap over stuffing, next fold thigh flap over the other flap.

Press *globi,* seam side down, onto table so that leg bone sticks straight up, with chicken forming a pear shape.

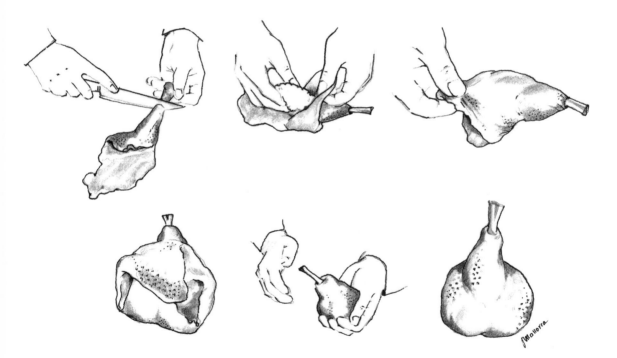

Alsatian Poussin   *Poussin à l'Alsacienne*

A poussin is a 3–4-week-old chicken. If poussins are not available, Rock Cornish hens, broiler-sized chickens (1½–2 pounds) or squab can be used. Partridge or quail can be cooked with this method—stuffing recipe will fill 12 quail, which can be cooked two in a paper pan.
One chicken weighing 1½–2 pounds will serve 2.

STUFFING:
2 tablespoons butter
2 tablespoons finely chopped onion
½ cup white rice or wild rice
1 cup chicken broth
1 sprig fresh thyme or a pinch dried
1 bay leaf
Salt and pepper

1 truffle, diced, or 2 dried mushrooms (use morels, if available)
2 ounces foie gras, diced, or 2 chicken livers sautéed briefly in 1 tablespoon butter and diced (fine pâté de foie gras preferred)
2 tablespoons Cognac or Armagnac

4 poussins, 12–14 ounces each

SAUCE:
½ cup port wine
¾ cup chicken broth or Brown Sauce (p. 39)

Paper frills for poussin legs (p. 230)

Parchment paper to make containers for poussins (p. 239)—heavy foil can be used, but birds brown better in parchment paper cases

1. Make rice pilaf for stuffing birds. If wild rice is used, cook in twice as much broth as for white rice and cook twice as long. In heavy casserole (with a tight lid) sauté chopped onion in butter on medium heat until transparent. Add rice and sauté until grains of white rice become milky, which means that the outside grains are seared. This prevents rice from sticking together. Add broth, thyme, bay leaf, salt, and pepper; bring to a boil, cover, and bake in a 325-degree oven for about 20 minutes (for white rice). Let cool before stuffing poussins. (If cooling must be hastened, spread pilaf out in a pan and put in freezer for 5 minutes.) Stir diced truffle, foie gras or diced liver, and Cognac into pilaf.

2. While pilaf is cooking, bone poussins from the back, leaving wings, thighs, and drumsticks intact. See directions for boning poussin (p. 233).

3. To season cavity of birds with salt and pepper, place 2–3 heaping tablespoons of stuffing in each bird. Fold skin over stuffing and place breast side up in parchment paper cases. (Directions for making cases are illustrated on page 239.) There is no need to sew cavity of birds closed—stuffing will remain in place.

4. Brush tops of poussins with butter or oil. Place prepared birds in shallow baking pan. Bake in a 400-degree oven for 25 minutes or until done. Baste once or twice. Remove poussins from parchment pans and keep warm on a platter in slow oven.

5. Prepare the sauce: Pour juice from individual pans into the large baking pan or a sauté pan, add ½ cup port, and reduce on medium high heat to about one quarter the amount. Add chicken broth or Brown Sauce and reduce again on medium high heat until juices have created a light sauce to pour around poussins.

6. Serve on individual dinner plates or a platter. Put frills on knob of legs. Serve with small steamed turnips and carrots.

Serves 4.

How to Bone Poussin or Any Bird for Alsatian Poussin

1. Using sharp boning knife, cut off outer wing joints and turn bird breast side down. Cut skin straight down backbone from neck to tail and scrape meat from each side of backbone. Remove tail.

2. Sever first joints of wings and thighs from carcass, leaving legs and wings intact. Scrape all meat from both sides of breast bone, being careful not to pierce the skin. Detach carcass by cutting along "keel" bone, leaving a little cartilage to keep from piercing skin. French chefs call the boat-shaped carcass the *bateau.*

3. Poussin is ready to be seasoned and stuffed before it is turned over on its back to regain its original shape as described in Step 3 of recipe.

The softness of small birds' bones makes them much easier to bone than larger poultry.

Poussin with Ewe Cheese
Chicken Stuffed under the Skin

Poussin au Fromage de Brebis
Poulet Farci sous la Peau

Rock Cornish hens can be substituted for poussins. A 3–4 pound chicken would require 4 ounces of cheese filling.

4 poussins (4-week-old chickens), about 1 pound each
8 ounces Boursin or Boursault cheese (French cream cheese with herbs and garlic)

2 tablespoons butter, softened
Salt and pepper to taste

1. Cut skin along the entire length of backbone, remove backbone, and flatten chicken by pressing down on breast bone from front. Secure drumsticks through vent end (see illustration below).

2. Loosen skin from breast meat to insert 2 ounces Boursin between skin and flesh.* Rub birds with softened butter, and season with salt and freshly ground black pepper.

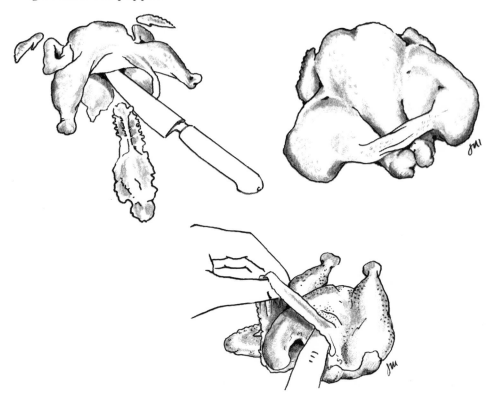

3. Roast in shallow pan in 400-degree oven for 30 minutes, basting three times. Serve hot with pan juices.

   Serve with braised vegetables in season, creamed spinach, or purée of white turnips or carrots.

Serves 4.

* Chicken was stuffed under the skin with grated Parmesan cheese several hundred years ago, according to J. Edmond Richardin in *L'Art du Bien Manger: La Cuisine Française du XIV au XX Siècle* (Cobeil, France: Ed. Crété, 1913), p. 445. (The recipe referred to is called *Poulet à l'Alexis* by G. Delafoy.)

Another filling using one ounce cheese for each poussin:

2 ounces Roquefort cheese
2 ounces (4 tablespoons) sweet
  butter, softened
1 tablespoon chives, snipped, or 1
  tablespoon parsley, chopped

Freshly ground white pepper to taste

If more stuffing is desired, ingredients can be increased by half the amount.

Pheasant with Cabbage Leaves and *Pâté* in Puff Pastry

Feuilletée Faisan aux Choux

1 pheasant, 2¹/₂ pounds
1 tablespoon Cognac
1 tablespoon port or Madeira
Freshly ground pepper to taste
1 small green cabbage

3 tablespoons butter
1 small onion, finely chopped
¹/₂ cup stock
Salt to taste

STUFFING (FARCE):

3 tablespoons butter
1 shallot, minced
2 legs and thighs of pheasant,
  skinned, boned, and cubed
1 pheasant liver, cut in half
3 ounces foie gras, fresh or canned
1 egg
2 tablespoons heavy cream

Salt and pepper to taste
2¹/₂ pounds Pâte Feuilletée (p. 307),
  prepared in advance
1 truffle (optional)
1 egg for glaze
1 cup Sauce Périgourdine(p. 44),
  prepared in advance

1. Remove breast, legs, and thighs of pheasant (carcass, wings, gizzard, and heart may be reserved to make stock for sauce). Skin breast meat and marinate both halves in Cognac, port or Madeira, and pepper for 2–3 hours, or overnight.

2. Cut cabbage into quarters and blanch in boiling water for 2 minutes. Drain, core, and detach large leaves, removing any tough sections (reserve center leaves for another use). Heat 2 tablespoons butter in heavy ovenproof skillet, and sauté chopped onion until soft and golden brown. Add cabbage leaves, stock, salt and pepper to taste. Leave in skillet, or transfer to shallow casserole, and bake in 350-degree oven for 20 minutes.

3. For the stuffing, heat 2 tablespoons butter in another heavy skillet and

235

sauté shallot, cubed leg and thigh meat, and pheasant liver for 2 minutes. Flame with juices from marinated breast. Allow to cool and place in bowl of food processor. Process to a paste, then add foie gras, egg, cream, salt and pepper, and remove to mixing bowl.

4. Heat remaining tablespoon of butter in small heavy skillet and sauté breast halves for 30 seconds on each side. Remove from pan and cut each into four diagonal slices, making eight slices in all.

5. Roll half *Pâte Feuilletée* to ⅛ inch thickness. Cut into two rectangles 4 inches by 7 inches. Roll out other half of dough and cut into two rectangles 5 inches by 8 inches. The top pieces of pastry are larger in order to accommodate filling when assembled.

6. To assemble: Lay two smaller rectangles of dough on cutting board—top each with two cabbage leaves, one quarter of stuffing, four slices of pheasant breast, another quarter of stuffing, and two more cabbage leaves, like a sandwich. If truffle is used, place thin slices between breast meat and stuffing. Top filling with larger rectangles of dough, first brushing edges with water so that they will seal together in the oven. Cup each assembled pastry in your hands and gently mold the shape as much like that of the original pheasant breast half as possible. Press edges together to seal; trim away excess dough, leaving two oval-shaped pastries. Be sure to use a sharp knife and cut straight down—dragging puff pastry at an angle will prevent proper rising. Form scalloped edge by pushing in slightly at 1-inch intervals with the back of a knife blade.

7. Brush tops with beaten egg and bake in 425-degree oven for 15 minutes, then reduce temperature to 375 degrees to bake for 10 minutes longer. Transfer to a warm platter and cut in half at the table.

   Serve with *Sauce Périgourdine*. A Confit of Pearl Onions (p. 272) also may be served.

Serves 4.

Dodine of Pheasant   *Dodine de Faisan St. Hubert*

2 pheasants, 2¹/₂ pounds each

MARINADE NO. 1:
¹/₄ cup Cognac
1 shallot
1 clove garlic
1 bay leaf
1 sprig fresh thyme or 1 pinch dried

STUFFING FOR BONED BREASTS:
Marinated meat from thighs and
   small breast filets of pheasants
1 egg
¹/₂ cup heavy cream
Pinch nutmeg
Salt to taste
¹/₄ teaspoon green peppercorns
¹/₄ teaspoon pink peppercorns

MARINADE NO. 2 FOR STUFFED BREASTS:
1–1¹/₂ cups dry red wine: Cabernet,
   Pinot Noir, or Zinfandel

STOCK FOR SAUCE:
Bones from pheasants
1 small carrot
1 small onion
¹/₂ rib celery
1 bouquet garni
3–4 cups chicken stock

SAUCE POIVRADE:
2 cups concentrated stock
¹/₂ cup red wine from Marinade No. 2
1¹/₂ tablespoons red wine vinegar
¹/₂ tablespoon crushed black
   peppercorns
2 cups Brown Sauce (p. 39)

Parchment paper for wrapping birds

1. Bone pheasants by cutting through skin along backbone and breast, then cutting meat away from carcass, leaving legs and breast attached to skin. Cut off wings and drumsticks and reserve for stock. Pull thigh meat carefully off skin, remove bones and reserve (see illustration, p. 213).

2. Each boned pheasant half will now have the breast meat attached to one side of large expanse of skin (a). Remove the small *filet* that runs along outer edge of breast and reserve for stuffing. Place left hand flat over breast meat and carefully cut in half horizontally, not quite all the way through

237

(butterfly cut) (b, c). Open meat out like a book so that it covers almost entire area of skin (d). Repeat with other three halves of pheasant, sprinkle with a little Cognac, and refrigerate overnight.

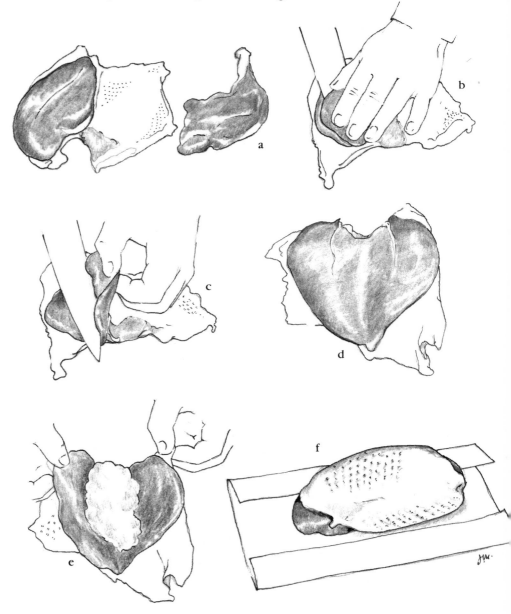

3. For Marinade No. 1, combine balance of Cognac, peeled shallot, garlic, bay leaf, and thyme. Add small breast fillets and boned leg meat. Cover and refrigerate overnight.

4. The next morning discard shallot, garlic, and herbs from Step 3. Put meat through meat grinder using fine blade. Transfer ground meat to food processor, process for a few seconds and add egg. Mix well and incorporate cream, nutmeg, and salt. Stir in green and pink peppercorns.

5. Lay butterflied breasts out flat and put one quarter of stuffing on each (e). Form oval "parcel" by wrapping skin around meat and stuffing, turn skin side up, and place on rectangle of parchment paper cut large enough to make case (f). (See illustration of technique below.) Marinate overnight in 1–1½ cups dry red wine.

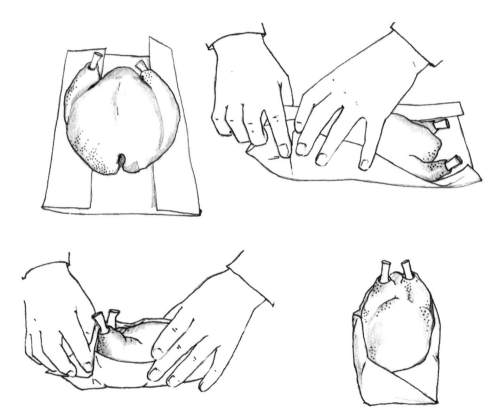

How to make a parchment paper case for poussin or Dodine of Pheasant

6. Prepare the stock: Combine carcasses and pheasants' bones, ½ cup red wine from Marinade No. 2, roughly chopped carrot, onion, and celery, and *bouquet garni.* Cover with chicken stock and simmer for 2 hours. Strain, degrease if necessary, and reduce to 2 cups. Reserve for sauce.

7. Place parchment cases containing dodines of pheasant in shallow casserole just large enough to hold them. Bring wine in which they were marinated to boil, pour over dodines, and braise, covered, in 350-degree oven for 45 minutes.

8. To make poivrade sauce, combine concentrated stock from Step 6, wine marinade, wine vinegar, peppercorns, and Brown Sauce. Reduce by about one half until sauce is thick and shiny.

9. Remove dodines from paper cases and place on warmed dinner plates. Before serving, slice dodines on individual plates or on platter. Nap with *Sauce Poivrade.*

    Serve with Chestnut Purée (p. 280) and Braised Red Cabbage with apples (p. 273).

Serves 4.

NOTE: This recipe sounds more complicated than it really is. In essence, the boned pheasant meat is marinated overnight, then the thigh meat is made into a stuffing for the butterflied breasts. Next, the stuffed breasts are marinated for 24 hours and a stock is made from the bones. Finally, the stuffed breasts, wrapped in pheasant skin and placed in parchment paper cases to keep them together, are braised in red wine, and a sauce is prepared from pheasant stock and Brown Sauce. The dish that results is deliciously full-flavored and well worth the effort involved.

Stewed Duck with Olives   *Etouffée de Canard aux Olives*

4–5 pound duckling, Long Island or
    female Muscovy, 5–6 pounds
Salt and pepper
1 carrot, sliced
1 small onion, sliced
1 celery rib, sliced
2 shallots, peeled and minced
1 garlic clove, peeled
3 sprigs parsley
1 bay leaf
Pinch thyme

1 tablespoon flour
1 bottle Vin Clos Vin Vougeot or a
    California Pinot Noir
1 cup chicken stock
1 tablespoon butter
1/4 cup Marc de Bourgogne, Cognac,
    or brandy
1/2 cup green cocktail olives,
    blanched*
1/4 pound mushrooms, quartered

1. Wash and dry duck; remove neck, wing tip, and first joint, and loose fat; reserve. Season inside of duck with salt and pepper. In shallow roasting pan place duck breast side up and roast in 350-degree oven for 45 minutes without basting. A large amount of fat should have melted from duck.

2. Remove duck from pan and cut into serving pieces. Cut breast meat from bone; remove skin and remaining fat.

3. Make sauce base while duck is roasting or ahead of time: Cut neck into several pieces, put some duck fat into a pot large enough to hold contents of a bottle of wine, add neck and wing pieces, gizzard, and heart, and brown with sliced carrot, onion, celery, shallots, garlic, parsley, bay leaf, and thyme. Remove excess fat, stir in flour, and cook for several minutes. Add wine and chicken stock, cook until reduced by one half, and strain.

4. In heavy skillet heat butter, add cut up duck, and brown lightly on all sides. Pour Marc de Bourgogne or brandy over duck and flame. As soon as flame has subsided, pour strained sauce base over duck.

5. Add blanched olives and quartered mushrooms, cover, and simmer until duck is tender, about 20–30 minutes.

    Serve with boiled potatoes, pasta such as noodles, spaghetti, or wild rice. A green vegetable or small turnips may be served on the side.

Serves 2.

NOTE: Clos Vougeot is a special wine made from the 125-acre vineyard surrounding the Château de Clos Vougeot owned by the Confrérie des Chevaliers du Tastevin, a world-wide brotherhood of Burgundy lovers. If it is not possible to use this wine, another Burgundy can be selected such as a Volnay or Chambertin. A California Pinot Noir is considered the American equivalent.

* To blanch olives, start them in cold water; boil for 1 minute. Change water if olives still taste salty; boil for another minute and drain.

Duck with Pineapple   *Canard aux Ananas*

---

1 duck, Long Island or Pekin,
*   4–5 pounds*
Salt and pepper
For duck cavity: sliced onion, sage,
*   celery rib, apple slices (optional)*
Basting liquid: a little stock, wine,
*   fruit juice or one part honey to two*
*   parts water*
1 onion and 1 carrot, sliced, for pan
1 large can pineapple slices
*   (1 pound, 13 ounces)*

1 tablespoon butter
1 tablespoon chopped shallots
¼ cup Kirsch
1 cup Brown Sauce (p. 39)
½ cup currant jelly
Confectioners' sugar for pineapple
*   slices*
Fritter Batter (Pâte à Frire, p. 243)

1. Wash inside and outside of duck, pat dry, and remove excess fat from neck and cavity. Cut off two first joints of wings and neck for making stock with duck giblets. Season inside with salt and pepper, and if desired, onion, sage, celery, and apples. Using a skewer, prick outside skin around thighs, back, and lower breast to let fat run out while baking. Duck can be trussed. Place in roasting pan correct size for duck—a low sided pan is better for browning poultry.

2. Start roasting duck on its back in 425-degree oven to brown for about 20 minutes, lower heat to 375 degrees, turn duck on one side, roast for 20 minutes, turn on other side, roast for 20 minutes, turn on back to finish browning and cooking for about 15 minutes. Remove fat from pan several times during baking and add sliced onion and carrot after first 20 minutes to flavor pan sauce. Roast duck 12 minutes to the pound, as a guide. Baste duck last 15 minutes with liquid of your choice to get a crispy skin.

3. Drain canned pineapple slices, reserving juice. In sauté pan heat butter and sauté shallots for 2 minutes. Add pineapple juice and Kirsch; reduce liquid over high heat to half the amount. Stir in 1 cup Brown Sauce and ½ cup currant jelly; bring to a boil and remove from heat.

4. Cut about two pineapple slices into quarters, sprinkle with confectioners' sugar, and bake in 450-degree oven just until lightly browned.

5. Place duck on warm platter, and arrange pineapple quarters on top and as a garnish around duck. Serve sauce in sauceboat.

    Serve with pineapple fritters made from remaining slices and green vegetables on a separate plate.

Serves 4.

Fritter Batter   *Pâte à Frire*

½ pound (1¾ cups) flour
Pinch salt
1 teaspoon sugar
1 tablespoon olive oil
3 eggs, separated
Dash vanilla extract or *dark rum*
7 ounces (1 cup plus 2 tablespoons)
  beer or *milk (if using milk,*
  dissolve ½ teaspoon granulated
  yeast in ¼ cup of the milk,
  warmed)

FRUIT:
20 canned pineapple rings or *4–5*
  large apples (peeled and cored),
  cut in rings, or *4–5 large pears*
  (peeled and cored), cut in quarters,
  or 6 large bananas (peeled), cut in
  half lengthwise and quartered
Confectioners' sugar
Kirsch or brandy to marinate fruit
Oil for deep frying

1. Put flour in mixing bowl; stir in salt and sugar. Make a well. Combine oil, egg yolks, vanilla or rum, and beer or milk (yeast mixture plus remaining 5 ounces milk). Slowly pour liquid into well of flour using a whisk to incorporate ingredients into a smooth batter. Cover with damp towel or plastic wrap and let batter rise 1–2 hours in a warm place.

2. Just before using, prepare fruit: dust with sugar, sprinkle with Kirsch or brandy, and steep ½ hour.

3. Heat oil 2 inches deep in a deep fryer to 375 degrees; beat egg whites to soft peaks and fold gently into batter.

4. Dry fruit on paper towels. Dip fruit one piece at a time in batter, coating thoroughly, and deep fry until golden brown. Do not crowd pan. Drain on paper towels and sprinkle with confectioners' sugar, if desired. Serve immediately.

Makes 3½–4 cups batter; serves 12.

Breast of Duck with Black Currant Sauce

Magret de Canard Baies de Cassis

It is important to use a meaty Muscovy or Moulard duck, as Long Island ducklings are much too fatty. Moulards are a cross between Muscovy and Pekin ducks and are sterile. They are now being bred in New York State and Healdsburg in the Napa Valley, California. The Muscovy duck is much leaner than the Mallard, which is also raised for its foie de canard frais.

1 duck breast from a 6¹/₂–8-pound
   Muscovy or Moulard duck (serves
   6) or a 5–6-pound Pekin duck
   (serves 4)
Salt and pepper to taste

INGREDIENTS FOR SAUCE:
2 tablespoons sugar
2 tablespoons raspberry vinegar
2 tablespoons black currant liqueur
   (crème de cassis) or black currant
   syrup (sirop de cassis)
2 cups Brown Sauce (p. 39)

1 cup fresh black currants or *canned*
   baies de cassis au sirop
3 fresh pears (ripe but firm Bosc or
   Comice are good), poached in
   white wine with Madeira and
   green peppercorns

1. To cut up duck: Disjoint and remove wings first, before removing breast, by cutting completely through center of breast bone to cut duck in half. Turn duck over, cut out backbone from each side, disjoint and remove thigh with leg attached. Remove shoulder bone from breast, leaving rib cage on each side of breast half to prevent shrinkage when cooking. Cut away any extra neck bone and skin. Remove flat breast bone (keel bone). Reserve legs and wings for Preserved Duck (*Confit de Canard,* p. 245). Save wing tips, neck, and backbone for stock.

2. In a preheated, heavy ovenproof skillet, sauté two duck breast halves for 3 minutes on each side, starting skin side down to release fat. (Duck breast can also be broiled, starting skin side up.) Transfer skillet to preheated 375-degree oven and roast for 6–10 minutes, depending on size of breast. Watch carefully! Duck meat, which is naturally a dark red color, should register 125–130 degrees on an instant meat thermometer. Season lightly with salt and pepper, and let rest in a warm oven for 10 minutes on a warm platter while preparing sauce.

3. Pour fat off pan, add the sugar, vinegar, and liqueur for sauce, deglazing pan over medium heat. Strain sauce, add Brown Sauce and black currants, and bring just to a boil when ready to serve.

4. Detach rib bones from duck breast meat and carve into thin slices on the diagonal, starting at the thinnest end to get slices as even as possible. Arrange slices attractively on plates, pour sauce around them, and serve with poached pears and freshly made pasta.

Serves 6.

How to Render Poultry Fat

3 pounds or 6 cups goose or duck fat with fatty skin pieces (grattons) *or fresh pork leaf fat*

1. Chop fat into small pieces. Set over low heat. When fat reaches 250 degrees, start timing. After 20–30 minutes, any solid pieces *(grattons)* left will be a light golden brown. Use in salads. This rendered fat should not be allowed to go too far above 325 degrees, or it will lose its white color when cold.

2. Strain through fine sieve, allow to cool, and refrigerate. It will keep for months.

Preserved Duck   *Confit de Canard*

1 teaspoon salt (Kosher, sea salt, or regular)
1 bay leaf
4 juniper berries, crushed
1 teaspoon thyme, dried or fresh
1/2 teaspoon cracked black pepper

2 legs, thigh, and upper wing portions from a 6 1/2 – 8 pound Muscovy, Moulard, Mallard, Pekin, or any other variety duck
2–3 cups rendered duck fat (see above)

1. Combine salt and seasonings in a shallow Pyrex or ceramic dish, arrange duck pieces, and sprinkle with the seasonings. Cover and refrigerate for 24 hours.

2. Wipe salt off duck pieces and dry carefully with paper towels. Liquify fat slowly in a heavy saucepan and put in duck. Fat should cover duck pieces by about 1 inch. Cook over gentle heat or bake at 300 degrees for 1–1½ hours.

3. Pack duck pieces into a bowl and cover with strained liquid fat. Gelatinous meat juice from duck will become rancid if not removed: it should be

245

separated from melted fat and saved to be used like a *demi-glace* to enrich sauces. When confit is cool, cover with plastic wrap and refrigerate. It will keep for at least 3 months. Remove pieces of duck as needed. Always cover remaining pieces with fat before refrigerating once more.

Confit can be eaten as soon as it is cooked, and is delicious with braised red or white cabbage (p. 273) and puréed potatoes (p. 267).

Serves 2–4.

NOTE: Confit is also made from turkey legs (remove tendons and cut thighs in half), cut up pheasant, goose, rabbit, and whole quail. Confit can be vacuum sealed. This very old method of preservation has been used in French farmhouses for centuries, particularly in regions where ducks and geese are raised commercially. Confit of duck and goose *(confit d'oie)* are used in cassoulet, the famous bean casserole.

Simmered Rabbit with Fresh Basil   *Lapin à l'Etuvée au Basilic Frais*

1 fresh rabbit, fryer 2¹/₂–3¹/₂ pounds, disjointed and fat removed
3 tablespoons flour for dredging
2–3 tablespoons Clarified Butter (p. 66)
4 shallots, peeled
1 clove garlic, peeled
1 bay leaf

¹/₂ teaspoon thyme, fresh or dried
Salt and pepper to taste
¹/₂ cup dry white wine
1 cup light Brown Sauce (p. 39) or brown stock
2 tablespoons chopped fresh basil
Basil sprigs for garnish

1. Cut up rabbit using boning knife: cut through hip joint on each side to remove leg sections, cut through shoulder joints to remove front legs after cutting saddle into 2–3 pieces, cut rack or rib cage into 2–3 pieces. Reserve liver and kidneys (remove any fat) to add last 5 minutes of cooking. Dredge rabbit pieces lightly in flour and sauté in Clarified Butter on medium high heat until golden brown, about 10 minutes. Add shallots and garlic and sauté for 3 minutes. Remove excess fat, add bay leaf, thyme, salt and pepper to taste, wine, and Brown Sauce.

2. Transfer to a casserole, cover, and simmer at 300–325 degrees for 30–45 minutes. Add liver and kidneys 5 minutes before rabbit is cooked. Rabbit should be very tender.

3. Remove rabbit and shallots from casserole, place on serving platter or plates and keep warm. Remove garlic clove from sauce, stir chopped fresh

basil into sauce, and taste to correct seasoning. (Do not serve neck.) Pour around rabbit and garnish each plate with a whole shallot and small sprigs of fresh basil.

Serve with fresh noodles, spaghetti, or white rice.

Serves 4.

NOTE: I do not recommend marinating rabbit, as the wine in the marinade gives an acid taste. A marinade gives a "gamey" taste to meat, if that is desired. It is also used to preserve meat, especially when it cannot be used right away.

Rabbit Roasted with Herbs, Whole Garlic Cloves, and Whole Shallots

Lapin Rôti aux Herbes, Gousses d'Ail, Echalotes

1 rabbit fryer, 3 pounds (approximate size)
1 tablespoon Dijon mustard
2 tablespoons white wine
2 tablespoons olive oil
Pinch oregano, lemon thyme, rosemary, and savory
Salt and pepper to taste

2 tablespoons butter
6 shallots, unpeeled
6 garlic cloves, unpeeled
½ cup white wine, such as Chardonnay
1 cup brown stock (fond brun, p. 6)

247

1. Wash and dry rabbit; rub or brush inside and out with mixture of mustard, white wine, and olive oil. Do not remove kidneys from cavity of rabbit, but trim away any fat around kidney and fillets. Cook liver last 5 minutes before rabbit is done.

2. Mix herbs together and sprinkle inside rabbit and over skin. Put prepared rabbit in a shallow roasting pan, sprinkle with salt and pepper, and place pats of butter on top and sides of rabbit. Place garlic cloves and whole shallots around rabbit. Roast in a 325-degree oven for 1–1½ hours, basting occasionally so that meat does not get dry, but remains moist and tender.

3. Remove rabbit with garlic cloves and whole shallots; put all on serving platter and keep warm.

   To make sauce: Discard any fat, deglaze baking pan with white wine and brown stock. Boil for 2–3 minutes. Serve in sauceboat or pour around rabbit after it has been cut up.

   To cut up rabbit, use sharp boning knife or poultry shears—cut off flank skin on both sides, cut through hip joint on each side to remove leg sections, cut saddle into 2–3 pieces, cut through shoulder joints to remove front legs, cut rack or rib cage into 2–3 pieces. Do not serve neck.

   Serve with Gratin of Potatoes Dauphinoise (p. 269) or Savoyard Potatoes (p. 270), steamed green beans or broccoli.

Serves 3–4.

Chapter Nine

VEGETABLES

Sorrel, Artichokes, and Potatoes Are Featured *Légumes;*
Subrics Are Formed from Vegetable Purées

In the hierarchy of chefs the person in charge of vegetables and eggs is called *le chef entremettier*. First on the agenda of each new day is the preparation of vegetables. This is called *couper,* and it requires great ability in peeling, slicing, chopping, and mincing.

The food processor is used about as much for vegetable cookery as it is for the preparation of terrines, *pâtés,* mousses, quenelles, and stuffings, not to mention the making of emulsified sauces, puréed soups, and doughs. Here, it is able to replace the knife to dice, grate, shred, julienne, and slice just as it replaces hand tools formerly used to purée vegetables, grind meat, and grate cheese. Another advantage of this miracle machine is that auxiliary bowls are available to help save cleaning time and effort.

Cooks must be careful handling the sharp steel blades and always be aware of overprocessing: vegetables to be chopped will turn into purées, and cream incorporated in delicate mixtures will turn into butter. Obviously, this machine still cannot replace the manual dexterity of the cook: It cannot peel fruit and vegetables, or grind anything too hard to be cut by a knife such as extra hard Parmesan, coffee beans, or grains.

Food processor aside, I have not yet abandoned my *mandoline* for slicing thin, even shapes when preparing souffléd potatoes, Potatoes Anna, shoestring potatoes for nests, and *Pommes Darphin*. The professional steel *mandoline,* freestanding or attached to a table, is a stainless steel oblong plate which rests at an angle on a folding steel frame. It has high carbon steel blades over which vegetables are pushed. The food is held down by a hinged lid with a knob which protects the fingers. Recently, the food processor has acquired discs which can slice about as thinly and evenly as the *mandoline,* but the potatoes, especially thin julienne cuts, may become more watery.

To make Potatoes Anna I use a deep, black cast-iron skillet or a heavy aluminum *sauteuse* about 2½ inches deep. One of the "tricks" I did not mention in the recipe is to save one pan for this dish only, cleaned with salt, to prevent potatoes from sticking. I do the same for omelet and crêpe pans.

The origin of souffléd potatoes may have been due to an accident, but there is no uncertainty in their preparation. I dry very thin evenly sliced baking potatoes and cook them in hot oil twice: the first time the oil is not as hot as the second time, which causes the potatoes to puff. This phenomenon originated in 1837 in Saint-Germain-en-Laye when the train was first brought there. The company responsible for the train had planned to lunch at the town's restaurant. Since they did not arrive on time, the fried potatoes became cold. When the company finally appeared, the chef quickly plunged the fried potatoes into hot oil. To his surprise, they puffed up.

Before cooking these potato dishes, I want to present some background information on vegetables. Careful preparation and presentation raise vegetables from the mundane to the sublime. Discovering that there are six types of vegetables helps explain why they display such a variety of colors, shapes, and tastes or flavors. *Nouvelle cuisine* has raised their decorative value to new heights, and the "eaters" concerned with nutrition are aware of their mineral, vitamin, and fiber content. Since the six types* of vegetables are not mentioned frequently, I will do so here:

1. Leaf vegetables: These are among the most nutritious because the leaves transform the energy of the sun into sugar, called photosynthesis. Some examples are spinach, Swiss chard, lettuce, mustard greens.

2. Stem vegetables: The stem contains the fiber which supports the plant and transports the nutrients between the roots and leaves. Asparagus and celery are examples.

3. Root vegetables: Roots, tubers, and bulbs store energy for the plant in the form of sugar and starch, causing some of these vegetables to have more calories. Beets, potatoes, salsify, carrots, and onions are examples.

4. Flower and bud vegetables: Broccoli has the highest nutrients, artichokes are the lowest in nutrients; other examples are cauliflower and Brussels sprouts.

5. Immature seed vegetables: Green peas, lima beans, and corn. Mature dry seeds such as legumes and cereals are not included in this explanation.

6. Fruit vegetables: The fruit vegetables are rather low in nutrients and they are *not* sweet—cucumbers, squash, eggplant, okra, tomatoes, and peppers. Winter squash, tomatoes, and okra are high in nutrients, however.

Ideally, vegetables should be cooked quickly in the least amount of water. Steaming fulfills both those requirements. The type of vegetable determines the amount of time necessary for steaming. Use a tight lid.

* "Fungi" are considered a seventh kind of vegetable by Alex O. Hawkes in *A World of Vegetable Cookery* (New York: Simon & Schuster, 1968, 1984), p.12.

Since the production of fruits and vegetables has become big business in the Western world, with California being the leading agricultural state, it is important to discuss the effects of early picking and shipping long distances on produce. Buyers seem to need instruction on selection, information which farmers and consumers seem to have known almost instinctively in the past. Tests have revealed that the freshest and best looking vegetables and fruits have the most vitamins and minerals. The longer they are stored or not used, the more nutrients they lose. Vegetables contain more vitamins and minerals and less calories than fruit. Vitamin C is the most easily lost nutrient since it is soluble in water and susceptible to chemical destruction. If vegetables are chilled rapidly after harvest, such as broccoli and green leafy vegetables, which are packed on crushed ice, they will not suffer as great a loss.

Avoid buying limp, old looking leaves and stalks. The stems of asparagus should not be shriveled or the tops spread out. Broccoli should not have yellowed flowerettes. Eggplants should have shiny purple skins with no brown spots, and the stem and cap should be bright green. Carrots and beets should be purchased with their green tops. The best tomatoes are vine-ripened. Tomatoes and cantaloupes should not be refrigerated until they are ripe. Most vegetables should be stored at 40 degrees in the "crisper" drawer of the refrigerator or in plastic bags with the exceptions of mushrooms (place these in open paper bags). New potatoes can be refrigerated, while mature potatoes should be stored in a dark, cool place. Garlic and onions are stored at room temperature in open containers.

If fruit is vine-ripened, the sugar content will be higher, creating a more characteristic flavor and a higher content of vitamin C. Some fruits will not ripen after they are picked: berries, cherries, grapes, and oranges. Some fruits give off ethylene gas as they ripen, such as bananas and tomatoes, which are sometimes treated with ethylene gas to hasten their ripening. Also, ripe fruits give off ethylene gas so they should not be stored in the vegetable drawer of the refrigerator with vegetables. The ethylene gas will have an adverse effect, causing green vegetables to yellow, asparagus to toughen, and lettuce to become spotted.*

Another controversial practice, besides treating with gas, is the use of wax to improve the appearance and prolong the life or retard spoilage of cucumbers, apples, or tomatoes. The two kinds of wax used on apples are from natural foods: tropical palm leaves or a food grade resin base mixed with a water solution together with whole milk or soybean caseins. One apple will receive about two drops, which is the same basic wax used to coat

* Consumers Coop of Berkeley, California, "All About Vegetables," *CO-OP News,* 12 May 1980, pp. 5 and 12.

confections and medicinal tablets. Waxing prevents apples from losing moisture, developing mold, and helps retain its malic acid content, which gives the apple its characteristic flavor.* The wax can be carefully washed off before using, or the fruit can be peeled. Ordinarily, it is best to restrain from washing fruits and vegetables until they are ready to be used, as water contributes to decay. The other elements which destroy the nutrients and appearance of vegetables are time, light, heat, air, and bruising.

I have singled out sorrel, potatoes, and artichokes for their unique attributes. It was a student cook's gift of homegrown sorrel which prompted my commentary on this aromatic, tart herb, which is both a substitute for lemon flavoring and lends a green tone to sauces for fish and meat dishes. Sorrel *(l'oseille),* which grows wild in the United States, is sometimes called sour grass. The scientific name of the American variety is *Rumex acetosa;* the French is *Rumex scutatus.* It is an arrow-shaped perennial that thrives in a sunny well-drained area of a vegetable or herb garden. Although it contains vitamins A and C plus iron, it has a high oxalic acid content, a substance one should not partake of too freely. Wash sorrel exactly as spinach is washed—remove the stem and center vein of the leaf by pulling them off together, rinse in three changes of cold water, and drain. Finally, chop or shred and sauté in butter before using in preparations such as soups or freezing for convenience. One pound melts down to ½ cup dark green purée. Several tender young leaves can be added to green salads; shredded sorrel plain or mixed with whipped cream gives an unexpected fresh flavor to omelets (p. 131) and quiches (p. 144). When fresh sorrel becomes wilted, soak in cold water to revive. This tendency to wilt partially explains why it is seldom found in produce markets. If cooks cannot find fresh sorrel, it is available preserved in glass jars. *Potage Crème Germiny* (p. 13) and *Potage Santé* (p. 19) feature sorrel, as do *Sole à l'Oseille* (p. 180), Salmon in Sorrel Sauce (p. 178), Braised Trout Stuffed with Sorrel (p. 180), and Veal Chop or Chicken Breast with Sorrel (pp. 220–221).

*Joe Carcione, "Don't Worry About the Wax on Apples," *San Francisco Chronicle,* 3 March 1982, Food section, p. 21. The article also states that the wax used is not a petroleum derivative. These natural solutions have been thoroughly tested by the United States Food and Drug Administration. They found them to be nontoxic.

Sorrel Sauce   *Sauce à l'Oseille*

½ pound sorrel
1–2 tablespoons butter
1 cup heavy cream

2–4 tablespoons stock or juice from
*   main course dish*
Salt and pepper to taste

1. Wash, devein, and chop sorrel. Sauté in butter in heavy saucepan on medium low heat until sorrel "melts."

2. Bring cream to a boil, and slowly pour into sorrel while stirring. Add stock or juice from fish, veal, or poultry dish with which it is to be served for added flavor, and to adjust consistency of sauce. Taste to correct seasoning, adding salt and pepper if necessary.

    Serve with poached or sautéed fish, veal chops, breast of chicken or turkey.

Makes 1½ cups.

Sorrel Purée   *Purée d'Oseille*

Sorrel is too acid to serve as a vegetable without adding about equal amounts of cooked spinach or lettuce. Use for soup, as it blends well with cream, for quiches and stuffing eggs (p. 135). Sorrel purée can be put in a Mason jar, covered with melted back fat, and refrigerated to use when it is out of season.

2 pounds sorrel
2 tablespoons butter (approximate
*   amount)*

Salt and pepper to taste
1–2 tablespoons consommé or white
*   stock*

1. Wash and devein sorrel and put in a large pot of boiling water. Cook in simmering water for about 10 minutes. Drain in strainer. The sorrel will shrink once cooked.

2. In saucepan, heat butter, add sorrel with salt and pepper to taste, and stir in consommé or stock. Simmer for 15–20 minutes.

Makes 1¼ cups.

Chiffonade of Sorrel

Chiffonnade d'Oseille

1–2 pounds sorrel   *1–2 tablespoons butter*

1. Wash, devein, and shred sorrel into a fine julienne.
2. In sauté pan on low heat cook sorrel with butter until all water has evaporated. Keep on hand to use as a garnish for soups and in sauces. Can use as an ingredient in a warm salad.

Makes approximately ½ cup.

Chiffonade of Sorrel with Cream

Chiffonade d'Oseille à la Crème

1 pound sorrel, deveined and washed
2 tablespoons heavy cream

Simmer sorrel in water that clings to leaves. When liquid has evaporated, stir in 2 tablespoons heavy cream. Simmer a couple of minutes.

Makes ½ cup.

The Artichoke
L'Artichaut

Some History and Lore

Perhaps the unique appearance of the artichoke can be explained by its derivation from the cardoon, a species of European thistle, which has been improved by scientific methods. The pine cone-shaped part of the artichoke plant, that which is edible, is really the flower. If it is left on the stalk, it turns into a purple thistle. The flower can be dried and used for decorative purposes. It has been cultivated in France since the beginning of the sixteenth century, when it was mentioned by Rabelais.

The three varieties which are most valued in France are:
1. the large green of Laon with a flat top
2. the large Camus of Brittany
3. the green of Provence with the longer shape

255

When it is young and tender, it is eaten raw or steamed:

1. as an hors d'oeuvre, *à la croque au sel,* dipped in salt
2. *à la poivrade* (also called *à la vinaigrette*) with *Sauce Poivrade:* an olive oil and wine vinegar sauce with salt, freshly ground pepper, minced garlic, and herbs*

The only variety produced commercially in the United States is the Green Globe (*Cynara scolymus,* an herbaceous perennial) where over ten thousand acres are under cultivation in California, with more acreage in artichokes being planted yearly. Castroville, California, is called the artichoke capital of the world, where the artichoke does best in a frost-free area with cool, foggy summers. In that climate the plant produces tender buds almost year-round. The plant grows to a height of three or four feet or more and spreads to cover an area about six feet in diameter.

How to Prepare the Artichoke   *La Méthode de Prépare l'Artichaut*

1. Soak the artichoke in cold water for a few minutes to remove debris.
2. Never cut the stem with a knife. Break stem by placing artichoke on edge of a table or counter, with stem over the edge. This allows pressure to be put on stem, which breaks it, tearing loose the fibers.
3. Twist the center to remove cone, which is saved to put back in artichoke after filling; sauce is put in center. The cone is then put back upside down.
4. Using a sharp French chef's knife, cut top off to second layer of leaves. Cut off sharp, thorny tips of leaves with kitchen shears.
5. The choke can be removed before or after cooking, depending on recipe instructions. To remove choke before cooking, turn artichoke upside down and apply pressure on it. Turn it right side up and take a small spoon or melon scoop to remove fuzzy choke. Scrape out as much of the hairs as possible.
6. To prevent the cut surface from turning brown while preparing artichokes, place in acidulated water. Acidulated water is enough water to cover the vegetables with the juice of half a lemon added.

* Prosper Montagné, *Larousse Gastronomique: The Encyclopedia of Food, Wine, and Cooking,* ed. Charlotte Turgeon and Nina Froud (New York: Crown Publishers, 1961), p. 56.

7. To demonstrate the special respect I hold for the artichoke, I place a round slice of peeled lemon on the bottom of the pared artichoke to prevent discoloration. I tie it on with a string going underneath and around the side of the whole artichoke.

8. To steam or boil artichokes *(artichauts bouillis):* Place artichoke upside down, if steamed. Or cover with boiling water in a large pot. Do not cover with a lid, but use some cheesecloth or a plastic plate to hold artichoke down. The size of the artichoke determines the cooking time— average time is 30–40 minutes. Test for doneness by pulling out a leaf or applying a pointed knife or toothpick to the heart or base.

9. Artichoke bottoms *(fonds d'artichauts)* are cooked in a *blanc:* mix several tablespoons of flour with ¼ cup water and stir into cooking water.

Artichokes Barigoule   *Artichauts Braisés Farcis à la Barigoule*

4 large artichokes

STUFFING:
¼ pound ham or *prosciutto*
½ pound fresh mushrooms
¼ cup butter
6 tablespoons olive oil or *vegetable oil*
½ cup minced onions

¼ cup minced shallots
Salt and freshly ground pepper to taste
Pinch of freshly grated nutmeg
8 anchovy fillets, drained
1 tablespoon freshly chopped parsley

257

4 slices bacon, fresh pork fat, or salt
   pork strips, blanched
2 cloves garlic, minced
1 bay leaf
1 cup coarsely chopped onion
1 cup chopped carrots
¼ cup chopped celery
½ teaspoon dried thyme or sprig of
   fresh thyme

1 cup dry white wine
2 tablespoons tomato paste
1 cup chicken broth
¼–½ cup Brown Sauce (p. 39) or 2
   tablespoons beurre manié or 1
   tablespoon cornstarch

1. Prepare artichokes for stuffing as explained on page 256, Steps 1 through 6. Drain artichokes by turning upside down. When they are thoroughly drained, they are ready for stuffing.

2. Chop ham until fine, making about ⅓ cup.

3. Clean, dry, and slice mushrooms. Either chop by hand as finely as possible or use food processor fitted with steel blade. Makes about 2 cups.

4. Use a large heavy casserole with high sides. Melt half of the butter and 2 tablespoons of oil in casserole, add finely chopped onion and shallots until they are wilted. Add mushrooms, salt, pepper, and nutmeg, stirring often until mushrooms have released most of their liquid. Add minced ham and blend well.

5. Chop anchovy fillets and add with chopped parsley and remaining butter. Stuff artichokes with equal portions of mixture and bard each artichoke with blanched bacon or salt pork or strips of fresh pork fat. Tie the bard around artichoke with string, going around the sides and underneath.

6. Heat remaining olive oil in casserole. Add garlic, bay leaf, coarsely chopped onion, carrots, celery, thyme, wine, tomato paste, and broth. Stir to blend. Place artichokes close together, bring liquid to a boil on top of stove, and cover. Place in a 350-degree oven and braise for an hour or until tender.

7. Remove the bards and place artichokes on a warm serving platter. Skim fat from casserole, strain sauce into a heavy saucepan, thicken with Brown Sauce, cornstarch, or *beurre manié*. Pour over artichokes.

   Serve as an appetizer for dinner or a main course luncheon dish in winter.

Serves 4.

Artichoke Bottoms Stuffed with Tomato Purée

Fonds d'Artichauts Farcis au Fondue de Tomates

6 large artichoke bottoms, cooked,
    trimmed, and warmed
6 large tomatoes, peeled, seeded, and
    chopped
1 clove garlic, finely chopped or
    minced (optional)
1/2 teaspoon tarragon, chopped, or
    1/2 teaspoon thyme, chopped

1 tablespoon butter
1/2 teaspoon sugar
1 tablespoon chopped parsley
2 black olives, pitted, thinly sliced
Salt and pepper to taste

1. Sauté tomatoes, garlic, and tarragon in butter on medium-low heat until most of moisture has evaporated and tomatoes have "softened," about 30 minutes. Stir in sugar.

2. Fill warm artichoke bottoms. Sprinkle with parsley and place thin slices of black olives on top. Salt and pepper to taste. Serve warm with roast chicken, Roast Prime Rib of Beef (p. 34), Roast Leg of Lamb (p. 33), or broiled steak.

Serves 6.

Since exact amounts of ingredients are not necessary to fill artichokes, the following recipes are a good way to use leftover fillings and sauces from other preparations.

Artichoke Bottoms Florentine

Fonds d'Artichauts Farcis à la Florentine

Cook or steam artichokes (p. 256), remove leaves, chokes, and trim bottoms. Large artichokes are preferred for holding more filling. Cook spinach (p. 271) and use plain or creamed (p. 278). Make Mornay Sauce (p. 52) and grate Parmesan cheese.

Fill artichoke bottoms with cooked spinach. Cover with Mornay Sauce, sprinkle with grated Parmesan cheese, and brown in 450-degree oven or under the broiler.

Serve as garnish on platter of roast meat or on dinner plates.

259

Artichoke Bottoms	*Fonds d'Artichauts*
Soubise	*Farcis Soubise*

Fill cooked artichoke bottoms with a thick *Sauce Soubise* (p. 55). Heat in a 350-degree oven before serving as a vegetable or garnish.

Artichoke Bottoms	*Fonds d'Artichauts*
Duxelles	*Farcis à la Duxelles*

Filled cooked artichoke bottoms with thick duxelles (p. 274), cover with a small amount of *Sauce Tomate* (p. 41) or Brown Sauce (p. 39). Sprinkle with bread crumbs and dot with a little butter. Brown in a 450-degree oven or under the broiler. Serve as a vegetable on the dinner plate.

Artichoke Bottoms	*Fonds d'Artichauts*
Stuffed with Chestnut and Soubise Purée	*Farcis à la Cévenole*

Heat cooked artichoke bottoms in butter, fill with Chestnut Purée (p. 280) that has been seasoned with soubise purée (p. 55). Sprinkle with grated Parmesan cheese and brown in 450-degree oven.

The Potato
La Pomme de Terre
The Adaptable Provider

Andre L. Simon wrote in his *Encyclopedia of Gastronomy* that there are more recipes and more varied methods of cooking potatoes than any other vegetable. *The World Atlas of Food* claims that the Incas of Peru were one of the earliest people to cultivate potatoes, even measuring units of time by how long it took a potato to cook. There are more than two hundred varieties of this tuber *(Solanum tuberosum),* which is said to have been brought by Sir Walter Raleigh from Virginia to Ireland. Largely due to the efforts of Parmentier, the potato became a staple food in France in the early 1800s.

The U.S. Department of Agriculture names the four basic types:

1. Russets (also known as Idaho, regardless of where raised)
2. California long whites (Russet Burbank and Norgold Russet, a new variety that has a light russet color with a long, block-like shape, grown mostly in Kern County)
3. Round whites (Katahdin)
4. Round reds (Red Pontiac and the Nordland, a new variety)

A "new" potato may be any one of these four types that has been harvested before the skin has "set" and thus is not fully mature.* Two of the best varieties grown in France are called the *Jaune longue de Hollande,* Dutch yellow long, and *Rouge longue de Hollande,* Dutch red long.

The yellow Finnish potato, produced in the state of Washington is now found in some supermarkets from October to February, according to Alex D. Hawkes.† He claims it is so moist that it can be eaten without butter, sour cream, or salt.

Since most of the nutrients (vitamins B and C and trace minerals) are in the skin, all potatoes should be boiled, steamed, or baked in their skin except very old ones, which should be peeled and soaked in cold water for an hour and then started in boiling, salted water. To preserve the flavor and minerals, they should be boiled in as little water as possible. Save cooking water for soup. Solid potatoes should be started in cold water; softer potatoes should be started in rapidly boiling salted water, boiled for about 25 minutes, drained, and allowed to finish cooking in the covered pan.

The U.S. Department of Agriculture also gives tips on handling and storage—potatoes are almost as delicate as apples, so they can be bruised on the way from the field to the kitchen. Use any bruised or cracked potatoes first, but do not wash until ready to cook. If stored in a cool, dark place with good ventilation (45–50 degrees F.), baking potatoes will keep for several months, and new ones for several weeks. Potatoes stored at 70–80 degrees F. should be used within a week.

Greening is caused by exposure to natural or artificial light. If only the skin is effected, peel all the green away. If the greening has penetrated the flesh, it contains the alkaloid solanin, which causes a bitter flavor and is said to be poisonous to some people. Do not use a potato with green flesh; discard it.

* "March in Your Garden" (*Sunset*'s Garden Guide), *Sunset Magazine,* March 1981 issue, p. 173, pictures five different varieties of homegrown potatoes: "Red Rose," "All Blue" (bluish color), "Bake King" (white), "Norgold Russett" (large brownish), and "Kennebec" (small white), which is the top favorite of home gardeners of the West.

† Alex D. Hawkes, *A World of Vegetable Cookery* (New York: Simon & Schuster, 1968, 1984), p. 187.

The above information is given to help restore respect for the potato and to supply the contemporary cook with the most up-to-date research. Dr. R. L. Sawyer, head of the International Potato Center founded in 1971 in Lima, Peru, said that potatoes yielded more protein and calories per unit of growing time and per unit of planted area than rice, wheat, or corn, the other three major food crops.*

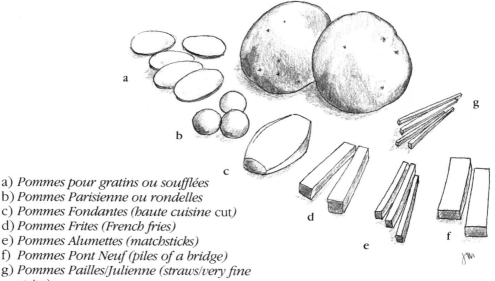

a) *Pommes pour gratins ou soufflées*
b) *Pommes Parisienne ou rondelles*
c) *Pommes Fondantes (haute cuisine cut)*
d) *Pommes Frites (French fries)*
e) *Pommes Alumettes (matchsticks)*
f) *Pommes Pont Neuf (piles of a bridge)*
g) *Pommes Pailles/Julienne (straws/very fine strips)*

Soufflé Potatoes   *Pommes de Terre Soufflées*

Large Idaho potatoes
Vegetable oil

EQUIPMENT:
Mandoline *(French slicer or shredder)*   *Thermometer for measuring*
Deep fat fryer (electric)   *temperature of fat or oil*
Large heavy pot with handles (4–4½ quarts)

1. Peel potatoes and trim edges to make an oval shape. Set in cold water. Potatoes can be cut or sliced by hand, but it is impossible to do as evenly as when using the *mandoline*. Cut pieces ⅛ inch thick the long way, using a *mandoline* to get even slices. Dry on a towel.

* *San Francisco Examiner and Chronicle,* 20 January 1980, This World section.

2. Use a deep-fat fryer for lower heat. It should be larger than the second fryer because it prevents the oil from cooling too fast. The first fryer should have handles in order to shake potatoes. Use a 4–4½ quart pot for 2 quarts of oil.

3. The temperature of oil in first pot should be 190 degrees. T   temperature of oil in second pot should be 250 degrees.

4. After putting potato slices in first pot, shake pan, which lets air inside. The oil will become foamy. Continue to shake pan off and on for about 7 minutes, when potatoes will start to puff.

5. Put potatoes in 250-degree fat or oil, which will cause potatoes to puff almost right away. Remove when puffed enough and put on paper towel or a dish towel until ready to serve. They can stand about 10–20 minutes in an open oven.

6. Right before serving, return them to deep-fat fryer to brown a little more. Soufflé potatoes can be covered in a towel and refrigerated for 2 days. They will deflate but can be inflated again by deep frying.

Allow 1 potato for each serving.

Potatoes Anna   *Pommes de Terre Anna*

2½–3 pounds red or *white potatoes*
1½ cups clarified butter
Salt and pepper to taste
Sprigs of watercress or *parsley*

8–9 inch heavy iron or aluminum
skillet with ovenproof handle
(season with oil on heat first, pour
off oil)
Parchment paper

1. Peel potatoes, place in cold water as briefly as possible. Do not soak—the natural starch needed to make them stick together should not be washed out. Trim edges of potatoes evenly.

2. Slice ⅛-inch-thick using a *mandoline* (French slicer or shredder) or correct size slicing blade of a processor. Dry slices in towels. Potato scraps can be used for mashed potatoes or in soups.

3. Skillet can be lined with parchment paper before pouring on layer of clarified butter, which is heated in pan. Arrange sliced potatoes in overlapping petal fashion, compactly, starting in the center. The direction of each layer should be reversed, clockwise to counterclockwise. Shake pan after two layers to settle potatoes and prevent sticking. Salt and pepper and

263

sprinkle 2 tablespoons hot butter on each layer, which should be pressed firmly against sides of pan.

4. Pour butter over top, press down on potatoes, and place a round piece of parchment, buttered, cut correct size to cover top. Bake in 400-degree oven for 1 hour. Remove parchment paper, shake pan, and put potatoes back in oven to brown a few minutes.

5. Remove when brown on top, place on high heat on stovetop for about 5 minutes, shaking pan several times to loosen potato cake. Drain butter out by turning pan upside down with a plate over top. Run knife around edge to loosen potatoes. Save butter for other uses.

6. Unmold by turning pan upside down on serving dish. Center Potatoes Anna and garnish sides with sprigs of watercress or parsley. Can be quartered like a cake.

Serves 6–8.

NOTE: Cooked quail is sometimes placed on top of the potato cake, or rock cornish hens are placed around it.

VARIATIONS:

Potatoes Salardaise   *Pommes de Terre Salardaise*

Prepare the same as Potatoes Anna, placing sliced truffles in alternate layers.

Potatoes Monselet   *Pommes de Terre Monselet*

Use the same method as the one for Potatoes Anna, making a layer of potatoes, a layer of raw, thinly sliced artichoke bottoms, and a layer of thinly sliced truffles.

Potatoes Massenet   *Pommes de Terre Massenet*

Prepare the same as Potatoes Anna, alternating rows of thinly sliced potatoes with previously sautéed sliced mushrooms.

Potato Cake   *Pommes Darphin*

3¹/₂ pounds potatoes, Idaho or large red

3 ounces (6 tablespoons) butter and vegetable oil (half of each), approximate amount

10¹/₂-inch frying pan (preferably a cast-iron skillet)

Mandoline or food processor fitted with julienne-cutting disc

1. Peel potatoes and cut into thin, julienne-style strips. Do not wash or put potatoes in water, which would remove the starch. The starch is needed to keep potatoes together. Potatoes will turn dark or discolor if cut ahead of time. Dry excess moisture from cut potatoes, and sprinkle with salt just before frying.

2. Heat two thirds butter and oil in skillet and add potatoes on medium heat, turning and stirring at first. Then let potatoes form a single mass. (Bake in 375-degree oven for about 20 minutes to cook inside of cake, if desired.) Return to stovetop. When a crust has formed on bottom of potatoes, turn out in one piece onto a plate. Add rest of butter and oil to pan, and return potatoes upside down to get a golden crust on other side. Pour off grease, place potato cake on board, and cut in wedges. Reshape on silver serving platter to prevent scratching silver with cutting knife.

   Serve with main course meat dish—Roast Prime Rib of Beef (p. 34), Tournedos (p. 223), Roast Turkey (p. 215), Roast Leg of Lamb (p. 33), or veal.

Serves 6.

VARIATIONS:

   Pommes Maxim: julienne or trimmings of truffles mixed with uncooked potatoes.

   Pommes Monselet or *Massena:* sliced, cooked artichokes mixed with uncooked potatoes.

   Pommes Massenet: sliced mushrooms added to uncooked potatoes.

Darphin potatoes can be made in crêpe or blini pans for individual servings:

1. Sauté julienned potatoes in a crêpe pan (6–7 inches in diameter) in butter several minutes, turning often; season with salt and pepper, then form a cake. Put in 375-degree oven for about 7–8 minutes, turning once. If potato cake is not crisp enough, put back on stovetop on medium heat for a few seconds. Pour off excess butter. Cut in quarters and serve as a garnish on dinner plates.

2. The same process described in Step 1 is used to make Darphin potatoes in blini pans (4–5 inches in diameter).

Serve 1 potato cake to a person on dinner plate.

Shoestring Potatoes for Potato Nests

Pommes Frites en Julienne pour Nids de Pommes de Terre

Idaho potatoes
Vegetable oil for frying
Deep fat fryer
Deep frying thermometer

Metal basket with a long handle and
second smaller basket attached,
called a nest mold

1. Cut potatoes into very thin strips or fine julienne ¼ inch thick or less. Dry well.
2. Line the larger basket with potato strips. Press smaller basket on top. Trim off pieces of potatoes extending above rim of mold.
3. Plunge into deep, hot fat—390 degrees. As soon as they start to get brown, remove smaller basket to let potatoes brown for 1 minute. Remove larger basket for about 1 minute. Drain on paper towel.
4. Soufflé potatoes can be placed in nests *(nids)* or fried potatoes can be served in potato baskets.

Allow 1 potato for each serving.

Duchess Potatoes

Pommes de Terre Duchesse

2 baked potatoes
2 egg yolks
2–3 tablespoons butter
1 tablespoon heavy cream (optional)
Salt and pepper to taste

Beaten egg for browning
Directions for baking potatoes are
given in recipe for **Pommes de**
Terre Dauphine *(p. 81)*

1. Cut potatoes in half and scoop potato flesh off potato skins, chop roughly, and return to oven briefly to dry out any remaining steam. Push through a potato ricer or coarse sieve, and then beat well with egg yolks and enough butter to give flavor and texture. Add cream to thin sufficiently for piping. Season with salt and white pepper to taste.
2. While mixture is still hot, pipe through a pastry bag fitted with a large star tube, forming border on platter, small rosettes, or other desired shapes. Brush with beaten egg and brown in 400-degree oven or under broiler.

Makes approximately 1 cup. Serves 4.

NOTE: The same mixture is used for forming potato croquettes, little patties, or cork shapes, in which case it must be left quite thick.

Potato Croquettes

Croquettes de Pommes de Terre
Pommes de Terre en Croquettes

1 cup Pommes de Terre Duchesse
   mixture (see preceding recipe)
Flour for dredging
1 egg
2 tablespoons milk

1 tablespoon salad oil
¼ teaspoon salt
Dried fine white bread crumbs
Oil for deep fat frying

1. Shape the cold *Pommes de Terre Duchesse* into small round flat cakes, or imitate wine corks, tiny pears, or other shapes.

2. Coat before frying with *à l'anglaise* coating. First, roll in flour. Next, beat whole egg with milk, oil, and salt. Dip croquettes in egg mixture, drain, and roll in bread crumbs.

3. Deep fry in 375-degree oil until golden brown.

Serves 4.

Potatoes Berny

Pommes de Terre Berny

These are made the same way as Potato Croquettes but are formed in shape of small pears enclosing a little chopped truffle and rolled in sliced, chopped almonds instead of bread crumbs. Deep fry until hazelnut brown. Garnish each with a "stem" of parsley stalk.

Potato Purée

Pommes de Terre en Purée

4 Idaho potatoes
4½–6 tablespoons butter to 1 pound
   potato purée
Several tablespoons milk to 1 pound
   potato purée

Salt to taste
Pinch nutmeg (optional)

1. Peel, quarter, and cook potatoes in rapidly boiling salted water. Drain.

2. Put in medium hot oven just long enough to evaporate extra moisture. Press through a sieve or potato masher.

3. Place mashed potatoes in a saucepan over low heat and blend in 4½–6

267

tablespoons fresh butter to each pound of purée. Lighten by adding a few tablespoons of *boiling* milk and stir well.

4. Keep warm in a *bain-marie* as short a time as possible. The potato purée should not be boiled after it is made. It goes well with roast pork, pork chops, sausages.

Serves 6–8.

Potatoes Mousseline
Pommes de Terre Mousseline or *Mousse Parmentier*

3½ ounces (7 tablespoons) grated Parmesan cheese (reserve some for top)
6 tablespoons heavy cream, whipped
2 pounds firm potato purée

5 egg whites
Few grinds nutmeg
Salt and pepper to taste

1. Mix grated Parmesan cheese and whipped cream into potato purée; season with nutmeg, salt and pepper to taste.

2. Beat egg whites until stiff. Fold into purée.

3. Butter and flour a large 2-quart soufflé mold. Spoon in mixture. Sprinkle top with grated Parmesan cheese. Bake in a 350-degree oven for about 20–30 minutes. Serve with broiled or roast meat.

Serves 6–8.

Potatoes Rissolé
Pommes de Terre Rissolées

2 pounds new potatoes (about 10 small potatoes to a pound)
4–6 tablespoons butter

Salt and freshly ground pepper to taste
Chopped parsley

1. Use a heavy 9-inch sauté pan or one the correct size for amount of potatoes. Peel potatoes, heat butter in pan, add potatoes, and cover. Cook on low heat so that butter does not burn.

2. Turn potatoes during cooking so that they brown evenly. Cooking time depends on size of potatoes—about 30 minutes for medium-small ones.

Add salt and pepper after they are cooked. Sprinkle with parsley. Serve with steaks and roasts.

If new potatoes are not available, trim larger Idaho potatoes in oval or round shapes, parboil several minutes, drain, and cook as above.

Serves 5–6.

Potatoes Noisette   *Pommes de Terre Noisette*

2 pounds Idaho baking potatoes
4 tablespoons butter

Salt and freshly ground pepper to taste
2 tablespoons chopped parsley

1. Use a melon baller about 1 inch in diameter to scoop out potato balls from peeled potatoes. Soak potatoes in cold water to remove excess starch.
2. Parboil potato balls for 1 minutes, drain, dry and cook the same way as Potatoes Rissolé. Use parsley as a garnish.

Serves 4–6.

Gratin of Potatoes Dauphinoise   *Gratin de Pommes de Terre Dauphinoise*

3–4 potatoes, new red or white, about 2 pounds*
1 egg beaten
3½ cups milk, boiled
5 ounces (10 tablespoons) Gruyère cheese, freshly grated

Few grinds nutmeg
Salt and freshly ground pepper to taste
1 clove garlic
Butter to grease gratinée dish and for tops of potatoes

1. Peel and slice potatoes ¼ inch thick. Put in mixing bowl with beaten egg, boiled milk, 4½ ounces (9 tablespoons) of the Gruyère, nutmeg, salt and pepper.
2. Cut garlic clove in half and rub it over the inside of gratinée dish. Butter dish liberally, and fill with potato mixture. Sprinkle top with rest of cheese, and dot with butter.

* New red potatoes have more flavor than the white, which should be parboiled first.

3. Bake at 350 degrees for 35–40 minutes, until potatoes are tender and top is golden brown. Serve with grilled steak or as a garnish with meat or poultry.

Serves 6–8.

Savoyard Potatoes   *Pommes de Terre à la Savoyarde*

Made in the same way as Gratin of Potatoes Dauphinoise, but omit egg and substitute coffee cream or half and half for the milk.

Serve with roast chicken, or broiled or roast meat.

Potatoes "Bakers' Style"   *Pommes de Terre Boulangère*

In the past, in French villages the family cook would prepare casseroles at home and take them to the baker to be placed in the great brick bread oven after the loaves had been removed. When cooked, the villagers would collect them and give the apprentis *a tip of a few centimes for this service. That is why a number of traditional country dishes are called* à la boulangère—*in the style of the baker. This custom still exists in small villages.*

*3–4 potatoes, new red or white,
    about 2 pounds
1 cup sliced smothered onions
Salt and freshly ground pepper to
    taste*

*3½ cups veal stock or consommé
Butter to grease gratinée dish and for
    top of potatoes*

Peel and slice potatoes ¼ inch thick. Alternate layers of potatoes and smothered onions in buttered baking dish, seasoning each layer with salt and pepper. Dot top layer of potatoes with butter and bake at 350 degrees for 35–45 minutes.

Serve with Roast Leg of Lamb (p. 33) or rack of lamb.

Serves 4–6.

Methods of Cooking for an Assortment of Vegetables

Artichokes *(artichauts):* To reheat chilled, cooked artichokes, place upside down in hot water for a few minutes.

String Beans *(haricots verts):* Cook briefly in large amount of boiling water. As soon as beans are crunchy, 4–5 minutes, drain and place in bowl of cold, running water to stop the cooking. Before serving, sauté in unsalted butter on medium-low heat. Season with salt and pepper and sprinkle with chopped parsley, if desired.

Spinach *(épinards):* Remove stems, and clean spinach in cold water. Cook in large amount of salted boiling water for about 2 minutes, drain, and squeeze out excess water. Serve with *beurre noisette* (butter cooked to a light hazelnut brown).

Washed spinach can also be cooked in the water which clings to its leaves, in a heavy sauté pan, covered on medium-high heat. Turn spinach once—its color will be a bright green and it will cook in a couple of minutes.

Mushrooms *(champignons):* Quarter or slice mushrooms, sauté quickly in heavy pan on high heat for about 2 minutes. Drain any liquid in pan, and add small amount of unsalted butter, chopped or crushed garlic, chopped parsley. Add salt and freshly ground pepper to taste. Liquid from sautéed mushrooms can be saved to flavor soup.

Confit of Onions or Shallots or Garlic
Confit d'Oignons ou Echalotes ou Ail

1 cup thinly sliced onions or *1 cup minced shallots*
1 tablespoon butter
Salt and pepper to taste
½ teaspoon sugar

¼ cup red wine
¼ cup red or *white wine vinegar*
1–2 tablespoons crème de cassis or brandy *(optional)*

1. Sauté sliced onions or minced shallots in butter until transparent. Season with salt, pepper, and sugar. Simmer until mixture caramelizes.
2. Add red wine, red or white wine vinegar, and *crème de cassis* or brandy. Simmer until liquid is absorbed.

Serve with game, beef, lamb.

Serves 2–3.

To make Confit of Garlic: Separate garlic head into cloves, parboil cloves for a few minutes, remove skins, and trim off base of cloves. Proceed with Steps 1 and 2 above.

To reduce garlic flavor, blanch unpeeled cloves in two or three changes of simmering water, if desired.

Confit of Pearl Onions   *Confit de Petits Oignons*

1 cup pearl onions, unpeeled
1 tablespoon wine vinegar

1–2 tablespoons butter
½ tablespoon sugar

1. In a saucepan cover onions with boiling water, add vinegar, and simmer until onions are beginning to soften, about 10–15 minutes.

2. Drain onions, peel if desired, and put in sauté pan with a little water (about a tablespoon), butter, and sugar. Cover, sauté slowly, stirring occasionally until butter and sugar start to caramelize. Remove cover to caramelize, if necessary.

   Serve with duck, turkey, chicken, other birds, and meat. If served around roast of beef, do not peel onions. If onions are boiled, as in Step 1, tearing will be avoided when they are peeled.

Serves 6–8.

There are three varieties of tiny button or pearl onions:
    red (Italian or Creole)—mild flavor
    white (Bermuda)—sweet flavor
    yellow (Spanish or Valencia)—strong flavor

Roast Shallots   *Echalotes Rôti*

16 large shallots
2 tablespoons olive oil or other
    vegetable oil

Salt and freshly ground black pepper
    to taste
Large pinch thyme

1. Peel any loose, dry outer skin from shallots, leaving only one layer to hold shallot together.
2. Place in a shallow baking pan, sprinkle liberally with oil, season with salt and pepper to taste, and add a large pinch of thyme. Bake at 350 degrees for about 1 hour, basting occasionally with the pan juices.

A slight pressure applied at one end will release the tender, baked shallot from the skin. Serve with duck or other poultry, or with steak.

Serves 4.

Roast Garlic   *Rôti d'Ail*   ·

Whole heads of garlic may be cooked in the same way; the garlic will become extremely mild and mellow. Peel away the outer skin, but leave the cloves attached to the root. The baked garlic purée may be eaten as a vegetable, or used to flavor sauces, soups, or soufflés.

Serve 1 head per person.

Braised Red Cabbage   *Choux Rouges Braisés*

2 tablespoons chopped fresh duck fat
or rendered duck or ham fat or
butter
1–2 large red onions, peeled, halved,
and thinly sliced
1 medium head red cabbage, cored
and sliced ½ inch thick

2 tart apples, unpeeled, cored, and
thinly sliced
½ cup Pinot Noir or other dry red
wine
½ cup red wine vinegar
Salt to taste

1. In a heavy dutch oven or casserole heat chopped duck fat over very low heat for about 5 minutes until enough fat has rendered to film bottom of pan.
2. Add onions and cook over medium low heat without browning until limp, about 3 minutes. Add sliced cabbage and then the sliced apple. Pour wine and vinegar over them; salt to taste. Cover, bring to a boil, reduce heat, and simmer about ¾ hour. Stir several times. Taste to check seasoning.

273

Cabbage should still be crunchy. It can be prepared in advance and reheated.

Serve with *Confit de Canard* (p. 245) and game.

Serves 8.

Basic Dry Duxelles Mushroom Mixture   *Duxelles*

1 pound mushrooms (stems can be substituted for tops)
4 tablespoons finely chopped onions
2 tablespoons each butter and oil or *4 tablespoons clarified butter*

2 tablespoons finely chopped shallots
Pinch nutmeg
Salt and freshly ground pepper to taste

1. Clean fresh mushrooms or stems and chop by hand or in food processor fitted with steel blade.
2. Place chopped mushrooms in clean towel and wring out moisture.
3. Sauté chopped onions in the butter until lightly browned. Add finely chopped shallots, sauté several minutes, add mushrooms, and sauté on medium heat until all liquid is gone and mixture has a light brown color.
4. Season to taste with nutmeg, salt, and pepper. Cool, refrigerate, or freeze.
    Use for flavoring sauces, as an ingredient in stuffings for meats, vegetables, or *pâtés.*

Makes 1 cup.

Duxelles as an Ingredient in Stuffings

1 cup dry duxelles
¼ cup Madeira or *dry wine*

¼ cup Brown Sauce (p. 39)
1 tablespoon chopped parsley

In a saucepan on medium heat cook duxelles with Madeira and Brown Sauce until liquid is absorbed. Add chopped parsley.

Makes 1½ cups.

Duxelles as a Filling for Vegetables

1 cup dry duxelles
1/2 cup Brown Sauce (p. 39)
1/4 cup dry wine

1/2 clove garlic
Fresh bread crumbs (optional)
1 tablespoon chopped parsley

Simmer first four ingredients until liquid has evaporated from duxelles; thicken with bread crumbs, if necessary. Remove garlic clove and stir in parsley.

Makes 1½ cups.

Mushroom Purée — *Purée de Champignons*

1 pound mushrooms, cultivated or
  wild such as morels
1–2 tablespoons butter
2/3 cup very thick Béchamel Sauce
  (p. 51)

1/4 cup heavy cream
Few grains nutmeg
Salt and freshly ground pepper to
  taste

1. Clean and dry mushrooms and purée in food processor fitted with steel blade. Put puréed mushrooms in clean towel and squeeze out moisture.
2. In a sauté pan heat butter, add mushrooms, and stir on medium heat until mixture is dry. Add Béchamel Sauce, cream, and seasonings. Reduce to correct consistency.

    Use for stuffing vegetables, for *subrics* or timbales, or as a puréed vegetable on dinner plate.

Makes 1½ cups.

Molded Mousse of Vegetables

Subrics de Légumes

¾ pound carrots
1 pound turnips
4 egg yolks
1 cup heavy cream
Few grinds nutmeg
Salt and pepper to taste
4 tablespoons Sauce Béchamel *(p. 51)*
Butter for molds

One cup of purée of any of the
following vegetables may be
substituted: broccoli, artichoke
bottoms, spinach and watercress,
green beans, or *peas. Molds may be*
filled with only one vegetable, or
they may be layered in contrasting
colors. However, keep proportions
of ingredients the same.
Foil to cover tops of molds
8 half-cup baba molds, 2 inches
diameter, 2 inches high
(approximately)

1. Boil or steam carrots and turnips until tender, then purée separately in a food processor or blender. You should have about 1 cup purée of each. Evaporate excess liquid from turnips by stirring purée over medium heat in a heavy saucepan; some vegetables contain more water than others.

2. Put 1 cup carrot purée in a food processor or blender and, with the motor running, add 2 egg yolks, ½ cup cream, nutmeg, salt and pepper, and 2 tablespoons *Sauce Béchamel*. Process just long enough to mix and set aside. Repeat Step 2 with the turnip purée.

3. Lightly butter molds and half fill with carrot purée, being careful not to drip it down the inside of the molds—the layers should be distinct and separate when unmolded. Fill molds to the top with turnip purée mixture.

4. Place molds in a *bain-marie* or a shallow baking pan and add enough boiling water to reach halfway up the sides of the molds. Cover molds with a sheet of buttered aluminum foil and bake at 350–375 degrees for 30–35 minutes. Let rest for 20 minutes before unmolding.

Molds can be served hot or cold (they look handsome arranged around roast meat or poultry, or a whole fish) and may be reheated by replacing in the *bain-marie* for a few minutes in a 350-degree oven. Unmolded vegetable mousse may be surrounded with another vegetable of contrasting color and texture, such as snap peas or asparagus tips.

Serves 8.

How to measure capacity of small molds, porcelain ramekins, etc.:
Fill with water and pour into glass measuring jar.

Vegetables That Require Special Cooking
for Molded Mousses or Timbales

Zucchini   *Courgettes*

*3 zucchini, each 6 inches long,
   weighing approximately 5 ounces
   each; slice in ¼-inch rounds or
   cubes*
1 tablespoon olive oil
1 teaspoon finely chopped onion

½ clove garlic
Pinch thyme
Few grinds nutmeg
*Salt and freshly ground pepper to
   taste*

1. Put all ingredients in sauté pan and simmer, covered, until zucchini is cooked, about 8–10 minutes. Remove lid to dry mixture.

2. Purée in processor and proceed with Step 2 of the recipe for Molded Mousse (p. 276). The additional seasoning may not be necessary.

Pumpkin   *Potiron*

*1 pound pumpkin pulp (fresh, if
   available) or yellow squash,
   crookneck, or banana squash*
2 tablespoons finely chopped onion
*1 cup milk or enough to cover half of
   vegetables*

Few grinds nutmeg
*Salt and freshly ground pepper to
   taste*

1. Peel pumpkin or squash, put in saucepan with onions, cover halfway with milk, and add nutmeg, salt and pepper to taste. Simmer uncovered until milk is evaporated and vegetable has thickened.

2. Purée 1 cup cooked pumpkin or squash in processor. There may be extra purée. Proceed with Step 2 of the recipe for Molded Mousse (p. 276)— additional seasoning may not be necessary.

Vegetable Purées
Purées des Légumes

Starchy or root vegetables: Steam or simmer in water until soft enough to purée. Drain, rub through a sieve, purée in food mill or food processor fitted with steel blade. When smooth, dry in saucepan on low heat with about 1 tablespoon butter to 1 cup purée or to taste. Season with nutmeg (optional), salt and pepper. Cream may be added at this stage; a few tablespoons cream are sometimes needed to add moisture while puréeing carrots. Rice can be cooked with carrots—1 tablespoon to 6 carrots.

Fresh or watery vegetables: Steam or cook in water such vegetables as green beans, broccoli, asparagus, cauliflower, or artichokes until fairly soft. Drain; purée in processor or push through a sieve. Heat with a little butter, stirring to remove any liquid. Add mashed potatoes, thick béchamel sauce, or steamed rice to thicken to desired consistency. Measurements are approximately ¼ cup thickener to 1 cup purée. Particularly watery purées such as asparagus may require more thickener: one third of the total volume or ⅓ cup thickener to ⅔ cup vegetable purée. Season to taste. Nutmeg is optional.

Serve as a vegetable or garnish with meats; use as a filling for other vegetables, in terrines or in mousses.

Spinach in Cream   *Epinards à la Crème*

1 bunch spinach, about 1 pound, stems removed
2 tablespoons butter
½ cup whipping cream
Salt and freshly ground pepper to taste
Pinch nutmeg

1. Blanch well-washed spinach in large pot of boiling salted water for 2 minutes. Drain and refresh with cold water. Chop and set aside until ready to serve, allowing spinach to cool completely.
2. Heat butter in a sauté pan until golden brown but not burned. Stir in spinach and add cream. Let cream reduce over medium high heat by about half, stirring spinach frequently, about 4 minutes. Season with salt, pepper, and a dash of nutmeg.

Serves 2–4.

Spinach Soufflé   *Soufflé aux Epinards*

Butter for soufflé dish
Grated Parmesan cheese or flour to
* line soufflé mold*
One 10-ounce package frozen
* spinach or 1 pound fresh*
4 tablespoons butter
4 tablespoons flour

1 cup milk
Salt and pepper to taste
⅛ teaspoon nutmeg
6 eggs, separated
Pinch salt for egg whites
Large soufflé dish (6½ inches wide
* and 3 inches high)*

1. Film mold with butter and refrigerate. When chilled, apply another coating of butter. Sprinkle sides and bottom with grated Parmesan cheese or flour and shake out excess.

2. Cook frozen or fresh spinach (p. 271) and cool immediately in cold water or use ice cubes. Drain spinach and press out *all* moisture.

3. To make béchamel sauce: Melt butter in a heavy saucepan, stir in flour with whisk, and cook for about 5 minutes. Bring milk to a boil and slowly stir with a whisk into butter and flour roux until thick and smooth. Season with salt, pepper, and nutmeg.

4. Chop spinach in processor fitted with steel blade. Add white sauce and mix. Add egg yolks and run machine just until incorporated. Remove to large mixing bowl.

5. Beat egg whites with a pinch of salt in large bowl of an electric mixer until soft peaks form. Fold one third of egg whites into spinach mixture. Fold in remaining egg whites, quickly using a spatula to mix.

6. Pour into prepared soufflé mold and set on baking sheet in 350-degree oven for 30–35 minutes or until firm. Serve immediately.

Serves 6–8.

Beet Mousse   *Mousse de Betteraves*

3 fresh beets, about 12 ounces
1 medium onion, about 4 ounces,
* sliced*
1 tablespoon butter
1 clove garlic, peeled

1 teaspoon red wine vinegar
¼ cup chicken or beef broth
¼ cup cream
Salt and pepper to taste

1. Remove tops of beets, clean beets with vegetable brush, dry, bake in 350-degree oven for about 1½ hours or until fairly soft. Peel and slice.
2. In a large skillet sauté sliced onion in butter on medium heat for about 5 minutes or until it starts to turn brown. Add sliced beets, garlic, vinegar, broth, and simmer until all liquid has evaporated.
3. Heat cream to a warm temperature. Put beet mixture in food processor fitted with steel blade. Slowly add heated cream while puréeing until mixture is smooth like mashed potatoes. Add salt and pepper to taste. Keep warm in a double boiler until ready to serve with main course.

   Goes well with duck and game.

Serves 4.

NOTE: The best way to cook beets for any purpose, even salad, is to bake them. Boiling always gives them a "muddy" taste.

Chestnut Purée   *Marrons en Purée*

1½–2 pounds chestnuts, shelled and peeled
2 cups milk or water (approximately)
2 cups stock or water (approximately)

1 rib celery
Salt to taste (pepper optional)
Butter to taste, about 3 tablespoons
Cream or milk to taste and for consistency, heated

1. Cover shelled and peeled chestnuts with half milk and half stock or water. Simmer with celery until soft enough to purée, about 20–30 minutes. Remove celery. When chestnuts are done, most of liquid will be absorbed. Purée in food processor or push through a strainer.
2. Put purée in top of double boiler; stir in a little butter and warmed cream. Salt lightly; if to be served with a roast, add some sauce from it. It should have the consistency of mashed potatoes. Serve with venison, pork chops, marinated lamb, Dodine of Pheasant (p. 237).

Serves 4–6.

How to Peel Chestnuts

METHOD 1:

Cut an X about ⅛ inch deep in rounded side of each chestnut, brush with oil, and bake in high oven (450 degrees) for about 20 minutes or until shells and skins can be removed. Rub chestnuts in a towel to remove skins. Do not let them cool off before peeling.

METHOD 2:

After a slit is cut in rounded side of chestnuts, put in boiling water until shells will peel, about 20 minutes. Remove a few at a time, leaving the rest in water until ready to peel.

METHOD 3:

Slit chestnuts, coat with oil, and place in a skillet over medium heat. Stir and cook until shells and skins can be removed with a sharp knife.

Grains
Riz

Boiled Rice   *Riz au Blanc*

American packaged rice is clean and does not require pre-washing. The process used affects amounts of water used in cooking and the time. Converted rice contains the same vitamins as brown rice, for it has been processed to drive those nutrients present in the husk into the center of the grain, where they are not removed by polishing.*

2 cups water   ½ teaspoon salt
1 cup regular or converted rice,
   unwashed

1. Use a heavy 3-quart saucepan with a tight fitting lid. Bring water to a boil, add salt, and pour in rice. Lower heat to a simmer, stir rice to distribute evenly, cover, and cook 15 minutes without removing lid. All the water should be absorbed. If not, cook a little longer.

2. If a moister rice is desired, use ½ cup more water and cook about 10 minutes longer.

Makes 3–4 cups cooked rice. Serves 6–8.

* William Laas, ed. *Cuisines of the Eastern World* (New York: Golden Press, 1967), p. 173.   **281**

Oven-Steamed Rice   *Riz à l'Etuvée*

2 cups rice   *1 teaspoon salt*
4 cups boiling water

Use a 3- or 4-quart ovenproof casserole with a tight lid. Put rice, boiling water, and salt in, cover, and bake in 350-degree oven for 20–30 minutes or until liquid is absorbed and rice is cooked.

Makes 7–8 cups cooked rice. Serves 10–12.

Rice Pilaf   *Riz Pilaf*

3 tablespoons butter   *4 cups chicken or veal stock*
2 tablespoons finely chopped onions   *Salt and pepper to taste*
2 cups regular or converted rice

1. Start with a large, heavy casserole with a tight lid or use a large, heavy sauté pan for Step 1 and transfer rice to ovenproof casserole in Step 2. Sauté chopped onions in 1½ tablespoons butter, on medium heat, until transparent. Add rice and stir until grains become milky in color, signifying the outside of grains of rice are seared to prevent rice from sticking together.
2. Bring stock to boil, pour over rice, add salt and pepper, cover, and bake in 325-degree oven for 18–20 minutes or until broth is absorbed and rice is soft enough.
3. Remove from oven, uncover, add 1½ tablespoons butter in pieces, and return to warm oven, where it can be kept for hours without losing its flavor or texture. Serve with poultry, meat, or fish.

Serves 10–12.

Wild Rice with Chicken Livers   *Riz Sauvage au Foies de Volaille*

Wild rice comes from the lakes and wilderness of the Northern woods of Minnesota and the Great Lakes area. It is believed to be found "nowhere else in the world." It was so prized by the Chippewa and Sioux Indians that they fought wars for possession of the areas where it grew. Wild rice is not a "true" rice—it is the grain of an aquatic grass found growing wild in shallow waters. Since it has always been scarce and the crop has been variable from year to year, the price is high. However, many wild rice paddies are now being cultivated in the Great Lakes area and California.

2 cups uncooked wild rice
2 tablespoons butter
1 cup finely chopped onion
Salt and pepper to taste
6 cups chicken stock or water
½ pound mushrooms, quartered or sliced

1 tablespoon oil and 1 tablespoon butter
1 pound (approximately) chicken livers (duck livers can substitute)

1. Wash wild rice in a strainer under cold running water until water is clear.

2. Melt butter in a large sauté pan, cook finely chopped onions until transparent. Stir in wild rice and cook on low heat for 2 or 3 minutes. Season lightly with salt and freshly ground black pepper.

3. Put rice in a large casserole, pour in boiling stock, cover, and cook in 350-degree oven for at least an hour or until rice is soft.

4. While wild rice is baking, sauté sliced or quartered mushrooms in butter and oil for several minutes. Remove from pan with juice, and cook chicken livers about 5 minutes, removing from fire while still pink. Cut into large dice. Duck livers should cook a little longer and be cut in fine dice.

5. Stir mushrooms and liver into cooked rice. Keep warm in oven or double boiler. More butter can be added. Serve with duck, other poultry, or meat.

One cup wild rice makes 3 cups cooked rice. Serves 6–8.

Chapter Ten

PASTRY CREAM

Crème Pâtissière Is Compared to
Cream Sauce—
Crème Anglaise; Soufflés, Custards, and
Butter Creams Follow

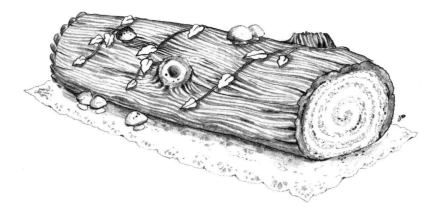

Now that *les pâtissiers* are eager to finish their *éclairs* of *pâte à choux, tartes* of *pâte brisée,* and *Religieuses,* made with both doughs, the time is ripe for fillings. I started with the simplest filling, *Crème Chantilly* (p. 79), in Chapter 3, and will end Chapter 10 with butter creams, the richest of all decorations for cakes. *Crème pâtissière,* usually vanilla flavored, is the basic pastry cream filling. It is closely related to the custard sauce, *crème à l'anglaise* shortened to *crème anglaise.* The ingredients and techniques are the same, except *crème anglaise* has no flour and a thinner consistency. I repeat the cooking law, "Always use a non-aluminum or non-reactive pot to prevent discoloration of the egg yolks."

Crème Pâtissière (below) is the basis for my dessert soufflés and Grand Marnier Sauce. I have been told my soufflés are the highest, lightest, and tastiest. Perhaps "my secrets" are selecting the correct size of soufflé mold, which is filled to the top, using fresh extra large eggs, and baking at the proper temperature. Soufflés can even be baked in hollowed out orange shells.

Crème à l'Anglaise (p. 287) is the basis for Bavarian creams—molded custards stabilized by gelatin and firmed by chilling. Other molded custards, *Crème Renversée* and *Crème Brûlée* (p. 292), are baked, served warm, or chilled.

If Bavarian creams are to be unmolded, the custard should be poured into a mold lightly coated with a tasteless oil or lined with ladyfingers or strips of génoise. To unmold, loosen edges of chilled cream with a sharp knife, place serving platter over top, and turn dessert upside down. If it does not unmold, place a damp hot towel over the mold until it loosens. Do not immerse mold in hot water.

French Pastry Cream   *Crème Pâtissière*

3 egg yolks	*4 tablespoons flour*
1 whole egg	*2 cups milk*
6 tablespoons sugar	*Confectioners' sugar*
1 teaspoon vanilla extract	

1. Put yolks, whole egg, sugar, and vanilla in a mixing bowl and beat until mixture becomes light in color and thick enough to form a slowly dissolving ribbon off a lifted beater.

2. Stir in flour. (Three ounces cornstarch is sometimes substituted, however, the resultant pastry cream will "set" and cannot be whipped. Soufflés are better made without cornstarch. As explained in the introduction, *Crème Pâtissière* is used as a base for dessert soufflés.)

3. Bring milk to the boil and whisk into pastry cream. Pour mixture into a large heavy pan and whisk for 1 minute over medium high heat. It should be very thick.

4. Cool pastry cream before adding optional flavorings to taste, such as coffee, praline, orange, lemon, mocha, or vanilla; or liqueurs chosen to taste—Grand Marnier, Cointreau, Kahlua, etc. While still warm, cover surface with plastic wrap or sprinkle with confectioners' sugar to prevent a skin from forming. *Crème Pâtissière* will keep for 3 or 4 days in the refrigerator.

Makes 2½–3 cups.

Custard Sauce   *Crème à l'Anglaise*

MODERN RECIPE:
6–8 egg yolks
½ cup sugar
1 teaspoon cornstarch

1 quart milk
1 vanilla bean, to infuse milk, or 1
   teaspoon vanilla extract

1. Whisk egg yolks and sugar together, or beat in an electric mixer until thick and lemon colored.

2. Mix cornstarch with a little cold milk and add to quart of milk. Scald milk with vanilla bean, and pour hot milk into egg yolks, whisking constantly. (Rinse and dry vanilla bean and store buried in sugar. It can be reused a number of times and will flavor the sugar also.)

3. Pour custard sauce into a heavy tin-lined copper pot or the porcelain insert of a double boiler. (Do not make *Crème Anglaise* in aluminum, which discolors it, or in a flimsy pan, which tends to scorch the mixture.)

4. Stir with wooden spoon over low to medium heat, or over hot water until custard starts to coat the spoon. In a double boiler it will take about 15 minutes to thicken, and must not be cooked at too high a heat or the eggs will curdle. To test, dip clean wooden spoon in mixture, turn it over and

287

run finger across back of spoon. If the two sides remain separated, it is ready. Or, if you blow on the back of the custard covered spoon, it should "make roses."

5. Strain into a bowl, stir in vanilla essence if used, and let cool. Stir from time to time to prevent a skin from forming.

Crème à l'Anglaise is served with *Gâteau Nancy* (p. 335), *Tarte aux Fruits Frais de Saison* (p. 153), *Gâteau Génoise* (p. 326), *Gratin de Pêches et Crème* (p. 333), or *Oeufs à la Neige* (p. 342), to name a few desserts.

Other flavorings may be added, such as caramel, mocha, pistachio, almond, anise—add flavor according to taste. Concentrated flavorings are added drop by drop. To flavor custard sauce with caramel, use 2 tablespoons caramelized sugar for each cup of sauce.

Makes 5–6 cups. Recipe can be halved.

TRADITIONAL RECIPE:

12 egg yolks
2 cups sugar
1 quart milk

1 vanilla bean, to infuse milk, or
1 teaspoon vanilla extract

Proceed with Steps 1–5 as in Modern Recipe above, omitting the cornstarch in Step 2.

Makes 5–6 cups. Recipe can be halved.

Chiboust Pastry Cream

Crème Chibouste, also called *Crème Saint-Honoré*

1½ cups Crème Pâtissière *(p. 286), heated*
1 heaping teaspoon unflavored gelatin
1 teaspoon vanilla extract or *other flavoring of choice*

3 egg whites
2 tablespoons sugar

1. Stir gelatin into *Crème Pâtissière,* which must be hot enough to dissolve the gelatin granules. Stir in vanilla.

2. Beat egg whites until stiff but not dry. Beat in sugar.

3. When pastry cream has cooled to lukewarm, fold into beaten egg whites.

Makes 2½–3 cups. Fills 8-inch diameter *gâteau.*

Praline Pastry Cream

Crème Chibouste Praliné

½ pint Crème Pâtissière *(p. 286), heated*
2 heaping tablespoons Pâte Praliné *(p. 289)*

1 heaping teaspoon unflavored gelatin
3 egg whites
2 tablespoons sugar

1. Stir *Pâte Praliné* into hot *Crème Pâtissière*.
2. Stir gelatin into hot pastry cream.
3. Beat egg whites until stiff but not dry and beat in sugar. Fold beaten egg whites into pastry cream after it has cooled to lukewarm.

If pastry is to be filled through a small opening such as an éclair (p. 75), it must be done immediately because gelatin will set and filling will not spread. If pastry cream has set, fill from top.

Use for *Gâteau Saint-Honoré (p. 154), Choux à la Crème, Paris-Brest* (p. 76).

Makes 2–2½ cups.

Praline Paste

Pâte Praliné

HANDMADE METHOD:
½ cup sugar
¼ cup almonds, shelled but not peeled

¼ cup hazelnuts (noisettes), *shelled but not peeled*

1. Place sugar and nuts in a heavy saucepan on medium high heat. Stir with a wooden spatula until the nuts are browned and the sugar turns a dark caramel color.
2. Place on an oiled marble surface and cool. Pound with a wooden mallet or use a rolling pin to pulverize or make a powder. Cover with heavy waxed paper to keep ingredients from flying off the marble.
3. Prolonged pounding is necessary to make a paste.

Praline powder, as opposed to paste, is easier to incorporate into butter cream.

Makes 1 cup.

FOOD PROCESSOR METHOD:
4 ounces (1 cup) hazelnuts
4 ounces (1 cup) almonds

8 ounces (approximately 1½ cups) confectioners' sugar

289

Toast nuts on a cookie sheet in a 350-degree oven for about 10 minutes, or until hazelnuts' skins start to split and nuts smell delicious. Place hot nuts in food processor (it is not necessary to remove skins) with sugar and process, using steel blade, until a paste is formed. This will take about 5 minutes. Add sugar and process until smooth, scraping down the bowl occasionally. Paste keeps almost indefinitely in the refrigerator, in an airtight container.

Praline can be used to stuff dried pitted California prunes or apricots. Fill, make a grid pattern on top, and brush with apricot glaze.

Makes 1½ cups.

Spanish Cream   *Crème Espagnole*

3 eggs, separated
⅓ cup sugar
1 cup milk
1 tablespoon unflavored gelatin

2 tablespoons Pâte Praliné *(p. 289)*
1 teaspoon vanilla extract
1 quart mold or individual glasses

1. Beat yolks and sugar together until thick and lemon colored. Put mixture in heavy saucepan.
2. Heat milk just to boiling point. Pour hot milk into yolks on low heat, stirring with whisk. Add gelatin and mix with wooden spoon until gelatin is dissolved and custard is thick enough to coat spoon.
3. Chill until it becomes slightly thicker; add *Pâte Praliné,* vanilla, and egg whites beaten to soft peaks. Grease mold lightly. Fill with Spanish Cream. Chill. Can be unmolded. Individual glasses can be used instead of one large mold. Decorate with candied violets or *Langues de Chat* (pp. 351–352) placed like rabbit ears on top.

Serves 6.

This is similar to a Bavarian Cream without whipping cream. It is a substitute cream for *Gâteau St. Honoré* (p. 154) and *Paris-Brest* (p. 76).

Serve with *Crème Anglaise* (p. 287) or *Coulis* of fresh raspberries or strawberries (p. 340).

Striped Chocolate and Vanilla Bavarian Cream

Crème Bavaroise au Chocolat et Vanille

8 egg yolks
1 cup superfine sugar, sifted
Pinch salt
1¾ ounces semi-sweet chocolate
2½ cups milk
1 vanilla bean or 1½ teaspoons vanilla extract

1½–2 tablespoons unflavored gelatin, softened in ¼ cup cold water
1 pint heavy cream, half-whipped
Sweet almond oil or tasteless oil to coat mold
2 quart mold, non-reactive, low or high sides.

1. In heavy saucepan or double boiler put yolks, sugar, and pinch of salt and stir until sugar is completely dissolved on low heat.

2. Melt chocolate in double boiler over hot water and let cool.

3. Bring milk with vanilla bean just to a boil. Pour milk into egg yolk mixture. Stir in softened gelatin using a spatula. Stir on low heat until custard coats a wooden spoon. Remove from heat.

4. Divide 4 cups custard equally in two bowls. Mix melted chocolate in one bowl using whisk to dissolve chocolate. Chill custards until they start to set.

5. Using chilled bowl and beaters, whip cream until it starts to thicken. Refrigerate until ready to fold into custard. When custard starts to set, divide partially whipped cream in half and fold into each bowl of flavored custard.

6. Oil mold lightly, pour custard onto mold, alternating flavors of chocolate and vanilla, making three to six layers depending on size of mold. If Bavarian Cream is served in a large glass bowl or individual glass dishes, the amount of gelatin may be reduced, resulting in a much lighter consistency. See Charlotte Russe (p. 332).

Serves 10–12.

Caramel Custard

Crème Renversée
Crème Moulée au Caramel

1 tablespoon water
½ cup sugar
1 pint milk or *half and half*

3 eggs
1 teaspoon vanilla extract
1 quart mold

1. In a small heavy saucepan put water and 3 tablespoons of the sugar; caramelize on medium high heat (p. 156).
2. Quickly pour caramelized sugar into the mold, coating the bottom of the mold or ovenproof bowl.
3. In a saucepan bring milk just to the boil.
4. Combine eggs, vanilla, and remaining sugar and beat for 1 minute using electric beaters or whisk. Slowly incorporate hot milk with a whisk.
5. Pour mixture into prepared mold. Skim off foam. Place in a *bain-marie* and bake in 375-degree oven for about 45 minutes or until a knife or toothpick comes out clean.
6. Chill in mold for 6–8 hours or overnight. Serve unmolded. Caramelized sugar will cling to custard better if it is chilled 24 hours.

Serves 6.

The texture is much better if you make two separate custards rather than double the recipe and bake in one mold.

Burned Custard

Crème Brûlée

6 egg yolks
6 tablespoons sugar
3 cups whipping cream
1 inch piece vanilla bean or 1
  teaspoon vanilla extract

½ cup light brown sugar
  (approximately)

1. Beat egg yolks with sugar until light and creamy. Heat whipping cream with vanilla bean in a double boiler or heavy saucepan until it is warm. Remove vanilla bean.
2. Stir warm cream into yolks very slowly. Put mixture in double boiler, and stir constantly until custard coats spoon. (Water should be boiling in bottom pot of double boiler.)

3. Pour into individual porcelain *ramequins* or a large white *ramequin*. Refrigerate 6 to 8 hours or overnight.

4. When ready to serve, cover entire top of custard with brown sugar. Place dish on a pan of crushed ice and put under the broiler until sugar melts and caramelizes. *Watch carefully to prevent sugar from burning!* Serve immediately.

      Serve with cookies (*Four-Secs,* p. 351).

Serves 10–12.

Grand Marnier Soufflé   *Soufflé au Grand Marnier*

Butter and sugar for molds
2 heaping tablespoons Crème
    Pâtissière *(p. 286), at room*
    temperature
1 egg yolk

1 tablespoon Grand Marnier
2–3 egg whites
2 individual soufflé molds, 4 inches
    diameter and 2 inches deep

1. Butter sides and bottom of molds well and coat generously with sugar.

2. Combine 2 heaping tablespoons *Crème Pâtissière* with egg yolk. Stir in Grand Marnier.

3. Beat egg whites until they stand in *moist* peaks; do *not* beat until dry. (Chocolate and lemon soufflés need more egg whites.) Fold quickly into *Crème Pâtissière* mixture.

4. Fill soufflé molds to the top and run index finger around edge about 1 inch from side of mold to form "hat" when baked. Bake in 375-degree oven for 7–10 minutes. Serve immediately!

Makes 2 individual soufflés.

Proportions for one large soufflé mold, 7–8 inches diameter and 2½ inches deep:

6 heaping tablespoons Crème
    Pâtissière
3 egg yolks

¼ cup Grand Marnier
8 egg whites

Bake in 350-degree oven for 25–30 minutes or until firm. Serves 5–6.

NOTE: This recipe can be used as a basic soufflé recipe by omitting the Grand

293

Marnier and substituting other liqueurs or flavorings, such as lemon, coffee, or rum.

A quarter cup of leftover Grand Marnier Soufflé mixture may be combined with ½ cup cream, whipped, ½ teaspoon confectioners' sugar, and 2 tablespoons Grand Marnier to make a sauce for the baked soufflé. If no leftover mixture is available, then use the following recipe.

Grand Marnier Sauce for Soufflés

Sauce Grand Marnier pour les Soufflés

½ cup heavy cream
½ teaspoon confectioners' sugar

½ cup Crème Pâtissière *(p. 286)*
2 tablespoons Grand Marnier

Whip cream and add confectioners' sugar. Fold whipped cream into *Crème Pâtissière* and add Grand Marnier.

Grand Marnier Sauce can be served separately, or spooned into an indentation made in the top of the baked soufflé.

Makes approximately 1½ cups.

Grand Marnier Sauce for Desserts

Sauce Grand Marnier pour les Desserts

5 egg yolks
8 ounces (1 heaping cup) sugar

1½ ounces (3 tablespoons) Grand Marnier
2¼ cups heavy cream

1. Put egg yolks in bowl, beat slightly, and set aside.
2. Combine sugar with ½ cup water in a heavy pan and cook until it reaches soft ball stage, 234–240 degrees F.
3. Pour sugar syrup over egg yolks, beating continuously, and beat until cool. Add Grand Marnier and let stand until cold.
4. Whip cream until firm, and fold in custard mixture.
   An outstanding sauce to serve with fresh berries or chocolate mousse.

Serves 10.

Cooking Tip about Use of Butter in Dessert Soufflés:

It is not strictly necessary to add butter to soufflé mixtures since in America a sauce is served with soufflés. However, a small amount of unsalted butter (1 teaspoon for every 4 egg whites) may be added to the *crème pâtissière* base for added moisture. Do not add too much, as it can cause the soufflé to run over.

Sauces to Serve with Soufflés:

1. *Crème à l'Anglaise* (p. 287) flavored with any kind of essence
2. *Sauce au Chocolat* (p. 80)
3. *Sauce Grand Marnier* (p. 294)
4. *Sauce au Fraises Fraîches Cuites* (Melba Sauce) (p. 340)

Harlequin Soufflé *Soufflé Arlequin*

*6 extra large eggs, separated, plus 2
  egg whites*
¼ cup sugar
¼ cup flour
1 cup milk
2 teaspoons vanilla extract
½ ounce unsweetened chocolate
1 tablespoon sugar

1½ cups Crème à l'Anglaise (p. 287)
Butter and sugar for molds
*12 individual soufflé dishes, 3 inches
  in diameter, or 2 soufflé dishes, 7
  inches in diameter. If extra large
  eggs are not used, there will not be
  as much soufflé batter.*
Aluminum foil

1. Film soufflé molds or dishes with butter and chill in refrigerator. After they are chilled, film again with butter and sprinkle with granulated sugar. Cut aluminum foil, fold to make a double sheet, and use to divide each dish in half.

2. In a small bowl beat 2 egg yolks until light. Add ¼ cup sugar and ¼ cup flour to beaten egg yolks and mix until they make a paste. Heat milk in a saucepan, add paste, and whisk over high heat until mixture becomes thick and smooth. Off heat, add vanilla.

3. Divide this in half by putting one half in another saucepan. Beat 2 yolks slightly, add to one saucepan with the chocolate, and stir on medium heat until chocolate is blended. (Chocolate can be melted beforehand.) Remove from heat.

4. Beat remaining 2 yolks slightly and add to other saucepan, stirring on medium heat until mixed. Remove from heat.

295

5. Beat the 8 egg whites in a large bowl until they are light and have *soft* peaks. Slowly add 1 tablespoon sugar and beat until completely dissolved. Fold about one third of beaten egg whites into vanilla mixture. Fold remaining beaten whites into chocolate mixture.

6. Pour vanilla mixture into half of each prepared soufflé mold and chocolate into the other half of each mold. Carefully remove foil.

7 Place soufflé molds or dishes on baking sheets and put in preheated 350–375-degree oven. Bake about 30 minutes or until firm for large soufflés. Bake at 375 degrees about 10 minutes for individual soufflés.

8. Serve at once with chilled *Crème à l'Anglaise.*

Serves 12.

Four Butter Creams for Fillings and Icings
Quatre Crèmes au Beurre pour Garnir

Butter Cream with Egg Whites

Crème au Beurre à la Meringue Italienne

16 ounces (approximately 2⅓ cups) sugar
8 egg whites, at room temperature
20 ounces (2½ cups) unsalted butter, creamed

Flavoring of choice (Grand Marnier, coffee, chocolate, vanilla extract, praline, etc.)

1. Combine sugar with ½ cup water and cook until it reaches the soft ball stage, 234–240 degrees F.

2. While sugar is cooking, beat egg whites until stiff, using an electric beater. Slowly pour boiling sugar syrup over egg whites, beating all the while, and beat until cool.

3. Blend creamed room temperature butter with meringue mixture. Add flavoring to taste. This is the lightest of all butter creams!

Makes approximately 6 cups.

Butter Cream with Egg Yolks

Crème au Beurre Mousseline (au Sucre Cuit)

6 egg yolks
1 cup sugar
1 cup unsalted butter, at room
*   temperature*

Flavoring of choice

1. Put egg yolks in top of double boiler and set aside.
2. Put sugar into heavy pan and add ½ cup water. Dissolve sugar, shaking pan by handle but not stirring, and cook sugar to 230 degrees F.
3. Cream butter in a large bowl and reserve.
4. Set egg yolks over simmering water and beat in sugar syrup very slowly until mixture is fluffy and almost double in bulk. Remove from heat and continue beating until cool.
5. Beat egg-sugar syrup mixture into creamed butter little by little, then beat in flavoring of choice.

Makes 2 cups.

Butter Cream with Whole Eggs

Crème au Beurre aux Oeufs Entiers

1 pound (4 sticks) unsalted butter, at
*   room temperature*
4 whole eggs

½ cup granulated sugar
Flavoring to taste

1. Cream room temperature butter and set aside. Beat eggs with electric beater, gradually adding sugar until mixture is thick. Beat over simmering water until double in volume.
2. Beat off heat until cool. Beat in creamed butter and add in flavoring.

Makes 3–4 cups.

Butter Cream with Pastry Cream

Crème au Beurre à la Crème Pâtissière

1 cup unsalted butter, at room temperature
1 cup Crème Pâtissière *(p. 286)*

Confectioners' sugar, to taste
Flavoring of choice

1. Cream room temperature butter in electric mixer. Bring pastry cream *(Crème Pâtissière)* to room temperature and slowly beat creamed butter into pastry cream. If a sweeter taste is desired, a small amount of confectioners' sugar can be added. Beat in flavoring. This butter cream recipe is obviously a good way to use up leftover pastry cream.

2. If mixture should curdle during process of mixing creamed butter and pastry cream, put butter cream in a slow oven for a *few seconds only.* Remove and stir with a whisk. Do not allow butter cream to get too warm, which will cause butter to clarify. This method can be used for all the butter creams. The same procedure is used to soften butter cream when it has been stored in refrigerator overnight or longer.

Makes 2 cups.

Assembling Cakes with Butter Cream Fillings and Frostings
Assemblement du Gâteau avec Crème au Beurre

Using butter cream and layers of génoise or sponge cake, and liqueur to perfume the cake, the chef—and the home cook—is in a position to assemble cakes of a flavor and quality far superior to those obtainable in any but a few of the finest and most expensive *pâtisseries.*

Different flavors of butter cream may be used in the same *gâteau.* For example, rum and chocolate may be used for the first layer; Cognac and praline for the second layer, and the top and sides can be masked with a thin coating of butter cream lightly flavored with coffee. Save a little of each kind for decorating the cake with the aid of a pastry bag and star tube. A *gâteau* moistened with Grand Marnier and filled and frosted with an orange-flavored butter cream may be decorated with preserved orange slices of candied orange peel. An Amaretto and almond combination could be completed with toasted sliced almonds around the sides of the cake.

Butter cream is used to fill rolled sheet cakes, *gâteaux roulées,* a traditional Yule Log being one example. This is simply a *Génoise* or *Génoise Mousseline* baked in a sheet cake pan, rolled up with one flavor of butter cream and frosted with another, usually chocolate. The outside covering is scored with a fork to resemble bark, and decorations of almond paste leaves and meringue mushrooms are often added (see illustration, p. 285).

Butter cream is also used for sandwiching small cookies together and filling *Cigarettes* (p. 353).

Fondant icing is often applied to butter cream-filled cakes over a layer of marzipan. The marzipan provides a smooth base, and also tastes good! When puff pastry crust is used as a Napoleon, for example, no marzipan is necessary.

Frosting
Glaçage

Fondant Icing   *Glaçage au Fondant*

2 cups sugar
2 tablespoons light corn syrup or
  glucose
1¼ cups water
1 teaspoon vanilla extract
Candy thermometer

1. Put all ingredients in a heavy saucepan of medium size. Mix well, and cook on high heat, swirling pan until sugar is dissolved. When boiling point is reached, cover, and cook for 3 minutes. Steam condensing on sides of pan will wash down any sugar crystals that may have formed.

2. Remove cover and place candy thermometer in pan without touching sides or bottom of pan. Cook without stirring until thermometer registers 238 degrees, or until a soft ball forms. (If a little syrup is dropped in cold water, it will form a ball.) Use a pastry brush dipped in cold water to wipe away any crystals that form above the syrup as it cooks. If crystals are not removed, it can cause crystals to form in the syrup.

3. Put a little oil on a marble slab and pour sugar on, letting it cool to tepid. Using a pastry scraper or a spatula, work fondant back and forth, folding edges toward the center until it becomes white and creamy.

4. Fondant should be made ahead of time. It can be preserved for months in a tightly covered jar kept in the refrigerator. It should be warmed up just enough to spread or dip cakes in. Warm up on very low heat, or set pot of fondant in a pan of simmering water. It will lose its shine if it is overheated.

5. The fondant can be colored when it is warmed up. Coffee, chocolate, pistachio, and other flavorings are used as well as food coloring.

Makes 1 pound (2 cups).

NOTE: A little water can be added if necessary when warming up the fondant. A thin layer of marzipan on top and sides of cake can be applied before icing to make a smooth base for frosting. Or, diluted apricot jam can be used for the same purpose.

Butterscotch Sauce   *Sauce au Beurre Ecossaise*

½ cup unsalted butter
1 pound (2 cups) brown sugar
1 tablespoon lemon juice

½ cup heavy cream
Small pinch salt

Combine all ingredients, and cook in covered double boiler over simmering water for 1 hour, stirring occasionally.

Serve hot with sliced *Gâteau Génoise* (p. 324) or ice cream. Since it is a rich sauce, it can be served as a contrast on the dessert plate with a *Coulis de Framboise* (p. 340). Maple sugar can be substituted for brown sugar.

Makes approximately 3 cups.

Creating a "Marbled" Pattern in Sauce
Décor Marbré

For an extra-special presentation of many desserts (*Gâteau Nancy,* Mango Mousse Cake, fresh raspberries), they may be centered on top of a pool or mirror of one sauce while a second sauce of a contrasting color is used to create a pattern around the edge.

For example, pour a mirror of *crème anglaise* onto a large dessert plate. Next, pipe three lines of raspberry *coulis* in circles of decreasing size around the edge of the *crème anglaise,* at half inch intervals. Finally, with the blade of a knife, draw lines through the circles, from center to edge, at 2-inch intervals, then reverse the procedure, "pulling" the knife blade through the circles (between the first set of knife marks) from edge to center. This procedure creates the marbled or feather design that is often seen on top of Napoleans, a familiar pastry decorated with white fondant icing and contrasting lines of chocolate.

Naturally, a raspberry or strawberry *coulis* can be used as the mirror, with contrasting lines of *crème anglaise;* the same technique is used with good effect for savory sauces when presenting seafood, poultry, or meat. The best utensil to use for piping out the contrasting lines of sauce is a simple plastic bottle with a nozzle tip (see illustration).

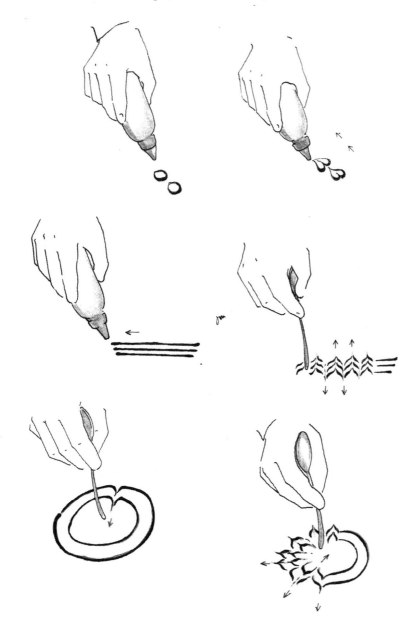

Chapter Eleven

PUFF PASTRY

Pâte Feuilletée, Classic and *Inversée; Les Pâtes Levées*—Croissants and Brioche

⚜

The best way to learn the art of the lightest *pâte* is to watch a master pastry chef perform this technique in his kitchen. It is customary for most young French student-chefs to learn from observing *un patissier* expertly make *la détrempe, le paton,* and *le tourage* to produce high, light-brown *bouchées, fleurons, palmiers,* or *chaussons.* This is the quickest way to learn, as well as by viewing video tapes. With the confidence you have gained from making the simpler doughs, my written instructions can serve as your next best guide to producing the ideal shape, texture, and taste of *pâte feuilletée,* whether you choose the recipe for *Pâte Feuilletée Fine* (p. 307) or *Inversée* (p. 308), in which the butter package is placed on the outside of *la détrempe* instead of inside it.

Feuille means leaf—the thinness of each layer resembles that of a leaf. The process of rolling and folding the dough is said to create over seven hundred layers when it is baked. Other characteristics of this *pâte feuilletée* are that it is never kneaded (nor is *pâte à choux*), it demands a cool kitchen, and it does not like a damp day (nor does *pâte à méringue*). These prerequisites can be partially fulfilled with a refrigerator nearby to chill the dough if it becomes too warm and to rest the dough if it becomes too elastic. In the modern kitchen, *la détrempe* and the butter package are often made in the processor or electric mixer. *Le tourage* is still made by hand, or there would be no more artistry. It is believed that the famous French artist Claude Lorrain (Claude Gellée) discovered the secret to successful puff pastry while he was working for a *pâtissier* in Paris sometime during the seventeenth century. Its origins were probably hundreds of years earlier, possibly in Persia, but there must be some truth in the persistent mention of Lorrain's name accompanied by stories that do not bear repeating here, except that he was a pastry chef in his youth and became an artist later.

It can be said that puff pastry is the most adaptable of all *pâtes*—it can be used for almost any recipe that calls for dough, which is possible in every course of the menu including *soupes. Fleurons* decorate platters and plates, cases are made to enclose meat or fish (*Loup en Croute,* p. 200); *petites bouchées, bouchées,* and *vol-au-vents* (wings of wind) are baked to hold fillings for hors d'oeuvres, first and main courses, and desserts. *Chaussons,* turnovers, are almost as versatile for fillings; cookies, *palmiers* and *papillons*, must not be overlooked.

Mille-Feuille, meaning a thousand leaves, is a rectangular pastry or cake called a Napoleon in America, filled with *crème pâtissière, Chantilly,* fruit jams or purées. *Gâteau de Pithiviers,* a specialty of the Loire, is a 9- or 10-inch round pastry filled with almond paste or frangipane *(crème d'amande)* and is recognized by its scalloped edges and domed top scored like the petals of a flower.

Puff pastry has adapted so well to the modern freezer that it can be frozen after four or more turns for several months; dough that is rolled, cut, and shaped into pastries is frozen to be baked directly from the freezer. Baked pastries are frozen to be reheated when needed. To make puff pastry, the equipment used is about the same as for all doughs:

1. a marble slab, 14 x 28 inches, a naturally cool surface; or a plastic cutting board which will fit on refrigerator shelf
2. a heavy ball bearing rolling pin or a *tutove*
3. heavy baking pans such as jelly roll pans (11 x 16 x 1-inch)
4. pastry scraper *(coupe-pâte)*
5. dough cutting knife
6. pastry brush
7. set of round pastry cutters with or without crinkled edges
8. a ruler
9. an oven thermometer

An Orientation to Puff Pastry
Pâte Feuilletée is generally made with the following proportions:

4 cups unbleached all purpose flour (bleached can be used)
1–1¼ cups cold water (ice water can be used)

1 pound (4 sticks) unsalted butter or margarine
¼ teaspoon salt

I usually use ⅓ cup more flour and 2 ounces (4 tablespoons) less butter. I still employ the same tool I used in France, a *tamis,* to sift the flour. It's a wooden frame shaped like a drum strung with fine wire mesh for sifting. To make the first step, *la détrempe,* the rough dough, I sift the measured flour on my marble slab, make a well, add salt, one-eighth of firm, room temperature butter, and just enough ice cold water by hand, to make the flour stick together. Do not work this dough. In the second step, *le paton,* the butter package is enclosed in *la détrempe*. The dough and the butter should be the same temperature, approximately 50 degrees F., because at the start butter that is too cold will lump or if too warm will leak out. The third step is *le tourage,* in which six "turns" are executed. Each turn involves rolling and folding the dough. Watch as I throw a little flour like fine white snow on the marble before rolling out the dough! As I make turns, I start with the open end facing me, rolling from the center away from me toward the top and then from the center toward me. Roll lightly over the edges at first, to even them and prevent bulges. Some rolling and pressing when making first turns can be done crosswise as well as lengthwise to get the right shape. The high gluten content or protein element of American flour may cause the dough to be elastic (that is my reason for putting some butter in *la détrempe*), which is controlled by resting in refrigerator. After making several turns, do not be afraid to press down on cold dough or hit it with the rolling pin to soften for rolling. This may help to prevent cracks from forming on the sides.

Five Methods for Making Puff Pastry
Cinq Méthodes pour Feuilletage

1. *Pâte Feuilletée Fine* (p. 307), Classic Method: General proportion of 20 ounces flour to 14 ounces butter.
2. *Méthod Inversée* or *Hollandaise* (Dutch Method, p. 308): Two thirds flour in *la détrempe,* ⅓ flour blended with butter for butter layer. Butter layer placed outside of flour layer for *le paton.*
3. *Ecossaise* or Scottish Method, also called *Méthode Rapide* and *Feuilletage Eclair:* Butter is cut in dice and mixed with flour at beginning.
4. *Méthode Anglaise:* One tablespoon lemon juice or vinegar to 1 pound flour.
5. *Méthode à la Viennoise* or *Danoise, Pâte Levée:* Whole eggs and yeast are used to make Danish pastries and croissants (p. 316).

General rules:

1. Use 20 grams (4 teaspoons) salt to 2 pounds (7 cups) flour (1 kilo).
2. If using salted butter, cut amount of salt in half.
3. Unsalted butter has less water than salted water.
4. Proportions of *détrempe* to butter:
   2½ pounds *détrempe* (average amount) to 1½ pounds (or a little more) butter

The Pastes
Les Pâtes

Classic Puff Pastry   *Pâte Feuilletée Fine*

21½ ounces (4⅓ cups) all purpose
  flour
¼ teaspoon salt
1 cup ice cold water

15 ounces (3¾ sticks) unsalted
  butter or unsalted margarine
  (lacks flavor of butter)

La Détrempe:

1. Sift flour with salt onto marble slab. Two ounces (4 tablespoons) butter may be incorporated here. Make a ring in which to pour water. Start pouring in water and quickly blend as little as possible to form a ball, using squeezing motion. Do not overwork dough! It should be pliable and have the same consistency as the butter. Make four little cuts in the top to "release the power." Let rest 20 minutes to 1 hour to deactivate the gluten.

2. While *la détrempe* is resting, mash cold butter with rolling pin to squeeze out any water. Unsalted butter can be beaten with a dough hook in a mixer for 5–6 minutes on low speed to let water come out. Unsalted margarine does not have water. Form butter into a cake quickly and chill if too warm.

Le Paton:

3. Roll *la détrempe* to a square shape large enough to encase butter completely, *or* roll in a circular fashion to make four petal-shaped ends for enclosing butter. Place butter in center of dough and fold four sides of *la détrempe* over butter to enclose it. Dust lightly with flour and begin to roll out. If butter starts to come out, refrigerate before making first turn so that butter and flour will be at the same temperature.

Le Tourage:

4. To make a turn, dust lightly with flour and roll dough out to a rectangle 14 inches long and 8 inches wide. If, while rolling, any butter starts to come out, dust the butter lightly with flour and chill dough briefly. To form three even layers, fold as for a business letter, bringing one-third to center and fold other third over first fold. With open end facing pastry chef, roll out again to 14 or more inches and fold to make second turn. Wrap in plastic wrap or bag to keep dough from getting dry. Always chill after two turns for 15–30 minutes. Instead of making two single turns at the beginning, a double turn can be made which gives more assurance that the butter will

307

not come out: bring both ends of dough to center where they just meet and then fold dough together like a book. If double turns are used, the order is: one double turn, one single turn, one double turn, one single turn.

5. Mark turns by punching two fingers in dough after two turns. Puff pastry requires a minimum of six turns; seven to eight turns would be the maximum number. The first four turns must be made the *same day* to ensure that the butter is evenly distributed inside the dough. After four turns dough can be frozen, or refrigerated for several hours or overnight. The last two turns should be made just before ready to use. I recommend baking temperature of 375 degrees F., as butter has to expand between layers. If temperature is too high they will not expand properly.

6. Comments: Correctly baked puff pastry should be a light brown color with a delicate flavor reminiscent of hazelnuts. To prevent dough from becoming too cold in refrigerator after wrapping in plastic wrap or bag, store in vegetable bin.

NOTE: Brush off excess flour during rolling and folding, as dry flour trapped in dough will make it tough. Work quickly to avoid excessive rolling and pressing which makes dough more elastic. After pastry is rolled out and cut into various shapes, rest in refrigerator or freezer, which prevents shrinkage during baking. I brush or sprinkle baking pan with water before baking pastries, to prevent sticking.

Makes approximately 2½ pounds.

Inverse Puff Pastry   *Pâte Feuilletée Inversée*

18 ounces (3¾ cups less 1 tablespoon) all purpose flour
2–3 teaspoons salt

15 ounces (3¾ sticks) cold unsalted butter
¾ cup cold water

1. In bowl of electric mixer machine, using flat beater, put 14 ounces (2¾ cups plus 2 tablespoons) flour, salt, and 5 ounces (1¼ sticks) of the butter. Mix on medium speed while adding the cold water, just enough to form a solid but flexible dough, *la détrempe*. This should take about 30 seconds. Remove from bowl and put on pastry board.

2. In same bowl put remaining 10 ounces (2½ sticks) cold butter (soften a little with rolling pin, if necessary) and remaining 4 ounces (¾ cup plus

2 tablespoons) flour. Mix about 1 minute on medium speed or until a mass is formed without melting butter. Wrap butter package and chill about 10 minutes if needed. Also chill *la détrempe* so that temperature will be the same for both.

3. On a lightly floured board roll out *détrempe* to a rectangle of 14–15 inches long, 5 inches wide, and at least ½ inch thick.

   How to place butter package (*le paton*) on outside of *la détrempe:* Roll out butter package to the same size, working quickly. Place *détrempe* on top of butter package, roll togther, and make a double turn—bring both ends of dough to center, where they must meet, and then fold dough together like a book. Rest dough 20 minutes in refrigerator. Lightly dust dough and board with flour, roll out to length of 22 inches, if dough is pliable enough, and make a single turn. Cover dough with plastic wrap and let rest in refrigerator for 20 minutes. (If dough ever becomes too warm, chill in refrigerator before making another turn.)

4. Make second double turn after rolling dough out about 20 inches long and 9 inches wide. Straighten ends when rolling out. The last two turns are the most important steps in making puff pastry: the dough has now become easier to work with, that is, to make it an even thickness throughout, including the edges. Chill and rest dough 20 minutes before making last single turn.

5. Dough can be cut in half or in thirds, rolled ¼ inch thick or less and shaped right away. Dough that is shaped in *bouchées, vol-au-vents,* and *tarte* shells can be frozen as well as the unrolled dough.

Makes 2½ pounds.

Pastries Made from *Pâte Feuilletée*

Patty Shells   *Bouchées*

1 recipe Pâte Feuilletée *(p. 307),*   *3½-inch round fluted cutter*
  approximately 2½ pounds   *2-inch round fluted cutter*
1 egg, slightly beaten

1. Roll out approximately one third of dough to ¼-inch thickness. This amount will make three *bouchées.* Save scraps.

309

2. Cut out two 3½-inch rounds of dough for one *bouchée*. Use one round for the base. The second round is made into a ring for sides of *bouchée* by removing center with 2-inch cutter. This center becomes the lid or top.

3. Rinse a baking pan in cold water, shake out excess, and place round base upside down on sheet or pan. Brush base with water before placing ring on. Seal ring to base by making slanting indentations ⅛ inch apart, supporting sides with fingers.

4. The pastry should rest 25 minutes in refrigerator or freezer before baking. When ready to put in oven, brush tops only of *bouchées* with beaten egg. Do not allow egg glaze to drip down sides because it would prevent proper rising of the *Pâte Feuilletée*.

5. Bake in 375-degree oven for approximately 15–20 minutes. One large sheet parchment paper may be placed over tops of pastries after 5 minutes of baking to make *bouchées* rise straight. The separate tops will require less baking time.

Makes 25–30 patty shells.

Fleurons

Roll dough to ⅛–¼ inch thickness. Use crescent-shaped cutter or round fluted pastry cutter which can then be used to cut fleurons in half. Put on pastry sheet, let rest ½ hour in refrigerator before baking. Then brush top with beaten egg. Bake 8–10 minutes in 375-degree oven. Oven temperature can be lowered after pastries have risen.

For square, individual-sized cases of puff pastry *(vol-au-vents)* proceed as follows:

1. Cut prepared puff paste into precise 6-inch squares.

2. Fold each into a triangle and make two cuts, ½ inch in from the "open" sides and stopping 1 inch short of the acute corner (see illustration).

3. Open pastry into a square once more and, beginning at an outer corner where the inner square is cut through completely, lift the border of dough and place its point over the opposite corner of the inner square. Then repeat the maneuver with the other border. The remaining two corners will be twisted into points like arrowheads by this operation.

4. Secure the border by lifting and brushing a little water underneath, then replace and press down gently.

5. Brush the top surface of the *vol-au-vent* cases with egg wash, making sure that it does not run down the sides of the pastry, as this would seal the leaves and prevent it from rising properly. Bake on a cookie sheet at 375 degrees for 25 minutes or until golden brown and well puffed. The inner square can be carefully cut out and used as a lid, or discarded. Remove any excess dough with a fork and return *vol-au-vents* briefly to a warm oven to dry out. Makes 4–5 *vol-au-vents* from 1 pound of dough.

Turnovers *Chaussons*

To avoid waste of puff pastry when forming small turnovers *(chaussons)*, make triangles instead of circles and thus avoid "trimmings." To achieve this, roll puff pastry into a long band 4–5 inches wide. Trim the long sides into a straight line and then make slanting cuts across the band, about every 4 inches, at an angle of 45 degrees. Roll the center part of each diamond a little thinner, place desired filling on one half, wet the edges of the pastry with water to seal, and fold over, forming a triangle out of the diamond. Repeat with the rest of the pastry.

Chaussons are filled with savory stuffings for a first course, and sweet mixtures like thick apple sauce, apple pie filling or jam for dessert. Fillings for turnovers are a good way to utilize a small amount of cooked poultry or seafood. Creamed mushrooms are a good choice.

FILLING FOR A FIRST COURSE: the proportions for 1 turnover are 2 teaspoons of Pacific shrimp blended with 1 tablespoon of Lobster Sauce (p. 199) or Cream Sauce (p. 53). The sauce *must be cold* before filling turnovers. Some omelet fillings (p. 132) recommended in Chapter 5 may be utilized.

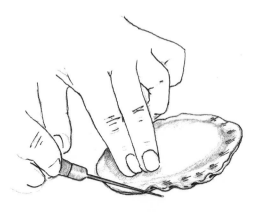

Three Pastries Made From Scraps
(Rognures) of Pâte Feuilletée

Cheese Sticks *Sacristains*

1. Trim scraps, overlap each scrap with horizontal strips of dough running in same direction. Roll very thin, cut into sticks 5–6 inches long and ½ inch wide. *Sacristains* can be twisted after they are cut out. Press ends onto

baking pan to make them stick and keep their shape. Season with paprika and sprinkle with grated Swiss or Parmesan cheese. Chill before baking. For a dessert, omit paprika and grated cheese and sprinkle with granulated sugar.

2. Bake in 375-degree oven for about 10–15 minutes or until done. Use for hors d'oeuvres, soup, or dessert. For soup make small and thin—4–5 inches long, called *paillettes.*

Fluted Ovals or Crescents   *Fleurons*

1. *Fleurons,* meaning flower shapes, are small and decorative. If made from scraps, add 6–8 ounces cold butter to ½ pound scraps. Make two turns, chilling dough as necessary. Roll dough ¼ inch thick. Make disks with round 3-inch fluted cutter. Cut each disk into a crescent or oval by cutting in half with pastry cutter.

2. Chill for about ½ hour. Brush tops with beaten egg. Bake in middle of 375-degree oven for 10–15 minutes.

3. Use as a garnish for fish or meat dishes.

Makes twenty to twenty-five 2½-inch *fleurons* from ½ pound dough.

Palm Leaves   *Palmiers*

1. Reconstruct scraps as described for cheese sticks or use fresh dough. Put a layer of granulated sugar on pastry board, when turns are made. Make two turns and roll dough very thin, ⅛ inch thick, into rectangle 8 × 10 inches long. Sprinkle granulated sugar on dough before folding.

2. With the 8-inch length facing you, fold one side into two layers toward the center. Fold the other side into two layers meeting the first side at the center. Now, bring the two rolled sides together the same way as a book is closed. Press with rolling pin to hold two sides together.

3. Cut dough crosswise into ⅜-inch thick pieces. Place on baking sheet about 3 inches apart, and arrange ends into desired shape. Ends can be turned inside to form two connecting swirls or turned outside going halfway up the sides of each *palmier.*

4. Chill about ½ hour. Bake in 375-degree oven for about 20 minutes, *turning over* after sugar has caramelized on the bottom in about 10 minutes.

Sprinkle with more sugar after turning, and watch carefully, as they burn easily. A piece of parchment paper can be placed over tops to encourage even baking. When baked, cool on rack. Palmiers can be stored several days in airtight container or may be frozen.

Makes 25–32 *palmiers* from ½ pound dough.

Puff Pastry for *Soupe en Croute*

Pâte Feuilletée pour Soupe en Croute

Consommé of Pheasant or
  Consommé Double ou Riche or
  Light Soupe de Poissons *(p. 22)*
2½ ounces puff pastry for each
  4½-inch marmite
3½–4 ounces puff pastry for each
  4½-inch marmite

*1 egg beaten with or without 1½
teaspoons water to seal rims and
to brush tops and sides of dough
covering marmites*

1. Prepare soup in advance. Consommé of Pheasant is finished with julienne of vegetables and truffles and Quenelles of Pheasant (p. 105). Soup must be cold before putting in bowls to cover with puff pastry.
2. Use ovenproof bowls called marmites—deep footed bowls about 4–5 inches in diameter with lug handles.
3. Roll puff pastry ⅛ inch thick, cut pastry in a round shape ½–1 inch larger than marmite rim. After cutting dough, chill about ½ hour.
4. Fill each marmite to within ½ inch of rim. Brush rim with beaten egg yolk and cover top of soup bowl with pastry, sealing edges tightly. Brush top and sides with beaten egg yolk or whole egg. Do not stretch or tear dough. Refrigerate before baking as long as 24 hours, if desired, covered with plastic wrap.
5. Place covered soup bowls on a rimmed cookie sheet and bake in 400-degree oven for 12–15 minutes or until pastry puffs up into a dome shape and is baked through. Remove from oven and serve immediately. Will hold in turned off oven for about 5 minutes.

Upside Down Apple Tart   *Tarte Tatin*

2 tablespoons butter
½ cup sugar
10–12 large, firm, green apples:
  California Pippin, Golden
  Delicious, or other non-watery
  variety

Pâte Feuilletée *(p. 307)—enough for*
  10-inch round pan (Pâte Brisée *or*
  Pâte Sucrée *can be used)*
Ovenproof frying pan or skillet (cast
  iron), 10 inches in diameter and
  2½ inches deep

1. Place butter and sugar in bottom of ovenproof pan.

2. Peel, core, and cut apples in half. Starting at outer edge of pan, stand each half of apple on end, lining outside edge of pan and continuing in circular pattern to fill pan. Pack apples tightly. Cut tops of apples even with height of pan, and use cut pieces to fill spaces left in pan.

3. Place pan on medium high heat until mixture is caramelized and apples are slightly cooked. Remove from heat and press down on top of apples.

4. Roll *Pâte Feuilletée* or *Brisée* very thin (¼–⅛ inch thick) into 11-inch circle. Place dough over top of apples, tucking edge inside pan. Prick top of dough to allow steam to escape. Bake in 375-degree oven, for 15–20 minutes or until crust is brown and cooked.

5. Place a large round platter on top of the crust and turn over quickly. Serve lukewarm.

Serves 10.

Serve with:

a. *Crème Fraiche:* One to 2 tablespoons buttermilk and 1 cup heavy cream put in a jar. Shake well and cover, leaving at room temperature until it thickens, approximately 24 hours. Shake again and refrigerate.

b. Vanilla ice cream or sour cream are also popular in America to serve with *Tarte Tatin,* which is said to have originated in the forested region called the Sologne in the pastry shop of two spinsters *(demoiselles)* named Tatin. Accidentally dropping a *tarte,* they decided to cover the damage with caramelized sugar over the top.

   This tart is sometimes called *Tarte Lamotte-Beuvron,* the name of the town of the Tatin sisters' Hotel Tatin.

315

Two Doughs Made with Yeast
Les Pâtes Levées

Crescents   *Croissants*

2 envelopes fresh dry yeast
¼ cup lukewarm water
1½ tablespoons sugar
4 cups all purpose flour, sifted
1 teaspoon salt

1½ cups lukewarm milk
¾ pound (3 sticks) unsalted butter
1 egg yolk beaten with 1 tablespoon
*   milk* (dorure)

1. Make the sponge: In a mixing bowl soften yeast in lukewarm water with 1 teaspoon sugar. Stir in 1 cup flour, shaping dough into a ball. Cut a cross in the top "to release the power," cover with damp cloth, and set in warm place (such as an 80–85-degree oven) to rise until double in size.

2. In large mixing bowl or bowl of a heavy-duty mixer, put 3 cups of flour, 1 tablespoon sugar, 1 teaspoon salt, and gradually add 1½ cups milk, stirring to make a dough. Add the sponge, beating well either by hand or in a heavy-duty electric mixer using a dough hook.

3. Remove dough from bowl and knead until smooth. Place dough in greased bowl, grease top of dough by turning over in bowl, and cover with damp cloth; let rise in warm place until double in bulk. Punch dough in center with fist to deflate, and chill in refrigerator for ½ hour.

4. At this stage follow directions given in Steps 2, 3, and 4 under classic *Pâte Feuilletée* (p. 307). Step 2 explains how to get water out of butter, Step 3 explains how to make the *paton*—form butter into correct shape and enclose in *détrempe*—and Step 4 describes how to make the turns.

   A marble or plastic board and rolling pin should be chilled if kitchen is warm.

5. Croissant dough is given two turns, wrapped in plastic wrap and a terry cloth, and refrigerated overnight. It requires only one or two more turns, in contrast to *pâte feuilletée,* which must be given six turns. Make the two turns and chill for about 1 hour. One more turn can be made before cutting dough in half.

6. Divide dough in half and roll into a rectangle ⅛ inch thick. Trim the edges with a pastry knife, and mark dough into triangles. Cut out triangles using rolling pin to roll out each triangle 6 inches long and 5 inches at base. Scraps of dough can be enclosed as you roll up each triangle. Starting from

the base, roll individually with palm of hand, pulling on the end at the same time. Twist to form a horseshoe or curve. Pinch ends to seal.

If you make a large amount of croissants, a croissant cutter is useful. Croissant dough can also be rolled into circles, which are cut in triangles like a cake or pie. First, cut dough in four equal parts. Then roll one part into a circle 12 inches in diameter. This will make about seven triangles 6 inches long with a 5-inch base.

7. Brush beaten egg and milk over the tops of croissants. Let rise in warm place until double in size. Or, croissants can be made through Step 5 and refrigerated overnight to be baked for breakfast. If they are to be baked for dinner, they can be refrigerated for 6–8 hours before being placed in a warm place to rise until double their size.

8. Bake in a 400-degree oven for 5 minutes. Reduce heat to 375–350 degrees and bake 15 minutes or until croissants turn light brown and test done.

Makes 2 dozen.

Brioche Dough   *Pâte à Brioche*

The two methods for making brioche are the same used to make bread:
1. with a sponge or starter *(levain)*
2. in one bowl *(méthode directe* or *Viennoise)*

The sponge method is used for making sourdough bread, one of San Francisco's hallmarks. For both methods it is necessary to have two risings or fermentations before shaping in brioche molds to rise for the third time. Before baking they are brushed on top with beaten egg mixed with milk *(dorure)* to give color and shine to their crust.

Pâte à Brioche Fine is made in two days. After the second rising it is refrigerated overnight. Chilling will make the dough easier to handle, as the warm dough is very sticky due to the large number of eggs incorporated. Chilling also makes the dough more mellow. Two kinds of brioche dough are: 1) *Pâte à Brioche Fine* (p. 319), which makes a small breakfast bread, *brioche à tête;* two different full-sized loaves, Parisian brioche loaf and Nanterre brioche loaf; as well as braided loaves, *brioche aux raisins secs* and *brioche au fromage.* My father, who came from the *département* of Vendée, was a specialist in baking *brioche Vendéenne,* a stollen-type loaf or a three-strand braided one. I also have twin brothers who are in the same profession —Alfred is a pastry chef, *un pâtissier,* and George is a baker, *un boulanger.*

317

Brioche mousseline is made in a cylindrical container such as a coffee can with a paper collar tied around. It rises twice as high as the can. The second style of brioche dough is 2) *Pâte à Brioche Ordinaire* or *Commune,* used for *en croute* dishes made with beef, lamb, or calves liver *(foie de veau)* and *coulibiac* of salmon.. The ingredients are:

2 packages (20 grams) dry yeast	*2 teaspoons (10 grams) salt*
¼ cup lukewarm water or *milk to soften yeast*	*3½ cups (453 grams) flour*
	2 eggs
2 teaspoons (10 grams) sugar	*1¼ sticks (150 grams) butter*

Pâte à Brioche Ordinaire is made the same as the recipe for *Pâte à Brioche Fine,* using the sponge or direct method. It contains less richness; that is, less sugar and butter and more salt because it is baked with fish or meat.

In France, two commonly used yeast doughs in restaurant and hotel kitchens for canapés, buffets, and desserts are:

Pain de Mie: Made with milk and no eggs in a closed container such as a Pullman loaf pan with a sliding top. Baked bread has no crust—it is used for rolled sandwiches or canapés (thin slices of bread are spread with filling, rolled, and chilled; when cut, the spiral of filling is revealed).

Petits Pains au Lait: Baked in cylindrical or baguette-style shapes, and rolls 3–4 inches long—may be slit across top with scissors held flat about four times (or cut with single stroke of razor blade across top before baking).

Pain au Lait: Baba and savarin doughs are all like brioche except they are less rich, more like a batter. The dough can be plain or with raisins, the same as brioche. German and French Christmas brioche contain candied fruit. Babas will keep in airtight containers 3–4 weeks, or they can be frozen. To serve, make a syrup of sugar, dip dry savarin or baba in, and they will swell up.

Fine Brioche Dough   *Pâte à Brioche Fine*

2 packages (20 grams) dry yeast
½ cup (125 grams) water or *milk*
4 tablespoons (50 grams) sugar
1 teaspoon (6 grams) salt
3½ cups (453 grams) flour
5 eggs, at room temperature
½–1 teaspoon orange flower water
¼ cup raisins macerated with rum
until softened and absorbed, then
flamed with Cognac or ¼ cup or
more candied fruit, chopped (both
optional)

2 sticks (226½ grams) butter, at
room temperature
Butter for molds
Glaze—1 beaten egg mixed with 1
tablespoon milk
Fluted brioche molds or muffin tins

1. To make sponge: In small, straight-sided bowl put contents of 2 packages of dry yeast, add ½ cup lukewarm (100 degrees) water or milk, and stir to dissolve yeast. Add 4 tablespoons sugar, salt, and 1 cup flour, and stir together quickly. Cover with damp cloth, set in warm spot such as a turned off oven, and let rise until double in size.

2. After sponge has risen to double its original size, place it in bowl of a heavy-duty electric mixer. Using flat beater mix in 2 cups flour and 2 eggs on low speed, then add rest of flour, remaining 3 eggs, and orange flower water. Beat until mixed, about 1–2 minutes. Change to dough hook and knead until smooth, about 8–10 minutes.

3. Using large rubber spatula put dough into large buttered bowl, cover with damp cloth, and place in a warm turned off oven. Let rise until double in size.

4. Punch dough down using a floured fist, turn over, cover, and let rise again in a warm area of the kitchen. After dough has risen again, mix in raisins or candied fruit (optional) and very soft butter by hand or by machine. Do not overmix after butter has been added.

5. Put in large buttered bowl, cover with damp kitchen towel or plastic wrap, and refrigerate overnight. When ready to form brioche, punch chilled dough down. It should now be easier to handle.

6. Heavily butter about 16 fluted molds. Place on pastry sheets. Break off pieces of dough the correct size to fill molds halfway, form into balls and place in molds. Punch a hole in center of dough, or cut a deep cross in which to insert a teardrop-shaped piece of dough to make *brioche à tête*. Let rise in warm place until double in size. Watch that they do not rise any higher. Glaze carefully with a mixture of 1 egg beaten with 1 tablespoon

319

milk. Do not let glaze drip down into molds. A second brushing with glaze may be applied.

7. Bake in 375–400-degree oven for about 20 minutes or until brioche are a deep brown color.

   Serve for breakfast, lunch, afternoon tea or as dinner rolls. Brioche can be served right away, reheated, or frozen. Leftover brioche may be sliced for French toast, used as a base for gratin of fresh fruit.

   Serve with terrine of foie gras, either fresh as a roll, or sliced horizontally, or cut in half and toasted. Brioche is also stuffed with cooked seafood or creamed chicken, and with fresh fruit for dessert.

Makes approximately sixteen 3-inch brioche.

Chapter Twelve

MORE ELABORATE DESSERTS

Pâte à Génoise Fine and *Mousseline;*
Ladyfingers; Mousses; Snow Eggs;
Cookies

Most of the desserts on my pastry cart reflect the season of the year. Whenever beautiful strawberries are in the market, I make *Tarte aux Fraises au Fromage Blanc,* a form of cheesecake in a long rectangular shape. It is built from a base of *pâte feuilletée,* lined with a thin layer of *gâteau génoise,* next a layer of cottage cheese mixed with yogurt and cream, another layer of *génoise,* with *Crème Chantilly* (p. 79) covering the top, decorated with precisely arranged strawberries or raspberries *(framboises).* The strawberries, pointed end up, are brushed with a strawberry jam glaze. I call a similar pastry Strawberry "Cheesecake" (without cheese) made of round layers of sponge cake with a filling of yogurt, sour cream, and gelatin (p. 341).

Year-round I bake *Gâteau Génoise* (p. 324) in an extra large low-sided rectangular pan. I then trim the cake to line the long loaf pan in which I pour my chocolate mousse. The top is covered with a layer of *Génoise,* which encases the entire thick dark mousse made of French chocolate. My most popular sauce, Grand Marnier (p. 294), is always nearby in a silver bowl. These two elongated pastries provide a sharp contrast in black and white.

A large crystal bowl of snow eggs, *Oeufs à la Neige* (p. 342), resting on a layer of *Crème Anglaise* (p. 287) topped with caramelized sugar, is a classic which rarely becomes tiresome. A variation is Molded Floating Island (*(Ile Flottante,* p. 344) baked in a charlotte mold lined with caramelized sugar. Unmolded, some of the caramelized sugar on the top slides down the sides and floats on the plate.

Meringues mimic cake and cookie doughs as they are baked in rounds, in shells like cookies, in rings which are glued together with unbaked meringue and baked to be filled with ice cream, fruit or whipped cream to become vacherins (p. 348). Unfilled vacherins will keep in tins for a week or more, whereas poached meringues (snow eggs) will keep only a few days in the refrigerator.

Recently, I devised a Lemon Soufflé Tart (p. 149), which by its nature is light and foamy, in line with the popular taste; but that does not detract from my *Tarte aux Citrons* for those people who like lemon-flavored custard tarts (p. 150).

Cold mousses or cold soufflés are as tempting as ice cream or sorbet for the host or hostess cook to make ahead. The trick to making my Avocado or Papaya Mousse and the Mango Mousse (pp. 337–39) spread between two layers of *Génoise Mousseline* (p. 326) is not to overbeat the egg whites or overwhip the cream. If the egg whites are beaten beyond the soft peak stage, they will not be absorbed properly to make a smooth mousse; and if the cream is overwhipped, the mixture could become buttery.

If by chance there is a reader who has not grasped the difference between a mousse and a mousseline, here are the official definitions:

MOUSSE: A cold dessert made in a large mold to serve a group of diners. It can have a collar to hold more mixture, giving the effect of a soufflé when removed.

MOUSSELINE: Made in an individual serving mold or dish like a quenelle. (This definition does not refer to a cake.)

COLD SOUFFLÉS: Small mousses molded in individual *cassolettes* or dishes.

Two new Bavarian cream type of *gâteaux* I make, *Miroir de Framboise* and *Gâteau Jacqueline,* ideally should be refrigerated overnight. If time does not allow this, the cakes may be put in the freezer for 15 minutes or longer. Remove from freezer ½ hour ahead of serving time and let thaw out in the refrigerator. If frozen solid, they will take longer to thaw out.

If I had time to bake only one *gâteau,* it would undoubtedly be *Gâteau Génoise,* which I am about to do now. It can be baked in round, rectangular, or square pans, and in ring molds for a *Mont-Blanc* (p. 334). Square pans are best for petits fours, usually cut in square shapes. The consistency of the cake is similar to the American sponge cake. Observe that I beat the delicate batter over simmering water until it is double in size, then I beat it off heat until the batter is cool. The "cooking law" or scientific reason for doing this is to create an additional volume, which occurs as it cools. The flour is sifted as it is folded in and the butter is gently folded in last. Before removing my cakes from the convection oven, I check the light brown color of the tops; then with my finger I give one last test to be sure the *gâteaux* spring back. After removing them from their baking pans, they must cool for a half day before they are decorated.

Ladyfingers (*Biscuits à la Cuiller* I and II, pp. 330 and 332) are composed of an even more delicate batter, as the egg whites are beaten separately. Special molds can be used to contain the batter. Ladyfingers I made with granulated sugar, cornstarch, and flour are crisper; while Ladyfingers II made with flour only, 2 more eggs, and powdered sugar are softer.

Biscuits à la Cuiller received their name *cuiller,* meaning spoon, because years ago they were used as "spoons" with desserts such as Bavarian creams. The main difference between a sponge or ladyfinger and a boudoir or Champagne biscuit is that the latter is crisp.

In step with the latest approach to cuisine, I make a lighter, more delicate version of the classic *Gâteau Génoise* called *Génoise Mousseline,* which I incorporate into several new desserts—*Le Miroir de Framboises* (p. 328), Mango Mousse (p. 337), and Gratin of Peaches and Cream (p. 333). The baked cake is cut to line the dessert pans or fit on top of the Mango Mousse, that I also make with papaya.

I also serve *Gâteau Nancy* (p. 335), one of the regional cakes of France, which range from the buttery shortbread of Normandy to the *Galette Breton* and the *Gâteau Nancy* of Lorraine. This wonderfully rich yet light chocolate soufflé cake is a specialty of the town of Nancy, and is baked on all special occasions and festivals. Sometimes I decorate the top with red and pink roses made of marzipan.

La pâtisserie probably receives more compliments than any other branch of cuisine. The visual effect lingers much longer than attractively garnished dinner plates so quickly consumed. The presentation of fine desserts is always a spectacle to be remembered, for by their nature many pastries can last for several hours on the pastry cart or buffet table. Now, I have disclosed one of the rewards of studying the art of pastry making!

Génoise Cake

Gâteau Génoise
Pâte à Génoise Fine or *Pâte à Biscuit*

---

8 large eggs
8 ounces (1 heaping cup) sugar
1 teaspoon vanilla extract
8 ounces (1½ cups plus 2 tablespoons) flour (all purpose, pastry, or cake flour)
4 ounces (1 stick) unsalted butter, melted

Butter and flour for pans
Three 8½-inch x 1½-inch-high round cake pans
Parchment paper

1. Butter and flour cake pans, line with circles of parchment paper, and set aside.

2. In large double boiler, or in 4–5 quart bowl set *over* but not *in* simmering water, beat eggs until well mixed. Beat in sugar, continuing to beat until light and thick, and temperature reaches 100 degrees. Add vanilla.

3. Remove from heat and continue beating until cold (the mixture will increase greatly in volume during this period) and batter forms a slowly dissolving ribbon from a lifted beater. This may be done in electric mixer, or using a hand-held electric mixer. Place flour in a fine sieve or *tamis* and sift onto mixture, folding it in lightly but thoroughly with a spatula. Pour lukewarm butter gently around edge of bowl and fold in. Be careful not to deflate mixture.

4. Fill prepared cake pans two thirds full. Bake at 350 degrees for 15–20 minutes or until top springs back when pressed and cake pulls away slightly from sides of pan. If cake starts to get too brown during baking, put parchment paper or foil over top.

5. Turn cakes out to cool on cake racks. Let rest until cool before decorating. Simple way to decorate top: Cut pattern in paper doily, place on top of cake and sprinkle confectioners' sugar over doily to serve for afternoon tea, breakfast, or with a *macédoine* of fresh fruit. Génoise cakes can be used in tiers for wedding cakes, or split and filled with *Crème Pâtissière* (p. 286), *Crème au Beurre* (pp. 296–298), or fresh purée of fruit. *Pâte à Génoise* is baked in square pans and cut into small shapes for petits fours *(les gâteaux petits)*. Decorate cakes with *Crème au Beurre, Crème Chantilly,* (p. 79), Fondant Icing (p. 299), fresh fruits with glaze made from jam that matches fruit used.

Other flavors for Genoise Cake *(Gâteau Génoise)* include:

1. Chocolate: Use only 6 ounces (1 cup plus 3 tablespoons) flour and add 2 ounces (½ cup) unsweetened cocoa.

2. Lemon: Use ½ teaspoon of vanilla extract and add the grated zest (colored part of the peel only) of 1 lemon.

3. Orange: Use ½ teaspoon of vanilla extract and add the grated zest of a small orange.

4. Almond: Omit vanilla extract and add 1 teaspoon almond flavoring.

A few notes on history and ways to use *Génoise* saturated with syrup:

1. In my youth in France the actual flat bone with cartilage from the front leg of the veal or lamb was used as a mixer and stirrer for cake batters. The plastic or rubber mixer (and scraper) without a handle called a

corne used today was designed from that bone. To mix the flour into the delicate inflated batter of the *Génoise,* use a plastic or rubber *corne,* a perforated skimmer, or a fine sieve.

2. Baked *Gâteau Génoise* is saturated with syrup just before:
    a. being filled with butter cream or fruit purées,
    b. being used to line bottom of charlotte mold, and
    c. when it is diced (first), saturated with raspberry liqueur or rum for instance, and placed in the center of a raspberry soufflé to give more flavor. English Trifle and Zuppa Inglese contain cake saturated with liqueurs.

Bavarian Cream Diplomat is a mold of alternating layers of vanilla Bavarian cream, finely chopped mixed candied fruit, and broken pieces of lady fingers or cake sprinkled with Kirsch.

Génoise Mousseline Cake

Extra Light Génoise Cake No. 1   *Gâteau Génoise Mousseline* No. 1

5 whole eggs
4 egg yolks
4 ounces (¹/₂ cup plus 1 tablespoon) sugar
¹/₂ teaspoon vanilla extract
2 ounces (¹/₂ cup less 1 tablespoon) flour
1¹/₂ ounces (¹/₃ cup plus 1 tablespoon) cornstarch

1 ounce (2 tablespoons) unsalted butter, melted and cooled to lukewarm
Three 8¹/₂-inch round cake pans (half-filled) or two 11 x 17-inch sheet cake pans
Baking parchment paper for pans

1. In large double boiler, or in a 4–5 quart bowl set *over* hot but not *in* simmering water, beat whole eggs and egg yolks until well mixed. Beat in sugar and continue beating until light and thick, and temperature reaches 100 degrees. Add vanilla.

2. Remove from heat and continue beating until mixture is cold (it will increase in volume dramatically) and forms a slowly dissolving ribbon from a lifted beater. This may be done in an electric mixer, or using a hand-held electric mixer. Place flour and cornstarch in a fine sieve or *tamis* and sift onto mixture, folding it in very lightly but thoroughly with a spatula. Pour butter gently around edge of bowl and fold in.

3. Pour mixture into prepared cake pans, which should be buttered, floured, and lined on the bottom with baking parchment.

This quantity of *Génoise Mousseline* mixture is sufficient for three 8½-inch round cake pans (bake at 375 degrees for 15 minutes) or two 11 x 17-inch sheet cake pans (bake at 375 degrees for 8 minutes.) Allow cake to rest in pan for 10 minutes before turning out on cooling rack. Peel off baking parchment. Let cool completely. Naturally, one thicker sheet cake instead of two thin ones may be prepared with this amount of batter. When preparing very thin sheet cakes, spread mixture evenly with a spatula. The round cakes, which freeze well, may be split in half for filling.

This cake is used to make roulades (jelly rolls): When rolled with jam it can be cut into "pinwheels" to line dessert molds; it serves as a base for mousses such as the *Miroir de Framboises* (p. 328) and Mango Mousse (p. 337).

Extra Light Génoise Cake No. 2   *Gâteau Génoise Mousseline* No. 2

IN QUANTITY FOR PROFESSIONAL KITCHEN:
9 whole eggs
9 yolks
½ pound (1 cup plus 2 tablespoons) sugar
3½ ounces (¾ cup plus 2 tablespoons) all purpose flour
3½ ounces (¾ cup) cornstarch
2 ounces (4 tablespoons) unsalted butter, melted
Dash vanilla extract

Butter and flour for pans
Two 9 x 2-inch high round cake pans, or two 25 x 17-inch sheet pans, or four 15½ x 10 x 1-inch jelly roll pans or baking sheets
Parchment paper to line pans

Instructions same as for *Génoise Mousseline* No. 1 (see preceding recipe).

NOTE: Number and size of round pans required to bake *Génoise Mousseline:*

Gâteau Génoise Mousseline No. 1, *whole* recipe, fills: three 8 x 2-inch round cake pans or two 9 x 2-inch round cake pans

Gâteau Génoise Mousseline No. 2, *halved* recipe, fills: one 9 x 2-inch round cake pan three quarters full* or two 9 x 2-inch round cake pans almost half full of batter if lower cakes are required.

After filling 9-inch round pan, leftover batter can be baked in smaller round pan.

---

* This size cake can be cut in half or in thirds after it is baked.

Number and size of "half sheet cake" pans to bake whole recipe *Gâteau Génoise Mousseline* No. 1:

one 17 x 11-inch half sheet cake pan bakes cake ½ inch thick *or*
two 17 x 11-inch half sheet cake pans bake cakes ¼ inch thick

To use a sheet pan that is too large for the amount of cake batter in a recipe, line the pan with parchment paper, fold one end underneath the liner, about 4–5 inches, and bend the folded end up to make an edge to contain the batter.

Glazed Raspberry Mousse Cake $\qquad$ *Miroir de Framboise*

3 ounces semisweet chocolate
1 layer Génoise Mousseline *No. 1*
(p. 326), 8½ x ½-inch
10 ounces (1¼ cups) purée of fresh raspberries (about 3 baskets)
½ tablespoon unflavored gelatin
2½ ounces (⅓ cup) sugar

2 ounces (4 tablespoons) unsalted butter
10 ounces (1¼ cups) heavy cream
4 ounces (¼ cup) raspberry jam
2 tablespoons Framboise (raspberry liqueur)
1 teaspoon red wine
8½ x 2½-inch flan ring

1. Melt chocolate over hot water, spread over top of cake with a spatula and refrigerate until firm. (This layer of chocolate forms the base of the *gâteau*. It prevents the liqueur from soaking through and keeps the cake from sticking to the plate.)

2. To make raspberry purée, grind berries in food processor, then put through a stainless steel sieve to remove seeds. Mix half of the purée with gelatin and sugar in a saucepan. Heat gently until sugar and gelatin dissolve, then cool to lukewarm.

3. Cream butter, whisk in lukewarm purée and the remaining half of cold purée, and blend well.

4. Beat cream until half whipped, then fold in raspberry mixture.

5. Place cake circle, chocolate side down, inside flan ring (or use sides of a springform pan, if unavailable) and pour in raspberry cream mixture, smoothing the top flat. Freeze for at least 3 hours.

6. To make *miroir,* combine jam and wine in a small saucepan and bring to boil. Unmold cake and sieve jam over top, smoothing out with a spatula.

Refrigerate overnight to let flavors mellow and allow cream to thaw—it is necessary to freeze it in order to allow the smooth spreading of the glaze, which is otherwise very difficult.

Serves 10–12.

NOTE: Purée of black currants and cassis may be substituted for the raspberries and Framboise.

Layered *Gâteau* with Chocolate-Praline Cream and Bavarian Cream with Grand Marnier
Gâteau Jacqueline

12 ounces semisweet chocolate
4 layers Génoise Mousseline No. 1 (p. 326), 11 x ¹/₂-inch
2 tablespoons Praline Paste (p. 289)

BAVARIAN CREAM WITH GRAND MARNIER:
4 egg yolks
2 cups milk
4 ounces (¹/₂ cup plus 1 tablespoon) sugar
1 tablespoon gelatin
3 cups heavy cream, half whipped
4 tablespoons Grand Marnier

3 ounces (6 tablespoons) unsalted butter
1 cup heavy cream, half whipped
¹/₂ cup Framboise (raspberry liqueur)

Cocoa or confectioners' sugar for decoration
2 metal rings, 11 inches diameter and 2¹/₂ inches deep (or use sides of springform pans)
Decorative stencil (see Step 6)

1. Melt chocolate over hot water and spread about half of it over two of the *Génoise* cake circles, using a spatula to achieve a thin, even layer. Refrigerate until chocolate has set.

2. Add praline and butter to remaining warm chocolate, and stir until smooth. Fold into half-whipped cream.

3. Place chocolate covered cake circles inside metal rings, chocolate side down, and sprinkle with ¼ cup raspberry liqueur. Divide chocolate cream evenly between both cakes and top with remaining two circles of cake. Sprinkle with remaining ¼ cup raspberry liqueur and refrigerate.

4. To make Bavarian cream, break egg yolks into a bowl and whisk. Combine milk, sugar, and gelatin in a saucepan and bring to a boil. Pour over egg yolks, whisking at the same time. Strain and cool, then fold into half-whipped cream and add Grand Marnier.

329

5. Pour Bavarian cream over cakes, dividing it equally and smoothing tops with a spatula. Refrigerate for 3 hours or overnight.

6. Cut out a stencil in parchment paper to decorate tops of cakes. A swan or a fleur-de-lis may be traced from the endpapers of this book, or some other design element may be used. Attach two loop handles with scotch tape on either side of the stencil to facilitate lifting off the cake later.

   Unmold cake and lay stencil on top. Sift cocoa over design, and then carefully remove stencil. Repeat with other cake.

   On a white cake use cocoa; on a chocolate cake use confectioners' sugar.

Serves 24. Recipe may be cut in half to make 1 cake.

Ladyfingers or Sponge Fingers I

Petits Gâteaux Secs
Biscuits à la Cuiller I

8 eggs, separated
8 ounces (1 cup plus 2 tablespoons) sugar
1 teaspoon vanilla extract
4½ ounces (1 cup) cornstarch

3½ ounces (¾ cup plus 2 tablespoons) flour
Confectioners' sugar
Baking parchment

1. Beat yolks in a large bowl until light, then slowly beat in 6 ounces (1 cup less 2 tablespoons) sugar until the mixture is thick, lemon-colored, and forms a slowly dissolving ribbon when beater is lifted. Stir in vanilla.

330

2. Fold in cornstarch and flour.

3. Beat egg whites until they form stiff peaks, then beat in remaining 2 ounces (⅓ cup less 2 teaspoons) sugar. Gently fold egg whites into batter with a large rubber spatula, without deflating mixture. (Cut down through mixture, then lift from underneath while rotating bowl.)

4. Line baking sheets with 5-inch wide strips of baking parchment, sticking them down with a tiny dot of sponge mixture under each corner. Using a pastry bag with a plain round ½-inch tube, form 3½-inch long "fingers" in lines along the parchment strips, at right angles to the length of the paper.

5. Slightly sift confectioners' sugar over tops of ladyfingers, sprinkle a little water on top with a brush, and let stand for 5 minutes so that sugar "pearls" will form during baking.

6. Bake in a preheated 325-degree oven for about 20 minutes. Allow to cool for 10 minutes—they will peel off paper very easily without breaking. Finish cooling on racks, then store in airtight tins.

Makes 5 dozen.

NOTE: This mixture can be used to make sheet cakes for a Yule Log *(Bûche de Noel)* (see pages 298–299) or a cake roll *(gâteau roulé).*

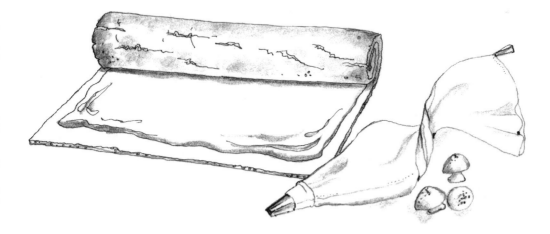

Ladyfingers II   *Biscuits à la Cuiller II*

10 eggs, separated
10 ounces (2⅓ cups) confectioners'
  sugar

1 teaspoon vanilla extract
10 ounces (2 cups) flour

1. In a large mixing bowl, beat egg yolks until light. Beat in sugar slowly, and continue beating until mixture forms a slowly dissolving ribbon when the beater is lifted. Add vanilla.
2. Fold in the flour, shaking it over the egg yolks through a *tamis* or fine sieve. Use a large rubber spatula to fold in lightly.
3. Beat egg whites until stiff. Fold lightly but thoroughly into batter.
4. Repeat Steps 4, 5, and 6 for *Biscuits à la Cuiller* I (see preceding recipe).

Makes 100. Recipe can be halved.

NOTE: Ladyfingers may also be baked in special ladyfinger pans, well buttered and floured. Let rest before trying to unmold.

Charlotte Russe   *Charlotte Russe*

1 recipe Bavarian Cream (p. 329)
1 recipe Ladyfingers I or II (above)
Sweet almond or other tasteless oil
  for mold

2-quart mold with high sides, non-
  aluminum

1. Make Bavarian Cream in advance in one or two flavors if alternate layers are desired.
2. Oil mold lightly. Line bottom of mold with ladyfingers cut in triangles or hearts, placing points toward center and pressing close together.
3. Next, cut off one rounded end of several ladyfingers and place around inside of mold, cut side resting on bottom and curved side against inside wall of mold. Trim even with top of mold to balance charlotte when unmolded.
4. Fill mold with Bavarian Cream. Chill in refrigerator for several hours or overnight.
5. Unmold on round platter covered with linen napkin.

Serves 12.

NOTE: Bottom of mold may be lined with *Gâteau Génoise* (p. 326), sliced ¼–½ inch thick, instead of ladyfingers.

Gratin of Peaches and Cream   *Gratin de Pêches et Crème*

Even if only six desserts are required, make the full amount of peach cream purée. It is delicious served as a frozen mousse on a later occasion.

14 ounces (2 scant cups) purée of peaches, fresh poached (approx. 5 small peaches) or canned (approx. 6 large peach halves, drained)
1 package unflavored gelatin
½ pound (1 cup plus 2 tablespoons) sugar
4 egg whites

1 cup heavy cream
¼ cup rum
Génoise Mousseline No. 1 (p. 326)
Small, fresh strawberries, halved
Confectioners' sugar
12 wax paper yogurt cups, to use as molds

1. Purée enough peeled and pitted peach halves to measure 14 liquid ounces and sprinkle with the gelatin. Let stand for 5 minutes, then heat to melt gelatin completely and allow to cool.

2. Make Italian meringue by heating sugar with ½ cup water until it reaches the soft ball stage. While sugar is boiling, beat egg whites until quite stiff. When ready, pour hot syrup onto beaten egg whites, beating continuously, and continue beating until mixture is cool.

3. Whip cream until very lightly thickened or "half whipped." Combine meringue mixture, peach purée, and half-whipped cream flavored with ¼ cup rum, folding them together lightly but thoroughly.

4. Cut bottoms off wax paper yogurt or ice cream cups, leaving molds that are open at both ends and which measure approximately 3–3½ inches across and 2½ inches deep. Cut 12 circles of ½-inch thick *Génoise Mousseline* cake to fit bottom of molds, which should be set on a baking sheet. Line sides of each mold with halved strawberries, cut side against mold, in a circle. Fill each mold to the top with peach mixture and chill for 4 hours, or more.

5. When ready to serve, carefully tear off paper molds and sieve a generous amount of confectioners' sugar over each portion. Preheat broiler and place close under broiler for 30 seconds. The sugar will caramelize into a thin, crackly layer, and a little will run down the sides. A salamander or *tatin* iron can be used to caramelize, *or* omit the sugar and finish with a strawberry on top of each.

   Pour strawberry *Coulis* (p. 340) or *Crème Anglaise* (p. 287) onto each dessert plate and place dessert in the center. The contrast of colors, temperatures, flavors, and textures is very seductive.

Serves 12.

Chestnut Dessert
Le Mont Blanc

Mont-Blanc aux Marrons

½ cup sugar
1 pound (2 scant cups) chestnut purée (if using imported canned purée, be sure to get purée de marrons, *not* crème de marrons *or* chestnut spread)
½ pound (2 sticks) unsalted butter, at room temperature

1 teaspoon vanilla extract
1 pint heavy cream, whipped
One 9-inch Génoise Cake (p. 326), baked in a savarin mold
2 tablespoons Kirsch
Strawberries, pineapple, or *other fresh fruit for center of dessert*

1. Heat sugar with ½ cup water to 220 degrees. Set sugar syrup aside to cool somewhat.

2. Cream chestnut purée with butter, beat in sugar syrup and vanilla. Chill for 30 minutes.

3. Split Génoise ring in two or three layers, and sprinkle the cut surfaces with Kirsch. Reassemble the cake, spreading each layer with a ⅓-inch layer of chestnut cream, and set on a serving platter. (A silver platter is traditional for *Mont-Blanc.*) Fill a pastry bag fitted with a plain ⅟₁₆-inch tube or a sprinkler head type of tube with the rest of the chestnut cream. Pipe this mixture in a random pattern (it will look like vermicelli) all over the cake, leaving only the inside of the ring uncovered.

4. Fill the center of the cake with fresh fruit, forming a cone shape.

5. Fill a pastry bag fitted with a large star tube with whipped cream and cover cone of fruit completely with lines of cream, to resemble snow. Chill briefly until ready to serve.

Serves 10–12.

Chocolate Soufflé Cake   *Gâteau Nancy*

*14 ounces semi-sweet chocolate,
   cut up
7 ounces (1¾ sticks) sweet butter
2 tablespoons Grand Marnier liqueur
1 teaspoon vanilla extract
1 tablespoon almond powder (finely
   ground almonds)
10 eggs, separated
9 ounces (1¼ cups plus 1
   tablespoon) sugar*

*Confectioners' sugar for top
1 quart Crème Anglaise (p. 287)
Two 10-inch x 2-inch-deep round
   cake pans, buttered and floured
   and lined with circles of
   parchment paper*

1. Put chocolate, butter, Grand Marnier, vanilla, and almond powder in double boiler. Melt over hot water, stirring occasionally. Remove from heat as soon as chocolate is melted.

2. Beat egg yolks with 5 ounces (¾ cup) sugar until thick and a slowly dissolving ribbon forms when beater is lifted, about 6 minutes. Blend into lukewarm chocolate mixture using a large rubber spatula.

3. Whip egg whites until foamy, then gradually add 4 ounces (½ cup plus 1 tablespoon) sugar, whipping until soft peaks are formed. Using large rubber spatula, blend lightly into chocolate-egg mixture, as if it were a soufflé.

4. Divide batter between two prepared pans and bake in preheated 275-degree oven for 1 hour and 20 minutes.

5. As soon as cakes test done (p. 323), loosen sides with a sharp knife and unmold on cake racks to prevent sogginess. Cakes will have a crisp "sugar bloom" on the outside, and will sink very slightly. The top surfaces will probably crack, which is normal. Let cool, and sprinkle with confectioners' sugar before serving.

    Serve with coffee-flavored *Crème Anglaise* surrounding wedge of cake on dessert plate.

Each cake serves 10–12. Recipe can be halved.

Poire William Cake   *Gâteau Poire William*

After watching me make pâte brisée, génoise mousseline, *and* crème chantilly, *Jackie Mallorca, who did the illustrations for this book, created this* gâteau. *I think you will agree that she is a good student.*

FOR CAKE AND FILLING:
Two 9-inch x 1-inch rounds Génoise
    Mousseline *No. 1 (p. 326)*
One 9-inch x ⅛-inch round of Pâte
    Brisée *(p. 141)*
¼ cup apricot jam, melted and sieved

1 recipe Crème Chantilly *(p. 79),*
    flavored with 2 tablespoons Poire
    William liqueur in addition to
    vanilla extract

FOR DECORATION:
8-ounce package dried pears
3 ounces (⅓ cup plus 2 tablespoons)
    sugar
Sugar for coating pears
Chocolate vermicelli
2 ounces bittersweet chocolate,
    melted and cooled

Pastry bag fitted with large star tube
    for cream
Pastry bag fitted with writing tube for
    chocolate

1. The day before the cake is required, make the *Génoise Mousseline,* the pastry, and the little pears for decorating the finished *gâteau.*

2. To make little pears, simmer soft dried pears (tough cores removed) in ½ cup water until tender, about 10 minutes, covered. Increase heat to evaporate any remaining water (watch carefully), and place in food processor. Purée with 3 ounces sugar and return paste to heavy pan. Stir over low heat until a thick, stiff paste is formed, about 3–4 minutes. When cool enough to handle, form into ½–¾-inch balls and roll in sugar. Elongate slightly to form a pear shape, and push a piece of chocolate vermicelli in top to simulate a stem. Allow to dry overnight on rack. Makes about 30— not all will be required to decorate cake.

3. Placed baked and cooled round of *Pâte Brisée* on flat platter and brush with apricot glaze. Top with layer of *Génoise Mousseline,* and sprinkle with Poire William liqueur. Spread cake with 1-inch thick layer of *Crème Chantilly* and top with second layer of *Génoise Mousseline.* Sprinkle with Poire William. Mask sides and top of cake with a smooth layer of *Crème Chantilly.*

4. Transfer balance of *Crème Chantilly* to pastry bag fitted with star tube and pipe a line of touching stars or shells around top of cake at outer edge, and around base.

5. Put melted and cooled but still liquid chocolate in pastry bag fitted with writing tube. Pipe out a spiraling vine stalk around edge of cake, just inside

star decoration. Form small heart-shaped leaves and dots for buds on either side of vine stalk. (See illustration below.)

6. Place a few small sugared pears on top of cake, and arrange more around the sides, two or three together in groups. Refrigerate until serving time.

Serves 10.

Mango Mousse   *Mousse de Mangue*

2 pounds ripe mangoes
2 tablespoons rum
1½ tablespoons (1½ envelopes) unflavored gelatin
3 ounces (6 tablespoons) sweet butter, at soft room temperature
1 cup sugar
4 egg whites
1 cup heavy cream, half-whipped

2 layers Génoise Mousseline *No. 1, 9 inches diameter and ¼–½ inch thick (p. 326) or 17¾ x 12¾-inch "half sheet cake" pan recommended for baking* Gâteau Génoise Mousseline *(p. 328)*
Confectioners' sugar for top
9-inch springform pan

1. Peel mangoes, slice flesh from stones, and cut in chunks.

2. In a heavy saucepan, put cut mangoes, rum, and ½ cup water, and simmer until mixture has texture of marmalade. Transfer to food processor and process until smooth. Return to rinsed pan, sprinkle with gelatin and let

337

dissolve over heat. Cool to lukewarm and stir in soft butter. (If fruit mixture is too warm, butter will clarify and turn oily.)

3. Heat sugar in heavy pot with ½ cup water until soft ball stage. While sugar is boiling, beat egg whites until just starting to get stiff. Beat boiling sugar mixture, when ready, into beaten egg whites.

4. Whip cream until just starting to thicken. Fold egg whites into cream, then fold into mango mixture.

5. Set sides of springform pan on a flat platter. Line bottom surface with a 9-inch diameter layer of *Génoise* cake (It is easiest to bake the cake in a 17¾ x 12¾-inch "half sheet cake" pan, then use the sides of the springform pan as a cutting guide.) Sprinkle with rum. Pour in mango mousse to within ½ inch of top of mold. Sprinkle underside of other cake layer with rum, reverse and fit on top of mousse. Refrigerate for at least 6 hours or overnight. When ready to serve, remove sides of springform pan and sprinkle cake generously with confectioners' sugar.

   Serve with raspberry or strawberry *Coulis* (p. 340) or *Crème Anglaise* (p. 287), optional.

Serves 12.

Avocado Mousse   *Mousse d'Avocat*

1 quart heavy cream
1 pint milk
2 tablespoons unflavored gelatin
3 ripe avocados, peeled, seeds
   removed (1½ cups)

Juice of ½ lemon
½ cup Amaretto
2 cups sugar, cooked to soft ball
   stage
12 eggs, separated

1. Whip heavy cream just to stage when it starts to thicken. Set aside in a cool place.

2. In a pot sprinkle gelatin over milk and heat just until it dissolves. In a blender or processor fitted with steel blade put peeled and seeded avocados, lemon juice, Amaretto, and milk—process until puréed.

3. Make sugar syrup, ½ cup water with 2 cups sugar, heating sugar to 238 degrees. In an electric mixer beat yolks while pouring in 1 cup syrup for about 6–7 minutes.

4. Beat egg whites until just starting to get stiff, slowly pour 1 cup sugar syrup into egg whites, beating until cool.

5. In a large bowl, mix yolks with avocado mixture, then fold in egg whites using large rubber spatula, and finish with partially whipped cream. Refrigerate for 6 hours or prepare the day before. This recipe will fill two large glass or Pyrex bowls.

Serve with *Crème Anglaise* (p. 287) or *Coulis* of raspberries (p. 340). (An ice cream scoop can be used to mold mousse into a ball for service.)

Serves 24. Recipe can be cut into thirds or half.

NOTE: Two papayas can be substituted for three avocados. Rum would then be substituted for Amaretto.

Lemon Mousse   *Mousse de Citron*

8 egg yolks
11 ounces (1²/₃ cups) sugar
1 pint half and half (light cream)
Vanilla bean or 1 teaspoon vanilla extract
2 tablespoons (2 packages) unflavored gelatin
1 quart heavy cream
4 teaspoons finely grated lemon peel (zeste râpé)

8 ounces (1 cup) lemon juice, freshly squeezed and strained
Lemon sections for decoration (see note)
Whole lemon for decoration (see note)
3-quart soufflé mold or large bowl

1. Make a rich *Crème Anglaise* (see p. 287 for method) with egg yolks, sugar, half and half, and vanilla. Dissolve gelatin in ½ cup hot water, add to *crème anglaise,* and chill, stirring occasionally. Remove from refrigerator before custard starts to set.

2. Whip heavy cream until it just starts to get thick (half-whipped stage); it should make 1½ quarts. Stir grated lemon peel and lemon juice into chilled custard, which should not have started to gel, and fold in half-whipped cream. There will be approximately 3 quarts of mousse.

3. Gently spoon into 3-quart soufflé mold or large bowl. Chill for 4 hours, or overnight. Decorate with lemon sections and notched lemon.

Serves 10–12.

NOTE: To prepare lemons for decoration, remove all peel and pith and then cut between the membranes to release sections of fruit. Place in a shallow

339

baking pan and sprinkle with sugar. Put under broiler for a few seconds or in a 450-degree oven for 2 minutes to kill acidity. To make notched lemons to decorate platter, stand lemon on wider or flatter end, and use a small sharp knife to cut deep, same-sized Vs or teeth around middle of lemon, cutting through to center. Pull halves apart.

Fresh Puréed Raspberry Sauce   *Coulis de Framboises Fraîches*

*1 pint fresh raspberries (strawberries
  can be substituted)*
*2 tablespoons raspberry jam
  (optional)*

¼ cup sugar or to taste
*2 tablespoons Kirshwasser or
  raspberry liqueur (liqueur de
  framboises)*

1. Wash raspberries in a strainer and drain. Put in container of blender or processor and purée with 2 tablespoons raspberry jam, if more flavor or thickness is needed.
2. Strain through a Chinese cap or fine sieve to remove seeds, add sugar to taste and liqueur.
3. Refrigerate until ready to serve.
    Serve with molded fruit mousses, Avocado Mousse (p. 338), custards, *Oeufs à la Neige* (p. 342), poached fruits, and sorbets.

Serves 6.

Cooked Puréed Strawberry Sauce (Melba Sauce)   *Sauce au Fraises Fraîches Cuites*

12-ounce box fresh strawberries
2 tablespoons strawberry jam
½ cup sugar, or to taste

1–2 teaspoons cornstarch
*2 tablespoons Kirsch, Framboise, or
  other liqueur*

1. Rinse strawberries, drain well, and remove hulls and stems. Cook on medium low heat until they can be mashed, about 2–3 minutes. Stir in jam and sugar to taste. Strain through fine sieve.
2. Mix a teaspoon of cornstarch with a tablespoon of water. Put puréed strawberries in a non-aluminum pot on medium low heat, stir in cornstarch,

and bring to a boil. The sauce will immediately clear and thicken slightly. Cool a little and add liqueur to taste. This sauce is preserved longer under refrigeration, but will not have as good a color as uncooked sauce.

Serve lukewarm or cold, depending on dessert it is served with. Sauce makes a mirror on plate with dessert on top, such as Mango Mousse (p. 337).

Serve with strawberries, ice cream, chilled molded charlotte desserts, soufflés.

Serves 4–6.

Strawberry "Cheesecake" (without cheese)

"Gâteau de Fromage" aux Fraises (sans fromage)

SPONGE CAKE LAYER:
2/3 cup sifted cake flour
3/4 teaspoon baking powder
2 eggs

2/3 cup sugar
1/4 cup water
1 teaspoon vanilla extract

1. Preheat oven to 375 degrees. Have ready a 9-inch springform pan, ungreased. Sift flour and baking powder together.

2. Beat eggs until thick and creamy using an electric mixer on high speed. Add sugar, a little at a time, on medium speed until mixture is very thick and makes "the ribbon." On low speed, add water, vanilla, and flour mixed with baking powder. Speed of mixer should correspond to folding technique. Pour into 9-inch springform pan.

3. Bake at 375 degrees for 10 minutes or until top springs back when lightly pressed with fingertip. Cool in pan on wire rack about 10 minutes. Loosen sides of cake with a sharp knife.

    Remove side of pan and let cake cool completely.

FILLING:
2 tablespoons lemon juice
1 envelope unflavored gelatin
8 ounces (1 cup) dairy sour cream
8 ounces (1 cup) plain yogurt
3 tablespoons sugar
2 teaspoons grated lemon rind

1 cup heavy cream, chilled
Strawberry liqueur
1/2 cup heavy cream
Dash vanilla extract
1/2 cup strawberry jam, melted
1 pint strawberries

341

1. In small saucepan, combine lemon juice and 1 tablespoon water. Sprinkle gelatin over the liquid, stirring to blend. Let soften 5 minutes. Dissolve gelatin on *very low* heat and continue cooking until mixture is clear. Let cool.

2. Beat until blended the sour cream, yogurt, 2 tablespoons of the sugar, lemon rind, and gelatin mixture. Beat chilled heavy cream until just starting to get stiff and fold in.

3. Split cooled sponge cake in half horizontally. Brush top of each layer with strawberry liqueur.

4. Line bottom of 9-inch springform pan with wax paper cut to fit. Place one of layers in pan. Spoon in sour cream and yogurt filling. Place second layer of sponge cake on top. Refrigerate until filling is solid, taking about 3 hours.

5. Remove side of springform pan. Beat ½ cup cream until almost whipped. Beat in remaining sugar and vanilla. Spread on side of cake. Brush top with melted strawberry jam. With pointed end up, place strawberries on top of cake in a circular pattern. Brush berries with melted jam. Refrigerate until ready to serve.

Meringues
Pâtes à Meringue

Snow Eggs   *Oeufs à la Neige*

SNOW EGGS OR MERINGUE BALLS:
3 quarts water
½ cup milk
1¾ cups sugar

1½ teaspoons vanilla extract
8 egg whites
Crème Anglaise *(modern or traditional) (p. 287)*

SPUN SUGAR (SUCRE FILÉ OU CHEVEUX D'ANGE):
1 cup sugar
1 tablespoon corn syrup

1. Fill large pan with water to a depth of 2 inches—the larger the pan, the more snow eggs can be made at one time. Add ½ cup milk to water.

2. Dissolve ¼ cup sugar to each quart of water used. Bring poaching liquid to a slow boil, reduce temperature to remain just below boiling or 170 degrees. Add vanilla.

3. Beat egg whites until stiff but not dry, and gradually add 1 cup sugar until mixture is smooth.

4. To form meringue balls use a large soup spoon, tablespoon, or pastry bag. Dip large spoon in cold water while forming snow eggs, which are then placed in simmering water.

5. Poach meringue balls approximately 8–10 minutes, turning over with a slotted spoon after about 4 minutes. When firm to the touch, place on paper towels to drain.

6. To assemble: Use a deep bowl, preferably crystal or glass; or a shallow Pyrex rectangular casserole to place the chilled *Crème Anglaise* in first. Arrange snow eggs on top, and cover with a web of spun sugar.

7. To make spun sugar: In a small heavy pot combine 1 cup sugar and 1 tablespoon corn syrup. Boil mixture on medium high heat until it turns golden brown, 310 degrees on a candy thermometer. Remove from heat instantly before it turns too dark.

8. Ahead of time, spread paper on work area where *Oeufs à la Neige* bowl is placed. Move sugar syrup next to it. Quickly, while syrup is still hot, hold 2 forks in one hand, side by side so that they appear to be 1 fork with 8 tines, and dip into hot syrup. Swing the sugar strands that drip from the forks over the meringue balls, covering them with a web of spun sugar.

Serves 8.

NOTE: To make *Cheveux d'Ange* to decorate a dessert, spin sugar over two broomstick handles placed 1 foot apart. (A turban shape can be made.) Cover floor with newspapers.

Floating Island in Raspberry Purée
Oeufs à la Neige au Coulis de Framboises

4 egg whites
1/3 cup sugar plus 3 tablespoons for other steps
Few drops vanilla extract
1 quart water

2 tablespoons milk
Grated peel of 1 orange
2 cups fresh raspberries
1/2 cup raspberry liqueur
Slivered almonds

1. Beat egg whites until firm. Gradually beat in 1/3 cup sugar and vanilla on high speed until egg whites are very stiff.

343

2. Using a large skillet, add water, 1 tablespoon sugar, milk, and orange peel; bring to a boil. Remove skillet from heat and let stand 1 minute.

3. Form egg whites with a large soup spoon dipped in cold water, making four to six mounds. Put skillet on low heat, carefully place egg whites on top of liquid, poaching a few minutes. Do not let water boil! Turn over with a spatula or skimmer, and poach about 1 more minute or until firm. Drain on paper towels.

4. Place on baking sheet, sprinkle 1–2 tablespoons sugar over tops of snow eggs or meringues, and place under broiler just long enough to melt sugar and brown tops delicately.

5. Wash and drain raspberries, reserving a few for garnishing. Purée the rest with raspberry liqueur in a blender or food processor. Add sugar to taste and blend. Strain through a sieve to remove seeds. Chill.

6. To serve, spoon raspberry purée onto chilled dessert plates. Place meringues in center with fresh raspberries and slivered almonds on top.

Serves 4–6.

Molded Floating Island   *Ile Flottante*

Caramelized Sugar (p. 156)
4 egg whites
Pinch salt
⅛ teaspoon cream of tartar (optional)
½ cup superfine or regular granulated sugar

Dash lemon juice
½ teaspoon vanilla extract
½ teaspoon cornstarch (optional)
1 quart charlotte mold

1. Line charlotte mold with Caramelized Sugar.

2. Beat egg whites with a pinch of salt until frothy. Add cream of tartar, if desired, and continue beating until stiff.

3. Slowly add sugar, using a spatula to push whites from side of mixing bowl. When meringue is thick and glossy, fold in lemon juice, vanilla extract, and cornstarch, if desired, with spatula. A few more tablespoons of sugar can also be folded in. Spoon into mold without packing.

4. Place in a *bain-marie* and bake in center of 300-degree oven for 30 minutes. Let cool in oven with door open for 30 minutes. Loosen sides with

knife and unmold on serving platter. Can refrigerate overnight, but no longer.

Serve with *Crème Anglaise* sauce (p. 287).

Serves 6.

Ordinary Meringue
French Meringue

Meringue Ordinaire
Meringue Française

This is the lightest of meringue mixtures and it melts in the mouth. Italian Meringue and Swiss Meringue are heavier. An alternative method of cooking (other than that used in these meringue recipes) is to leave the formed meringues in a 150-degree oven overnight. Technically meringue does not bake. It simply dries out.

8 egg whites, at room temperature
16 ounces (2¼ cups) sugar, superfine or granulated
Dash vanilla extract (optional)
Baking sheets, buttered and floured or lined with baking parchment

16–18-inch long pastry bag
½–1-inch tip or nozzle: round, fluted, and star-shaped (for decoration)

1. *Beat* egg whites until stiff peaks form, then gradually *beat* in half of the sugar and vanilla extract for about 3 minutes or until mixture is firm and glossy.

2. *Fold* in other half of sugar, and quickly form into desired shapes. A pastry bag fitted with ½–1-inch plain or fluted tube is used to control the shapes piped onto prepared baking sheets. Some meringue shapes include ovals, rounds, fingers, shells of various sizes (to be filled), small and large vacherins (p. 348), *Oeufs à la Neige* (p. 342), and Meringue Mushrooms (p. 346). Round or oval shapes are made by starting in the center, piping ever-widening spirals.

3. Bake in a very slow oven, 200 degrees F., for 2 hours or until dry and crisp. Meringues should not color, but a pale ivory is permissible. Let cool in turned-off oven and store airtight.

Makes four 9-inch round cake layers piped in spirals. Recipe can be halved.

NOTE: The proportions for meringue are always the same: 2 ounces (4 tablespoons) granulated sugar for every large egg white (1 ounce); one half of the sugar is beaten in and the other half folded in.

345

Meringue Mushrooms

Champignons en Meringue

¹/₂ recipe Meringue Ordinaire *(p. 345)*
4 baking sheets, lightly buttered and floured or lined with baking parchment
16–18-inch long pastry bag

¹/₂–³/₄-inch round tip or nozzle
Chocolate or *butter cream for gluing stalks*
Unsweetened cocoa for decoration (optional)

1. Follow *Meringue Ordinaire* recipe to Step 2. As soon as all the sugar is folded in meringue mixture, quickly spoon meringue in pastry bag fitted with round tip, and form mushrooms on prepared pans. Pipe 1½-inch diameter rounds for the caps, smoothing off any "points" with the tip of a knife.

2. Pipe an equal number of ½-inch diameter by 1-inch high "stalks," pulling the pastry bag upward so that the stalks will be upright and have pointed ends.

3. If speckled meringue mushrooms are required, sprinkle lightly with unsweetened cocoa *before* baking.

4. Bake in a 200-degree oven for about 1½ hours or until mushrooms are dry. To assemble, make a small hole in the underside of the baked cap, fill with butter cream or melted chocolate, and insert a stalk. Store in an airtight container.

Makes approximately 30 mushrooms.

Italian Meringue   *Meringue à l'Italienne*

*8 extra large egg whites, at room
    temperature*
Dash vanilla extract (optional)

16 ounces (2¼ cups) sugar

Using an electric mixer on a stand, beat egg whites until stiff and add vanilla
after sugar syrup has started to cook. Cook sugar with 1 cup water to soft ball
stage: 240 degrees F. Pour over egg whites, beating constantly, and continue
beating until cold.

Makes 16 cups meringue. Recipe can be halved.

Italian meringue is used for petit fours and certain meringue-topped
pastries, and can be beaten into whipped cream or butter cream to give added
lightness.

Swiss Meringue
(Cooked Meringue)

*Meringue à la Suisse
(Meringue Cuite)*

*8 extra large egg whites, at room
    temperature*
16 ounces (2¼ cups) sugar

Dash vanilla extract

Add sugar to egg whites in top of large double boiler. Using electric beater,
beat over simmering water using same method as used when making Génoise
Cake (p. 324). As soon as volume has doubled, remove from heat, add vanilla,
and continue beating until cold.

**Makes 8 cups meringue: thirty-two 3-inch circles or approximately sixteen
3-inch shells. Recipe can be halved.**

Use for making petit fours and for giving lightness to whipped cream and
butter cream, if desired.

NOTE: Today, *Meringue Ordinaire* is called Swiss Meringue by some cooks.
This is incorrect, as the classic Swiss Meringue is cooked over hot water with
a sugar syrup. Another method for making Swiss Meringue is to heat the sugar
without melting it (it must remain dry) and incorporate it slowly into half-
whipped egg whites. This method replaces the use of a *bain-marie,* or double
boiler.

Chocolate Meringue Mixture

Meringue au Chocolat

As far as I can surmise, chocolate meringue originated in Germany.

8 egg whites, at room temperature
8 ounces (1 cup plus 2 tablespoons)
  granulated sugar
Dash vanilla extract (optional)
8 ounces (1¾ cups) confectioners'
  sugar

2½ ounces (1 scant cup) cocoa
Baking parchment paper
Baking sheets

1. Beat egg whites until stiff, then beat in granulated sugar and vanilla, if used. Beat about 3 minutes until mixture is firm and glossy.

2. Sift together confectioners' sugar and cocoa, then sift over beaten egg whites one-quarter at a time, and fold in with rubber spatula. It is easier to fold in the cocoa if the beaten egg whites are placed in a wide bowl.

3. Line cookie sheets with baking parchment, sticking it down with dabs of meringue mixture on underside of each corner. Form into desired shapes and bake in a very slow oven, 200 degrees F., until dry and crisp. Let dry out in turned-off oven overnight, and store in an airtight container.

Halved recipe makes approximately 30 fingers about 2 inches long and 1 inch wide. Whole recipe makes 26–30 shells about 2½ inches in diameter.

Two Kinds of Vacherin
Deux Sortes de Vacherin

Large Vacherin Shell with Fresh Fruit

Grand Vacherin aux Fruits Frais

SHELL:
6 egg whites
12 ounces (1¾ cups) sugar
Dash vanilla

FILLING AND GLAZE:
1 pint vanilla ice cream
Fresh fruit: strawberries, raspberries,
  blackberries, sliced peaches, or
  pears, or other fresh fruit in season

DECORATION:
2 egg whites
4 ounces (½ cup plus 1 tablespoon)
  sugar

1 cup apricot or raspberry jam (to
  suit fruit chosen)
1 tablespoon liqueur of choice

348

1. Make up ordinary meringue mixture with above ingredients as directed on page 345, and place in pastry bag fitted with plain ½-inch tube.

2. Butter and flour two cookie sheets. Using a flan ring or cake pan, make five 9-inch circles in flour.

3. Pipe out base of shell first, filling in one 9-inch circle with a spiral of meringue and smoothing out with spatula. Next pipe out four even 9-inch diameter rings.

4. Bake at 200 degrees F. for 3–4 hours. Let cool in turned off oven.

5. When meringue base and circles are cool, make up second batch of *meringue ordinaire* mixture with 2 egg whites and 4 ounces sugar as directed on page 345. (A fresh batch must be made, as it will become watery if left to stand for several hours.) Place small dots of mixture around edge of vacherin base, and set one ring on top. Apply more dots of uncooked meringue to secure second, third, and fourth rings in place.

6. Using spatula, smooth uncooked meringue mixture thinly over sides of shell, forming a smooth surface. Transfer balance of mixture to a pastry bag and apply continuous bands of shell or star decoration around sides.

7. Bake at 200 degrees F. for 30 minutes to 1 hour. Let cool in turned off oven or other dry place.

8. When ready to serve, fill shell two thirds full with slightly softened ice cream. Fill shell to top with fresh fruit arranged in decorative pattern. Melt jam, stir in liqueur, sieve, and brush over fruit to glaze.

Serves 12–14.

Meringue and Ice Cream Layer Cake

Gâteau aux Méringues et Glace

CAKE LAYERS:
8 egg whites
16 ounces (2¼ cups) sugar
Dash vanilla extract

FILLING:
1 pint each chocolate, coffee, and vanilla ice cream (or any three different colors and flavors of choice)

DECORATION:
1 recipe Crème Chantilly (p. 79)

1. Make four 9-inch meringue layers as directed in large vacherin shell recipe (see above, Steps 3 and 4), forming continuous spirals using a pastry bag fitted with a plain ½-inch tube, and then smoothing out with a spatula.

349

2. Spread baked and cooled meringue layers with slightly softened ice cream, ½ inch thick. Return cake to freezer for 1 hour to set ice cream hard.

3. Cover outside of cake with smooth layer of *Crème Chantilly,* then decorate using a star tube.

4. Return to freezer if not using immediately. Can be made 1 or 2 days ahead of time. Remove from freezer 10 minutes before serving time.

Serves 12–14.

COMPARISON OF RECOMMENDED TEMPERATURES FOR BAKING CAKES, PASTRIES, COOKIES, AND BREADS	
Gâteau Génoise	350 degrees
Gâteau Génoise Mousseline	375 degrees
Ladyfingers	325 degrees
Puff Pastry	375 degrees
Pâte à Choux	375 degrees
Brioche	400 degrees
Croissant	375–400 degrees
Tuiles	375 degrees
Tulipes and *Cigarettes*	400 degrees
Meringues	200 degrees

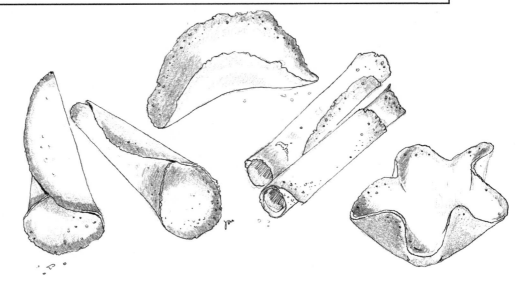

Seven Petits Fours
Sept Petits Fours Secs

Rum-Raisin Wafers   *Palets aux Raisins*

*4¹/₂ ounces (1 scant cup) seedless
   raisins*
¹/₃ cup rum
4¹/₂ ounces (9 tablespoons) butter
4¹/₂ ounces (²/₃ cup) sugar

2 eggs
¹/₂ teaspoon vanilla extract
*5 ounces (1 cup plus 1 tablespoon)
   flour*

1. Put raisins and rum in a saucepan and let stand for 30 minutes, then warm gently and flame. Most of the rum will evaporate. Set aside to cool.
2. Cream butter and sugar, and beat in eggs one by one.
3. Add vanilla, fold in flour, and raisins.
4. Butter and flour cookie sheets, and drop batter by teaspoonfuls, allowing room for the cookies to spread. Flatten each mound into a neat circle with the back of a small spoon.
5. Bake in a 375-degree oven for 6–8 minutes. Cookies will start to brown around the edges. Cool on racks and store airtight. *Palets aux Raisins* are meant to be somewhat soft, not crisp.

Makes approximately 5 dozen.

NOTE: Currants may be substituted for raisins or chocolate chips.

Cats' Tongues I   *Langues de Chat I*

10 tablespoons butter
1 cup sugar
1 teaspoon vanilla extract

8 egg whites
2 cups flour

1. Cream butter and sugar and add vanilla. Add egg whites one by one, beating on medium speed.
2. Fold in flour. Transfer mixture to a pastry bag fitted with a plain round ¼– ½-inch tube.
3. Form 3¼-inch cookies on buttered baking sheet, pressing a little harder at

351

each end to form a slight "hourglass" shape. Allow 1½ inches of space between cookies as they spread. Bake in a preheated 400-degree oven for 6–8 minutes, until lightly browned around the edges. Cool on a rack and store in an airtight container.

Serve with tea or coffee, with ice cream or fruit cups or compotes.

Makes approximately 65 cats' tongues. Recipe can be halved.

Cats' Tongues II   *Langues de Chat II*

7 ounces (1¾ sticks) butter, softened
8½ ounces (1 cup plus 2 tablespoons) confectioners' sugar
1 teaspoon vanilla extract

3 eggs
10 ounces (2 cups) flour

1. Cream butter and sugar and add vanilla. Add eggs, one by one, beating on medium speed.
2. Fold in flour. Transfer mixture to a pastry bag fitted with a plain round ¼–½-inch tube.
3. Form 3¼-inch cookies on buttered baking sheet, pressing a little harder at each end to form a slight "hourglass" shape. Allow 1½ inches of space between cookies as they spread during baking. Bake in a preheated 375-degree oven for 6–8 minutes, until lightly browned at edges. Cool on rack and store in an airtight container.

Makes approximately 60 cats' tongues.

NOTE: These cookies can be served plain with desserts such as ice cream or fruit cups, or offered with afternoon tea or morning coffee sandwiched together with butter cream (*Crème au Beurre,* p. 296) or jam.

"Roof Tiles"   *Tuiles aux Amandes*

9 ounces (2¼ cups) grated almonds
8 ounces (1¾ cups) confectioners'
  sugar
4 egg whites
2 whole eggs

4 ounces (1 scant cup) flour
3 ounces (6 tablespoons) unsalted
  butter, melted
Few drops vanilla extract

1. Put grated almonds (this can be done in a food processor) in a mixing bowl. Add confectioners' sugar, egg whites, and whole eggs. Stir in flour, melted butter, and vanilla.

2. Drop by teaspoonfuls at 3-inch intervals on greased baking sheet. (Cookies will spread to about 2 inch diameter.) Press lightly with fork dipped in water. Bake at 375 degrees for about 8 minutes. Cookies should brown slightly around the edges.

3. Immediately remove from baking sheet with a short spatula or paint scraper and curve into the shape of old-fashioned clay roof tiles by placing inside 9-inch diameter savarin or ring molds, or pressing lightly over a rolling pin.

4. Cookies will "set" almost immediately. Remove from savarin molds and continue cooling on rack. Store in airtight container.

Makes approximately 120.

Rolled Wafer Cookies   *Cigarettes*

6 ounces (1½ sticks) butter, at room
  temperature
12 ounces (1½ cups) confectioners'
  sugar
8 egg whites

Few drops vanilla extract
7 ounces (1½ scant cups) pastry
  flour

1. Cream butter and sugar together.

2. Add egg whites and vanilla

3. Fold in flour.

4. Drop batter by teaspoonfuls onto well-buttered cookie sheets—they will spread to about the size of a silver dollar, so leave plenty of space.

5. Bake at 400 degrees about 7 minutes; cookies will start to brown around edges. Remove from oven and, while cookies are still hot and pliable,

353

remove from baking sheet with a short spatula or paint scraper and roll around a pencil or the handle of a wooden spoon. Cool on rack and store airtight.

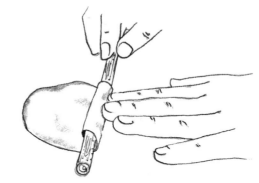

Makes about 150.

Rolled cookies may be served plain; have one end dipped in melted chocolate; or be filled with flavored butter cream (p. 296).

Rum-Raisin Wafers   *Palais aux Dames*

These are made in the same way as *Cigarettes,* with the addition of 5 ounces (1 heaping cup) seedless raisins and 4 tablespoons rum, and the cookies are left flat. Soak raisins in rum for 30 minutes, then warm gently and flame. Most of the liquid will evaporate. Add raisins to batter after folding in flour and proceed as above. Store airtight, recrisping in low oven if necessary.

Tulip-shaped Cookie Cups   *Pâte pour Tulipes*

3 ounces (6 tablespoons) butter
4½ ounces (½ cup plus 3 tablespoons) sugar
7 egg whites

4½ ounces (1 scant cup) flour
Butter for greasing pan

1. In bowl of mixer, cream butter and sugar together, beat in egg whites one by one, and blend in flour, working as little as possible.
2. For each cookie cup, drop 2 tablespoonfuls batter onto large buttered baking sheet, allowing 3–4 per sheet. Spread the batter out into 5-inch

circles (size depends on size of mold to be used). Leave plenty of space between each.

3. Bake in a 400-degree oven for 2–5 minutes. Have ready four custard cups or Chinese tea bowls turned upside down to use as molds. Using short spatula or paint scraper, remove one of the cookies from baking sheet and press over the back of cup; or mold in place by immediately placing a second cup on top. Repeat with the other three cookies. As the cookies become crisp very quickly and will no longer be pliable enough to mold, it is necessary to work with only three or four at a time.

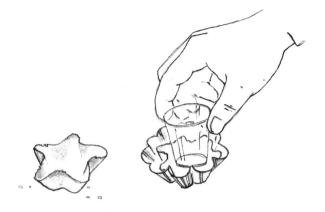

4. Repeat with the rest of the dough. Allow to cool, then fill with mousse, sorbet, ice cream, or fresh fruit. *Pâte pour Tulipes* can be rolled around a French horn mold to make cornets. This recipe is a good way to use leftover egg whites and to make plain cookies.

Makes approximately sixteen 5-inch *tulipes.*

Chapter Thirteen

Composing Menus; Choosing Wines for Menus

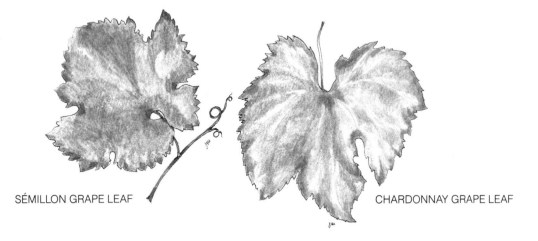

SÉMILLON GRAPE LEAF

CHARDONNAY GRAPE LEAF

The Five Flavors, Five Senses, and Four Seasons All Contribute to the Composition of Menus

Before I discuss how I compose menus in the 1980s, I would like to invoke the past and travel to the East. We will visit the Chinese, who discovered the five basic flavors:

1. salt
2. sour (tart, acidic)
3. sweet (white, brown and malt sugar, honey, molasses)
4. hot (black, white, red pepper—bitter would be similar for the Western palate)
5. fragrant (garlic, onion, cilantro, herbs and spices)

The Chinese were also the first to record that cuisine should appeal to all five senses:

1. the eye—in an aesthetic way
2. the nose—to be pleasant to smell
3. the touch—feel good in the mouth
4. the ear—create the correct sound when being chewed
5. the tongue—taste exceptionally good

There are more than five aromas, however, for the nose can make thousands of distinctions in food and wine. The mind integrates and stores the tastes, learns from the palate and the smells caught by the nose, to organize the concepts referred to as flavors. This phenomenon brings about the ability to discriminate and appreciate the subtleties of fine food and wine. Since modern scientists have learned that the eye can distinguish nearly eight million differences in color and the ear more than three hundred thousand tones, it is not surprising that one person can make thousands of differentiations in wine and food.

It is this ability to discriminate that puts a burden on the chef to supply variety and newness in menus to satisfy man's craving for innovation, an inherent part of his being. That is why the goal of the student chef is to learn to compose delectable and appropriate menus—the culmination of his determination to perfect the fundamentals and advance in due time to *chef des cuisines.*

The season of the year, the purpose or the occasion for the dinner, the number of guests, the location of the event, and the budget all contribute to the decisions for a formal or informal dinner party. A formal dinner has, sometimes, nine to ten courses. These use all of the kitchen's resources of sous-chefs, food storage, make-ahead dishes, not to mention marketing, and *mise en place.* The courses in present day dinner parties or banquets are alternated with lighter and heavier dishes: hors d'oeuvre; appetizer or first course (Chapters 4, 5, 6, 7, 9—all three discussed in Introduction to Chapter 4); soup course (Chapter 1); fish course (Chapters 4 and 7); sorbet course; main course (Chapters 2, 5, 7, 8 and 9); salad course (Chapter 4); cheese course; dessert course (Chapters 3, 6, 10, 11, 12).

With these ideas in mind, let me present a few dos and don'ts to remember when planning a menu:

1. Do not repeat the same ingredients: If serving *Sole Bréval* (p. 176) with a cream sauce, do not follow with *Poularde Maison Blanche* also with a cream sauce (p. 226). If a light sauce is served first, *Paillarde de Saumon* (p. 188), a heavy sauce may follow, *Poulet au Fleurie* (p. 227).

2. Do not have two game or poultry dishes on the same menu. If serving a duck salad (p. 123), do not serve a main course with chicken such as *Globi de Volaille au Poivre Rose* (p. 229). Do serve as a first course sautéed goose or duck liver with mushrooms or cooked corn kernels (p. 103) before a main course of Veal Chop Trianon (p. 218); a green salad may come afterwards. It would be inappropriate to serve Duck with Pineapple (p. 242) after a *Salade au Foie Gras de Canard* (pp. 107–108).

3. In the past, salad was always served after the main course, presumably to aid digestion. In our time a composed salad *(salade composée)* is often served first as stated above—cooked duck or foie gras salad or to mention other salads: Warm Scallop Salad Carlo (p. 116) and Crayfish Salad with Chicory and Radicchio (p. 115). I do not believe in serving salad again if it is served as a first course.

4. Do not repeat textures: If *Soupe en Croute, Feuilletée d'Asperges* or *Chaussons d'Homard* are served as a first course, do not have a main course with dough.

5. Serve a sorbet or granité before main course of a five- to six-course dinner. A lemon sorbet is enhanced with a little Vodka on top; cantaloupe or pear sorbet is pleasant with a few drops of Port wine on top. A granité is made similarly to a sorbet or sherbert—freeze the mixture, then for a granité stir until it makes slivers of ice.

6. I recommend make-ahead desserts for an elaborate dinner party or any meal that requires most of the chef's time and attention on the day it is served. Some pastries that even benefit from being assembled ahead of time are my *Miroir de Framboise* (p. 328), *Gâteau Jacqueline* (p. 329), Linzer Tarte (p. 152). A light dessert is made from *Les Tulipes* (p. 354) filled with ice cream and fresh fruit on top, Avocado Mousse (p. 338) served with a *Coulis* of raspberries (p. 340).

Menus—Motivation of the Cook's Art and Inspirational Goal

The following menus are included to give examples of how I plan menus. They have not been selected on the basis of recipes appearing in this cookbook. However, dishes and preparations marked with an asterisk (*) can be found here in their appropriate category of cuisine. When composing your own menus, similar dishes in the book can substitute for ones in the restaurant menus. For example, Alsatian Poussin (p. 232) may be substituted for *Squab Braisé* (p. 368) or *Pigeon en Cocotte* (p. 364), and *le fond d'artichaut* may be filled with a purée preferred by the cook. Seasonal availability of ingredients also influences the menu maker. Since fresh vegetables appear in the market year round, it is always possible to make Molded Mousse of Vegetables (p. 276), a colorful and flavorful presentation on dinner plates. When a Confit of Onions, Shallots, or Garlic (p. 271) is served with an appropriate lamb or beef dish, all the flavors are intensified. You can refer to "dos and don'ts to remember when planning a menu" (above) for constructive ideas.

Fourteen Restaurant Menus Spanning Twelve Years

Opening Night Dinner of Le Trianon Restaurant, *Le Premier Soir,* March 23, 1972. Menu cover: pen and ink drawing of the White House
First Growth Group Dinner, November 3, 1974
Château Pétrus Dinner, April 4, 1975

Dinner Party for Six Guests, November 9, 1973
Dinner Menu for Small Party, July 14, 1978
Dinner Menu for Four, Giving Choices of Main Course, February 1980
Dinner Menu for Four, February 1981
Dinner for Alan Shepard, May 5, 1981
Dinner Menu for Eight, October 1981
Dinner Menu, April 21, 1982
Dinner Party for Six, May 7, 1982
Dinner Party for Four, February 7, 1983
Dinner to Benefit KQED (public television), December 5, 1983
Dinner for the American Institute of Wine and Food, June 29, 1984

PINOT NOIR GRAPE LEAF

Opening Night Dinner of Le Trianon Restaurant
Le Premier Soir, March 23, 1972

MENU COVER: PEN AND INK DRAWING OF THE WHITE HOUSE

Réception: *Pendant le chuchotement des invités des amuse-bouche seront servis.*

Le Menu: *Consommé* du Printemps*
(Consommé* with Spring Vegetables)
Ballotine du Roi Soleil
Casserolette de Sole Pompadour
(Sole Served in Individual Casseroles of Puff Pastry)
    Moët et Chandon
    Brut Imperial

Intermède: *Granité au Lime*

*Globi de Volaille au Poivre Vert**
(Boned Chicken Stuffed with Veal and
Green Peppercorns*)
*Haricots Vert Frais**
(Fresh Green Beans*)
Feuilles Vertes de Saison
(Salad of Seasonal Green Leaves)

L'Apothéose: *Surprise Glacée Trianon:*
Gratin de Fruits au Sabayon
Petits Fours

Liqueurs

Café

First Growth Group Dinner
November 3, 1974

Le Fond d'Artichaut* Jeannette
(Artichoke Bottom* Filled with Garden Vegetables)

Les Goujonettes de Saumon Trianon*
(Fried Fish Sticks of Salmon*)

Le Coeur de Filet de Boeuf* en Chevreuil
(The Heart of the Filet of Beef* Marinated Like Venison)
Sauce Grand Veneur*
(Pepper Sauce with the Marinade*)
Les Pommes Surprises

La Salade de Saison*

Les Fromages Selectionnes

La Coupe Nancy

Quelques Gourmandises
(Assorted Petits Fours)

Les Aperitifs
Le Porto Da Silva
Le Xeres G. Byass

Vins
Le Riesling d'Alsace

Les Grand Crus Classes 1947
Château Lafite Rothschild
Château Mouton Rothschild
Château Margaux
Château Haut-Brion
Château Latour
Château Pétrus
Château Cheval Blanc
Château Ausone

Champagne
Dom Ruinart 1966
Blanc de Blancs

Liqueurs, Cognacs

Château Pétrus Dinner
April 4, 1975

L'Oeuf Lucullus*
(Quail and Chicken Eggs Stuffed with Foie Gras Mousse*)
Le Loup en Croute "René"*
(Bass in Puff Pastry*)
Beurre Blanc aux Fines Herbes*
(White Butter Sauce with Herbs*)
Le Pigeon en Cocotte Gastronome
(Squab Stuffed with *Foie de Volailles, Demi-Glace* Sauce)
Fond d'Artichaut Printanier*
(Artichoke Bottom Filled with Purée of Spinach and Carrots*)
La Salade de Saison*
(Limestone Lettuce, Watercress, and Walnuts with Vinaigrette Dressing*)
La Brie de Meaux
Le Gâteau Mascotte*
(Round Cake with Alternating Layers of Meringue* and Génoise* with Mocha
Butter Cream*—Toasted slivered almonds on icing)

Champagne
Deutz Cuvée William
Magnum 1966

Vins
Montrachet-Romanée Conti, 1965
Château Pétrus 1947
Château Pétrus 1949
Château Pétrus 1950
Château Pétrus 1952
Château Pétrus 1953
Château Pétrus 1959
Château Suduiraut 1959

**Dinner Party for Six Guests
November 9, 1973**

Saucisson Chaud de Lyon au Porto en Croute
(Warm Handmade Sausage with Port in a Pastry Crust)

Choice of:
Pigeonneau Stanislas
(Stuffed Baby Pigeon)
or
Etouffée de Canard aux Olives*
(Stewed Duck with Olives*)
Salade Yvette

Charlotte* aux Framboises
(Molded Bavarian Cream* with Raspberries)
Mousse de Citrons*
(Lemon Mousse*)
Linzer Tart*

Dinner Menu for Small Party
July 14, 1978

Quenelles de Faison Sauce Périgourdine*
(Pheasant Quenelles*) (Madeira Sauce with Chopped Truffles*)
Mousseline de Coquilles St. Jacques Sauce Nantua*
(Mousseline of Scallops*) (Crayfish Sauce*)

Poussin Farcis Sauce Madère*
(Alsatian Poussin*)
Salade Verte

Desserts du Chariot (pastry cart)
Vacherin Crème de Noisette*
(Meringue Cake* Filled with Hazelnut Pastry Cream)
Tarte Tatin
Crème Bavaroise au Chocolat et Vanille
Mousse au Chocolat
Sauce Grand Marnier
Ile Flottante au Coulis de Framboises*
(Molded Floating Island* with Puréed Raspberry Sauce*)

Dinner Menu for Four, Giving Choices of Main Course
February 1980

Baked Oysters* in Curry Sauce

Bouillabaisse with Rouille*
(Fish Soup with Rouille*)
Carré d'Agneau au Miel
(Rack of Lamb with Honey Sauce)

*Pommes de Terre Dauphine**

Dodine de Faison Sauce Poivrade**
(Dodine of Pheasant*) (Pepper Sauce*)
Lamb Niçoise

*Gâteau de Fromage aux Fraises (sans fromage)**
(Strawberry Cheesecake [without cheese])
*Gâteau Saint Honoré**

Dinner Menu for Four
February 1981

Terrine de Truite Sauce Verte**
(Terrine of Trout*) (Green Sauce*)

Médaillons de Veau Confit d'Oignons**
(Boned Loin or Leg of Veal*) (Caramelized Onion Sauce*)
*Asperges Fraîches Sauce Hollandaise**
(Fresh Asparagus) (Hollandaise Sauce*)

Limestone Lettuce Salad*

Grand Marnier Soufflé* in Orange Shells

Dinner for Alan Shepard
May 5, 1981

Consommé* Romanoff

Cervelas aux Fruits de Mer* aux Deux Sauces*
(Seafood Sausage with Two Sauces)

Squab Braisé Sauce Bordelaise*
(Braised Squab) (Bordelaise Sauce*)

Coeur de Filet de Boeuf* Sauce Périgourdine*
Endive Braisées

Salade de Mâche*
(Lamb's Lettuce or Corn Salad)* Hazelnut Dressing

Tulipe* de Mousse de Papaya Fraiche* Sauce aux Fraises*

Comment: This dinner was a repeat performance of the one I prepared at the White House to celebrate the United States' first manned space flight on May 5, 1961. The *cervelas* were made up of fresh scallops, lobster, and pistachio nuts as the principal ingredients.

Dinner Menu for Eight
October 1981

*Oeufs à la Coque au Saumon Fumé**
(Eggs in the Shell with Smoked Salmon*)

Seafood Quenelle* (sole and scallops) *Sauce Beurre Blanc**
(White Butter Sauce)

Rouen Duck (*Canard de Rouen,* France), slices of breast cooked rare*

Purée de Salsifi, Purée d'Haricots Verts,* Purée de Marron**
(Purée of Salsify,* Purée of Green Beans,* Purée of Chestnuts*)

*Filet de Boeuf Baies de Cassis**
(Filet of Beef with Black Currants*)

Desserts du Chariot
Gâteau Trianon (version of *Gâteau Marjolaine*)
*Gâteau Nancy** (round shape, chocolate color and flavor:
Chocolate Soufflé Cake*)
*Sauce Crème Anglaise**
*Charlotte Russe**
*Tarte aux Myrtilles**
(Tart with Juicy Summer Fruits*)
Mousse au Chocolat
*Sauce Grand Marnier**

Dinner Menu
April 21, 1982

Gâteau Foie de Volaille Sauce Tomate (Tomato Sauce*)
(Mousse of Chicken Livers on a Bed of Spinach Surrounded with Fresh
Tomato Sauce Topped with a *Coulis* of Tomatoes)

Sorbet of Passion Fruit
Cailles Farcies (Stuffed Quail with Chopped Shiitake Mushrooms, Bread
Crumbs, Raspberry Vinegar)
Sauce au Jus
Two Quail Served on Nest of Julienned Vegetables:
Zucchini and *Haricots Verts Frais**
(Fresh Green Beans*)

Salade de Chèvre Chaude (Crotin Lezay)
(Limestone Lettuce, Warm Goat Cheese, Tiny Croutons, Walnut Oil)

Les Desserts du Chariot:
Gâteau de Mousse aux Framboise et Chocolat*
(Glazed Raspberry Mousse Cake*)
Sauce Crème Anglaise*
Tarte aux Citrons*
(Lemon Tart*)
Mille-Feuilles aux Fraises
(Thousand Leaves Cake with Strawberries)
(Chocolate Soufflé Cake) *Gâteau Nancy**
La Religieuse*

Dinner Party for Six
May 7, 1982

Fresh Poached Salmon Slice* *Sauce Genevoise**
(Sauce prepared from head of salmon, parsley stems, red wine)
*Mousseline de Saumon Saint-Jacques**
(Scallop and Salmon Mousse*)

Sliced Moulard Duck Magret from Napa Valley*
*Sauce au Poivre Vert**
(Fresh Green Peppercorn Sauce*)
Purée of Chestnut and Turnip*

*Salade Alice**
(Stuffed Apple Salad*)

Dessert du Chariot
Gâteau Marron avec Cognac
*Mousse au Chocolate Sauce Grand Marnier**
*Tarte Tatin** *Sauce Crème Anglaise** or *Chantilly**
*Charlotte Russe**
Tarte aux Fraises Pérouges-style

Dinner Party for Four
February 7, 1983

Cervelas aux Fruits de Mer * *Sauce Aurore* (Fish *Velouté* * and Tomato)
(Seafood Sausage* Made of Sole, Flounder, Lobster, and Scallops,
Stuffed Zucchini in Center of Plate)

Vol au Vent de Pâte Feuilletée * *Sauce Beurre Fondu (Beurre Monté)* *
(Square Puff Pastry Case* Filled with Creamed Mushrooms, Topped with
Asparagus Spears)

Médaillons d'Agneau * *Sauce au Jus* * *et Les Truffes*
(Boned and Trimmed Loin of Lamb* with Pan Juices* and Truffles)
Pommes Darphin * (Potato Cake*)
Confit d'Ail * (Garlic Confit*)
Légumes Variés * *en Alumettes*
(Mixed Vegetables* Cut in Match-Stick Shapes)

Salade d'Endives et de Champignons *
(Belgian Endive and Mushroom Salad*)

Les Desserts

Gratin de Pêches et Crème *
(Gratin of Peaches and Cream*)
Gâteau Génoise * *Crème Fraiche* *
(Topped with julienne of reddened orange peel)
Tarte Soufflé aux Citrons *
(Lemon Soufflé Tart*)

Dinner with Julia Child, René Verdon, and Brooks Firestone
to Benefit KQED (Public Television)
Monday, December 5, 1983

Les Canapés Assortis
(Assorted Canapés)
1982 Gewürztraminer

Le Saumon Soufflé aux Courgettes
Piments Rouge et Vert et Vermouth*
(Salmon Soufflé with Zucchini, Red and Green Peppers, and Dry Vermouth*)
1981 Chardonnay

Le Filet d'Agneau* en Croute Trianon avec sa Garniture de Petits Légumes
(Filet of Lamb* Trianon in Crust Garnished with Vegetables *Subrics**)
1978 Pinot Noir (magnums)

La Salade de Saison avec son Crottin de Chavignol Roti
(Hot Salad with Goat Cheese)
1979 Ambassador's Vineyard Merlot

Le Miroir aux Framboises*
(Raspberry Mousse*)

Assortiments de Petits Fours Secs*
1981 Ambassador's Vineyard
Select Harvest Johannisberg Riesling

Moka
(Coffee)

Dinner for the American Institute of Wine and Food
June 29, 1984

Paillarde de Saumon à la Moutarde de Meaux*
(Filet of Salmon with Whole Grain Mustard*)
Sauce Vièrge*

Feuilletée* *d'Asperges*
(Asparagus in a Puff Pastry Case*)

Noisette d'Agneau Ail Confits*
(Boned Loin of Lamb—Garlic Confit*)
Gratin de Pommes de Terre Dauphinoise*
(Gratin of Potatoes Dauphinoise*)
Chicorée Salade avec Fromage de Chèvre de Californie

Trois Mousses aux Trois Sauces:
Mousse de Papaya,* *d'Avocat,** *et de Fruits de la Passion*
Sauces Coulis de Framboise,* *d'Abricot, Crème Anglaise**

Petits Fours Secs*

Café

Choosing Wines for Menus

There are four basic characteristics of wine: color, bouquet, taste, and age. The first course of a meal usually begins with a dry wine, proceeds to a more robust wine for the main course, and finishes with a sweet wine served with dessert. Wines should be chosen to complement the flavor of the dish chosen for each course. If the main course is the heartiest, the wine should match in richness—proceed from diminuendo to crescendo to a climax. For an haute cuisine dinner, one rarely begins with a red wine because it is reserved to be served with the main course. The quality of the wine should match the occasion—serve high quality wines for a black tie dinner. However, too many great wines served at one dinner de-emphasize the enjoyment of the best one. For a birthday celebration, it is memorable to serve a great bottle of the year of the person's birth. Begin with a good Champagne, proceed to a better white wine, then a comparably great Bordeaux or Burgundy. A dinner party can begin with Champagne, and it can continue to be served with all the courses. The four types of Champagne are *brut, sec, demi-sec,* and *doux.* Sherry, a fortified wine, can also be served with more than one course. Dry sherry is served with the hors d'oeuvre and the soup course, while sweet sherry is served with dessert.

SELECTING WINES FOR EACH COURSE

I. **Hors d'Oeuvre**: Fine Champagne, *brut* or extra dry, is recommended as most connoisseurs believe no wine surpasses it. Sparkling wines may be served instead of Champagne. An alternative would be a dry white wine such as Chenin Blanc or Sauvignon Blanc from California or other wine-making regions. French equivalents are Vouvray, Pouilly Fumé, or white Bordeaux. Some aperitifs are dry sherry, Kir, or Campari.

II. **Soup Course**: A dry sherry is preferred, if a fortified white wine is served. Any of the white wines mentioned for aperitifs can be served with the soup or fish course. A young, crisp, white wine can be served with a highly seasoned dish or soup such as *Soupe de Poissons* (p. 22).

III. **First Course**: The quality of the wine should match the elegance of the dish. Chardonnay, the queen of white wines, deserves to be served with haute cuisine dishes. Montrachet, one of the finest French white wines made with the Chardonnay grape, should not be served with a Provençal dish—that dish should be served with a

Muscadet (a less expensive wine). Chablis and Chardonnay complement Salmon Soufflé with Zucchini, Green and Red Peppers, and Dry Vermouth (p. 178), Salmon or Trout Quenelles (pp. 189 and 196), or *Cervelas aux Fruits de Mer* (p. 193). The overall favorite white wine is Chardonnay; its quality depends on the region in Burgundy from which it comes—in Macon or Montagny the quality is not as good. The quality may be expected to improve in the regions of Beaujolais (Pouilly-Fuissé), to Chablis, Meursault, and Montrachet. A properly aged white wine five years of age has elegance, but it is the vintage year which decides its final quality or excellence. A white wine may be served with an entire dinner, if the main course is a chicken or veal dish and no red wine has been used in preparation of the dish, such as in *Blanquette de Veau* (p. 216).

IV. **Main Course:** The choice of a red or white wine is optional. A red wine is correct for game and meat dishes, which tend to be highly seasoned or have been cooked with red wine. Although red wine is rarely served with seafood, it may be if the dish is prepared with red wine or is highly seasoned. The intensity of red wine depends on the grape and the age of the wine—wines made from the Gamay Beaujolais grape tend to be drunk very young, while Petite Sirahs or Zinfandels are enjoyed young or old. Old Zinfandel and old Rhone wines are far less common than old Cabernets, Bordeaux, or Burgundies. For an informal dinner, you may choose a young Cabernet or a young Bordeaux rather than a classified wine of a great vintage year. It is a convention among connoisseurs to have a Cabernet or Bordeaux precede a California Pinot Noir or a red Burgundy. The most exalted red Burgundies are wines of Romanée–Conti, Chambertin, and Musigny; the next best are Gevrey-Chambertin and Pommard. Although a truly mature and fine Pinot Noir is rare in California, there are now a few that compare favorably with the red Burgundies of France. If California and French wines are served at the same dinner, they should be selected so as not to overshadow or underscore one another.

If Champagne is to be served exclusively for an entire dinner, the Champagne served first or with the hors d'oeuvre should be a *brut,* proceeding to a luxury bottle such as Moët et Chandon Dom Perignon for the high point of the dinner—the main course. A dry Champagne is the *only* dry white wine that is a pleasant companion to a sweet dessert. A *demi-sec* or *doux* is also correct. Champagne should be sipped chilled in a flute glass or long-stemmed tulip shaped glass. *Blanc de Blancs* Champagne is made with all white grapes. The amount of sugar syrup added to wine, called the *dosage,* determines its type.

V. **Salad Course**: Wines are not usually served with this course due to the vinegar in the vinaigrette dressing. If wine, or part wine and part wine vinegar, or fresh lemon juice are substituted for vinegar, a dry white or red wine (red is drier) can be served.

VI. **Cheese Course**: Choose wine according to intensity of flavor of variety of cheese selected. A Burgundy or Pinot Noir are popular choices. If cheese replaces the dessert course, a red port is appropriate.

VII. **Desserts**: A favorite here is a sweet Sauternes, such as Château d'Yquem (king of wines and wine of kings), Château Suduiraut, or a Barsac such as Château Coutet. Other suitable sweet wines from California are Moscato Amabile or Mission del Sol or a late harvest Riesling; from Italy a Muscato or Asti Spumanti; from Germany a Beerenauslese or Trockenbeerenauslese. California vintners are emulating German winemakers by producing late harvest wines from a variety of grapes including Reisling, Gewürztraminer, and even Zinfandel, which is a red wine. Tokay, a Hungarian wine, is another dessert wine.

VIII. **Coffee**: Spirits are preferred with coffee or after coffee is served. The Cognac or Armagnac should match the quality of the dinner. A 1920 Armagnac is reserved for the end of a festive dinner. An American brandy is served on a lesser occasion. The choice of spirit can be either sweet or dry.

NOTE: The wine glass should be filled less than halfway in order to be able to swirl the wine to enjoy the bouquet or aroma. It also enables one to test the "legs" of the wine—streams which descend down the inner side of glass after wine has been tipped away, showing the heaviness of the wine. The glass should be held at the base. Two reasons for this are so the glass does not get warm and to prevent fingerprints. The wine glass should be held in the light to test the color of the wine, revealing whether the wine is clear or cloudy (cloudiness indicates a defect in the wine). Briefly, a wine is judged on its appearance, color, aroma and bouquet, total acid, sugar, body, flavor, astringency, and general quality.

Appendix:

Batterie de Cuisine: Pots, Pans, and Utensils, Weights and Measurements

Tools of the Kitchen
Batterie de Cuisine

For any pursuit it is necessary to have the right tools to produce a successful piece of work. Cooking is not only made easier when the proper tools are used, but it is also aesthetically more pleasing to work with well-made, well-cared-for kitchen equipment. As I explained in my Introduction, a well organized kitchen facilitates the application of *mise en place* (p. xvi). In turn the *mise en place* is improved with the possession of the correct pots and pans.

This collection of cooking equipment *(batterie de cuisine)* is put together to represent the requirements of the fairly advanced home cook. Naturally, this equipment can be acquired over a period of time as more elaborate dishes are undertaken. The choice of cookware available today is overwhelming. A good rule of thumb is to buy the best quality because it is a lifetime investment. For reasons of clarity, this list has been divided into 3 categories: 1) Stovetop and Oven-Cooking Utensils: pots, pans, and casseroles; 2) Cooking Utensils: cooks' hand tools and electrical machines; 3) Baking Pans and Tools: equipment for baking and pastry making.

Stovetop and Oven-Cooking Utensils   *Ustensiles à l'Etuve et le Four*

Two or three pans for sautéing *(sauteuse)*, 9 x 10 x 12 inches. It represents a transition between a skillet and a saucepan. Materials can be copper lined with tin, stainless steel, aluminum of heavy gauge with or without Calphalon finish.

Two or three frying pans or skillets *(poêle à frire)*, 8 x 9 x 10 inches in diameter, made of cast iron, enameled cast iron, heavy gauge aluminum with cast aluminum handle, stainless steel with aluminum or copper. Lids.

Two or three saucepans, 6 or 7 inches, 8½ inches, and 9 inches in diameter; enameled cast iron (Le Creuset has a lip), heavy gauge hammered aluminum, heavy gauge copper with tin lining, stainless steel with aluminum on the bottom or copper used by Revere Ware. Lids.

One large oval pot roaster and braising pot, 10 x 12 inches, called a *doufeu, marmite,* or *pot-au-feu;* enameled cast iron, heavy gauge aluminum, or Magnalite with lids.

One large round casserole, 9–11 inches in diameter, also called a *cocotte;* enameled cast iron, heavy gauge stainless steel, or earthenware (clay *marmite*) with lids.

Two double boilers, 2 and 3 quarts; stainless steel, enamel, or Pyrex.

One stockpot, 12½–16-quart capacity; stainless steel or heavy duty aluminum.

One **tall saucepan,** 8½ inches in diameter and 6½ inches deep; 6½-quart capacity recommended for making Brown Sauce. Heavy gauge aluminum or stainless steel.

One **oval gratin pan** *(plat à gratin),* 14 inches long, 9 inches wide, 1¾ inches deep. Used for baking and presentation dishes—porcelain, aluminum with cast iron handles, copper with tin lining and brass handles, enameled cast iron all found in various sizes without lids.

Eight small gratin dishes *(plat à gratin),* oval or round; porcelain.

One **baking pan,** 15½ x 10½ x 2¼ inches—aluminum or stainless steel used for a *bain-marie.*

One or two **frying pans for crêpes** *(poêle à crêpes),* about 7 inches in diameter— long handle, heavy flat base.

One **omelet pan** *(poêle à omelette),* 10 inches in diameter for three- or four-egg omelet—heavy iron or Teflon-lined with sloping sides. One omelet pan about 7 inches in diameter for a two egg omelet—fairly long handle, heavy enameled cast iron or teflon lined aluminum, sloping sides.

One **vegetable steamer,** deep cannister type; stainless steel or aluminum.

One **fish poacher** *(poissonnière* or *saumonnière),* 20 x 6½ inches or size that will fit in oven—tinned steel or stainless steel (optional utensil).

Pâté mold, terrine, *(pâté en terrine),* **loaf pan,** or **oval casserole,** 11 x 4 x 3 inches deep, enameled cast iron, or porcelain mold.

Charlotte mold *(moule à charlotte),* 6 inches in diameter, 3½ inches deep, 1-quart capacity—tinned steel. One-and-a-half- or two-quart available. Also pudding molds.

Hinged pâté mold *(moule à pâté),* 11 x 4 x 3 inches deep—tinned steel.

Cooking Utensils   *Ustensiles de Cuisine*

One set long-handled, stainless steel implements:
  a large spoon *(cuiller à bouche)*
  a spatula *(spatule)*
  a perforated spoon and skimmer *(écumoire)*
  a small and large ladle used for soup *(louche)* and batter *(cuiller à pot)*
  a fork *(fourchette maître d'hôtel)*

Two wooden spoons with long handles, one with flat tip, used for stirring *(mouvette)*

One wire whisk *(fouet à purée),* heavy wire stainless steel

One wire whisk *(fouet à sauce),* thin wire stainless steel

Two screen sieves or strainers *(passoires),* rounded 5-inch and 8-inch in diameter, stainless steel or nylon

One screen sieve *(chinois)*, conical 7½ inches in diameter for straining sauces and purées

One grater, stainless steel for cheese, citrus peel, vegetables

One set mixing bowls, stainless steel, Pyrex, or ceramic

One vegetable mill *(Moulinette* or *mouli-légumes)*

One electric mixer

One food processor

One electric blender

One deep-fat fryer *(bassine à friture* or *poêle à friture)*

One wire basket for deep frying *(panier à friture)*

One *mandoline* (p. 000) for slicing potatoes, cucumbers, etc.

One potato nest maker *(panier à nid)*, optional

One potato ricer

One kitchen scale *(balance)*

Two chopping boards or blocks *(planche à hacher)*, one for meat and one for vegetables, 18 x 24 inches (approximate)

One carving board *(planche a découper)*, with groove for juices *(tranchoir)*

Five or six knives *(couteaux)*—small paring knives *(couteaux d'office)*, French chef's knife *(couteau de cuisine)* 6–8–10 inches long for general kitchen work, boning knife *(couteau à désosser)*, carving knife *(couteau à découper)* 15 inches long, knife for fine slicing *(couteau à émincer)*, long narrow carving knife *(couteau à trancher)*

One trussing needle, 8 or 10 inches long, stainless steel

One larding needle *(lardoire)*, 7½–17½ inches long

One deep-frying thermometer

One candy-jelly-frosting thermometer

One oven thermometer, to check accuracy of oven temperature

One meat thermometer, instant type to insert in meat after removing from oven

One set skewers, tinned steel or stainless steel

One package cheesecloth, to wrap fish, poultry, or meat before cooking

One parchment paper roll, 20 square feet long, 15 inches wide

One ball polished twine, for trussing poultry, tying meat and vegetables

Baking Pans and Tools   *Matériel pour la Pâtisserie*

One marble slab, approximately 18 x 28 inches, or pastry board *(planche à pâtisserie)*; plastic cutting board can be used

Two sets measuring spoons

Two sets measuring cups

One set mixing bowls

One wire whisk, balloon whisk for beating egg whites *(fouet à blancs),* stainless steel wire with tinned-steel or wooden handles, 10–16 inches long

One egg beater

One ball bearing rolling pin *(rouleau à pâtisserie)* for *pâte feuilletée,* roller length 10½ x 15 inches

One French rolling pin *(rouleau à pâtisserie)* without handles or straight, 19 inches long

Two rubber spatulas, one large blade, 4½ x 3 inches, and one smaller blade, 3¼ x 2 inches

One copper bowl with brass ring *(bassine à blancs d'oeufs)* used for beating egg whites, 11 inches diameter, 4½ inches deep, 5-quart capacity

Two layer cake pans *(moule à manqué),* 8- or 9-inch sets, aluminum or heavy-gauge tinned steel, round or square

Two baking sheets or pans *(plafond* or *plaque à pâtisserie),* heavy aluminum, 11 x 16 x 1 inch

One large cake rack *(grilles à pâtisserie),* metal, 10 x 16 inches

Two small cake racks, metal, round or square, 10 x 10½ inches

One dough scraper *(coupe-pâte),* stainless steel with wooden handle

One dough cutting knife

One pastry brush, natural bristle with wooden handle

One ruler, aluminum, 15–25 inches long

One set puff paste cutters *(découpoirs),* round (also available in oval shape), fluted edges

Two pie pans, 9 inches diameter, 1¼ inches deep, aluminum and Pyrex

One tart pan *(tourtière),* 8 or 9½ inches diameter, 1 inch deep, tinned steel or black steel with fluted sides and removable bottom

Eight tartlet tins, 4 inches diameter, fluted, removable bottoms or small pie tins

One soufflé dish *(timbale à soufflé),* 7 or 8 inches diameter, 3 inches deep, 1½-quart capacity, porcelain or Pyrex

Six soufflé dishes, 3¼ or 4½ inches diameter, porcelain—for individual servings

Two tins for storing baked pastry

Two pastry bags *(poche),* 10–15½ inches long, canvas or plastic-lined fabric

One basic set tips *(douille),* or ½-inch round, ¾-inch round, No. 6 star tubes

Equivalent Measures

"dash"	=	less than ⅛ teaspoon or 8 drops
"pinch"	=	⅛ teaspoon
60 drops	=	1 teaspoon
3 teaspoons	=	1 tablespoon
2 tablespoons	=	1 liquid ounce
8 tablespoons	=	½ cup = 4 ounces
16 tablespoons	=	1 cup = 8 ounces
1 cup	=	½ pint or 8 ounces
2 cups	=	1 pint = 16 ounces = 1 liquid pound
2 pints	=	1 quart = 32 ounces
4 quarts	=	1 gallon
16 fluid ounces	=	2 cups
16 ounces (dry meaure)	=	1 pound
1 stick butter	=	½ cup = 8 tablespoons = 4 ounces
4 sticks butter	=	2 cups = 1 pound
2 cups (unsifted) flour	=	10 ounces
3½ cups flour	=	1 pound
2 cups granulated sugar	=	approx. 1 pound (less 2½ ounces)
2⅔ cups (not packed) brown sugar	=	1 pound
3¾ cups (unsifted) powdered sugar	=	1 pound (confectioners' sugar)
2 cups water	=	1 pound
4 cups grated cheese	=	1 pound
1 cup uncooked rice	=	2 cups cooked (long grain rice)
8–10 large egg whites	=	1 cup
12–14 large egg yolks	=	1 cup
5 whole eggs	=	1 cup
1 large egg	=	2 ounces (approximately)

One cup ingredient weight in ounces:

1 cup cake flour	=	3½ ounces
1 cup unsifted all purpose flour	=	5 ounces
1 cup sugar (granulated)	=	7 ounces
1 cup confectioners' sugar	=	4 ounces
1 cup brown sugar (well packed)	=	8 ounces
1 square chocolate	=	1 ounce
1 envelope gelatin	=	¼ ounce = ¾ tablespoon

Metric Measurements:

Liters measure liquid or volume; grams measure mass or weight.

To make multiples of the base units, add deca-, hecto-, or kilo- to designate 10, 100, or 1000 times the base unit. Example: A kilogram (or kilo) is 1000 grams. In France meat is sold by the kilo, which is 2.2 pounds. An ounce is 28 grams. One pound is 454 grams.

To make fractions of the base unit, add deci-, centi-, or milli- to designate .1, .01, or .001 of a gram or liter. Example: A milliliter is one-thousandth of a liter. A teaspoon of vanilla is about 5 milliliters (ml). A tablespoon is 15 ml. A cup is 250 ml.

Approximate Conversion to Metric Measures:

For teaspoons, multiply by 5 to get milliliters (ml)
For tablespoons, multiply by 15 to get milliliters
For dry ounces, multipy by 28 to get milliliters
For fluid ounces, multiply by 30 to get milliliters
For cups, multiply by 250 to get milliliters

INDEX